Davinder Kumar's
Just Kebabs
Celebration of 365 Kebabs & One for a Leap Year
(Vegetarian & Non Vegetarian)

Davinder Kumar's
JustKebabs
Celebration of 365 Kebabs & One for a Leap Year
(Vegetarian & Non Vegetarian)

Shubhi Publications
Gurgaon - India

First Published - 2010

Copyright: Author

©All rights reserved. Neither this book nor any part may be reproduced or transmitted in any form or by any form or by any means, electronic or mechanical, including photocopying, microfilming and recording or by any information storage and retrieval system, without permission in writing from the author & publisher.

Published by: Shubhi Publications
240, 2nd floor, City Centre, Gurgaon - 122 002, Haryana, India

Photographs by Dinesh Gaur.

Designed by SN GRAPHIX

Printed in India by
Aegean Offset Printers
F-17, Mayapuri, Industrial Area,
Phase II, Delhi - 64

Distributed by
Variety Book Depot
M-3, AVG Bhawan, Connaught Circus
New Delhi-1

CONTENTS

FOREWORD	11
PREFACE	12
ACKNOWLEDGEMENTS	15
A WORD ABOUT RECIPES	18
COOKERY TERMS	20
WEIGHT & MEASURE	23
BASIC KITCHEN EQUIPMENT	26
CONTENTS AS PER LIST	5
POULTRY	27
Murg Toofani Tikka	37
Lahori Murg Tikka	37
Murg Dhaniya Tikka	38
Peeli Mirch Ka Tikka	38
Murg Bikaneri Tikka	39
Hari Mirch Kebab	39
Murg Haryali Tikka	40
Julandhari Chatpate Murg Tikke	40
Tandoori Tikka Hakka Style	41
Murg Tulsi Tikka	41
Pista Murg Tikka	42
Zaffrani Murg Kebab	42
Murg Sarson Tikka	43
Murg Tikka Thai Style	43
Murg Elaichi Tukra	44
Murg Potli Kebab	45
Murg Nizami Kebab	46
Chicken And Cheese Kebab	46
Pudine Wala Murg Seena	47
Murg Malai Tikka	47
Chandi Murg Tikka	48
Bakarkhani Seekh Kebab	48
Murg Reshmi Tikka	49
Tawa Murg Kulfi	49
Shan-E-Murg	50
Reshmi Seekh	50
Murg Kastoori Kebab	51
Murg Shammi Kebab	51
Tandoori Kukkar Patiala Shahi	52
Murg Methi Malai	52
Murg Anmol Rattan	53
Murg Methi Seekh	53
Murg Lapeta Kebab	54
Harre Pyaaz Ka Murg Tikka	55
Murg Haider Ali Kebab	55
Kesari Murg Ke Tukre	56
Reshmi Murg Tikka	56
Peshawari Murg Tikka	57
Murg Kalonji Seekh	57
Tandoori Murg Chettinad	58
Phuljhari Seekh Kebab	58
Murg Choppati Tikka	59
Khatta Meetha Tikka	59
Murg Dalcha Kebab	60
Murg Rogani Tikka	60
Murg Ka Sula	61
Kadak Seekh Kebab	62
Murg Achari Tikka	62
Khasta Seekh Kebab	63
Teekha Murg Tikka	63
Kandhari Murg Tikka	64

Nasheela Murg	64	Murg Ke Paarchey	90
Szechwan Murg Tikka	65	Murg Hazarvi Kebab	90
Tandoori Murg Bemisal	65	Murg Pasanda Kebab	91
Murg Noorani Kebab	66	Kalmi Shirazi	92
Murg Sikandari Kebab	66	Tandoori Bater Kali Mirch	101
Punjabi By Nature	67	Khatta Meetha Tandoori Duck	101
Murg Lolly Pop Kebab	67	Murg Tikka Kandhari	102
Tandoori Duck Chettinad	68	Murg Anmol Tikka	103
Chatpate Kaleji Kebab	68	Lahsuni Murg Tikka	104
Gazab Ka Seena	69	Lagan Ka Teetar	105
Shahjahani Murg Kebab	70		
Murg Nagina	70	**SEAFOOD**	**107**
Lazeez Murg Shashlik	71	Machhli Ke Shammi Kebab	117
Lime And Coconut Chicken Kebab	71	Sarson Wali Machhli	117
Raan - E - Murg	72	Khatti Meethi Machhli	118
Murg Burra Kebab	72	Dalchini Machhli Tikka	118
Lagan Ke Kebab	73	Goanese Mahi Kebab	119
Rajasthani Murg Burra	73	Tandoori Khusk Machhli	119
Raan - E - Patiala Shahi	74	Amchur Machhli Ke Tikke	120
Murg Mulayam Kebab	74	Tandoori Methi Machhi	120
Tandoori Chicken Lolly Pops	75	Haryali Machhi Tikka	121
Dum Ka Murg Seena	75	Mahi Tikka Ajwaini	121
Murg Karara	76	Afghani Fish Tikka	122
Surkh Lal Tangri	76	Mahi Dil Se	121
Murg Shehnaz	77	Kastoori Mahi Tikka	123
Narial Ka Murg Tukra	77	Malika-E-Dariya	123
Tandoori Murg Frontier	78	Lahori Mahi Kebab	124
Tandoori Chooza Masaledar	79	Malabari Mahi Tikka	124
Seekh - E - Noorani	80	Tandoori Achari Machhli	125
Murg Badshahi	80	Tandoori Ajwaini Lobster	125
Malika - E - Hussn	81	Tandoori Kalyera Lobster	126
Bharwan Gulmohar Tangri	82	Samundari Manthan	126
Murg Chilgoja Kebab	82	Jugal Bandi Seekh	127
Bharwan Murg Tangri	83	Tandoori Machhli Seekh	127
Til Wali Tangri	84	Methi Machhli Seekh	128
Tandoori Murg Zaffrani	84	Tandoori Paatrani Machhli	128
Tandoori Pankhari Kebab	85	Tandoori Pomfret	129
Murg Kalmi Kebab	85	Amritsari Machhi	129
Harra Tandoori Pankhari	86	Puddine Wali Tandoori Pomfret	130
Chatpate Tandoori Gurdey	86	Samundar Ki Rani	130
Haryali Murg Tangri	87	Ajwaini Tandoori Pomfret	131
Tandoori Khatta Murg	88	Haryali Tandoori Pomfret	131
Bhatti Da Murg Pindiwala	89	Lobster of The Raj	132
Murg - A - Pa	89	Tandoori Haryali Lobster	132

Jhinga Adraki	133	Champ – E – Charminar	172		
Zameen Ki Machhi	133	Hussaini Seekh Kebab	173		
Tandoori Chilli Prawns Chinese Style	134	Raan – E – Patialashahi	173		
Kasoori Jhinga	134	Keema Goli Kebab	174		
Aatish-E-Jhinga	135	Nawabi Pasande	174		
Tandoori Achari Jhinga	135	Kebab – E – Baluchistan	175		
Jhinga Haldi Mirch	136	Shalimar Raan	175		
Ajwain Aur Lahsun Wale Jhinge	136	Gosht Elaichi Pasanda	176		
Haryali Tandoori Jhinga	137	Lahsuni Burra Kebab	176		
Anmol Tandoori Jhinga	137	Majedar Tandoori Champen	177		
Tandoori Jhinga Goanese Style	138	Gosht Puddina Champen	177		
Tandoori Jhinga Shashlik	138	Kabuli Gosht Tikka	178		
Surkh Lal Tandoori Jhinga	139	Raan – E – Gulistan	179		
Tandoori Lemon Chilli Prawns	139	Lamb Kufta Kebab	179		
Nashila Tandoori Jhinga	140	Turkish Boti Kebab	180		
Kolmi Na Kebab (Parsi)	140	Chatpate Narial Gosht Ke Tikke	180		
Mahi Mussallam	149	Tandoori Raseeli Botian	181		
Adraki Mahi Shashlik	150	Gosht Puddina Champen	181		
Crab Aur Jhinga Kebab	150	Kebab – E – Mehfil	182		
Jhinga Mahi Jugal Bandi	151	Sunheri Tandoori Anda	182		
Machhli Tawa Kebab	151	Sunheri Boti Kebab	183		
Lajawab Tandoori Mahi Tikka	152	Lahori Seekh Kebab	183		
Jhinga Samrat	155	Lajawab Gosht Ke Tikke	184		
Mahi Tikka Noorani	153	Lajawab Methi Tikka	184		
Samundari Sher	153	Kasoori Gosht Tikka	185		
Tandoori Mahi Bharwan	154	Lamb Chilgoja Seekh	185		
Salmon Ali Shaan	154	Akbari Seekh Kebab	186		
		Gosht Boti Kaliyan	186		
LAMB	155	Hyderabadi Kaleji Kebab	187		
Jahangiri Seekh Kebab	165	Peshawari Boti Kebab	187		
Sangam Seekh Kebab	165	Rajasthani Boti Kebab	188		
Seekh Patialashahi	166	Gosht Dalcha Kebab	188		
Malai Seekh Kebab	166	Multani Seekh Kebab	189		
Lucknowi Seekh Kebab	167	Joshiley Boti Kebab	189		
Khusk Seekh Kebab	167	Gosht Kashmiri Tikke	190		
Kebab - E - Gulmarg	168	Lazeez Dohra Kebab	190		
Dum Ke Awadhi Kebab	168	Boti Keema Kebab	191		
Kasoori Seekh Kebab	169	Gilawat Ke Kebab	191		
Lagan Ke Gosht Kebab	169	Dum Keema Kebab	192		
Dhania Wali Tandoori Champen	170	Patiala Seekh	192		
Bhyankar Tandoori Champen	170	Gosht Kebab Wajid Ali	193		
Methi Seekh Kebab	171	Dum Ka Kebab	193		
Adrak Ke Panje	171	Seekh - Pa	194		
Hyderabadi Seekh Kebab	172	Pathar Ka Gosht	194		

Tandoori Rogani Champen	195	Mungphali Aur Paneer Kebab	233
Shahi Gosht Tikke	195	Doranga Paneer Tikka	234
Joshiley Tandoori Pasliyan	196		
Chatpate Tandoori Gurdey	196	VEGETABLES	235
Kashmiri Shammi Kebab	201	Tandoori Shakar Kandi	236
Shikampuri Kebab	201	Shakar Kandi Seekh	236
Shahi Shikampuri Kebab	202	Jimikand Seekh Kebab	237
Tabakh Maaz	202	Bharwan Tandoori Tinda	237
Balti Muthi Kebab	203	Seeta Phal Ke Shammi	238
Champ - E - Gulistan	203	Tandoori Bharwan Parmal	238
Pasanda Kebab	204	Tandoori Shimla Mirch	239
Chapli Kebab	205	Gajab Ka Phool	239
Kakori Kebab	206	Vilayati Seekh Kebab	240
Purdah Nashin Kebab	207	Mazedaar Broccoli Seekh	240
Tunde Ke Kebab	207	Shikampuri Subz Kebab	241
Maas Ke Sule	208	Parsi Subz Kebab	241
Dori Ke Kebab	208	Tandoori Tamatar Ka Dolma	242
		Tandoori Surkh Lal Aloo	242
PANEER	211	Jaipuri Bharwan Aloo	243
Lahsuni Paneer Tikka	212	Tandoori Phalon Ki Chaat	243
Paneer Tikka Shashlik	212	Palak Bhutte Ki Seekh	244
Tandoori Sikandari Paneer	213	Dahi Ke Shammi	244
Khatta Meetha Paneer Tikka	213	Till Ke Khaas Kebab	245
Paneer Ka Sula	214	Subz Galouti Kebab	245
Lajawab Paneer Seekh	214	Kadak Sabudana Tikka	246
Chandi Paneer Tikka	215	Khus Ke Khaas Kebab	246
Tandoori Paneer Tikka Kalimmirch	215	Harra Tawa Kebab	247
Harra Bharra Paneer Tikka	216	Bharwan Aloo Tikki	247
Tandoori Amchurwala Paneer	216	Khasta Subz Kebab	248
Tandoori Til Wala Paneer	217	Til Mill Seekh Kebab	248
Saunphia Paneer Tikka	217	Tandoori Aloo Nazakat	249
Bharwan Paneer Tikka	218	Muttar Kaju Kebab	249
Tandoori Ghungroo Paneer De	218	Harre Muttar Ki Seekh	250
Jaipuri Paneer Tikka	219	Til Ke Khaas Soya Kebab	250
Makhmali Paneer Seekh	219	Khaas Soya Seekh	250
Tiranga Paneer Tikka	220	Tandoori Achari Aloo	251
Noorani Paneer Seekh	220	Achari Bharwan Khumb Shashlik	251
Lajawab Paneer Roll	221	Mewey Aur Mawey Ki Kakori	252
Kandhari Paneer Tikka	221	Soya Shammi Kebab	252
Tandoori Paneer Gulnar	222	Saunphia Soya Kebab	253
Tandoori Paneer Pasanda	223	Tandoori Lahsuni Broccoli	253
Saunphia Dum Paneer	223	Khaas Palak Seekh	254
Tutti Frutti Paneer Seekh	224	Shahi Tandoori Gobhi	254
Bharwan Tandoori Paneer	224	Vilayati Shammi Kebab	255

Bharwan Subz Kebab	255	Bhutta Seekh Kebab	283
Aloo Makai Seekh	256	Khumb Mutter Ke Shammi	284
Tawa Bhutta Kebab	256	Tandoori Aloo Sarson Wale	284
Multani Khumb Ki Shaan	257	Kale Moti Ke Shammi	285
Bhutta Seekh Kebab	257	Makkai Akhrot Ki Seekh	285
Broccoli Bhutta Ke Shammi	258	Kathal Ke Galouti Kebab	286
Tandoori Baby Bhutta	258	Tandoori Subz Bahar	286
Navrattan Seekh Kebab	259	Tandoori Bharwan Achari Baigan	287
Makkai Khumb Ki Kakori	259		
Lazawab Tandoori Gobhi	260	LENTILS	289
Tandoori Dhingri Shashlik	260	Channa Dal Ke Shammi	290
Subz Kakori Kebab	261	Kurkure Malka Kebab	291
Shahi Khumb Galouti	261	Ankurit Dal Ke Kebab	291
Tandoori Lahsun Wali Gobhi	262	Kabuli Shammi Kebab	292
Tandoori Adraki Gobhi	262	Kale Moti Kebab	292
Lauki Ki Seekh	263	Kale Channe Ke Shammi	293
Kathal Aur Kacche Kele Ke Kebab	263	Kurkure Dal Shammi	293
Tori Ke Shammi	264	Malka Dal Shammi	294
Toofa - E - Zameen	264	Lajawab Rajma Kebab	294
Bhein Ki Kakori	273	Rajma Ke Galouti	295
Kacche Kele Anar Ke Kebab	273	Harra Chholia Kebab	295
Kathal Ke Shammi	274	Lobia Galouti Kebab	296
Akhrot Ki Galouti	274		
Lajawab Achari Arbi	275	SPICES	297
Arbi Khumb Ke Kebab	275		
Arbi Akhrot Ke Kebab	276	GARAM MASALA (MIX SPICE)	300
Tandoori Malai Arbi	276		
Nadru Chop	277	MARINADES	303
Lauki Ki Galouti	278		
Phaldari Seekh Kebab	278	TENDERIZERS	306
Syalkoti Subz Kebab	279		
Tandoori Bharwan Karela	279	PASTES	306
Khumb Palak Seekh	280		
Basmati Aur Bhutta Seekh	280	INGREDIENTS	309
Chawal Bhutte Ke Shammi Kebab	281		
Dahi Ke Kebab	281	IMPORTANT COOKING TIPS	312
Palak Dal Ke Shammi	282		
Shahi Dahi Palak Ke Shammi	282	GLOSSARY	316
Tarkari Shammi Kebab	283		

FOREWORD

Khushwant Singh is a prominent Indian novelist and journalist. An important Indo-Anglian novelist, Singh is best known for his trenchant secularism, his humor, and an abiding love of poetry. He served as editor of several well-known literary and news magazines, as well as two major broadsheet newspapers, through the 1970s and 1980s.

PREFACE

In Arabic the word "KAB" implies as turning movement. KAAM AAB (aab means water and kaam means little water or semidry).

Although the word kebab is derived from the Persion "Cabob" means a piece of meat, fish or vegetable roasted or grilled over charcoal.

We usually associate kebabs with the advent of the mughals into India. Which is probably not true and the kebabs in many froms were already existing. It is also said that probably kebabs originated in the Caucasus where mountain people speared meat pieces & then cooked them over on open fire.

The Rajputs, for example, made sule or smoked kebabs long before the Muslim invasion. Hunting being a popular sport of the Maharajas, game meat was a favourite. This meat was often cooked over an open fire in the forest. Meat that was not consumed immediately was pickled and preserved for another day. The origin of the kebab was probably just a hunk of freshly killed animal meat smoked or cooked over a simple wooden fire with a little salt and may be some chilli powder added to it. The subtle addition of flavours, textures and tastes was an art form that evolved over a period of time.

Rajasthan known for its kebabs was the state of Palanpur. The Nawabs of Palanpur were of Afghan descent who came to India in the twelfth century. Surrounded on all sides by Hindu Rajputs, they were microscopic but important Muslim state in that area. The food was pure Mughal and their pulaos and kebabs were renowned.

Finest cuisine of the nizams of Hyderabad was blended with the fiery spices of Andhra Pradesh. Large chunks of meat, heavily spiced, unlike the delicate kebabs of Awadh, where meat is ground so fine that even a toothless person could eat it without difficultes besides subtle flavours, fragrances used. I have included famous recipes of Hyderabad PATHAR Gosht, a tongue searing kebab so named because it is cooked on heated stone. It is a fact that heated stone releases minerals that mix with the spices on the meat and give the kebab its special flavours. From the state of Kishengarh in Rajasthan comes the dahi ka kebab, made with yoghurt and chickpea flour flavoured with saffron.

Awadh (Lucknow) is a city synonymous with Nawabi Culture. Known for its Adab and Tehzeeb (cultural refinement) Lucknow is also associated with its legendary hospitality, leisurely moods of life, fabled edifices steeped in history, world-renowned cuisine and exquisite Sham-e-Avadh.

The Moghuls brought with them their culture and their cuisine. Ingredients hitherto not generally used formed a fusion with the local foods. They were the first to use dried fruit, fragrances such as rose and kewda and nuts. These ingredients were brought from Turkey, Persia and Afghanistan and soon adapted to the local cuisine.

The culinary art of Awadh was raised to a fine art under royal patronage. The royal chefs of Awadh, by their expertise of blending spices achievedhigh degreeof finesse in cooking and the presentation of food. They also gave birth to various types of cooking namely Zamin Doz, Dum Pukht.

The development of Awadhi cuisine started off with the rule of monarch after the battle Buxar. The Nawabs left behind their culinary excellence. Their Bawarchis became the master creators of culinary delights. The royal recipes traveled to the ordinary people. The kabab traveled with No mads, innovated and presented in the present form by the Bawarchis. Its in Awadh alone 150 varieties of bread have been developed depending upon the fat, khameer, raising agents, nuts.

Royal chefs also inventd specific method such as Zamin Doz, which imparts the wonderful earthy flavour to the dish and various blends of spices were used, which still stays as a secret to the inventor families.

The equipments used also enhance the flavour of the secret spices added to the dish. For example - Degchi impart a typical Awadhi flavour to the dish kept for dum. Earthy flavour from earthen ware in Zamin Doz.

In north perhaps the most famous cuisine was that of the Nawabs of Avadh. Images of a time of gracious living where the culinary arts were at their most evolved. This was the birth place of some of the finest food in the land. The Nawabs of Avadh were indulgent lot and had always craved the best foods even when old and toothless.

Moving back to north, we have the princely state of Kashmir and Patiyala both of which have contributed greatly to the popularity of the kebab. The robust cuisine of punjab has spawned a tandoori revolution that is still going strong all over the world. Kashmiri Muslim Cuisine on the other hand though entirely based on lamb is characterized by its use of delicate flavours such as saffron, cardamom and yoghurt. Kashmiri Tabak maaz, a kebab made of tender ribs of lamb is a gourmet delight.

Some of the most popular kebabs from Awadh have also been incorporated in the book. Example, Gilawat Ka Kebab, Kakori Kebab, Shikumpur Kebab etc.

'Kebab corner' a famous cookery show hosted by me on ETC Channel Punjabi has been a huge success. Its uniqueness in presenting array of recipes on kebabs both vegetarians and non-vegetarian in a simple way using varieties of ingredients. In view of the overwhelming response from viewers of the program, prompted me to write this book.

True to my reputation of burying my nose into cuisine-related literature of the past, I have unearthed a treasure of 365 kebab recipes one for each day + 1 for leap year.

Each recipe is different in taste, texture and colour. My passion for kebabs began a couple of years ago when I was looking for a professional book on this subject, was not found on any bookshelf as reference book. My first book "Kebab, chutney & bread" has been well appreciated and considering its success I decided to pen down this book which will be ideal for any professional or housewife or gourmet of kebabs.

This book is an attempt to encourage people to prepare kebabs with confidence and make it a part of daily life.

A delectable kebab possess the prefect blend of taste, aroma, succulence and lingering smokey flavour.

Recipes have been created by using simple ingredients, presented in a format that makes cooking systematic.

Variety of tips have been added to enable the reader understand and achieve better results. Keeping in view the changing health-friendly food culture & life styles, health-friendly kebabs have been created.

A detailed glossary in English and Hindi, various ingredients that are commonly used in making kebabs, utensils, cooking methods and culinary terms widely used have been listed.

All recipes have been formatted in such a way that even a novice would get the desired results, if steps are followed.

It has been my desire to standardize recipes of kebabs and create history in variety. Myth that kebabs are only non-vegetarian has been buried and I am proud to present large number of vegetarian kebabs as well.

I am sure the readers will enjoy the recipes and don't forget that to prepare good food one needs Patience-Love-Attitude.

Happy kebabing!!!

ACKNOWLEDGEMENTS

I am indebted to the following associates for their help, support, dedication & hard work.

Master Chef Anil kumar & Om Prakash Sharma, true connoisseurs of kebabs, their contribution is commendable.

Special thanks to Chefs Karan Mehta for food styling. Virender Kumar for editing, Vinod Kumar, Rahul Sharma, Alok Kumar who prepared all recipes to perfection.

Mr. A.S. Ahuja for high standard & quality products. Ms. Kiran Nath my secretary for formatting the recipes.

Special thanks to my kitchen team.

Photography by Dinesh Gaur.

Last but not the least thanks to my family who had to sacrifice lot during the creation of the book.

A
DEEP DEBT
OF
GRATITUDE

At the outset, I would like to express my deep debt of gratitude to the crafter of the masterpiece that is **Le Meridien** today……
our late Chairman, Charanjit Singh—whose vision, dedication and management skills were its building blocks.

He literally translated his vision of 'a hotel which will shine like a jewel in the heart of the capital and be the pride of the city' into a reality that has put **Le Meridien** in the select class of the top hotels in the world.

It is my pleasure and privilege to be associated with the legacy of our illustrious late Chairman as part of the gourmets team that provides select cuisines as hospitality of **Le Meridien,** New Delhi.

A Word About Recipes

All the recipes in this book have been written in a manner that makes easy to follow. Each recipe has been tried out personally to ensure that it is accurate and perfect.

To make preparation simple/easy, the ingredients in this book have been listed in the order in which they are to be used.

All weights are net not gross. If the recipe says 100gms chicken it implies that weights of the ingredients after clearing and deboning. Similarly any vegetable that is required should be weighed after clearing, washing and cutting.

Each recipes yields one portion and is sufficient to be served as a main course or single dish besides accompaniments, i.e, salad, chutney. Full portion can be easily shared by more persons depending upon the menu.

Each preparation has its own distinguishing taste, not only because of the different texture of the meat but also because of the varying fragrances of different combinations of spices in the marination.

The quantities are mentioned in gross, tablespoon, teaspoon, and cups. I have allowed our imagination free reign at times nevertheless the final product came out to be delicious and sometimes beyond expectations.

To the Memory of my
Beloved Mother
who has always been a source of inspiration, and who believed that preparing good food does not only require spices and condiments—it is the personal touch and the way you cook that makes the food a gourmet's delight.

Cookery Terms

The reader must familiarize himself/herself with some of the culinary terms which specifically lend this cuisine its distinctive character. These are described below:

Smoking (Dhuanaar): This is a quick procedure used to flavour a meat dish. In this process smoke imparts a subtle aroma to the meat or vegetable, which enhances the quality of kebab. The method is as follows. In a shallow utensil in which meat has been marinated, a small bay is made in the center and a small bowl or onion skin is placed. A small piece of burning charcoal is placed in it and hot ghee is poured on charcoal. Sometimes mixed aromatic herbs or condiments are used for additional flavour, and immediately covered with a lid to prevent the smoke from escaping. It is left covered for about 10 – 15 minutes so as to allow the smoke to work on the ingredients inside. The coal is then removed from the utensils and meat put through further cooking process.

Fry: Talna or frying is done in a kadai. For kebabs use clean refined oil preferably groundnut. Use sufficient quantity of oil to ensure proper and even frying.

Baste: Moisten with fat or ghee or melted butter during roasting. For tandoori kebabs basting acquires special significance. Application of butter or oil seals in the juices and the kebabs remain succulent.

Roast: Cook in clayoven or oven.

Broil: Dry roast on griddle plate.

Grill: To cook on an open iron grill fired with charcoal.

Knead: To work a dough lightly by bringing the outside dough into the center, using the knuckles of the hand.

Batter: A mixture of flour and liquid of such consistency that it can be used as a coating or for baking.

Bake: Cook in an oven or on a hot surface without direct exposure to a flame.

Devein: Remove the main central vein from cray fish.

Blanch: Immerse briefly in boiling water to ease removed of skin like almonds or tomatoes.

Puree: Make a soft pulp of vegetables or fruit & reduce to a smooth paste.

Saute: Quickly fry in a little hot oil.

Par boil: To simmer or boil till partially cookies.
Fermentation: Effervescence caused by enzymes. Usually yeast is added to bread dough in order to raise it. Some batters are kept overnight to ferment.
Refresh: To cool hot food quickly either under running water or by dipping in ice cold water to stop further cooking.
Tadka (Tempering): Which boosts the flavours, heat up the reserved ghee / clarified butter or oil in a large ladle over a flame (or in a small pan) add the reserved cloves or cumin seeds and red chillies. Fry for few seconds until spices change colours and flavours released, pour the condiments quickly over the marinade.
To make hung curd: Tie the yoghurt in muslin cloth. Hung it for one hour and allow the water to drop in a container. (The whey is nutritious and can be used in other dishes or to make dough).
Bharwan: Stuffed.
Tikka: Small chunks of meat, chicken or fish, usually chicken, which can be skewered before roasting in the tandoor.
Kebab: Fish, chicken lamb or vegetable, usually skewered (whole cubes or mince) and roasted in a tandoor or grilled on charcoal iron grill. Also shallow fried on a griddle plate (e.g. Galouti, Shammi, etc.)
Marination: To soak meat, fish, vegetable before cooking in a mixture with spices, oil, yoghurt, cream to ensure that spices, herbs penetrate into the food item for flavour.
Marinade: Mixture in which spices, herbs, oil, yoghurt, cream, egg, as per choice have been mixed together for marination of meat, fish or vegetables.
Masala: In marination of kebabs one uses different kinds of masalas such as Garam masala, Tandoori masala etc.
Galavat: Refers to the use of softening agents such as PAPAIN (Raw Papaya), or Kalmi Shora to tenderize meat.
Clarified butter (Ghee): Over a medium flame heat some unsalted butter until it melts and froths in a heavy-bottomed skillet or saucepan. Remove the foam that rises from the top and once clear, pour the melted butter into a heat-proof container. Discard the milk solids that are left behind. Leave to cool at room temperature and then chill. When the chilled fat rises to the top, spoon it off, leaving the ghee further, then heat the ghee and strain it through a muslin cloth.
Note: In India, cooking oils with distinctive flavours, are used, depending on the region. In eastern

India, mustard oil and coconut oil are very popular, while in the south, til or sesame seed oil and coconut oil are used. It is recommended that a tasteless refined oil be used. Refined peanut oil is also suitable.

Gram flour: besan is used in certain dishes, snacks and in the making of Indian breads. Besan has a very distinctive flavour and must not be substituted with any other flour.

Roast yellow split peas in pan, stirring constantly, so that they do not burn. Remove the pan from the heat and cool. Then blend the roasted peas at a high speed or pound with a mortar and pestle. Sieve, the keep in an airtight container.

Baghar: Aromatic spices play a very important role in Indian cooking. These spices include cloves, cumin seeds, cardamom seeds and pods, and cinnamon sticks, just to name a few. When these spices are added to a heated cooking medium, they release their flavours into the cooking medium. This process of flavouring is called baghar. One can also experiment doing baghar with dry red and green chillies, and garlic cloves.

Heat the cooking medium until it is almost smoking; reduce the heat to medium and add the spices or condiments. Wait till the spices or condiments change color and float upon the oil, then remove the pan from the heat. This highly flavoured cooking medium can be added at either the beginning or at the end of cooking.

Mussallam: Any meat (chicken, leg of meat, goat or lamb, fish.........) or vegetable (cauli flower, bitter gourd ....) that is cooked whole is called mussallam.

Weights and Measures

WEIGHT EQUIVALENTS

Ounces	Grams
½ oz	14 gm
1 oz	28 gm
2 oz	57 gm
3 oz	85 gm
4 oz (¼ B)	113 gm
5 oz	142 gm
6 oz	170 gm
7 oz	198 gm
8 oz (½ B)	227 gm
9 oz	255 gm
10 oz	284 gm
11 oz	312 gm
12 oz (¾ B)	340 gm
13 oz	369 gm
14 oz	397 gm
15 oz	425 gm
16 oz (1 1B)	454 gm
24 oz	680 gm
32 oz (2 1B)	908 gm

LIQUID MEASURES EQUIVALENTS

Liquid Measures	Cup Measures	Liquid Measures
1 fl oz		30 ml
2 fl oz	¼ cup	60 ml
3 fl oz		100 ml
4 fl oz	½ cup	125 ml
5 fl oz		150 ml
6 fl oz	¾ cup	185 ml
8 fl oz	1 cup	240 ml
10 fl oz	(½ pt.)	1½ cups

Ounces		Grams	
1 tsp	=	5 gm	
2 tsp	=	10 gm	
3 tsp	=	15 gm	= 1 tbsp = ½ fl oz

Measurements

To convert the commonly used ingredients in this book, the following chart will be a convenient guide:

SPICES & POWDER

1.	Red chilli powder	1tsp	5gm
2.	Yellow chilli powder	1tsp	5gm
3.	Garam masala	1tsp	5gm
4.	kasoori methi powder	1tsp	5gm
5.	Cardamom powder	1tsp	5gm
6.	Mace powder (javitri)	1tsp	5gm
7.	Clove powder	1tsp	5gm
8.	Saunf powder	1tsp	5gm
9.	White pepper powder	1tsp	5gm
10.	Turmeric powder	1tsp	5gm
11.	Cinnamom powder	1tsp	5gm
12.	Galouti masala	1tsp	5gm
13.	Lucknowi masala	1tsp	5gm

SEEDS

14.	Cumin seeds	1tsp	3gm
15.	Fennel Seeds	1tsp	3gm
16.	Fenugreek seeds	1tsp	4gm
17.	Black peppercorn	1tsp	3gm
18.	Black onion seeds (kalonji)	1tsp	3gm
19.	Coriander seeds	1tsp	2gm
20.	Sesame seeds	1tsp	3gm
21.	Carom seeds (ajwain)	1tsp	3gm
22.	Mustard seeds	1tsp	3gm
23.	Poppy seeds	1tsp	3gm
24.	Royal cumin seeds	1tsp	3gm
25.	Pomegranate seeds	1tsp	3gm

VEGETABLES

26.	Green chilli (chopped)	1tsp	2gm
27.	Fresh coriander (chopped)	1tsp	1gm
28.	Fresh mint (chopped)	1tsp	1gm
29.	Onion (chopped)	1tsp	3gm
30.	Garlic (chopped)	1tsp	3gm
31.	Ginger (chopped)	1tsp	3gm

DRY FRUITS

#	Item	Measure	Weight
32.	Almonds (chopped)	1tsp	3gm
33.	Cashewnuts (chopped)	1tsp	3gm
34.	Pistachio (chopped)	1tsp	3gm
35.	Walnuts (chopped)	1tsp	3gm
36.	Raisins (chopped)	1tsp	3gm

FLOUR

#	Item	Measure	Weight
37.	Corn flour	1tbsp	5gm
38.	Gram flour	1tbsp	10gm
39.	Wheat flour	1tbsp	10gm

DAIRY

#	Item	Measure	Weight
40.	Processed cheese (grated)	1tbsp	8gm
41.	Cream	½ cup	120ml
42.	Hung curd	1tbsp	15gm
43.	Milk	½ cup	120ml
44.	Coconut oil	½ cup	120ml

OILS

#	Item	Measure	Weight
45.	Mustard oil	1tsp	5ml
46.	Refined oil	1tsp	5ml
47.	Clarified butter	1tsp	5gm
48.	Desi ghee	1tsp	5gm
49.	Olive oil	1tsp	5ml

LENTILS

#	Item	Measure	Weight
50.	All daals	½ cup	100gm
51.	All dry beans	½ cup	100gm
52.	All grams	½ cup	100gm

PASTES

#	Item	Measure	Weight
53.	Ginger garlic paste	1tsp	5gm
54.	Cashewnut paste	1tbsp	15gm
55.	Almond paste	1tbsp	15gm
56.	Poppy seed paste	1tbsp	15gm
57.	Red chilli paste	1tsp	5gm
58.	Raw papaya paste	1tsp	5gm
59.	Brown onion paste	1tbsp	15gm

OTHERS

#	Item	Measure	Weight
60.	Soya sauce	1tbsp	15ml
61.	Thai green paste	1tbsp	15gm

Basic Kitchen Equipments

Tandoor: The clay-oven is the most versatile kitchen equipment and plays a prominent part in the preparation of kebabs and Indian breads. The traditional tandoor is a clay oven fired by charcoal. Lately iron gas tandoors have been invented but these are not successful and nothing to match the versatility of clay oven. It is the charcoal aroma which is important. Temperature plays an important part in tandoor cooking. If the temperature is too high the charcoal is moved to one side with the help of a skewer. If the temperature is low then both the openings are shut off.

Tawa: A thick heavy iron griddle plate, slightly concave and used for making Tak-a-Tak kebabs, chapatis and paranthas etc.,

Paraat: A flat, round utensil with a border mostly preferred in brass otherwise in stainless steel. It is used for kneading flour dough for breads.

Chakla Belan: Chakla is a small marble or wooden platform, belan is a rolling pin, usually made of wood. This pair is used for rolling chapatis.

Kadhai: A deep frying pan similar to the Chinese wok. It is either made in brass or iron or stainless steel. Most common in iron.

Degchi/pateela/handi: All of these belong to the same family. They are traditionally made from brass or copper. Nowadays stainless steel is also used. A pateela has stright sides and a horizontal rim. The bottom is lightly rounded. A handi has a neck that is narrower than the base. A Degchi is a bigger version of the Handi.

Pauni: A small perforated frying spoon.

Karchhi: A ladle used for stirring.

Hamam-Dasta: A mortar and pestle, used to pound dry masalas and pastes.

Lohe ka Tandoor: It is an iron tandoor, as distinct from the clay tandoor. It has a kind of dome shape. Iron oven used for making most breads served as shermal, taftan, bakerkhani, etc.

And the usual graters, sieves, stainers, knives, lemon squeezers, etc.

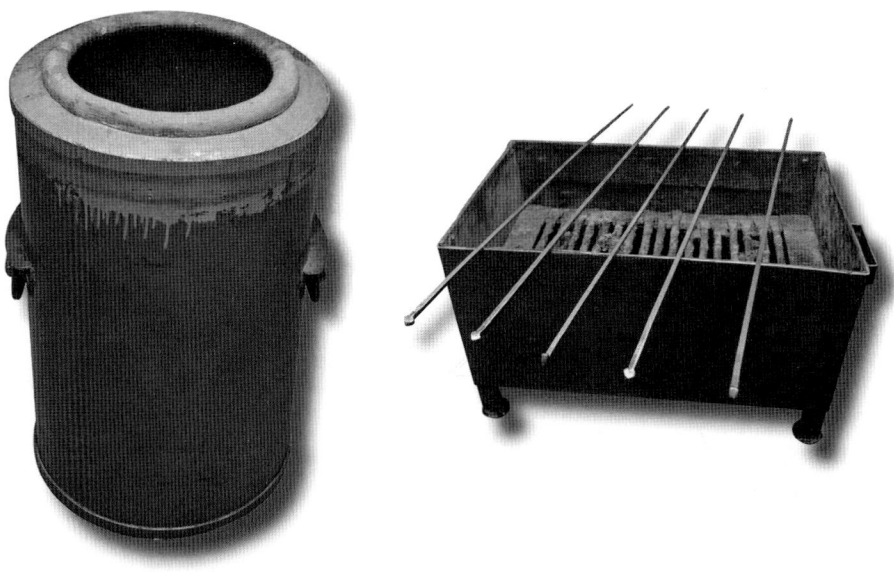

Poultry

POULTRY

Poultry is a misleading word; many people associate only chicken with poultry. No doubt, chicken is more universal, and in India it certainly is the most popular bird, but many other varieties of birds that come under poultry are eaten all over the world.

Other types of poultry commonly used in tandoori cuisine are partridge (teetar) and quail (bater). These are rare delicacies.

An important consideration in choosing chicken for kebabs will vary on the type of kebab to be made.

Whole Chicken - Use small birds (skinless)
Weight approx 650 – 700 gms
(ideal for tandoori chicken)

Large Pieces On Bone- Use medium size broiler (skinless)
Weight approx = 750-850 gms
4 in number, i.e., 2 breast and 2 legs.
8 in number, i.e., 4 each on breast and leg
(ideal for banquet menus)

Boneless - Use large broilers (skinless)
Weight approx = 1000-1250 gms
2 inch pieces from the leg and breast.

Mince- Use large broilers (skinless)
Finely minced

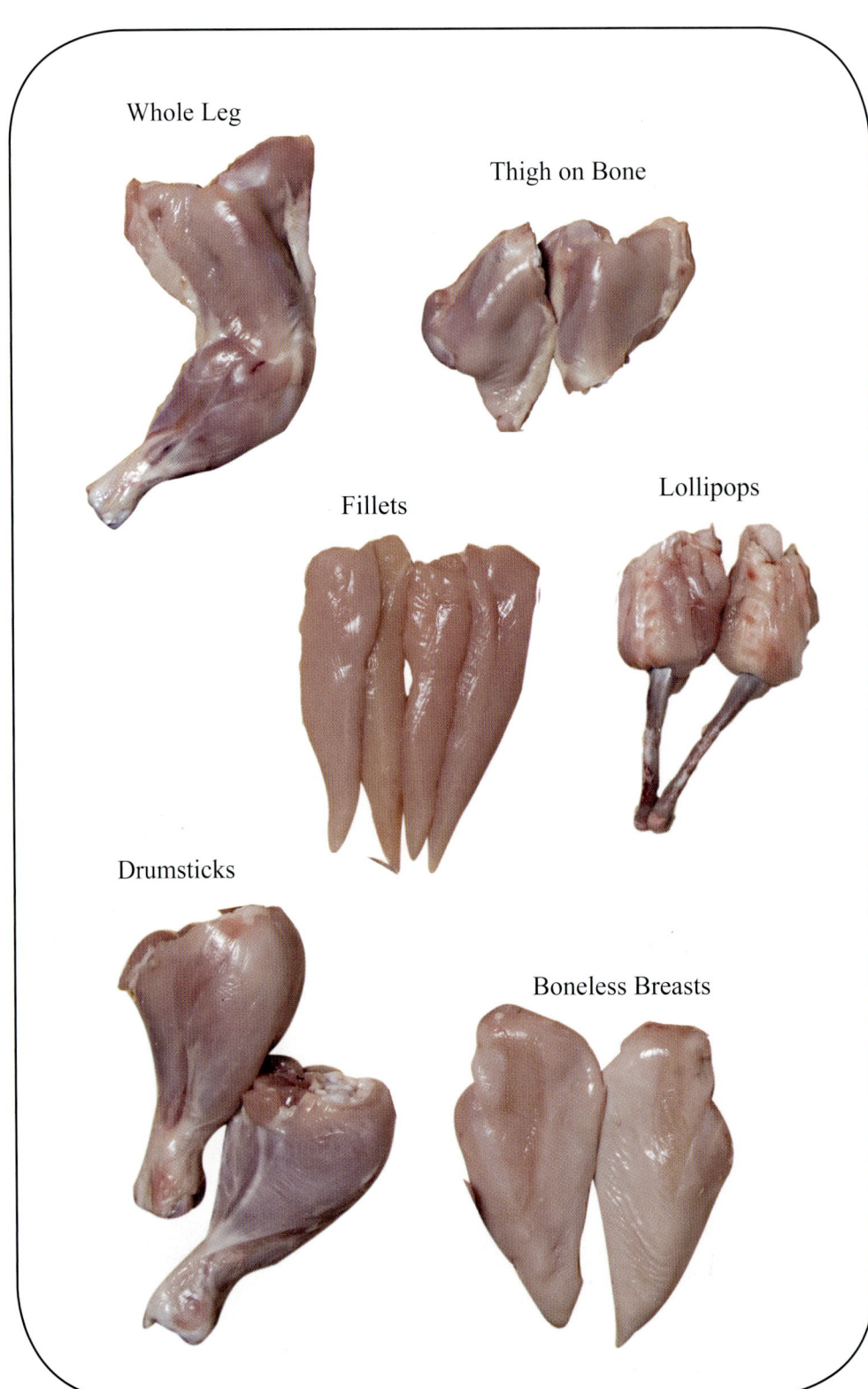

Pista Murg Tikka (for recipe turn to page no: 42)

Zaffrani Murg Kebab (for recipe turn to page no: 42)

Murg Methi Malai (for recipe turn to page no: 52)

Murg Potli Kebab (for recipe turn to page no: 45)

Chandi Murg Tikka (for recipe turn to page no: 48)

Shan - E - Murg (for recipe turn to page no: 50)

Tandoori Murg Chettinad (for recipe turn to page no: 58)

Murg Toofani Tikka

HOT AND SPICY CHICKEN KEBAB
Cooking time 10-12 minutes Serves 1-2

INGREDIENTS

200-225 gm-Chicken leg boneless (2 no.)

First marination

½ tsp	- Garlic paste
To taste	- Salt
½ tsp	- Yellow chilli powder
1 tsp	- Lemon juice

Second marination

4 tbsp	- Hung curd
To taste	- Salt
½ tsp	- Yellow chilli powder
1 tsp	- Garlic (chopped)
1 tsp	- English mustard paste
1/3 tsp	- Garam masala
A pinch	- Turmeric powder
2 tsp	- Khus-khus (poppy seeds)
2 tsp	- Lemon juice
2 tsp	- Refined oil

For basting - Clarified butter

METHOD

1. Clean, cut each chicken leg into 3 pieces each, wash, pat dry and keep aside.

First marination

2. In a bowl mix garlic paste, salt, yellow chilli powder and lemon juice. Apply this to chicken pieces, rub well and keep aside for at least 45 minutes.

Second marination

3. In a bowl whisk hung curd, add salt, yellow chilli powder, garlic chopped, English mustard paste, garam masala, turmeric, khus-khus, lemon juice, oil and mix well.
4. Put chicken pieces into this marinade, coat well and keep aside for at least 1 hour.

Cooking

5. Take a skewer and skew the marinated chicken pieces, keep a tray underneath to collect drippings.
6. Roast in a moderately hot tandoor or over charcoal grill for 7-8 minutes.
7. Baste with clarified butter and further roast for 3-4 minutes or till tender.
8. Serve hot with choice of a salad and chutney.

Lahori Murg Tikka

SUCCULENT CHICKEN KEBAB PREPARED WITH ROCK SALT IN TRUE LAHORI STYLE
Cooking time 10-12 minutes Serves 1-2

INGREDIENTS

200-225 gm-Chicken leg boneless (2 pcs)

First Marination

½ tsp	- Ginger garlic paste
1 tsp	- Lemon juice
To taste	- Lahori salt

First Marination

2 tsp	- Processed cheese (grated)
4 tbsp	- Hung curd
To taste	- Lahori salt
½ tsp	- Ginger garlic paste
1/3 tsp	- Yellow chilli powder
½ tsp	- Garam masala
2 tsp	- Brown onion paste
2 tsp	- Refined oil
A pinch	- Saffron

For basting - Clarified butter

METHOD

1. Clean, wash, and cut the chicken leg into 3 pieces each, pat dry and keep aside.

First Marination

2. In a bowl mix ginger garlic paste, lahori salt, lemon juice and apply this to chicken pieces, rub well and keep aside for at least 45 minutes.

Second Marination

3. Mash processed cheese in a bowl, add hung curd, Lahori salt, ginger garlic paste, yellow chilli powder, garam masala, brown onion paste, oil and saffron and mix well.
4. Put the chicken pieces into this marinade, coat well and keep aside for at least 1 hour.

Cooking

5. Take a skewer and skew the marinated chicken pieces, keep a tray underneath to collect drippings.
6. Roast in a moderately hot tandoor or over charcoal grill for 7-8 minutes.
7. Remove and baste with clarified butter and further roast for 3-4 minutes or till tender.
8. Serve hot with choice of a salad and Chutney.

Murg Dhaniya Tikka

FRESH CORIANDER FLAVOURED CHICKEN KEBAB
Cooking time 10-12 minutes Serves 1-2

INGREDIENTS

200-225 gm-Chicken leg boneless (2 pcs)

First Marination
½ tsp	- Ginger garlic paste
A pinch	- Yellow chilli powder
To taste	- Salt
1 tsp	- Lemon juice

Second Marination
4 tbsp	- Hung curd
To taste	- Salt
½ tsp	- Ginger garlic paste
½ tsp	- Yellow chilli powder
A pinch	- Garam masala
½ tsp	- Dhaniya powder
2 tsp	- Whole dhaniya (crushed)
2 tsp	- Refined oil

For basting - Clarified butter

METHOD

1. Clean, cut chicken leg into 3 pcs, wash, pat dry and keep aside.

First Marination
2. In a bowl mix ginger garlic paste, yellow chilli powder, salt, lemon juice and apply this to the chicken pieces, rub well and keep aside for at least 45 minutes.

Second Marination
3. In a bowl whisk hung curd and add salt, ginger garlic paste, yellow chilli powder, garam masala, dhaniya powder, whole dhaniya crushed, oil and mix well.
4. Put chicken pieces into this marinade, coat well and keep aside for at least 1 hour.

Cooking
5. Take a skewer and skew the marinated chicken pieces, keep a tray underneath to collect drippings.
6. Roast in a moderately hot tandoor or over charcoal grill for 7-8 minutes.
7. Remove and baste with clarified butter and further roast for 3-4 minutes or till tender.
8. Remove and serve hot along with choice of a salad and chutney.

Peeli Mirch Ka Tikka

YELLOW CHILLI FLAVOURED DELICIOUS CHICKEN KEBAB
Cooking time 10-12 minutes Serves 1-2

INGREDIENTS

200-225 gm-Chicken leg boneless (2 pcs)

First Marination
½ tsp	- Ginger garlic paste
To taste	- Salt
1 tsp	- Lemon juice
½ tsp	- Yellow chilli powder

Second Marination
4 tbsp	- Hung curd
To taste	- Salt
½ tsp	- Ginger garlic paste
½ tsp	- Yellow chilli powder
A pinch	- Turmeric powder
2 tsp	- Refined oil

For basting - Clarified butter

METHOD

1. Clean, cut chicken leg into 3 pieces, wash, pat dry and keep aside.

First Marination
2. In a bowl mix ginger garlic paste, salt, lemon juice, yellow chilli powder and apply this to chicken pieces, rub well and keep aside for at least 45 minutes.

Second Marination
3. In a bowl whisk hung curd, add salt, ginger garlic paste, yellow chilli powder, turmeric powder, oil and mix well.
4. Put the chicken pieces into this marinade, coat well and keep aside for at least 1 hour.

Cooking
5. Take a skewer and skew the marinated chicken pieces.
6. Roast in a moderately hot tandoor or over a charcoal grill for 7-8 minutes.
7. Remove and baste with clarified butter and further roast for 3-4 minutes or till tender collect drippings.
8. Remove and serve hot with choice of a salad and chutney.

Murg Bikaneri Tikka

SUCCULENT CHICKEN KEBAB FROM THE ROYAL KITCHEN OF BIKANER

Cooking time 10 – 12 minutes Serves 1-2

INGREDIENTS

200- 225 gm-Chicken leg boneless(2 pcs)

First Marination

To taste	- Salt
1/3 tsp	- Yellow chilli powder
2 tsp	- Ginger juice

Second Marination

4 tbsp	- Hung curd
To taste	- Salt
½ tsp	- Yellow chilli powder
2 tsp	- Ginger garlic paste
½ tsp	- Green chilli (chopped)
1 tsp	- Green coriander (chopped)
2 tsp	- Khus khus paste
2 tsp	- Refined oil
For basting	- Clarified butter

METHOD

1. Clean, wash and cut each chicken leg into 3 pieces, pat dry and keep aside

First Marination

2. In a bowl mix salt, yellow chilli powder, ginger juice and apply this to chicken pieces, rub well and keep aside for at least 45 minutes.

Second Marination

3. In a bowl whisk hung curd, add salt, yellow chilli powder, ginger garlic paste, green coriander, green chilli, khus-khus paste, oil and mix well
4. Put chicken pieces into this marinade, coat well and keep aside for at least 1 hour.

Cooking

5. Take a skewer and skew the marinated chicken pieces. Keep a tray underneath to collect the drippings
6. Roast in a moderately hot tandoor or over charcoal grill for 6-7 minutes
7. Remove and hang skewer to let excess moisture drain out for 1-2 minutes. Baste with clarified butter and further roast for 3-4 minutes or till tender.
8. Serve hot with choice of a salad and chutney.

Hari Mirch Kebab

JUICY CHICKEN TIKKA WITH GREEN CHILLI

Cooking time 10-12 minutes Serves 1-2

INGREDIENTS

200-225 gm-Chicken leg boneless (2 pcs)

First Marination

½ tsp	- Ginger garlic paste
To taste	- Salt
A pinch	- White pepper powder
1 tsp	- Lemon juice

Second Marination

2 tsp	- Processed cheese (grated)
½ tsp	- Ginger garlic paste
5 tsp	- Cream
To taste	- Salt
1/3 tsp	- White pepper powder
1 tsp	- Green chilli paste
For basting	- Clarified butter

METHOD

1. Clean, wash and cut chicken leg into 3 pcs, pat dry and keep aside.

First Marination

2. In a bowl mix ginger garlic paste, salt, white pepper powder, lemon juice and apply this to the chicken pieces, rub well and keep aside for at least 45 minutes.

Second Marination

3. In a deep tray mash cheese, add ginger garlic paste, cream, salt, white pepper powder, green chilli paste and mix well.
4. Put chicken pieces into this marinade, coat well and keep aside for at least 1 hour.

Cooking

5. Take a skewer and skew the marinated chicken pieces, keep a tray under neath to collect drippings.
6. Roast in a moderately hot tandoor or over charcoal grill for 7-8 minutes.
7. Remove and baste with clarified butter and further roast for 3-4 minutes or till tender.
8. Remove and serve hot along with choice of a salad and chutney.

Murg Haryali Tikka

CHAR-GRILLED CHICKEN MORSELS WITH DELICATE FLAVOUR OF MINT AND CORIANDER

Cooking Time 10-12 minutes Serves 1-2

INGREDIENTS

200-225gm - Chicken leg boneless (2 pcs)

First Marination
To taste	- Salt
½ tsp	- Ginger garlic paste
2 tsp	- Lemon juice
½ tsp	- Yellow chilli powder

Green Paste
10 gm	- Mint leaves
50 gm	- Coriander leaves
50 gm	- Boiled spinach
2 no	- Green chilli (chopped)

Second Marination
4 tbsp	- Hung curd
To taste	- Salt
1/3 tsp	- Yellow chilli powder
½ tsp	- Garam masala
2 tsp	- Mustard oil

For basting - Clarified butter

METHOD

1. Clean, wash and cut each chicken leg into 3 pieces, pat dry and keep aside.

First Marination

2. In a bowl mix salt, ginger garlic paste, lemon juice, yellow chilli powder and apply this to the chicken pieces, rub well and keep aside for at least 45 minutes.

Green Paste

3. Put mint leaves, coriander, spinach and green chillies in a processor and make a thick paste. Transfer it to a bowl.

Second Marination

4. In a bowl Whisk hung curd, add green paste (4tsp), salt, yellow chilli powder, garam masala, mustard oil and Mix well.
5. Put the chicken pieces into this marinade, coat well and keep aside for at least 1 hour.

Cooking

6. Take a skewer and skew the marinated chicken pieces. Keep a tray underneath to collect drippings
7. Roast in moderately hot tandoor or over charcoal grill for 7-8 minutes, till half done.
8. Remove and baste with clarified butter and further roast for 3-4 minutes or till tender.
9. Serve hot along with a choice of a salad and chutney.

Julandhari Chatpate Murg Tikke

HOT AND SPICY CHICKEN TIKKA FROM THE CITY OF PUNJAB

Cooking time 10-12 minutes Serves 1-2

INGREDIENTS

200-225 gm - Chicken leg boneless (2 pcs)

First Marination
To taste	-Salt
½ tsp	-Ginger garlic paste
1 tsp	-Lemon juice

Second Marination
4 tbsp	-Hung curd
To taste	-Salt
½ tsp	-Ginger garlic paste
½ tsp	-Red chilli paste
2 tsp	-Mint chopped
2 tsp	-Lemon juice
½ tsp	-Garam masala
2 tsp	-Refined oil

For basting -Clarified butter

METHOD

1. Clean, cut chicken leg into 3 pieces, wash, pat dry and keep aside.

First Marination

2. In a bowl mix salt, ginger garlic paste, lemon juice and apply this to chicken leg, rub well and keep aside for at least 45 minutes.

Second Marination

3. In a bowl whisk hung curd, add salt, ginger garlic paste, red chilli paste, mint chopped, lemon juice, garam masala, oil and mix well
4. Put the chicken pieces into this marinade, coat well and keep aside for at least 1 hour.

Cooking

5. Take a skewer and skew the marinated chicken pieces, keep the tray underneath to collect drippings.
6. Roast in a moderately hot tandoor or over a charcoal grill for 7-8 minutes.
7. Remove and baste with clarified butter and further roast for (3-4 minutes) or till tender.
8. Serve hot with choice of a salad and chutney.

Tandoori Tikka Hakka Style

CHICKEN KEBAB PREPARED WITH CHINESE TOUCH

Cooking time 10-12 minutes Serves 1-2

INGREDIENTS

200-225 gm-Chicken leg boneless (2 pcs)

First Marination
To taste	- Salt
½ tsp	- Ginger garlic paste
1 tsp	- HP sauce
2 tsp	- Lemon juice
1/2 tsp	- Red chilli paste

Second Marination
4 tbsp	- Hung curd
To taste	- Salt
½ tsp	- Ginger garlic paste
1 tsp	- Lemon juice
½ tsp	- Red chilli paste
1 tsp	- Soya sauce
2 tsp	- Cornflour

For basting - Clarified butter

METHOD

1. Clean, cut each chicken leg into 3 pieces, wash, pat dry and keep aside.

First Marination

2. In a bowl mix salt, ginger garlic paste, HP sauce, lemon juice, red chilli paste and apply this to the chicken pieces, rub well and keep aside for at least 45 minutes.

Second Marination

3. In a bowl whisk hung curd, add salt, ginger garlic paste, lemon juice, red chilli paste, soya sauce, corn flour and mix well.
4. Put the chicken pieces into this marinade, coat well and keep aside for at least 1 hour.

Cooking

5. Take a skewer and skew the marinated chicken pieces. Keep a tray underneath to collect drippings.
6. Roast in a moderately hot tandoor or over a charcoal grill for 7-8 minutes.
7. Remove and baste with clarified butter and further roast for 3-4 minutes or till tender.
8. Serve hot with choice of a salad and chutney.

Murg Tulsi Tikka

LOW CALORIE BASIL FLAVOURED DELICIOUS CHICKEN KEBAB

Cooking time 10-12 minutes Serves 1-2

INGREDIENTS

200-225 gm-Chicken leg boneless (2 pcs)

First Marination
To taste	- Salt
½ tsp	- Ginger garlic paste
½ tsp	- Yellow chilli powder

Second Marination
4 tbsp	- Hung curd
To taste	- Salt
1/3 tsp	- Yellow chilli powder
1 tsp	- Lemon juice
1 tsp	- Cashewnut paste
2 tsp	- Basil paste
2 tsp	- Olive oil

For basting - Olive oil

METHOD

1. Clean, cut each chicken leg into 3 pieces each, wash, pat dry and keep aside.

First Marination

2. In a bowl mix salt, ginger garlic paste, yellow chilli powder and apply this to chicken pieces, rub well and keep aside for at least 45 minutes.

Second Marination

3. In a bowl whisk hung curd, add salt, yellow chilli powder, lemon juice, cashewnut paste, basil paste, olive oil and mix well.
4. Put the chicken pieces into this marinade, coat well and keep aside for at least 1 hour.

Cooking

5. Take a skewer and skew marinated chicken pieces. Keep a tray underneath to collect drippings.
6. Roast in a moderately hot tandoor or over a charcoal grill for 7-8 minutes.
7. Remove and baste with olive oil and further roast for (3-4 minutes) or till tender.
8. Serve hot with choice of a salad and chutney.

Pista Murg Tikka

CHAR-GRILLED CHICKEN MORSELS WITH DELICATE FLAVOUR OF GREEN PISTACHIO
Cooking time 10-12 minutes **Serves** 1-2

INGREDIENTS

(200-225 gm)-Chicken leg boneless (2 pcs)

First Marination
To taste	- Salt
½ tsp	- Ginger garlic paste
½ tsp	- Yellow chilli powder

Paste
15 gms	- Pistachio
2 no	- Green chilli
5 no	- Curry leaves
35 gm	- Processed cheese (grated)
20 gm	- Green coriander (chopped)

Second Marination
4 tbsp	- Hung curd
To taste	- Salt
1/3 tsp	- Yellow chilli powder
2 tsp	- Lemon juice
1 tsp	- Cream
2 tsp	- Refined oil
1 tsp	- Pista flakes

For basting - Clarified butter

METHOD

1. Wash, clean and cut chicken leg into 3 pieces each, pat dry and keep aside.

First Marination
2. In a bowl mix salt, ginger garlic paste, yellow chilli powder, and apply this to chicken pieces, rub well and keep aside for at least 45 minutes.

Paste
3. In a processor make a fine paste of pista, green chilli, curry leaf, cheese, green coriander and remove in a bowl.

Second Marination
4. In a bowl whisk hung curd and add salt, yellow chilli, lemon juice, cream, oil, pista flakes 4 tsp of pista paste and mix well.
5. Dip chicken into this marinade, coat well and keep aside for at least 1 hour.

Cooking
6. Take a skewer and skew the marinated chicken pieces, keep a tray underneath to collect drippings.
7. Roast in a moderately hot tandoor or over a charcoal grills for 7-8 minutes.
8. Remove and baste with clarified butter and further roast for 2-3 minutes or till tender.
9. Serve hot with a choice of a salad and chutney.

Zaffrani Murg Kebab

A DELICATE SAFFRON FLAVOURED KEBAB MADE WITH CHICKEN FILLET AND MILDLY SEASONED
Cooking time 3-4 minutes **Serves** 1-2

INGREDIENTS

150-175 gms-Chicken fillet (8 pcs)

3 tsp	- Processed cheese
1 no	- Egg yolk
To taste	- Salt
2 tbsp	- Cream
½ tsp	- White pepper powder
½ tsp	- Ginger garlic paste
A pinch	- Elaichi powder
1/3 tsp	- Saffron
2 tsp	- Roasted channa powder

For frying - Refined oil

METHOD

1. Clean the chicken fillets, pat dry and keep aside.

Marination
2. In a deep tray mash processed cheese with your palm till smooth, add egg yolk, salt, cream, white pepper powder, ginger garlic paste, elaichi powder, saffron, roasted channa powder and mix well to smooth consistency.
3. Put chicken fillets in the marinade and coat well and keep aside for at least 1 hour.

Cooking
4. Take a wooden stick and skew marinated chicken pieces.
5. Heat oil in a non-stick pan and shallow fry the chicken pieces till golden brown on both sides.
6. Remove and serve hot with choice of a salad and chutney.

Murg Sarson Tikka

CHICKEN CHUNKS RESERVED IN A YOGHURT MARINADE WITH SYMPHONY OF EXOTIC SPICES INCLUDING EXTRA TOUCH OF MUSTARD GRAINS

Cooking time 10-12 minutes Serves 1-2

INGREDIENTS

(200-225 gm) Chicken leg boneless (2 pcs)

First Marination
To taste	- Salt
½ tsp	- Ginger garlic paste
½ tsp	- Yellow chilli powder
1 tsp	- Mustard paste

Second Marination
4 tbsp	- Hung curd
To taste	- Salt
½ tsp	- Ginger garlic paste
½ tsp	- Green chilli (chopped)
1 tsp	- Lemon juice
A pinch	- Turmeric powder
½ tsp	- Mustard paste
1 tsp	- Mustard oil

For basting - Clarified butter

METHOD

1. Wash, clean and cut chicken leg into 3 pieces each, pat dry and keep aside.

First Marination
2. In a bowl mix salt, ginger garlic paste, yellow chilli powder, mustard paste, apply this to the chicken pieces, rub well and keep aside for at least 45 minutes.

Second Marination
3. In a bowl whisk hung curd, add salt, ginger garlic paste, yellow chilli powder, green chilli, lemon juice, turmeric powder, mustard paste, mustard oil and mix well.
4. Put the chicken pieces into this marinade, coat well and keep aside for at least 1 hour.

Cooking
5. Take a skewer and skew the marinated chicken pieces. Keep a tray underneath to collect drippings.
6. Roast in a moderately hot tandoor or over a charcoal grill for 7-8 minutes.
7. Remove and baste with clarified butter and further roast for 2-3 minutes or till tender.
8. Serve hot with choice of a salad and chutney.

Murg Tikka Thai Style

JUICY CHICKEN KEBAB WITH THAI SPICES

Cooking time 10-12 minutes Serves 1-2

INGREDIENTS

(200-225 gm) - Chicken leg boneless (2 pcs)

First Marination
½ tsp	- Ginger garlic paste
To taste	- Salt
2 tsp	- Lemon juice

Second Marination
4 tbsp	- Hung curd
To taste	- Salt
4 tsp	- Coconut milk
2 tsp	- Thai green paste
1/2 tsp	- Lemon grass (chopped)
2 tsp	- Refined oil

For basting - Clarified butter

METHOD

1. Clean, wash and cut each chicken leg into 3 pieces, pat dry and keep aside.

First Marination
2. In a bowl mix ginger garlic paste, salt, lemon juice and apply this to the chicken pieces, rub well and keep aside for 45 minutes

Second Marination
3. In a bowl whisk hung curd, add salt, coconut milk, Thai green paste, lemon grass, oil and mix well.
4. Put the chicken pieces into this above marinade, coat well and keep aside for 1 hour.

Cooking
5. Take a skewer and skew the marinated chicken pieces. Keep a tray underneath to collect drippings.
6. Roast in a moderately hot tandoor or over a charcoal grill for 7-8 minutes.
7. Remove and baste with clarified butter and further roast for 3-4 minutes or till tender.
8. Serve hot with choice of a salad and chutney.

Murg Elaichi Tukra

A SUCCULENT BONELESS CHICKEN KEBAB FLAVOURED WITH GREEN CARDAMOM

Cooking time 8-10 minutes Serves 1-2

INGREDIENTS

200-225 gm-Boneless chicken breast (3 no)

First Marination
½ tsp	- Ginger garlic paste
To taste	- Salt
1/3 tsp	- White pepper powder

Second Marination
4 tbsp	- Hung curd
To taste	- Salt
½ tsp	- Ginger garlic paste
3 tsp	- Cream
1 tsp	- Elaichi powder
1/3 tsp	- White pepper powder
1 tsp	- Corn flour

For basting - Clarified butter

METHOD

1. Clean, wash and cut each chicken breast into 2 pieces each, pat dry and keep aside.

First Marination
2. In a bowl mix ginger garlic paste, salt, white pepper powder and apply this to chicken breast, rub well and keep aside for at least 45 minutes.

Second Marination
3. In a bowl whisk hung curd, add salt, ginger garlic paste, cream, elaichi powder, white pepper powder, corn flour and mix well.
4. Put chicken pieces into this marinade, coat well and keep aside for at least 1 hour.

Cooking
5. Take a skewer and skew the marinated chicken pieces, keep a tray underneath to collect drippings.
6. Roast in a moderately hot tandoor or over a charcoal grill for 6-7 minutes.
7. Remove and baste with clarified butter and further roast for 2-3 minutes or till tender.
8. Serve hot with choice of a salad and chutney.

Murg Potli Kebab

FUSION OF CHICKEN BREAST BUNDLED WITH EXOTIC LAMB MINCE AND ROASTED IN CLAY OVEN

Cooking time 8-10 minutes Serves 1-2

INGREDIENTS

175 gms - Chicken breast boneless (3 nos)

First Marination
To taste	- Salt
A pinch	- White pepper powder
½ tsp	- Ginger garlic paste

Stuffing
2 tsp	- Refined oil
1 tsp	- Cashewnut (chopped)
75 gm	- Lamb mince
To taste	- Salt
½ tsp	- White pepper powder
½ tsp	- Green chilli (chopped)
½ tsp	- Green coriander (chopped)
A pinch	- Saffron

Second Marination
3 tsp	- Processed cheese
2 tsp	- Egg white
4 tbsp	- Cream
2 tsp	- Cashewnut paste
To taste	- Salt
½ tsp	- White pepper powder
½ tsp	- Green chilli (chopped)
A pinch	- Elaichi powder
A pinch	- Shahi jeera

For basting - Clarified butter

METHOD

1. Clean and flatten each breast with a hammer till thin, pat dry and keep aside.

First Marination
2. In a bowl mix ginger garlic paste, salt, white pepper powder, rub well and apply this to chicken breast and keep aside for at least 45 minutes.

Stuffing
3. Heat oil in a pan, saute cashewnut, add lamb mince, salt, white pepper powder, green chilli, green coriander, saffron and saute till mince is cooked and water evaporates. Keep it aside for cooling.
4. Stuff each breast with this mince and tie it with a thread to make a potli. (Round balloon shape).

Second Marination
5. In a deep tray mash grated cheese and egg white, ginger garlic paste and mix it gradually with your palm. Pour cream and further mix it, so that it becomes a smooth paste. Add cashewnut paste, salt, white pepper powder, green chilli, elaichi powder, shahi jeera and mix well.
6. Put the chicken pieces into this marinade, coat well and keep aside for at least 1 hour.

Cooking
7. Take a skewer and skew the marinated chicken pieces. Keep a tray underneath to collect drippings.
8. Roast in a moderately hot tandoor or over a charcoal grill for 6-7 minutes.
9. Remove and baste with clarified butter and further roast for 2-3 minutes or till tender.
10. Serve hot with choice of a salad and chutney.

Murg Nizami Kebab

A CREAMY AND GENTLY SPICED CHICKEN KEBAB FLAVOURED WITH SAFFRON PRESENTED IN THE WAY NIZAMS OF HYDERABAD ENJOYED IT

Cooking time 8-10 minutes **Serves** 1-2

INGREDIENTS

200-225 gm-Chicken breast boneless (3 No)

First Marination
½ tsp	- Ginger garlic paste
To taste	- Salt
1/3 tsp	- White pepper powder

Second Marination
4 tsp	- Processed cheese (grated)
1 no	- Egg white
½ tsp	- Ginger garlic paste
4 tbsp	- Cream
To taste	- Salt
2 tsp	- Tamarind pulp
1/3 tsp	- White pepper powder
A pinch	- Elaichi Powder
½ tsp	- Green chilli (chopped)
A pinch	- Shahi jeera
2 tsp	- Almonds (chopped)
A pinch	- Saffron

For basting - Clarified butter

METHOD

1. Clean, cut chicken into 2 pieces each, wash, pat dry and keep aside.

First Marination

2. In a bowl mix ginger garlic paste, salt and white pepper powder and apply this to chicken breast, rub well and keep aside for atleast 45 minutes.

Second Marination

3. In a deep tray mash grated cheese and add egg white, ginger garlic paste and rub it well to make a smooth paste then add cream, salt, tamarind pulp, white pepper powder, elaichi powder, green chilli, shahi jeera, chopped almonds and saffron, mix well
4. Put the chicken pieces into this marinade, coat well and keep aside for at least 1 hour.

Cooking

5. Take a skewer and skew marinated chicken pieces, keep a tray underneath to collect drippings.
6. Roast in a moderately hot tandoor or over a charcoal grill for 6-7 minutes.
7. Remove and baste with clarified butter and further roast for 2-3 minutes or till tender.
8. Serve hot with choice of a salad and chutney.

Chicken And Cheese Kebab

A DIFFERENT AND UNIQUE BOILED CHICKEN SMOTHERED WITH PROCESSED CHEESE INFUSED WITH ROYAL CUMIN AND CRISP FRIED

Cooking time 2-3 minutes **Serves** 1-2

INGREDIENTS

75 gm	- Boiled chicken (chopped)
	- (Chicken Brest)
100 gm	- Boiled potatoes (grated)
30 gm	- Processed cheese (grated)
5 gm	- Green chilli (chopped)
1 tsp	- Fresh coriander (chopped)
To taste	- Salt
1/3 tsp	- White pepper powder
1 no	- Egg
A pinch	- Shahi jeera (black cumin)
For binding	- Dry breadcrumbs

For frying - Refined oil

METHOD

1. Clean, remove shoulder bone of the chicken breast, boil and chop.
2. Put chicken in a deep tray, add potatoes, cheese, green chilli, coriander, salt, white pepper, egg, shahi jeera, dry breadcrumbs, mix well and keep aside for at least 45 minutes.
3. Divide the mixture into 6-8 equal parts and make balls using wet hands and give it a shape of medallion (tikki) shape.

Cooking

1. Heat oil in a kadhai and deep fry till golden brown colour and crisp.
2. Serve hot with choice of a salad and chutney.

Puddine Wala Murg Seena

A JUICY KEBAB MADE FROM BREAST OF CHICKEN STEEPED IN RICH MINT MARINADE

Cooking time 8-10 minutes Serves 1-2

INGREDIENTS

200-225 gm - Chicken breast boneless (3 no)

First Marination
To taste	- Salt
½ tsp	- Ginger garlic paste
½ tsp	- White pepper powder

Second Marination
4-5 tbsp	- Hung curd
To taste	- Salt
½ tsp	- Ginger garlic paste
2 tsp	- Cashewnut paste
1/3 tsp	- White pepper powder
2 tsp	- Fresh mint (chopped)
1 tsp	- Dry puddina (powder)
1 tsp	- Vinegar

For basting - Clarified butter

METHOD

1. Clean and cut each chicken breast into 2 pieces each, wash, pat dry and keep aside.

First Marination
2. In a bowl mix salt, ginger garlic paste, white pepper powder and apply this to the chicken, rub well and keep aside for at least 45 minutes.

Second Marination
3. In a bowl whisk hung curd, add salt, ginger garlic paste, cashewnut paste, white pepper powder, puddina chopped, dry puddina, vinegar and mix well.
4. Put the chicken pieces into this marinade, coat well and keep aside for at least 1 hour.

Cooking
5. Take a skewer and skew marinated chicken breast pieces one by one leaving a gap of an inch between. Keep a tray underneath to collect drippings.
6. Roast on a moderately hot tandoor or over a charcoal grill for 6-7 minutes.
7. Remove and baste with clarified butter and further roast for 2-3 minutes or till tender.
8. Serve hot with choice of a salad and chutney.

Murg Malai Tikka

A CREAMY KEBAB MADE FROM BREAST OF CHICKEN, THE MURG MALAI COMBINES THE JOY OF THE TRADITIONAL KEBAB, HERBS AND SPICED WITH PROCESSED CHEESE. AN ALL TIME FAVOURITE

Cooking time 8-10 minutes Serves 1-2

INGREDIENTS

200-225 gms-Chicken breast boneless (3 no.)

First Marination
½ tsp	- Ginger garlic paste
1/3 tsp	- White pepper powder
To taste	- Salt

Second Marination
4 tsp	- Processed cheese (grated)
2 no	- Egg white
½ tsp	- Ginger garlic paste
3 tbsp	- Cream
To taste	- Salt
A pinch	- White pepper powder
¼ tsp	- Green chilli (chopped)
½ tsp	- Green coriander (chopped)
A pinch	- Elaichi powder

For basting - Clarified butter

METHOD

1. Clean and wash the chicken breast, cut into 2 pieces each, pat dry and keep aside

First Marination
2. In a bowl mix ginger garlic paste, white pepper powder, salt and apply this to chicken breast, rub well and keep aside for at least 45 minutes.

Second Marination
3. In a bowl mash grated processed cheese, rub it with palm and then add egg white, ginger garlic paste. Rub it well then add cream, salt, white pepper powder, green chilli, green coriander, elaichi powder and mix well to smooth consistency.
4. Put the marinated chicken in this mixture, coat well and keep aside for at least 1 hour.

Cooking
5. Take a skewer and skew the marinated chicken pieces. Keep a tray underneath to collect the drippings.
6. Roast in a moderately hot tandoor or over a charcoal grill for 6-7 minutes till half done.
7. Remove and baste with clarified butter and further roast for 2-3 minutes or till tender.
8. Serve hot with choice of a salad and chutney.

Chandi Murg Tikka

THIS IS A MAGNIFICENT KEBAB OF TENDER CHICKEN BREAST ENHANCED WITH HOME GROUND SPICES AND ROLLED IN SILVER LEAVES

Cooking time 8-10 minutes **Serves** 1-2

INGREDIENTS

200–225 gm Chicken breast boneless (03 no)

First Marination
½ tsp	- Ginger garlic paste
To taste	- Salt
½ tsp	- White pepper powder

Second Marination
3 tsp	- Processed cheese (grated)
2 tsp	- Egg white
½ tsp	- Ginger garlic paste
4 tbsp	- Cream
To taste	- Salt
½ tsp	- Green chilli (chopped)
1 tsp	- Fresh coriander (chopped)
½ tsp	- White pepper powder
A pinch	- Elaichi powder
A pinch	- Shahi jeera (black cumin)
3 tsp	- Mixed dry fruit (chopped)
2 tsp	- Cornflour

For basting - Clarified butter

For coating - Chandi ka varq (silver leaves)

METHOD

1. Wash, clean, and cut chicken breast, into 2 pieces each, pat dry and keep aside.

First Marination

2. In a bowl mix ginger garlic paste, salt, white pepper powder and apply this to the chicken pieces, rub well and keep aside for at least 45 minutes.

Second Marination

3. In a deep tray mash grated cheese, egg white, ginger garlic paste and mix gradually with your palm, pour cream and mix further so that it becomes a smooth paste. Add cream, salt, green chilli, green coriander, white pepper, elaichi powder, shahi jeera, mix dry fruits, corn flour and mix well.
4. Put chicken pieces into this marinade, coat well and keep aside for at least 1 hour.

Cooking

5. Take a skewer and skew the marinated chicken pieces, keep tray underneath to collect drippings.
6. Roast over a charcoal grill or in a moderately hot tandoor for 6-7 minutes.
7. Remove and baste with clarified butter and further roast for 2-3 minutes or till tender.
8. Transfer chicken to a plate and, coat with chandi ka varq completely.
9. Serve hot with choice of a salad and chutney.

Bakarkhani Seekh Kebab

AN IMPRESSIVE CHICKEN MINCE SKEWER, ENRICHED WITH ALMONDS, WITH FLORAL AROMA AND SUBTLE SPICES

Cooking time 7-8 minutes **Serves** 1-2

INGREDIENTS

2 tbsp	- Processed cheese (grated)
½ tsp	- Ginger garlic paste
200 gm	- Chicken mince
To taste	- Salt
½ tsp	- White pepper powder
A pinch	- Ajwain
1/3 tsp	- Roasted jeera powder
A pinch	- Elaichi powder
½ tsp	- Baking powder
2 tsp	- Almond paste
1 no	- Egg
1 tsp	- Green chilli (chopped)
1 tsp	- Green coriander (chopped)
2 tsp	- Refined flour

For basting - Clarified butter

METHOD

1. Mash processed cheese in a deep tray rub it well add ginger/garlic paste add chicken mince, salt, white pepper powder, ajwain, jeera powder, elaichi powder, baking powder, almond paste, egg, green chilli, green coriander and mix well to smooth consistency and keep aside for at least 1 hour.
2. Divide the mixture into 4 equal parts and make balls.

Cooking

3. Spread this mixture on skewer using wet palm to press each ball along the length of the skewer in a cylindrical shape an inch apart and making each kebab 4-5 inches long.
4. Roast in a tandoor or over a charcoal grill at a moderate temperature for 5-6 minutes. Baste with clarified butter and further roast for 1-2 minutes.
5. Serve hot with choice of a salad and chutney.

Murg Reshmi Tikka

ABSOLUTELY SOFT CHICKEN KEBAB RESERVED IN A NON YOGHURT MARINADE WHICH IS RICH IN TASTE AND FLAVOUR

Cooking time 8-10 minutes Serves 1-2

INGREDIENTS

200-225 gm Chicken breast (Boneless) (3 no)

First Mariantion
1 tsp	- Ginger garlic paste
To taste	- Salt
½ tsp	- White pepper powder

Second Marination
2 tbsp	- Refined oil
1 tsp	- Garlic (chopped)
1 tbsp	- Onion (chopped)
2 tbsp	- Gram flour
3 tbsp	- Cashewnut paste
1 tbsp	- Cream
½ tsp	- Ginger garlic paste
To taste	- Salt
½ tsp	- White pepper powder

For basting - Clarifid butter

METHOD

1. Clean and wash each chicken breast and cut into 2 pieces, pat dry and keep aside.

First Mariantion

2. In a bowl mix ginger paste, salt, white pepper powder and apply this to chicken pieces, rub well and keep aside for at least 45 minutes.
3. Heat oil in a pan, add garlic chopped, chopped onion and sauté, add gram flour and slightly saute so that it does not change its colour. Leave it for cooling.

Second Marination

4. In a bowl take cashewnut paste, roasted gram flour mixture, cream, ginger garlic paste, salt and white pepper powder and mix well.
5. Put the marinated chicken into this mixture, coat well and keep aside for at least 1 hour.

Cooking

6. Take a skewer and skew the marinated chicken pieces. Keep a tray underneath to collect drippings.
7. Roast in a moderately hot tandoor or over a charcoal grill for 6-7 minutes till half done.
8. Remove and baste with clarified butter during cooking and further roast for 2-3 minutes or till tender.
9. Serve hot with choice of a salad and chutney.

Tawa Murg Kulfi

AN UNUSUAL CHICKENMINCE KEBAB SKEWERED AN A WOODEN BAMBOO STICKS IN THE SHAPE OF A POPULAR INDIAN ICE-CREAM (KULFI)

Cooking time 4-5 minutes Serves 1-2

INGREDIENTS

2 tbsp	- Processed cheese (grated)
200 gm	- Chicken mince
1 tsp	- White pepper powder
3 tsp	- Cream
To taste	- Salt
1 tsp	- Green coriander (chopped)
½ tsp	- Green chilli (chopped)
1/3 tsp	- Elaichi powder
2 tbsp	- Refined oil

METHOD

1. In a deep tray mash processed cheese with palm, add chicken mince, white pepper, cream, salt, green coriander, green chilli, elaichi powder and mix well to a smooth consistency and keep aside for at least 1 hour.
2. Divide the mixture into 4-5 equal parts.

Cooking

1. Apply this mixture on a wooden bamboo stick with the help of wet palm and shape it in cylindrical form (kulfi) 4" – 5".
2. Heat oil in a flat pan, put kulfi-shaped chicken stick and cook it on slow fire till golden brown colour (4 – 5 minutes).
3. Serve hot with a choice of a salad and chutney.

Shan - E - Murg

AN IMPRESSIVE KEBAB OF TENDER CHICKEN BREAST STUFFED WITH MANGO FLAVOURED DELICIOUS FILLING

Cooking time 8-10 minutes Serves 1-2

INGREDIENTS

225-250 gm - Chicken breast (2 No) (with shoulder bone)

First Marination

½ tsp	- Ginger garlic paste
To taste	- Salt
1/3 tsp	- White pepper powder

Stuffing

2(slit)	- Mango slice

Second Marination

3 tsp	- Processed cheese (grated)
2 tsp	- Egg white
½ tsp	- Ginger garlic paste
4 tbsp	- Cream
½ tsp	- Green chilli (chopped)
A pinch	- Elaichi powder
1/3 tsp	- White pepper powder
To taste	- Salt

METHOD

1. Clean each chicken breast with sharp knife, slit it from the centre, wash, pat dry and keep aside.

First Marination

2. In a bowl mix ginger garlic paste, salt, white pepper powder and apply this to chicken breast, rub well and keep aside for at least 45 minutes.

Stuffing

3. Stuff each chicken breast with a mango slice and seal the breast with the back of knife.

Second Marination

4. In a deep tray mash processed cheese and rub with the help of your palm. Add egg white, ginger garlic paste. Mix it well then add cream, green chilli, elaichi powder, white pepper powder, salt and mix well to smooth consistency.
5. Remove the extra moisture from the chicken breast, put it in the marinade, coat well and keep aside for at least 1 hour.

Cooking

6. Take a skewer and skew marinated chicken breast an inch a part from the edge of the shoulder bone. Keep a tray underneath to collect drippings.
7. Roast in a moderately hot tandoor for 6-8 minutes.
8. Remove and baste with clarified butter during cooking and further roast for 2-3 minutes or till tender.
9. Serve hot with choice of a salad and chutney.

Reshmi Seekh

SAFFRON FLAVOURED CHICKEN SEEKH KEBAB

Cooking time 7-8 minutes Serves 1-2

INGREDIENTS

2 tbsp	- Processed cheese (grated)
½ tsp	- Ginger garlic paste
200 gm	- Chicken mince
To taste	- Salt
½ tsp	- White pepper powder
2 tsp	- Cream
1 tsp	- Green coriander (chopped)
½ tsp	- Green chilli (chopped)
1 gm	- Saffron
A pinch	- Elaichi powder
For basting	- Clarified butter

METHOD

1. In a deep tray mash processed cheese, add ginger garlic paste, add chicken mince, salt, white pepper powder, cream, green coriander, green chilli, saffron, elaichi powder and mix well to smooth consistency and keep aside for at least 1 hour.
2. Divide the mixture into 4 equal parts and make balls.

Cooking

3. Spread this mixture on skewer using wet palm to press each ball along the length of the skewer in a cylindrical shape an inch apart and making each kebab 4 inches long.
4. Roast in a tandoor or over a charcoal grill at a moderate temperature for 5-6 minutes. Baste with clarified butter, further roast for 1-2 minutes.
5. Transfer on to a plate and serve hot with a choice of a salad and chutney.

Murg Kastoori Kebab

AN EGG-COATED VARIATION OF THE MURG TIKKA, SPICED WITH BLACK PEPPER AND FLAVOURED WITH SAFFRON

Cooking time 6-8 minutes **Serves** 1-2

INGREDIENTS

200-225 gm Chicken breast (boneless) (03 no)

First Marination
½ tsp	- Ginger garlic paste
1/3 tsp	- Yellow chilli powder
To taste	- Salt
1/3 tsp	- Black pepper (crushed)

Second Marination
50 gm	- Yellow butter
4 tsp	- Besan
A pinch	- Saffron
A pinch	- Kasoori methi powder
½ tsp	- Ginger garlic paste
½ tsp	- Green chilli (chopped)
To taste	- Salt

Coating
2 no	- Egg yolk
A pinch	- salt
A pinch	- Turmeric powder
½ tsp	- Fresh coriander (chopped)

METHOD

1. Clean, wash and cut each chicken breast into 2 pieces, pat dry and keep aside

First Marination
2. In a bowl mix ginger garlic paste, yellow chilli powder, salt, crushed black pepper and apply this to the chicken pieces, rub well and keep aside for at least 45 minutes.

Second Marination
3. Heat butter in a non-stick pan, add besan and saute it for some time, add saffron, kasoori methi, ginger garlic paste, green chilli, salt and mix it well.
4. Add the chicken to it and saute till water dries and besan sticks to chicken. Keep it aside to cool.

Coating
5. In a bowl whisk egg yolk, add salt, turmeric and fresh coriander and keep aside.

Cooking
6. Take a skewer and skew the marinated chicken breast very near to each other.
7. Roast in tandoor at moderate temperature for 4 – 5 minutes.
8. Apply the egg yolk mixture all over and put it back in tandoor for further 2 – 3 minutes or till tender.
9. Serve hot with choice of a salad and chutney.

Murg Shammi Kebab

ANOTHER CONCOCTION OF LUCKNOWI SHAMMI PREPARED WITH CHICKEN AND CONDIMENTS

Cooking time 2-3 minutes **Serves** 1-2

INGREDIENTS

20 gm	- Channa dal (pre soaked in water)
200 gm	- Chicken mince
To taste	- Salt
2 no	- Cloves
2 no	- Black pepper
2 no	- Green cardamom
1 no	- Black cardamom
1no	- Bay leaf
1 no	- Cinnamon stick
1 tsp	- Coriander (chopped)
½ no	- Egg
A pinch	- Elaichi javitri powder

METHOD

1. Boil channa dal with salt, cloves, black pepper, green cardamom, black cardamom, bay leaf, cinnamon stick when 3/4th cooked then add chicken mince, cook on slow fire till water evaporates.
2. Remove whole condiments and keep it for cooling
3. In a processor put the cooked mixture and make a fine paste. Transfer this to a bowl and add chopped coriander, egg, elaichi javitri powder and mix well to a smooth consistency and keep aside for 1 hour.
4. Divide the mixture into 5 equal parts and make balls. Apply a little melted ghee on palm and flatten the mince balls into a round medallion (tikki) shape.

Cooking
1. Heat oil in a kadhai/ pan and deep fry till golden brown and crisp.
2. Serve hot along with a choice of a salad and chutney.

Tandoori Kukkar Patiala Shahi

SUCCULENT PIECES OF CHICKEN MARINATED WITH SPICY MASALA, A DELICACY FROM KITCHEN OF THE ROYAL HOUSE OF PATIALA

Cooking time 12-14 minutes Serves 1-2

INGREDIENTS

325-350 gm - Chicken ½ no. (leg and breast)

First Marination
To taste	- Salt
½ tsp	- Ginger garlic paste
½ tsp	- Red chilli paste
1 tsp	- Vinegar

Second Marination
4 tbsp	- Hung curd
To taste	- Salt
½ tsp	- Ginger garlic paste
½ tsp	- Red chilli paste
A pinch	- Kastoori methi powder
1 tsp	- Lemon juice
½ tsp	- Garam masala
1 tsp	- Mustard oil

For basting - Clarified butter

METHOD

1. Clean, wash and make three incisions with a sharp knife on breast and leg, pat dry and keep aside.

First Marination

2. In a bowl mix salt, ginger garlic paste, red chilli paste, vinegar and apply this to chicken pieces and keep aside for at least 45 minutes.

Second Marination

3. In a bowl whisk hung curd, add salt, ginger garlic paste, red chilli, kasoori methi, lemon juice, garam masala, oil and mix well.
4. Put chicken pieces into this marinade, coat well and keep aside for at least 1 hour.

Cooking

5. Take a skewer and skew the marinated chicken. Keep a tray underneath to collect drippings.
6. Roast in a moderately hot tandoor or over a charcoal grill for 7-8 minutes.
7. Remove and hang the skewer to let extra moisture drain out completely (2-3 minutes).
8. Baste with clarified butter and further roast for 2-3 minutes or till tender.
9. Serve hot with choice of a salad and chutney.

Murg Methi Malai

CUBES OF CHICKEN, STEEPED IN CREAMY FENUGREEK MARINADE

Cooking time 8-10 minutes Serves 1-2

INGREDIENTS

200-225 gms - Chicken breast (boneless) (3pcs)

First marination
½ tsp	- Ginger garlic paste
1/3 tsp	- White pepper powder
To taste	- Salt

Second marination
3 tsp	- Processed cheese (grated)
2 no	- Egg white
½ tsp	- Ginger garlic paste
3 tbsp	- Cream
To taste	- Salt
A pinch	- White pepper powder
¼ tsp	- Green chilli (chopped)
½ tsp	- Corn flour
4 tsp	- Methi (chopped)

For basting - Clarified butter

METHOD

1. Clean and wash chicken breast, cut into 2 pieces each, pat dry and keep aside.

First marination

2. In a bowl mix ginger garlic paste, white pepper powder, salt and apply this to chicken pieces, rub well and keep aside for at least 45 minutes.

Second marination

3. In a bowl take grated processed cheese rub it with your palm and then add egg white, ginger garlic paste. Mix it well then add cream, salt, white pepper powder, green chilli, corn flour, chopped methi and mix well to smooth consistancy.
4. Put the marinated chicken pieces into this mixture, coat well and keep aside for at least 1 hour.

Cooking

5. Take a skewer and skew the marinated chicken pieces. keep a tray underneath to collect the drippings.
6. Roast in a moderately hot tandoor or over charcoal grill for 6-7 minutes.
7. Remove and baste with clarified butter and further roast for 2-3 minutes or till tender.
8. Serve hot with choice of a salad and chutney

Murg Anmol Rattan

ANOTHER AMAZING CREATION OF CHICKEN MORSELS MARINATED WITH SYMPHONY OF SPICES AND NUTS

Cooking time 10-12 minutes Serves 1-2

INGREDIENTS

(200-225 gm) Chicken leg (boneless) 2 pcs

2 tsp	- Refined oil
15 no	- Curry leaves
3 g	- Mint leaves

First Marination
To taste	- Salt
½ tsp	- Ginger/garlic paste
½ tsp	- White pepper powder

Second Marination
4 tbsp	- Hung curd
To taste	- Salt
½ tsp	- Ginger/garlic paste
2 tsp	- Cream
1 tsp	- Almond paste
1 tsp	- Cashewnut paste
1 tsp	- Brown onion paste
A pinch	- Garam masala
A pinch	- Kasoori methi powder
1/3 tsp	- Curry powder
A pinch	- Elaichi javitri powder

For basting - Clarified butter

METHOD

1. Clean, wash and cut chicken into 3 pieces each, pat dry and keep aside.
2. Heat oil and fry curry leaves, mint leaves till crisp, crush & keep aside.

First Marination

3. In a bowl mix salt, ginger/garlic paste, white pepper and apply this to chicken pieces, rub well and keep aside for at least 45 minutes.

Second Marination

4. In a bowl whisk hung curd, add salt, ginger/garlic paste, cream, almond paste, cashewnut paste, brown onion paste, garam masala, kasoori methi, curry powder, elaichi javitri powder, oil and mix well.
5. Put chicken pieces into this marinade, coat well, sprinkle crushed fried curry, mint leaves and keep aside for at least 1 hour

Cooking

6. Take a skewer and skew the marinated chicken pieces, keep a tray underneath to collect drippings.
7. Roast in a moderately hot tandoor or over charcoal grill for 6-7 minutes.
8. Remove and baste with clarified butter and further roast for at least 2-3 minutes or till tender.
9. Serve hot with choice of a salad and chutney.

Murg Methi Seekh

DRIED FENUGREEK AND SPICES COMBINED TO MAKE THIS SUCCULENT KEBAB OF CHICKEN MINCE AN EXTRAORDINARY ONE

Cooking time 7-8 minutes Serves 1-2

INGREDIENTS

2 tbsp	- Processed cheese (grated)
½ tsp	- Ginger garlic paste
200 gm	- Chicken mince
To taste	- Salt
½ tsp	- White pepper powder
1 tsp	- Green coriander (chopped)
½ tsp	- Green chilli (chopped)
2 tsp	- Kasoori methi (chopped)
1 tsp	- Kasoori methi powder
2 tsp	- Hung curd

For basting - Clarified butter

METHOD

1. In a deep tray mash processed cheese, add ginger garlic paste. Rub it again then add chicken mince, salt, white pepper, green corriander, chilli, kasoori methi chopped, kasoori methi powder, hung curd and mix well to smooth consistency and keep aside for at least 1 hour.
2. Divide the mixture into 4 equal parts and make balls.

Cooking

3. Spread this mixture on skewer using wet palm to press each ball along the length of the skewer in a cylindrical shape an inch apart and making each kebab 4 inches long.
4. Roast in a tandoor or over a charcoal grill at a moderate temperature for 5-6 minutes. Baste with clarified butter, further roast for 2-3 minutes.
5. Transfer on to a plate and serve hot with choice of a salad and chutney.

Murg Lapeta Kebab

THIS IS A MAGNIFICIENT KEBAB OF TENDER CHICKEN BREAST STUFFED WITH CHICKEN MINCE AND DRY FRUITS

Cooking time 8-10 minutes **Serves 2**

INGREDIENTS

(225- 250 gm) - Chicken breast boneless 4 pcs

First marination
To taste	- Salt
½ tsp	- Ginger/garlic paste
½ tsp	- Yellow chilli powder

Stuffing
2 tsp	- Refined oil
2 tsp	- Onions (chopped)
75 gm	- Chicken mince
1 tsp	- Green chilli (chopped)
1 tsp	- Green coriander (chopped)
2 tsp	- Dry fruits (chopped)
To taste	- Salt
1/3 tsp	- Red chilli powder
1/3 tsp	- Kasoori methi powder
A pinch	- Garam masala
3 tsp	- Processed cheese (grated)

Second Marination
4 tbsp	- Hung curd
Salt	- To taste
½ tsp	- Ginger/garlic paste
½ tsp	- Yellow chilli powder
1 no	- Egg yolk
2 tsp	- Roasted channa powder
A pinch	- Turmeric powder
1 tsp	- Vinegar
2 tsp	- Mustard oil

For basting - Clarified butter

METHOD

1. Clean, wash and cut the chicken breast and slightly beat it with hammer, pat dry and keep aside.

First marination
2. In a bowl mix salt, ginger/garlic paste, yellow chilli powder and apply this to chicken pieces rub well and keep aside for at least 45 minutes.

Stuffing
3. Heat oil in pan put onions and saute it for a while, then add chicken mince, green chilli, green coriander, salt, green chilli, kasoori methi, garam masala and cook it till water/moisture from chicken evaporates, keep aside for cooling, after cooling add processed cheese and mix well.
4. Divide this mixture into 4 equal portions and place a portion of mince on each breast and roll it like roulade and tie with thread.

Second Marination
5. In a bowl whisk hung curd, add salt, ginger/garlic paste, yellow chilli powder, egg yolk, roasted channa powder, turmeric, vinegar, mustard oil and mix well
6. Put the chicken pieces into this marinade, coat well and keep aside for at least 1 hour.

Cooking
7. Take a skewer and skew marinated chicken pieces one by one horizontally. Keep a tray underneath to collect drippings
8. Roast in a moderately hot tandoor or over charcoal grill for 6-7 minutes.
9. Remove and baste with clarified butter and further roast for 2-3 minutes or till tender.
10. Serve hot with choice of a salad and chutney.

Harre Pyaaz Ka Murg Tikka

A DIFFERENT CREATION OF KEBAB GENTLY MASSAGED WITH COMPOUND OF SPICES AND EXTRA FLAVOUR OF SPRING ONION

Cooking time 8-10 minutes Serves 2

INGREDIENTS

(200 – 225 gm) - Chicken leg boneless 2 pcs

First Marination
To taste	- Salt
½ tsp	- Ginger garlic paste
½ tsp	- Yellow chilli powder

Second Marination
3 tsp	- Processed cheese
1 no	- Egg white
2 tsp	- Cashewnut paste
To taste	- Salt
2 tsp	- Spring onion (chopped)
1 tsp	- Green chilli (chopped)
1 tsp	- Green coriander (chopped)
½ tsp	- Yellow chilli powder
1 tsp	- Ginger (chopped)
A pinch	- Garam masala
A pinch	- Elaichi powder

For basting - Clarified butter

METHOD

1. Clean, wash and cut each chicken leg into 3 pieces and pat dry.

First Marination

2. In a bowl mix salt, ginger garlic paste, yellow chilli powder and apply this to chicken pieces, rub well and keep aside for at least 45 minutes.

Second Marination

3. In a deep tray mash processed cheese, rub it well then add egg white, cashewnut paste, salt, spring onion, green chilli, green coriander, yellow chilli, ginger, garam masala, elaichi powder and mix it well to smooth consistency.
4. Put chicken pieces into this marinade, coat well and keep aside for at least 1 hour.

Cooking

5. Take a skewer, skew marinated chicken pieces one by one leaving an inch gap.
6. Roast in moderately hot tandoor or over charcoal grill for 6-7 minutes.
7. Remove and hang so that excess moisture drains out completely.
8. Baste with clarified butter and further roast for 2-3 minutes or till tender.
9. Serve hot with a choice of a salad and chutney.

Murg Haider Ali Kebab

LEG OF CHICKEN MARINATED WITH FLORAL AROMA AND SUBTLE SPICES, A UNIQUE DELICACY FROM THE ROYAL STATE OF AWADH

Cooking time 14-15 minutes Serves 1-2

INGREDIENTS

300-325 gm - Chicken leg (with thigh) (2 no.)

4 tbsp	- Hung curd
To taste	- Salt
½ tsp	- Ginger garlic paste
1 tsp	- Black pepper powder
½ tsp	- Red chilli powder
A pinch	- Turmeric powder
2 tsp	- Lemonjuice
1 tsp	- Cloves, shahi jeera, javitri
1 tsp	- Jaiphal powder
1 tsp	- Roasted channa powder
2 tsp	- Mustad oil

For basting - Clarified butter

METHOD

1. Clean, wash and make 3 incisions on both sides of chicken leg, pat dry and keep aside.

Marination

1. In a bowl whisk hung curd, add salt, ginger garlic paste, , black pepper, red chilli, turmeric, lemon, whole masala powder, roasted channa powder, oil and mix well
2. Put chicken pieces into this marinade, coat well and keep aside for at least 2 hours.

Cooking

2. Take a skewer and skew marinated chicken pieces along the skewer, keep a tray underneath to collect drippings.
3. Roast in a tandoor or over charcoal grill at a moderate temperature for 8-10 minutes.
4. Remove and hang the skewer so that the moisture drains out completely (1-2minutes). Baste with clarified butter and further roast for 2-3 minutes or till tender.
5. Serve hot along with choice of a salad and chutney.

Kesari Murg Ke Tukre

A DELICATE SAFFRON FLAVOURED CHICKEN MORSELS IN RICH MARINADE
Cooking time 10-12 minutes Serves 1-2

INGREDIENTS

(200-225 gm) - Chicken leg boneless 2 pcs

First Marination
To taste	- Salt
½ tsp	- Ginger/garlic paste
½ tsp	- Yellow chilli powder
1 tsp	- Vinegar

Second Marination
3 tbsp	- Almond, Cashewnut, Chaar magaz (paste)
To taste	- Salt
A pinch	- Garam masala
1/3 tsp	- Yellow chilli powder
A pinch	- Saffron
2 tsp	- Refined oil

For basting - Clarified butter

METHOD

1. Clean, wash and cut each chicken leg into 3 pieces and pat dry.

First Marination
2. In a bowl mix salt, ginger/garlic paste, yellow chilli powder, vinegar and apply this to chicken pieces, rub well and keep aside for at least 45 minutes.

Second Marination
3. In a bowl mix almond, cashewnut, chaar magaz paste, salt, garam masala, yellow chilli powder, saffron, oil and mix well.
4. Put chicken pieces into this marinade, coat well and keep aside for at least 1 hour.

Cooking
5. Take a skewer, skew marinated chicken pieces one by one leaving an inch gap in between.
6. Roast in moderately hot tandoor or over charcoal grill for 7 - 8 minutes.
7. Remove and baste with clarified butter and further roast for 3 – 4 minutes or till tender.
8. Serve hot with choice of a salad and chutney.

Reshmi Murg Tikka

RICH CHICKEN MORSELS SPICED WITH POUNDED YELLOW CHILLI AND GARLIC
Cooking time 10-12 minutes Serves 1-2

INGREDIENTS

2 no (200-225 gm) - Chicken leg boneless

First Marination
To taste	- Salt
To taste	- Ginger/garlic paste
½ tsp	- Yellow chilli powder
1 tsp	- Vinegar

Second Marination
3 tsp	- Refined oil
3 tsp	- Besan (gram flour)
1 no	- Egg
To taste	- Salt
½ tsp	- Yellow chilli powder
1 tsp	- Chopped garlic
2 tbsp	- Cream
2 tbsp	- Cashewnut paste

For basting - Clarified butter

METHOD

1. Clean, wash and cut each chicken leg into 3 pieces and pat dry and keep aside.

First Marination
2. In a bowl mix salt, ginger/garlic paste, yellow chilli powder, vinegar and apply this to chicken pieces. Rub well and keep aside for at least 45 minutes.
3. Heat oil in a pan, add besan and cook it for a while till raw smell goes, keep aside for cooling.

Second Marination
4. In a bowl mix cooked besan, egg, salt, yellow chilli powder, chopped garlic, cream, cashewnut paste and mix well.
5. Put chicken pieces into this marinade, coat well and keep aside for at least 1 hour.

Cooking
6. Take a skewer, skew marinated chicken pieces one by one leaving an inch gap in between.
7. Roast in moderately hot tandoor or over charcoal grill for 7 - 8 minutes.
8. Remove and baste with clarified butter and further roast for 3 - 4 minutes or until tender.
9. Serve hot with a choice of a salad and chutney.

Peshawari Murg Tikka

SUCCULENT AND SPICY CHUNKS OF CHICKEN WITH EXTRA FLAVOUR OF POMEGRANATE SEEDS PREPARED IN PESHAWARI STYLE

Cooking time 10-12 minutes Serves 1-2

INGREDIENTS

200- 225 gm (2 no) - Chicken leg (boneless)

First Marination
½ tsp	- Ginger garlic paste
½ tsp	- Red chilli paste
To taste	- Salt
1 tsp	- Lemon juice

Paste
25 gm	- Roasted khus khus
4 tsp	- Pomegranate seeds

Second Marination
4 tbsp	- Hung curd
½ tsp	- Ginger garlic paste
½ tsp	- Red chilli paste
To taste	- Salt
1/3 tsp	- Garam masala
A pinch	- Kasoori methi powder
2 tsp	- Refined oil

For basting - Clarified butter

METHOD

1. Clean, wash and cut each chicken leg into 3 pieces, pat dry and keep aside.

First Marination

2. In a bowl mix ginger/garlic paste, red chilli paste, salt, lemon juice, apply this to chicken and keep aside for at least 45 minutes.

Paste

3. In a processor make a paste of khus khus pomegranate seeds and keep aside.

Second Marination

4. In a bowl whisk hung curd and add ginger/garlic paste, red chilli paste, salt, garam masala, kasoori methi, 5 tsp of khus khus paste and mix well.
5. Put chicken pieces into this marinade, coat well and keep aside for at least 1 hour.

Cooking

6. Take a skewer and skew marinated chicken pieces, keep a tray underneath to collect drippings.
7. Roast in a moderately hot tandoor or over a charcoal grill for 7-8 minutes.
8. Remove and baste with clarified butter and further roast for 3-4 minutes or till tender.
9. Serve hot with a choice of a salad and chutney.

Murg Kalonji Seekh

MINCED CHICKEN SKEWER FLAVOURED WITH EXTRA TOUCH OF BLACK ONION SEEDS

Cooking time 7-8 minutes Serves 1-2

INGREDIENTS

2 tbsp	- Processed cheese (grated)
½ tsp	- Ginger garlic paste
200 gm	- Chicken mince
To taste	- Salt
½ tsp	- Ginger (chopped)
1/3 tsp	- White pepper powder
1 tsp	- Green coriander (chopped)
½ tsp	- Green chilli (chopped)
½ tsp	- Kalonji (onion seeds)

For basting - Clarified butter

METHOD

1. In a deep tray mash processed cheese, rub it well, add ginger garlic paste, add chicken mince, salt, ginger chopped, white pepper powder, green corriander, green chilli, kalonji mix well to smooth consistency and keep aside for at least 1 hour.
2. Divide the mixture into 4 equal parts and make balls.

Cooking

3. Take a skewer and spread the mixture using a wet palm along the length of the skewer in a cylindrical shape one inch apart and make each kebab 4 inches long.
4. Roast in a moderately hot tandoor or over a charcoal grill for 5-6 minutes, baste with clarified butter and further roast for 1-2 minutes.
5. Serve hot with choice of a salad and chutney.

Tandoori Murg Chettinad

TANGY CHICKEN KEBAB PREPARED WITH CHETTINARD SPICES

Cooking time 10-12 minutes Serves 1-2

INGREDIENTS

200-225 gm (2 no) Chicken leg boneless

First Marination
½ tsp	- Ginger garlic paste
To taste	- Salt
½ tsp	- Yellow chilli powder
1 tsp	- Lemon juice

Paste
½ tsp	- Mustard seeds
2-3 cloves	- Garlic
5 gm	- Ginger
1 tsp	- Coriander whole
1 tsp	- Cumin (jeera)
2 no	- Green cardamom
3 no	- Clove
½ tsp	- Nutmeg (crushed)
2 tsp	- Poppy seeds
1 spring	- Curry leaves
2 no	- Red chilli (whole)
2 tsp	- Coconut (grated)
25 gm	- Roasted channa

Second Marination
2 tbsp	- Hung curd (Low fat)
A pinch	- Turmeric powder
To taste	- Salt
2 tsp	- Coconut milk
3 tsp	- Tamarind pulp

For basting - Olive oil

METHOD

1. Clean, wash and cut each chicken leg into 3 pieces, pat dry and keep aside.

First Marination

2. In a bowl mix ginger garlic paste, salt, lemon juice and yellow chilli powder, apply this to chicken pieces, rub well and keep aside for at least 45 minutes.

Paste

3. Heat pan, put all listed ingredients and roast for a minute, cool it. Put this into a blender and make a fine paste by adding a little water.

Second Marination

4. In a bowl whisk hung curd and add 5 tsp paste, a pinch of turmeric powder, salt, coconut milk, tamarind pulp and mix well.
5. Remove extra moisture from the chicken pieces, put this into marinade, coat well and keep aside for at least 1 hour.

Cooking

6. Take a skewer and skew the marinated chicken pieces. Keep a tray underneath to collect drippings.
7. Roast in a moderately hot tandoor or over a charcoal grill for 7-8 minutes. till half done.
8. Remove and baste with olive oil and further roast for 3-4 minutes or till tender.
9. Serve hot with choice of a salad and chutney.

Phuljhari Seekh Kebab

A DELICATE FLAVOURED CHICKEN MINCE ROLLED ON A SKEWER COATED WITH COLOURFUL BELLPEPPERS AND CHAR-GRILLED)

Cooking time 7-8 minutes Serves 1-2

INGREDIENTS

2 tbsp	- Processed cheese (grated)
½ tsp	- Ginger garlic paste
200 gm	- Chicken mince
½ tsp	- Green chilli (chopped)
1 tsp	- Green coriander (chopped)
½ tsp	- Ginger (chopped)
½ tsp	- White pepper powder
To taste	- Salt
A pinch	- Elaichi javitri powder
A pinch	- Kasoori methi powder
2 tbsp	- Onion, red, yellow, green capsicum (chopped)

For basting - Clarified butter

METHOD

1. In a deep tray mash processed cheese, rub it well, add ginger garlic paste, add chicken mince, green chilli, green coriander, ginger chopped, white pepper powder, salt, elaichi javitri powder, kasoori methi and mix well to a smooth consistency and keep aside for at least 1 hour.
2. Divide this mince into 4 equal parts and make balls.

Cooking

3. Take a skewer, using a wet palm, spread each ball along the length of skewer in a cylindrical shape, 2 inches apart, making each kebab 4 inches long.
4. Apply finely chopped onion, capsicum on top of the seekh with a light hand and roast in a tandoor or over a charcoal grill for 5-6 minutes.
5. Baste it with clarified butter and further roast it in a tandoor for 1-2 minutes.
6. Serve hot along with a choice of a salad and chutney.

Murg Choppati Tikka

CHICKEN KEBAB FROM THE FAMOUS CHOPPATI (BEACH) IN MUMBAI

Cooking time 10-12 minutes Serves 1-2

INGREDIENTS

200-225 gm (2 No) - Chicken leg (boneless)

First Marination
½ tsp	- Ginger garlic paste
To taste	- Salt
½ tsp	- Red chilli paste

Second Marination
4 tbsp	- Hung curd
To Taste	- Salt
½ tsp	- Garam masala
½ tsp	- Lemon juice
½ tsp	- Curry powder
A Pinch	- Turmeric powder
1 tsp	- Corn flour
1 tsp	- Refined oil

For basting - Clarified butter

METHOD

1. Clean, wash and cut each chicken leg into 3 pieces, pat dry and keep aside.

First Marination

2. In a bowl mix ginger garlic paste, salt, red chilli paste apply this to the chicken, rub well and keep aside for at least 45 minutes.

Second Marination

3. In a bowl whisk hung curd and add salt, garam masala, lemon juice, curry powder, turmeric, corn flour, oil and mix well.
4. Put the chicken pieces into this marinade, coat well and keep aside for at least 1 hour.

Cooking

5. Take a skewer and skew marinated chicken pieces, keep a tray underneath to collect drippings.
6. Roast in a moderately hot tandoor or over a charcoal grill for 7-8 minutes.
7. Remove and baste with clarified butter and further roast for 3-4 minutes or till tender.
8. Serve hot with a choice of a salad and chutney

Khatta Meetha Tikka

SOUR AND SWEET CHICKEN TIKKA PREPARED WITH MANGO PULP

Cooking time 10-12 minutes Serves 1-2

INGREDIENTS

200-225 gms - Chicken leg (boneless) (2 pcs)

First Marination
½ tsp	- Ginger garlic paste
½ tsp	- Yellow chilli powder
To taste	- Salt
2 tsp	- Lemon juice

Second Marination
4 tbsp	- Hung curd
½ tsp	- Ginger garlic paste
1/3 tsp	- Yellow chilli powder
To taste	- Salt
A pinch	- Turmeric powder
2 tsp	- Boiled raw mango (puree)
1 tsp	- Mango chutney (fine chopped)
2 tsp	- Refined oil

For basting - Clarified butter

METHOD

1. Clean, wash and cut each chicken leg into 3 pieces, pat dry and keep aside.

First Marination

2. In a bowl mix ginger garlic paste, yellow chilli powder, lemon juice, salt and apply this to the chicken, rub well and keep aside for at least 45 minutes.

Second Marination

3. In a bowl whisk hung curd, add ginger garlic paste, yellow chilli powder, salt, turmeric powder, mango puree, mango chutney, oil and mix well.
4. Remove extra moisture from the chicken pieces, put them into this marinade, coat well and keep aside for at least 45 minutes.

Cooking

5. Take a skewer and skew marinated chicken pieces, keep a tray underneath to collect dripping.
6. Roast in a moderately hot tandoor or over a charcoal grill for 6-7 minutes.
7. Remove and baste with clarified butter and further roast for 3-4 minutes or till tender.
8. Serve hot with choice of a salad and chutney.

Murg Dalcha Kebab

SUCCULENT CHICKEN MORSELS BLENDED WITH YELLOW LENTIL FLAVOURED WITH SPICES AND CHAR-GRILLED

Cooking time 10-12 minutes Serves 1- 2

INGREDIENTS

200-225 gm - Chicken leg boneless (2 Pcs)

First Marination
½ tsp	- Ginger garlic paste
½ tsp	- Yellow chilli powder
To taste	- Salt
2 tsp	- Lemon juice

Paste
50 gm	- Boiled channa dal
A pinch	- Nutmeg powder

Second Marination
4 tbsp	- Hung curd
½ tsp	- Ginger garlic paste
1/3 tsp	- Yellow chilli powder
To taste	- Salt
A pinch	- Turmeric powder
1 tsp	- Corn flour
A pinch	- Elaichi javitri powder
2 tsp	- Roasted besan
2 tsp	- Refined oil

For basting - Clarified butter

METHOD

1. Clean, wash and cut each chicken leg into 3 pieces, pat dry and keep aside.

First Marination

2. In a bowl mix ginger garlic paste, yellow chilli powder, salt, lemon juice apply this to chicken pieces, rub well and keep aside for at least 45 minutes.

Paste

3. Put boiled channa dal in a food processor, make a paste, add nutmeg powder and keep aside.

Second Marination

4. In a bowl whisk hung curd, add all the remaining ingredients listed in order, add 3 tsp of dal paste and mix well.
5. Squeeze extra moisture from marinade chicken and put them into this marinade, coat well and keep aside for at least 1 hour.

Cooking

6. Take a skewer and skew marinated chicken pieces.
7. Roast in a moderately hot tandoor or over a charcoal grill for 7-8 minutes.
8. Remove and baste with clarified butter and further roast for 3-4 minutes or till tender.
9. Serve hot with choice of a salad and chutney.

Murg Rogani Tikka

HOT AND FIERY CHICKEN TIKKA WITH EXTRA TOUCH OF RED CHILLI

Cooking time 10-12 minutes Serves 1-2

INGREDIENTS

200-225 gm (2 No) - Chicken leg (boneless)

First Marination
½ tsp	- Ginger garlic paste
To taste	- Salt
½ tsp	- Red chilli paste

Second Marination
4 tbsp	- Hung curd
To taste	- Salt
½ tsp	- Garam masala
1/3 tsp	- Kasoori methi powder
½ tsp	- Red chilli paste
1 tsp	- Lemon juice
2 tsp	- Refined oil
1 tsp	- Red chilli powder

For basting - Clarified butter

METHOD

1. Clean, wash and cut each chicken leg into 3 pieces, pat dry and keep aside.

First Marination

2. In a bowl mix ginger garlic paste, salt, red chilli paste, apply this to chicken, rub well and keep aside for at least 45 minutes.

Second Marination

3. In a bowl whisk hung curd and add salt, garam masala, kasoori methi, red chilli, lemon juice and mix well.
4. Heat oil in a pan, put red chilli powder and immediately add this to marinade.
5. Put the chicken pieces into this marinade, coat well and keep aside for at least 1 hour.

Cooking

6. Take a skewer and skew marinated chicken pieces, keep a tray underneath to collect drippings.
7. Roast in a moderately hot tandoor or over a charcoal grill for 7-8 minutes.
8. Remove and baste with clarified butter and roast for another 3-4 minutes.
9. Serve hot with choice of a salad and chutney.

Murg Ka Sula

DELICACY OF BONELESS CHICKEN PICATTA PREPARED IN AUTHENTIC RAJASTHANI STYLE

Cooking time 10-12 minutes Serves 1-2

INGREDIENTS

200-225 gm - Chicken leg boneless (2 no)

First Marination
To taste	- Salt
A pinch	- White pepper powder
½ tsp	- Ginger garlic paste

Second Marination
3 tbsp	- Hung curd
To taste	- Salt
A pinch	- Elachi javaitri powder
½ tsp	- Ginger garlic paste
½ tsp	- Green chilli (chopped)
1/3 tsp	- White pepper powder
1 tsp	- Brown onion paste
½ tsp	- Ginger (chopped)
1/3 tsp	- Shahi jeera
1 tsp	- Cornflour
2 tsp	- Cream
1 tsp	- Ghee
2 no	- Cloves

For basting - Clarified butter

METHOD

1. Clean, wash and cut each chicken leg 3 pieces each, pat dry and keep aside.

First Marination
2. In a bowl mix salt, white pepper, ginger garlic paste apply this to chicken pieces, rub well and keep aside for at least 45 minutes.

Second Marination
3. In a bowl whisk hung curd and add salt, elaichi javitri powder, ginger garlic paste, green chilli, white pepper, brown onion paste, ginger, shahi jeera, corn flour, cream and mix well.
4. Squeeze extra moisture from marinade chicken, put them into this marinade and coat well.
5. Take small bowl and place in the centre of the chicken, put 1-2 pieces of burning charcoal, put 2-3 cloves and pour ghee on charcoal, immediately cover bowl with lid for 2-3 minutes.
6. Remove the lid from the bowl keep chicken into this marinade for at least 1 hour.

Cooking
7. Take a skewer, skew marinated chicken legs one by one leaving an inch gap between each leg.
8. Roast in moderately hot tandoor or over charcoal grill for 7 - 8 minutes.
9. Remove and baste with clarified butter and further roast for about 3 – 4 minutes or till tender.
10. Serve hot with choice of a salad and chutney.

Kadak Seekh Kebab

CHARGRILLED CHICKEN SKEWER, DIPPED IN BATTER AND CRUNCHY FRIED

Cooking time 8-10 minutes Serves 1-2

INGREDIENTS

2 tbsp	- Processed cheese (grated)
½ tsp	- Ginger garlic paste
200 gm	- Chicken mince
To taste	- Salt
1/3 tsp	- White pepper powder
1 tsp	- Green coriander (chopped)
½ tsp	- Green chilli (chopped)
A pinch	- Elaichi javitri powder
3 tsp	- Cream
A pinch	- Shahi jeera
4 tbsp	- Cornflour
4 no	- Prcessed cheese (sticks)
For basting	- Clarified butter

METHOD

1. In a deep tray mash processed cheese, rub it well, add ginger garlic paste, rub well again, then add chicken mince, salt, white pepper, green corriander, green chilli, elaichi javitri powder, cream, shahi jeera and mix well to a smooth consistency, keep aside for at least 1 hour.
2. Divide them into 4 equal parts and make balls.

Cooking

3. Take a skewer and spread this mixture along the length of the skewer in a cylindrical shape an inch apart from each other 4-5 inches long.
4. Roast in a moderately hot tandoor or over a charcoal grill for 5-6 minutes.
5. Remove and baste with clarified butter and further roast till tender (1-2 minutes)
6. Transfer on to a plate and then make a slight cut in the centre of seekh and put a stick of cheese, make batter of corn flour and flour to coating consistency, dip stuffed seekh kebab into this batter and deep fry for 1-2 minutes till crisp.
7. Serve hot with choice of a salad and chutney.

Murg Achari Tikka

PICKLE FLAVOURED CHICKEN MORSELS COOKED IN CLAY OVEN

Cooking time 10-12 minutes Serves 1-2

INGREDIENTS

200-225 gm - Chicken leg (boneless) (2 Nos)

First Marination

½ tsp	- Ginger garlic paste
To taste	- Salt
½ tsp	- Yellow chilli powder
1 tsp	- Lemon juice

Second Marination

3 tbsp	- Hung curd
To taste	- Salt
½ tsp	- Ginger garlic paste
2 tsp	- Achar paste
2 tsp	- Garam masala
1 tsp	- Lemon juice
3 tsp	- Mustard oil
2 tsp	- Whole achar masala (saunf, kalonji, mustard seeds, methi dana)
½ tsp	- Turmeric powder
For basting	- Clarified butter

METHOD

1. Wash, cut each chicken leg into 3 pieces cubes, pat dry and keep aside.

First Marination

2. In a bowl mix ginger/garlic paste, salt and yellow chilli powder, lemon juice, apply this to chicken pieces rub well and keep aside for at least 45 minute.

Second Marination

3. In a bowl whisk hung curd add salt, ginger gralic paste, achari masala, garam masala, lemon juice and mix well.
4. Heat oil in a pan, add whole achar masala saute for a while and immediately put it in to marinade, add turmeric powder and mix well.
5. Squeeze extra moisture from the marinated chicken, put it into this marinade, coat well and keep aside for at least 1 hour.

Cooking

6. Take a skewer and skew marinated chicken pieces, keep a tray underneath to collect dripping.
7. Roast in a moderately hot tandoor or over a charcoal grill for 7-8 minutes.
4. Remove and baste with clarified butter and further roast for 2-3 minutes or till tender.
5. Serve hot with choice of a salad and chutney.

Khasta Seekh Kebab

SOFT CHICKEN MINCE SEEKH KEBAB MILDLY FLAVOURED COATED WITH CORNFLAKES AND CRISPY FRIED
Cooking time 8-10 minutes Serves 1- 2

INGREDIENTS

2 tbsp	- Processed cheese (grated)
½ tsp	- Ginger garlic paste
200 gm	- Chicken mince
To taste	- Salt
1 tsp	- Green coriander (chopped)
½ tsp	- Green chilli (chopped)
½ tsp	- White pepper powder
3 tsp	- Cream
For coating	- Crushed cornflakes
4 tbsp	- Cornflour
For basting	- Clarified butter
For frying	- Refined oil

METHOD

1. In a deep tray mash processed cheese, rub well with palm, add ginger garlic paste add chicken mince, salt, green coriander, green chilli, white pepper powder, cream and mix well to smooth consistency and keep aside for at least 1 hour.
2. Divide the mixture into 4 equal parts and make balls.

Cooking

3. Take a skewer using a wet hand, spread this mixture along the length of the skewer in a cylindrical shape and an inch apart to make each kebab 4 – 5 inches long.
4. Roast in a moderately hot tandoor or over a charcoal grill for 5-6 minutes
5. Remove and baste with clarified butter and further cook for 1-2 minutes.
6. Remove from the skewer and leave to cool.
7. Take cornflour in a bowl, add water and make a batter to coating consistency, dip seekh kebab one by one and roll in crushed cornflakes.
8. Heat oil in a kadhai and deep fry seekh kebab for 1-2 minutes till golden brown and crisp.
9. Serve hot with choice of a salad and chutney.

Teekha Murg Tikka

ABSOLUTE HOT RED CHICKEN KEBAB, BEST SERVED WITH DRINKS
Cooking time 10-12 minutes Serves 1 – 2

INGREDIENTS

200-225 gm (2 Nos) - Chicken leg boneless

First Marination

½ tsp	- Ginger garlic paste
To taste	- Salt
½ tsp	- Red chilli paste
2 tsp	- Lemon juice

Second Marination

4 tbsp	- Hung curd
To taste	- Salt
½ tsp	- Ginger garlic paste
½ tsp	- Red chilli paste
½ tsp	- Garam masala
½ tsp	- Kasoori methi powder
½ tsp	- Red chilli (crushed)
1 tsp	- Refined oil
For basting	- Clarified butter

METHOD

1. Wash and cut each chicken leg into 3 pieces and pat dry.

First Marination

2. In a bowl mix ginger garlic paste, salt, red chilli paste, lemon to chicken pieces and keep aside for at least 45 minutes.

Second Marination

3. In a bowl whisk hung curd, add all the remaining ingredients listed in order and mix well.
4. Put chicken pieces into this marinade, coat well and keep aside for at least 1 hour.

Cooking

5. Take a skewer and skew marinated chicken pieces, keep a tray underneath to collect drippings.
6. Roast in a moderately hot tandoor or over a charcoal grill for 7-8 minutes.
7. Remove and baste with clarified butter and further roast for 3-4 minutes or till tender.
8. Serve hot with choice of a salad and chutney.

Kandhari Murg Tikka

CHICKEN CHUNKS MARINATED IN A BLEND OF FRESH POMEGRANATE AND SYMPHONY OF EXOTIC SPICES AND PREPARED IN TRUE KANDHARI STYLE

Cooking time 10-12 minutes Serves 1-2

INGREDIENTS

200-225 gm - Chicken leg (boneless) (2 pcs)

First Marination
½ tsp	- Ginger garlic paste
To taste	- Salt
2 tsp	- Anar juice (pomegranate)
1 tsp	- Lemon juice

Second Marination
4 tbsp	- Hung curd
½ tsp	- Ginger garlic paste
To tast	- Salt
½ tsp	- Red chilli paste
A pinch	- Kasoori methi powder
2 tsp	- Anar juice
3 tsp	- Pomegranate seeds(crushed)
1 tsp	- Refined oil

For basting - Clarified butter

METHOD

1. Clean, wash and cut each chicken leg into 3 pieces each (large cube) pat dry and keep aside.

First Marination

2. In a bowl mix ginger/garlic paste, salt, anar juice, lemon juice, apply this to chicken pieces, rub well and keep aside for at least 30 minutes.

Second Marination

3. In a bowl whisk hung curd, add the ingredients in the order listed above and mix well
4. Squeeze extra moisture, put chicken pieces into this marinade, coat well and keep aside for at least 1 hour.

Cooking

5. Take a skewer and skew marinated chicken pieces, keeping a tray underneath to collect drippings.
6. Roast in a moderately hot tandoor or over a charcoal grill for 7-8 minutes till half done.
7. Remove and baste with clarified butter and further roast for 3-4 minutes or till tender.
8. Serve hot with choice of a salad and chutney.

Nasheela Murg

RUM FLAVOURED CHICKEN MORSELS COOKED IN CLAY OVEN

Cooking time 10-12 minutes Serves 1-2

INGREDIENTS

200-225 gm - Chicken leg boneless (2pcs)

First Marination
To taste	- Salt
½ tsp	- Red chilli paste
2 tsp	- Lemon juice
½ tsp	- Ginger garlic paste

Second Marination
3 tbsp	- Hung curd
½ tsp	- Ginger garlic paste
½ tsp	- Red chilli paste
A pinch	- Kasoori methi powder
½ tsp	- Garam masala
To taste	- Salt
1 tsp	- Lemon juice
2 tsp	- Refined oil
30 ml	- Rum

For basting - Clarified butter

METHOD

1. Clean, wash and cut the chicken leg into 3 pieces each, pat and keep aside.

First Marination

2. In a bowl mix salt, red chilli paste, lemon juice ginger garlic paste, apply this to chicken pieces, rub well and keep aside for at least 45 minutes.

Second Marination

3. In a bowl whisk hung curd and add all the remaining ingredient in the order listed, mix well, red chilli can be adjusted according to taste.
4. Put the chicken pieces into this marinade, coat well and keep aside for at least 2 hours.

Cooking

5. Take a skewer and skew the marinated chicken pieces, keeping a tray underneath to collect drippings.
6. Roast in a moderately hot tandoor or over a charcoal grill for 7-8 minutes, till half done.
7. Remove and baste with clarified butter and further roast for 3-4 minutes or till tender.
8. Serve hot with choice of a salad and chutney.

Szechwan Murg Tikka

JUICY CHICKEN KEBAB MARINATED WITH SZECHWAN PEPPER, CHINESE SPICES AND CHAR-GRILLED

Cooking time 10-12 minutes Serves 1-2

INGREDIENTS

(200-225 gm) - Chicken leg (boneless) 2 pcs

First Marination
To taste	- Salt
½ tsp	- Ginger garlic paste
½ tsp	- Red chilli paste
2 tsp	- Lemon juice

Second Marination
1 tsp	- Szechwan pepper (crushed)
1 tsp	- Soya sauce
To taste	- Salt
1 tsp	- Worcestershire sauce
1 tsp	- Tomato ketchup
1 tsp	- Vinegar
½ tsp	- Sugar
3 tsp	- Corn flour

For basting - Refined oil

METHOD

1. Clean and cut each chicken leg into 3 pieces, pat dry and keep aside.

First Marination

2. In a bowl mix ginger garlic paste, salt, red chilli paste, lemon juice, apply this to chicken pieces, rub well and keep aside for at least 45 minutes.

Second Marination

3. In a bowl take soya sauce, add the remaining ingredients in the order listed and mix well.
4. Put chicken pieces into this prepared mixture and keep aside for at least 1 hour.

Cooking

5. Take a skewer and skew marinated chicken pieces. Keep a tray underneath to collect drippings.
6. Roast in a tandoor or over a charcoal grill at equal moderate temperature for 7-8 minutes.
7. Remove and baste with refined oil and further roast for at least 2-3 minutes or till tender.
8. Serve hot with choice of a salad and chutney.

Tandoori Murg Bemisal

THIS INNOCENT, VERY DELICATELY FLAVOURED KEBAB OF CHICKEN BREAST FLAVOURED WITH SYMPHONY OF SPICES AND FRESH MINT

Cooking time 8-10 minutes Serves 1-2

INGREDIENTS

2no (200-225 gm) - Chicken breast (with shoulder bone)

First Marination
To taste	- Salt
½ tsp	- Ginger garlic paste
1/3 tsp	- Yellow chilli powder

Second Marination
5 tsp	- Hung curd
To taste	- Salt
½ tsp	- Ginger garlic paste
½ tsp	- Yellow chilli powder
½ tsp	- Green chilli (chopped)
1 tsp	- Mint (chopped)
1 tsp	- Green coriander (chopped)
2 tsp	- Lemon juice
1 no	- Egg yolk
1 tsp	- Cream
2 tsp	- Refined oil

For basting - Clarified butter

METHOD

1. Clean, wash and make 3 incisions on chicken breast, pat dry and keep aside.

First Marination

2. In a bowl mix salt, ginger garlic paste, yellow chilli powder, rub well and keep aside for at least 45 minutes.

Second Marination

3. In a bowl whisk hung curd, add salt, ginger garlic paste, yellow chilli powder, green chilli, mint, green coriander, lemon juice, egg yolk, cream, oil and mix well.
4. Put chicken pieces into this marinade, coat well and keep aside for at least 1 hour.

Cooking

5. Take a skewer and skew the marinated chicken pieces, keep a tray underneath to collect drippings.
6. Roast in a moderately hot tandoor or over a charcoal grill for 6-7 minutes.
7. Remove and baste with clarified butter and further roast for 2-3 minutes or till tender.
8. Serve hot with choice of a salad and chutney.

Murg Noorani Kebab

DELICIOUS, SIMPLE TO MAKE, SUCCULENT CHICKEN KEBAB FLAVOURED WITH FRESH GARLIC IN ABUNDANCE AND ROASTED IN CLAY OVEN

Cooking time 12-14 minutes Serves 1-2

INGREDIENTS

325-350 gm - Chicken ½ no. (breast and leg)

First Mariantion
To taste	- Salt
½ tsp	- Garlic paste
½ tsp	- White pepper powder

Second Marination
4 tbsp	- Hung curd
To taste	- Salt
½ tsp	- Garlic paste
1/3 tsp	- White pepper powder
1 tsp	- Garlic (chopped)
1 no	- Egg
2 tsp	- Cashewnut paste
2 tsp	- Cream
1 tsp	- Corn flour
2 tsp	- Refined oil

For basting - Clarified butter

METHOD

1. Clean, wash, give 3 incisions on chicken breast and leg, pat dry and keep aside.

First Mariantion

2. In a bowl mix salt, garlic paste, white pepper powder, apply this to chicken, rub well and keep aside for at least 45 minutes.

Second Marination

3. In a bowl whisk hung curd add salt, garlic paste, white pepper powder, garlic chopped, egg, cashew nut paste, cream, cornflour, oil and mix well.
4. Put the chicken into this marinade, coat well and keep aside for at least 1 hour.

Cooking

5. Take a skewer and skew the marinated chicken pieces. Keep a tray underneath to collect drippings.
6. Roast in a moderately hot tandoor or over a charcoal grill for 6-7 minutes.
7. Remove and hang the skewer to let excess moisture drain out completely (2-3 minutes) baste with clarified butter and further roast for 3-4 minutes or till tender.
8. Serve hot with choice of a salad and chutney.

Murg Sikandari Kebab

SUCCULENT PIECES OF CHICKEN INFUSED WITH CINNAMON

Cooking time 12-14 minutes Serves 1-2

INGREDIENTS

325–350 gm Chicken ½ no (breast and leg)

First Mariantion
To taste	- Salt
½ tsp	- Ginger garlic paste
½ tsp	- White pepper powder

Second Marination
4 tbsp	- Hung curd
To taste	- Salt
½ tsp	- Ginger garic paste
1/3 tsp	- White pepper powder
2 tsp	- Cream
½ tsp	- Garam masala
½ tsp	- Cinnamon powder
2 tsp	- Lemon juice
2 tsp	- Refined oil

For basting - Clarified butter

METHOD

1. Clean, wash, make incisions on chicken breast and leg, pat dry and keep aside.

First Mariantion

2. In a bowl mix ginger garlic paste, salt, white pepper powder, apply this to the chicken and keep aside for at least 45 minutes.

Second Marination

1. In a bowl whisk hung curd add salt, ginger garlic paste, white pepper powder, cream, garam masala, cinnamon powder, lemon juice, oil and mix well.
2. Put marinated chicken pieces into this marinade, coat well and keep aside for at least 1 hour.

Cooking

1. Take a skewer and skew the marinated chicken pieces. Keep a tray underneath to collect drippings.
2. Roast in a moderately hot tandoor or over a charcoal grill for 6-7 minutes till half done.
3. Remove and hang the skewer to let excess moisture drain out completely (2-3 minutes) baste with clarified butter and further roast for 3-4 minutes or till tender.
4. Serve hot with choice of a salad and chutney.

Punjabi By Nature

THE FIRE AND SPICE OF INDIA, SPRING CHICKEN MARINATED OVERNIGHT IN YOGHURT, GINGER, GARLIC AND AROMATED WITH HOME MADE SPICE MIX AND ROASTED IN CLAY OVEN

Cooking time 14-15 minutes Serves 2-4

INGREDIENTS

700-750 gm - Chicken

First Mariantion
To taste	- Salt
1 tsp	- Ginger garlic paste
1 tsp	- Red chilli paste
2 tsp	- Malt vinegar

Second Marination
½ cup	- Hung curd
To taste	- Salt
1 tsp	- Ginger garlic paste
1 tsp	- Red chilli paste
A pinch	- Turmeric powder
1 tsp	- Garam masala
½ tsp	- Kasoori methi powder
2 tsp	- Lemon juice
2 tsp	- Mustard oil

For basting - Clarified butter

METHOD

1. Clean, wash, make 3 incisions on chicken, breast and leg pat dry and keep aside.

First Mariantion

2. In a bowl mix the ginger garlic paste, salt, red chilli paste, malt vinegar, apply this to chicken pieces, rub well and keep aside for at least 45 minutes.

Second Marination

3. In a bowl whisk hung curd add salt, ginger garlic paste, red chilli paste, turmeric powder, garam masala, kasoori methi, lemon juice, oil and mix well.
4. Put the chicken into this marinade, coat well and keep aside for overnight.

Cooking

5. Take a skewer and skew the marinated chicken pieces. Keep a tray underneath to collect drippings.
6. Roast in a moderately hot tandoor for 10-12 minutes till half done.
7. Remove and hang the skewer to let excess moisture drain out completely (2-3 minutes) baste with clarified butter and further roast for 3-4 minutes or till tender.
8. Serve hot with choice of a salad and chutney.

Murg Lolly Pop Kebab

CHICKEN WINGS SHAPED LIKE LOLLYPOP FLAVOURED WITH CINNAMON AND CHAR-GRILLED

Cooking time 6-8 minutes Serves 1-2

INGREDIENTS

(200-225 gm) 12 pcs - Chicken wings

First Marination
To taste	- Salt
½ tsp	- Ginger garlic paste
½ tsp	- White pepper powder

Second Marination
4 tbsp	- Hung curd
To taste	- Salt
½ tsp	- Ginger garlic paste
1/3 tsp	- White pepper powder
1/3 tsp	- Cinnamon powder
1 no	- Egg white
1 tsp	- Cornflour
2 tsp	- Refined oil

For basting - Clarified butter

METHOD

1. Wash, clean and cut chicken wings, pat dry and keep aside.

First Marination

2. In a bowl mix salt, ginger garlic paste, white pepper, apply this to chicken wings and keep aside at least for 45 minutes.

Second Marination

3. In a bowl whisk hung curd, add salt, ginger garlic paste, white pepper, cinnamon powder, egg white, corn flour, oil and mix well.
4. Put chicken pieces into this marinade, mix well and keep aside for at least 1 hour.

Cooking

5. Take a skewer and skew the marinated chicken pieces, keep a tray underneath to collect drippings.
6. Roast in a moderately hot tandoor or over a charcoal grills for 5-6 minutes.
7. Remove and baste with clarified butter and further roast for 1-2 minutes.
8. Serve hot with choice of a salad and chutney.

Tandoori Duck Chettinad

DELICIOUS DUCK DELICACY PREPARED WITH CHETTINAD SPICES
Cooking time 12-14 minutes Serves 1-2

INGREDIENTS

350-375 gm - Duck ½ no (leg and breast)

First Marination
½ tsp	- Ginger/garlic paste
To taste	- Salt
½ tsp	- Yellow chilli powder
1 tsp	- Lemon juice

Chettinad Paste
½ tsp	- Mustard seeds
2-3	- Cloves, garlic
5 gm	- Ginger
1 tsp	- Coriander whole
1 tsp	- Cumin (jeera)
2 no	- Green cardamom
3 no	- Clove
½ tsp	- Nutmeg (crushed)
2 tsp	- Poppy seeds
1 sprig	- Curry leaf
2 no	- Whole red chilli
2 tsp	- Coconut (grated)
2 tsp	- Roasted channa powder

Second Marination
3 tsp	- Hung curd
A pinch	- Turmeric powder
To taste	- Salt
2 tsp	- Coconut milk powder
1-2 tsp	- Tamarind pulp

For basting - Olive oil

METHOD

1. Clean, wash the duck, make 2 incisions each side of the duck, pat dry and keep aside.

First Marination

2. In a bowl mix ginger garlic paste, lemon juice, yellow chilli powder, salt, apply this to duck pieces, rub well and keep aside for at least 45 minutes.

Chettinad Paste

3. In a pan add all whole garam masala boil for a while. Cool it and make a paste by adding a little water in a food processor.

Second Marination

4. In a bowl whisk hung curd, add chettinad paste (4 tsp), turmeric, salt, coconut milk, tamarind pulp and mix well.
5. Put duck pieces into this marinade, coat well and keep aside for at least 2 hours

Cooking

6. Take a skewer and skew the marinated duck pieces. Keep a tray underneath to collect drippings.
7. Roast in a moderately hot tandoor or over a charcoal grill for 6-7 minutes till half done.
8. Remove and hang the skewer to let excess moisture drain out completely (2-3 minutes). Baste with olive oil and further roast for 2-4 minutes or till tender.
9. Serve hot with choice of a salad and chutney.

Chatpate Kaleji Kebab

HOT AND FIERY DELICATE KEBAB MADE WITH CHICKEN LIVER AND INFUSED WITH DRY FENUGREEK
Cooking time 5-6 minutes Serves 1-2

INGREDIENTS

200-225 gm - Kaleji (chicken liver-large pieces)

4 tbsp	- Hung curd
To taste	- Salt
1 tsp	- Ginger/garlic paste
1 tsp	- Red chilli paste
1/3 tsp	- Garam masala
1/3 tsp	- Kastoori methi powder
1 tsp	- Lemon juice
1 tsp	- Cornflour
1 tsp	- Refined oil

For basting - Clarified butter

METHOD

1. Clean, wash chicken liver, pat dry and keep aside.

Marination

2. In a bowl whisk hung curd, add salt, ginger garlic paste, red chilli paste, garam masala, kasoori methi, lemon juice, corn flour and mix well.
3. Remove excess moisture from kaleji and put kaleji into this marinade and keep aside for at least 1 hour

Cooking

4. Take a skewer and skew marinated kaleji pieces, keep a tray underneath to collect drippings.
5. Roast in a moderately hot tandoor or over charcoal grill for 4-5 minutes.
6. Remove and baste with clarified butter and further roast for 1-2 minutes or till tender.
7. Serve with a choice of a salad and chutney.

Gazab Ka Seena

A CREAMY GENTLY SPICED CHICKEN BREAST FLAVOURED WITH CARDAMOM

Cooking time 10-12 minutes Serves 1-2 portion

INGREDIENTS

200-225 gm (2 no.) - Chicken breast (with shoulder bone)

First Marination
½ tsp	- Ginger garlic paste
To taste	- Salt
A pinch	- White pepper powder

Stuffing
1 tsp	- Refined oil
5 gm	- Cashewnut (chopped)
75 gm	- Chicken mince
To taste	- Salt
½ tsp	- White pepper powder
½ tsp	- Green Chilli (chopped)
1 tsp	- Fresh coriander (chopped)
1 pinch	- Saffron
A pinch	- Elaichi powder
2 tsp	- Processed cheese (grated)

Second Marination
3 tsp	- Processed cheese (grated)
2 tsp	- Egg white
½ tsp	- Ginger garlic paste
4 tbsp	- Cream
1 tsp	- Cornflour
2 tsp	- Cashewnut paste
To taste	- Salt
½ tsp	- White pepper powder
A pinch	- Green chilli (chopped)
A pinch	- Elaichi powder
½ tsp	- Fresh coriander(phopped)

For basting - Clarified butter

METHOD

1. Clean and with tip of a knife make deep slit along the base of chicken breast from the centre to make a hole taking care not to penetrate from the opposite side for the stuffing, pat dry and keep aside.

First Marination

2. In a bowl mix ginger garlic paste, salt, white pepper powder and apply this to chicken breast, rub well and keep aside for at least 45 minutes.

Stuffing

3. Heat oil in a pan, put in cashewnuts, fry till light brown and add chicken mince, salt, white pepper powder, green chilli, green coriander, saffron, elaichi powder and saute till chicken gets cooked and water get evaporates. Keep aside to cool, then add processed cheese, mix well.
4. Divide mixture into 2 parts and stuff it into each breast and seal with the back of knife.

Second Marination

5. In a deep tray mash grated cheese, add egg white, ginger garlic paste and mix with the palm gradually, pour cream and further mix till it becomes a smooth paste, add corn flour, cashewnut paste, salt, white pepper powder, green chilli, elaichi powder, green coriander and mix well.
6. Put the chicken pieces into this marinade, coat well and keep aside for at least 1 hour.

Cooking

7. Take a skewer and skew chicken breast leaving a gap of at least an inch between each breast. Keep a tray underneath to collect drippings.
8. Roast in a moderate hot tandoor or oven for 7-8 minutes. Remove and hang so that the excess moisture drains out completely (1-2)
9. Baste with clarified butter and further roast for 3-4 minutes or till tender.
10. Serve hot with choice of a salad and chutney.

Shahjahani Murg Kebab

THIS IS A MAGNIFICENT RICH KEBAB OF TENDER CHICKEN BREAST STUFFED WITH SAFFRON FLAVOURED ROYAL STUFFING – GREAT KEBAB OF MUGHAL ERA

Cooking time 10-12 minutes Serves 1-2

INGREDIENTS

200-225 gm (2no) Chicken breast (with shoulder bone)

Stuffing
40 gm	- Khoya (grated)
20 gm	- Paneer (grated)
½ tsp	- Green chilli (chopped)
1 tsp	- Green coriander (chopped)
½ tsp	- Raisins (chopped)
A pinch	- Garam masala
A pinch	- Elaichi powder
To taste	- Salt

Marination
5 tbsp	- Hung curd
To taste	- Salt
1 tsp	- Ginger garlic paste
½ tsp	- Yellow chilli powder
2 tsp	- Lemon juice
A pinch	- Saffron
1/3 tsp	- Roasted jeera powder
A pinch	- Garam masala
A pinch	- Turmeric powder
1 tsp	- Mustard oil

For basting - Clarified butter

METHOD

1. Clean, wash and with help of knife slit chicken breast from the top and make a hole with the help of a finger, pat dry and keep aside.

Stuffing
2. In a bowl put khoya, paneer, green chilli, green coriander, raisins, garam masala, elaichi powder, salt and mix well.
3. Stuff each breast with this mixture and seal the top with the back of a knife and keep aside.

Marination
4. In a bowl whisk hung curd, add salt, ginger garlic paste, yellow chilli, lemon juice, saffron, jeera powder, garam masala, turmeric, mustard oil, mix well.
5. Put chicken breast into this marinade, coat well and keep aside for at least 1 hour.

Cooking
6. Take a skewer and skew marinated chicken breast as much apart from the edge of shoulder bone. Keep a tray underneath to collect drippings.
7. Roast in moderately hot tandoor for 5-6 minutes
8. Remove and hang skewer to let excess moisture drain out completely (1-2 minutes)
9. Baste with clarified butter and further roast for (3-4 minutes) or till tender.
10. Serve hot along with choice of a salad and chutney.

Murg Nagina

ANOTHER VERSION OF CHICKEN TIKKA INFUSED WITH CRUSHED BLACK PEPPER

Cooking time 10-12 minutes Serves 1-2

INGREDIENTS

(200-225 gm) 2pcs - Chicken leg (bone less)

4 tbsp	- Hung curd
2 tsp	- Cornflour
1 no	- Egg
1 tsp	- Ginger garlic paste
½ tsp	- Green chilli (chopped)
1 tsp	- Fresh coriander (chopped)
1 tsp	- Lemon juice
½ tsp	- White pepper powder
1/3 tsp	- Black pepper (crushed)
To taste	- Salt

For basting - Clarified butter

METHOD

1. Clean, wash and cut each chicken leg into 3 pieces, pat dry and keep aside.

Marination
2. In a bowl whisk hung curd and add ginger garlic paste and all the remaining ingredients listed in order above, mix well.
3. Put the chicken pieces into this marinade and keep aside for 1 hour.

Cooking
4. Take a skewer and skew marinated chicken pieces, keep a tray underneath to collect drippings.
5. Roast in a moderately hot tandoor or over a charcoal grill for 8-9 minutes.
6. Remove and baste with clarified butter and roast for another 3-4 minutes.
7. Serve hot with choice of a salad and chutney.

Lazeez Murg Shashlik

JUICY MORSELS OF CHICKEN SKEWERED WITH BELL PEPPERS AND CHAR-GRILLED

Cooking time 12-14 minutes Serves 1-2

INGREDIENTS

325-350 gm Chicken ½ no
(leg and breast with bone)

First Marination

1 tbsp	- Ginger garlic paste
To taste	- Salt
½ tsp	- White pepper powder
1 tsp	- Vinegar
1 tsp	- Refined oil

Second Marination

4 tbsp	- Hung curd
To taste	- Salt
½ tsp	- Ginger garlic paste
½ tsp	- White pepper powder
½ tsp	- Green chilli (chopped)
1 tsp	- Green coriander (chopped)
A pinch	- Elaichi javitri powder
½ tsp	- Crushed peppercorn
½ tsp	- Garam masala
2 tsp	- Refined oil
3no.each (1 ½ "/ 1 ½ ")	- Capsicum, tomato, onion (dices)

For basting - Clarified butter

METHOD

1. Wash, clean and cut leg and breast into 2 pieces, make 2-3 deep incisions on breast and leg with sharp knife, pat dry and keep aside.

First Marination

2. In a bowl mix ginger garlic paste, salt, white pepper powder, vinegar, oil and apply this to chicken pieces, rub well and keep it for at least 45 minutes.

Second Marination

3. In a bowl whisk hung curd, add salt, ginger garlic paste, white pepper, green chilli, green coriander, elaichi javitri powder, pepper corn, garam masala, oil and mix well.
4. Put chicken into this marinade, coat well and keep aside for at least 1 hour.

Cooking

5. Take a skewer and skew the marinated chicken pieces and the vegetables along the skewer alternatively, keep tray underneath to collect drippings.
6. Roast in a moderately hot tandoor or over a charcoal grill for 6-7 minutes.
7. Remove and hang the skewer to let excess moisture drain out completely (2-3 minutes). Baste with clarified butter and further roast for 3-4 minutes or till tender.
8. Serve hot with choice of a salad and chutney.

Lime And Coconut Chicken Kebab

AN UNUSUAL FUSION OF THAI AND INDIAN SPICES

Cooking time 8-10 minutes Serves 1-2

INGREDIENTS

(225-250 gm) 3no - Chicken breast (boneless)

3 tsp	- Processed cheese (grated)
2 tsp	- Onion (chopped)
1 tsp	- Garlic (chopped)
1 tsp	- Ginger (chopped)
1 tsp	- Spring onion (chopped)
1 tsp	- Lemon grass (chopped)
2 tbsp	- Coconut milk powder
½ tsp	- Rosated cumin powder
A pinch	- Turmeric powder
½ tsp	- Yellow chilli powder
A pinch	- Black cumin
To taste	- Salt

For basting - Clarified butter

METHOD

1. Clean, wash chicken breast, pat dry and keep aside.

Marination

2. In a bowl, combine all the ingredients in the order listed above, put chicken breast in this marinade, rub well and keep aside for at least 2 hours.

Cooking

3. Take a skewer, skew marinated chicken breast one by one.
4. Roast in a moderately hot tandoor or over a charcoal grill for 10-12 minutes and baste with clarified butter chicken breast during cooking.
5. Serve hot with choice of a salad and chutney

Raan – E – Murg

LEG OF CHICKEN RESERVED IN YOGHURT MARINADE, THAT IS VERITABLE SYMPHONY OF EXOTIC SPICES INCLUDING THE CLOVES

Cooking time 14-15 minutes Serves 1-2

INGREDIENTS

300-325 gm (2 no) - Chicken leg on bone (with thigh)

First Marination
To taste	- Salt
½ tsp	- Red chilli paste
½ tsp	- Ginger garlic paste
3 no	- Black pepper (whole)
1 no	- Big cardamom (crushed)
2 no	- Small cardamom (crushed)
A pinch	- Nutmeg (grated)

Second Marination
5 tbsp	- Hung curd
To taste	- Salt
½ tsp	- Red chilli paste
½ tsp	- Ginger garlic paste
1/3 tsp	- Kasoori methi powder
A pinch	- Clove powder
2 tsp	- Refined oil
For basting	- Clarified butter

METHOD

1. Clean, wash and make 3 incisions on both sides of chicken leg, pat dry and keep aside.

First Marination

2. In a bowl mix salt, red chilli paste, ginger garlic paste, black pepper whole, small and big cardamom, nutmeg and apply this to chicken pieces, rub well and keep aside for at least 1 hour.

Second Marination

3. In a bowl whisk hung curd, add salt, red chilli paste, ginger garlic paste, kasoori methi, clove powder and mix well.
4. Heat oil in a pan and put the marinade and cook it on slow flame till oil comes on top, keep aside for cooling.
5. Put the chicken pieces into this marinade, coat well and keep aside for at least 2 hours.

Cooking

6. Take a skewer and skew marinated chicken pieces along the skewer lengthwise. Keep a tray underneath to collect drippings.
7. Roast in a tandoor or over charcoal grill at a moderate temperature for 9-10 minutes.
8. Remove and hang the skewer so that the excess moisture drains out completely (1-2 minutes). Baste with clarified butter and further roast for 2-3 minutes or till tender.
9. Serve hot along with choice of a salad and chutney.

Murg Burra Kebab

JUICY AND SPICY KEBAB MADE OF CHICKEN SHANKS, INFUSED WITH CINNAMON AND HOME GROUND SPICES

Cooking time 8-10 minutes Serves 1-2

INGREDIENTS

(275-300 gm) 6 no. - Chicken leg

3 tbsp	- Hung curd
1 tsp	- Ginger garlic paste
½ tsp	- Cinnamon powder
½ tsp	- Yellow chilli powder
½ tsp	- Garam masala
½ tsp	- Kasoori methi powder
1 tsp	- Mustard oil
To taste	- Salt
For basting	- Clarified butter

METHOD

1. Clean, wash and cut each chicken leg and give burra shape, pat dry and keep aside.

Marination

2. In a bowl whisk hung curd, add ginger garlic paste, yellow chilli powder, cinnamon powder, garam masala, kasoori methi powder, mustard oil, salt and mix it well.
3. Put chicken pieces in this marinade, rub well and keep aside for at least 2 hours.

Cooking

4. Take a skewer and skew the marinated chicken pieces and keep a tray underneath to collect drippings.
5. Roast in a moderately hot tandoor or over a charcoal grill for 5-6 minutes.
6. Remove and hang the skewer to let excess moisture drain out completely (1-2minutes). Baste with clarified butter and roast for another 3-4 minutes.
7. Serve hot with choice of a salad and chutney.

Lagan Ke Kebab

FOR THIS DELICACY OF CHICKEN, KEBAB IS MARINATED WITH LUCKNOWI SPICES AND COOKED IN LAGAN (THICK BOTTOMED PAN)

Cooking time 16-18 minutes Serves 1-2

INGREDIENTS

325-350 gm - Chicken ½ no. on bone (leg and breast)

First Marination
To taste	- Salt
½ tsp	- Ginger garlic paste
½ tsp	- Red chilli paste
2 tsp	- Lemon juice

Second Marination
4 tbsp	- Hung curd
To taste	- Salt
½ tsp	- Ginger garlic paste
½ tsp	- Red chilli paste
1/3 tsp	- Garam masala
1/3 tsp	- Kasoori methi powder
1 tsp	- Lemon juice
A pinch	- Elaichi javitri powder
1 tsp	- Green chilli (chopped)
A few	- Big cardamom (crushed)
1 tsp	- Green coriander (chopped)
3 tsp	- Brown onion paste
2 tsp	- Refined oil

For garnishing - Mint chopped

METHOD

1. Clean, wash and cut leg and breast into 2 pieces and make 3 incisions on chicken pieces with a sharp knife, pat dry and keep aside.

First Marination

2. In a bowl mix salt, ginger garlic paste, red chilli paste, lemon juice and apply this to the chicken, rub well and keep aside for at least 45 minutes.

Second Marination

3. In a bowl whisk hung curd, add salt, ginger garlic paste, red chilli paste, garam masala, kasoori methi, lemon juice, elaichi javitri powder, green chilli, big caradamom, green coriander, brown onion paste, oil and mix well.
4. Put the chicken pieces into this marinade, coat well and keep aside for at least 1 hour.

Cooking

5. Heat oil in a thick bottmed pan or lagan, place the chicken pieces, cover with a lid and cook on slow fire for 15-16 minutes or till chicken is tender, sprinkle chopped mint on top.
6. Serve hot with choice of a salad, chutney and bread.

Rajasthani Murg Burra

SPRING CHICKEN MARINATED WITH BLEND OF SPICES INFUSED WITH CINNAMON AND ROASTED IN CLAY OVEN

Cooking time 12-14 minutes Serves 1-2

INGREDIENTS

325-350 gm - Chicken ½ no. on bone (leg and breast)

First Marination
½ tsp	- Ginger garlic paste
To taste	- Salt
2 tsp	- Mustard oil
1 tsp	- Vinegar

Second Marination
4 tbsp	- Hung curd
To taste	- Salt
½ tsp	- Yellow chilli powder
1/3 tsp	- Garam masala
1/3 tsp	- Kasoori methi powder
1/3 tsp	- Cinnamon powder
2 tsp	- Mustard oil

For basting - Clarified butter

METHOD

1. Clean, wash and make 3 incisions on chicken both leg and breast, pat dry and keep aside.

First Marination

2. In a bowl mix ginger garlic paste, salt, mustard oil, vinegar and apply this to chicken pieces, rub well and keep aside for at least 45 minutes.

Second Marination

3. In a bowl whisk hung curd, add salt, yellow chilli powder, garam masala, kasoori methi, cinnamon powder, oil and mix well.
4. Put the chicken pieces into this marinade, coat well and keep aside for at least 1 hour.

Cooking

5. Take a skewer and skew the marinated chicken pieces. Keep a tray underneath to collect drippings.
6. Roast in a moderately hot tandoor or over charcoal grill for 7-8 minutes.
7. Remove and hang the skewer to let the excess moisture drain out completely (2-3 minutes). Baste with clarified butter and further roast for 2-3 minutes or till tender.
8. Serve hot with choice of a salad and chutney.

Raan - E - Patiala Shahi

CHICKEN LEGS PREPARED WITH SECRET RECIPE FROM THE KITCHEN OF THE ROYAL HOUSE OF PATIALA
Cooking time 10-12 minutes Serves 1-2

INGREDIENTS

(300-325 gm) 2 no - Chicken leg on bone (with thigh)

First Marination
To taste	- Salt
½ tsp	- Ginger garlic paste
½ tsp	- Red chilli paste
2 tsp	- Lemon juice

Second Marination
4 tbsp	- Hung curd
To taste	- Salt
½ tsp	- Ginger garlic paste
½ tsp	- Red chilli paste
1/3 tsp	- Kasoori methi powder
A pinch	- Clove powder
1 tsp	- Vinegar
20 ml	- White wine
2 tsp	- Refined oil

For basting - Clarified butter

METHOD

1. Clean, wash and make 3 incisions on both side of chicken, pat dry and keep aside.

First Marination
2. In a bowl mix salt, ginger garlic paste, red chilli paste, lemon juice and apply this to chicken pieces, rub well and keep aside for at least 1 hour.

Second Marination
3. In a bowl whisk hung curd, add salt, ginger garlic paste, red chilli paste, kasoori methi, clove powder, vinegar, white wine, oil and mix well.
4. Put the chicken pieces into this marinade, coat well and keep aside for at least 2 hours.

Cooking
5. Take a skewer and skew marinated chicken pieces along the skewer, keep a tray underneath to collect drippings.
6. Roast in a tandoor or over a charcoal grill at a moderate temperature for 7-8 minutes.
7. Remove and hang the skewer so that the moisture drains out completely (1-2 minutes). Baste with clarified butter and further roast for 2-3 minutes or till tender.
8. Serve hot along with choice of a salad and chutney.

Murg Mulayam Kebab

A CREAMY KEBAB MADE FROM CHICKEN FLAVOURED WITH ROYAL CUMIN AND CARDAMOM
Cooking time 10-12 minutes Serves 1-2

INGREDIENTS

(200-225) 2 no. - Chicken leg (bone less)

First marination
½ tsp	- Ginger garlic paste
1 tsp	- Lemon juice
To taste	- Salt

Second marination
2 tbsp	- Processed cheese (grated)
1 tsp	- Ginger garlic paste
1 no	- Egg white
2 tbsp	- Cream
½ tsp	- Green chilli (chopped)
1 tsp	- Fresh coriander (chopped)
A pinch	- Shahi jeera
½ tsp	- White pepper powder
A pinch	- Elaichi powder
To taste	- Salt

For basting - Clarified butter

METHOD

1. Clean, wash, cut the chicken leg into 3 pieces, pat dry and keep aside.

First marination
2. In a bowl mix ginger garlic paste, lemon juice, salt, apply this to chicken pieces, rub well and keep aside for at least 45 minutes.

Second marination
3. In a deep tray mash grated cheese, add ginger garlic paste, egg white and mix it gradually with your palm. Pour cream and further mix it, so that it becomes a smooth paste, add green chilli, fresh coriander, shahi jeera, white pepper powder, elaichi powder, salt and mix well.
4. Put the chicken pieces into this marinade and keep aside for at least 2 hours.

Cooking
5. Take a skewer and skew marinated chicken pieces, keep a tray underneath to collect drippings.
6. Roast in a moderately hot tandoor or over a charcoal grill for 6-7 minutes.
7. Remove and baste with clarified butter and further roast for 3-4 minutes or till tender.
8. Serve hot with choice of a salad and chutney.

Tandoori Chicken Lolly Pops

SUCCULENT KEBAB MADE OF CHICKEN THIGH, SPECIAL BLEND OF SPICES AND CHAR-GRILLED

Cooking time 10-12 minutes Serves 1-2

INGREDIENTS

325-350 gm (4 no) - Chicken thigh

First Marination
To taste	- Salt
½ tsp	- Red chilli paste
1 tsp	- Lemon juice
½ tsp	- Ginger garlic paste

Second Marination
4 tbsp	- Hung curd
To taste	- Salt
½ tsp	- Ginger garlic paste
½ tsp	- Red chilli paste
1 tsp	- Lemon juice
1/3 tsp	- Garam masala
½ tsp	- Kasoori methi powder
1 tsp	- Refined oil

For basting - Clarified butter

METHOD

1. Cut the thigh from one side and open it across the bone without disjoining from other side. Pat dry and keep aside.

First Marination

2. In a bowl mix salt, red chilli paste, lemon juice, ginger garlic paste, apply this to chops, rub well and keep aside for at least 45 minutes

Second Marination

3. In a bowl whisk hung curd, add salt, ginger garlic paste, red chilli paste, lemon juice, garam masala, kasoori methi, oil and mix well.
4. Put the chicken chops into this marinade, coat well and keep aside for at least 1 hour.

Cooking

4. Take a skewer and skew marinated chops one by one keeping a distance in between. Keep a tray underneath to collect drippings.
5. Roast in moderately hot tandoor or over a charcoal grill for 7-8 minutes.
6. Remove and let extra moisture drain out completely (1-2 minutes)
7. Baste with clarified butter and further roast for 2-3 minutes or till tender.
8. Serve hot with choice of a salad and chutney.

Dum Ka Murg Seena

CHICKEN BREAST INFUSED WITH ORIENTAL SPICES AND COOKED ON LAGAN AS SLOW FIRE

Cooking time 8-10 minutes Serves 1-2

INGREDIENTS

(200-225 gm) 3 no. - Chicken breast (boneless)

2 tbsp	- Hung curd
½ tsp	- Ginger (chopped)
½ tsp	- Garlic (chopped)
1 tsp	- Dark brown sugar
2 tsp	- Sesame seeds
1 tbsp	- Soya sauce
1 tbsp	- Dry sherry
1 tsp	- Crushed black pepper
To taste	- Salt
For cooking	- Oil (refined)

METHOD

1. Clean, wash, pat dry chicken breast and keep aside.

Marination

2. In a bowl whisk hung curd and add all the ingredients listed in order, mix well, put in chicken breast, coat evenly and keep aside for at least 2 hours.

Cooking

3. Heat oil in a thick bottomed pan (lagan), put chicken breast and cook it on absolutely slow fire, occasionally baste with oil and cook for 8-10 minutes or till tender and crispy.
4. Remove and cut into slices, each breast into 2 or 3 parts.
5. Serve hot with mint chutney and salad.

Murg Karara

HOT AND SPICY VARIATION OF SPRING CHICKEN FLAVOURED WITH SELECTED SPICES AND HERBS

Cooking time 12-14 minutes Serves 1-2

INGREDIENTS

325-350 gm - Chicken ½ no. on bone (leg and breast)

First Marination
To taste	- Salt
½ tsp	- Ginger garlic paste
2 tsp	- Lemon juice

Second Marination
4 tbsp	- Hung curd
To taste	- Salt
½ tsp	- Ginger garlic paste
1 tsp	- Red chilli powder
1/3 tsp	- Garam masala
1 tsp	- Green chilli (chopped)
1 tsp	- Green corriander (chopped)
1 tsp	- Spring onion (chopped)
1 tsp	- Corn flour
2 tsp	- Egg powder
1 tsp	- Soya sauce
1 tsp	- Vinegar
2 tsp	- Mustard oil

For basting - Clarified butter

METHOD

1. Clean, wash, cut chicken leg and breast into 2 pieces and make 3 incisions on both sides of chicken pieces, pat dry and keep aside.

First Marination
2. In a bowl mix salt, ginger garlic paste, lemon juice and apply this to chicken pieces, rub well and keep aside for at least 1 hour.

Second Marination
3. In a bowl whisk hung curd, add salt, ginger garlic paste, red chilli powder, garam masala, green chilli, coriander, spring onion, corn flour, egg powder, soya sauce, vinegar, oil and mix well.
4. Put the chicken pieces into this marinade, coat well and keep aside for at least 2 hours.

Cooking
5. Take a skewer and skew marinated chicken pieces along the skewer, keep a tray underneath to collect drippings.
6. Roast in a tandoor or over charcoal grill at a moderate temperature for 6-8 minutes.
7. Remove and hang the skewer so that the moisture drains out completely (1-2 minutes), baste with clarified butter and further roast for 3-4 minutes or till tender.
8. Serve hot along with choice of a salad and chutney.

Surkh Lal Tangri

RED AND HOT CHICKEN DRUMSTICKS- BEST TO ENJOY WITH DRINKS

Cooking time 10-12 minutes Serves 1-2

INGREDIENTS

4 no. (250-275) - Chicken drumsticks

First Marination
To taste	- Salt
½ tsp	- Ginger garlic paste
½ tsp	- Red chilli paste
1 tsp	- Malt vinegar

Second Marination
4 tbsp	- Hung curd
To taste	- Salt
½ tsp	- Ginger garlic paste
½ tsp	- Red chilli paste
1 tsp	- Cashewnut paste
3 tsp	- Beetroot puree
1/3 tsp	- Garam masala
1 tsp	- Refined oil

For basting - Clarified butter

METHOD

1. Clean, wash and make 3 incisions on both sides of chicken drumsticks, pat dry and keep aside.

First Marination
2. In a bowl mix salt, ginger garlic paste, red chilli paste, malt vinegar, and apply this to chicken drumsticks, rub well and keep aside for at least 1 hour.

Second Marination
3. In a bowl whisk hung curd, add salt, ginger garlic paste, red chilli paste, cashewnut paste, beet root puree, garam masala, oil and mix well.
2. Put chicken pieces into this marinade, coat well and keep aside for at least 2 hours.

Cooking
4. Take a skewer and skew marinated chicken pieces along the skewer length wise. Keep a tray underneath to collect drippings.
5. Roast in a tandoor or over a charcoal grill at a moderate temperature for 7-8 minutes.
6. Remove and hang the skewer so that the moisture drains out completely (1-2 minutes). Baste with clarified butter and further roast for 2-3 minutes or till tender.
7. Serve hot along with choice of a salad and chutney.

Murg Shehnaz

MUSTARD FLAVOURED JUICY LEG OF CHICKEN INFUSED WITH ROYAL CUMIN AND CHAR-GRILLED
Cooking time 14-15 minutes Serves 1-2

INGREDIENTS

300-325 gm (2 no) - Chicken leg on bone (with thigh)

First Marination
To taste	- Salt
½ tsp	- Ginger garlic paste
½ tsp	- Yellow chilli powder
1 tsp	- Lemon juice

Second Marination
4 tbsp	- Hung curd
To taste	- Salt
½ tsp	- Ginger garlic paste
½ tsp	- Yellow chilli powder
A pinch	- Turmeric powder
1 tsp	- Mustard paste
A pinch	- Shahi jeera (black cumin)
1 tsp	- Lemon juice
1 no	- Egg yolk
2 tsp	- Refined oil

For basting - Clarified butter

METHOD

1. Clean, wash, cut chicken leg into 2 pieces with a sharp knife and make 3 incisions on both sides of chicken, pat dry and keep aside.

First Marination

2. In a bowl mix salt, ginger garlic paste, yellow chilli powder, lemon juice and apply this to chicken, rub well and keep aside for at least 1 hour.

Second Marination

3. In a bowl whisk hung curd, add salt, ginger garlic paste, yellow chilli powder, turmeric powder, mustard paste, shahi jeera, lemon juice, egg yolk, oil and mix well.
4. Put chicken pieces into this marinade, coat well and keep aside for at least 2 hours.

Cooking

5. Take a skewer and skew marinated chicken pieces along the skewer, keep a tray underneath to collect drippings.
6. Roast in a tandoor or over charcoal grill at a moderate temperature for 8-10 minutes
7. Remove and hang the skewer so that the moisture drains out completely (1-2 minutes). Baste with clarified butter and further roast for 2-3 minutes or till tender.
8. Serve hot along with choice of a salad and chutney.

Narial Ka Murg Tukra

SUCCULENT CHICKEN MORSELS WITH EXTRA FLAVOUR OF COCONUT
Cooking time 10-12 minutes Serves 1-2

INGREDIENTS

(200 225 gm Pcs) - Chicken leg (Boneless)

First Marination
1 tsp	- Ginger garlic paste
1 tsp	- lemon juice
To taste	- Salt

Second Marination
3 tbsp	- Hung curd
2 tbsp	- Coconut (grated)
2 tbsp	- Coconut powder
2 no	- Egg white
2 tbsp	- Cream
1 tbsp	- Green chilli (chopped)
1 tsp	- Green coriander (chopped)

For basting - Coconut oil

METHOD

1. Clean, wash and cut each chicken leg into 3 pieces. Pat dry and keep aside.

First Marination

2. In a bowl mix ginger garlic paste, lemon juice, salt, apply this to chicken pieces, rub well and keep aside for at least 1 hour.

Second Marination

3. In a bowl whisk hung curd, add grated coconut, coconut powder, egg white, cream, chopped green chilli and coriander, squeeze excess moisture from chicken and put them into this marinade, coat well and keep aside for at least 2 hours.

Cooking

4. Take a skewer and skew the marinated chicken pieces. Keep a tray underneath to collect drippings.
5. Roast in a moderately hot tandoor or over a charcoal grill for 10-12 minutes, till done, baste with coconut oil during cooking
6. Serve hot with choice of a salad and chutney.

Tandoori Murg Frontier

SPICY CHICKEN MARINATED WITH VARIETY OF SPICES AND PREPARED EXACTLY IN FRONTIER STYLE

Cooking time 12-14 minutes Serves 1-2

INGREDIENTS

325-350 gm (½ no) - Chicken on bone (leg and breast)

First Marination
To taste	- Salt
½ tsp	- Ginger garlic paste
½ tsp	- Red chilli paste
1 tsp	- Lemon juice

Second Marination
4 tbsp	- Hung curd
To taste	- Salt
½ tsp	- Ginger garlic paste
½ tsp	- Red chilli paste
A pinch	- Small cardamom powder
A pinch	- Cinnamon powder
½ tsp	- Coriander powder
1 tsp	- Lemon juice
2 tsp	- White wine
2 tsp	- Mustard oil

For basting - Clarified butter

METHOD

1. Clean, wash, cut chicken breast and leg into 2 pieces each and make 3 incisions on both sides of chicken pieces, pat dry and keep aside.

First Marination
2. In a bowl mix salt, ginger garlic paste, red chilli paste, lemon juice and apply this to chicken pieces, rub well and keep aside for at least 1 hour.

Second Marination
3. In a bowl whisk hung curd, add salt, ginger garlic paste, red chilli paste, small cardamon powder, cinnamon powder, coriander powder, lemon juice, oil, wine and mix well.
4. Put the chicken pieces into this marinade, coat well and keep aside for at least 2 hours.

Cooking
5. Take a skewer and skew marinated chicken pieces along the skewer, keep a tray underneath to collect drippings.
6. Roast in a tandoor or over charcoal grill at a moderate temperature for 7-8 minutes.
7. Remove and hang the skewer so that the moisture drains out completely (1-2 minutes), baste with clarified butter and further roast for 3-4 minutes or till tender.
8. Serve hot along with choice of a salad and chutney.

Tandoori Chooza Masaledar

WHOLE SPRING CHICKEN STUFFED WITH DRY FRUITS AND CHICKEN MINCE ENHANCED WITH SPICES AND ROASTED IN CLAY OVEN

Cooking time 14-15 minutes Serves 2-4

INGREDIENTS

1 no. (700-750 gm) - Whole chicken (without skin)

First Marination
To taste	- Salt
½ tsp	- Ginger/garlic paste
½ tsp	- White pepper powder
2 tsp	- Malt vinegar

Stuffing
2 tsp	- Refined oil
2 tsp	- Onions (chopped)
150 gm	- Chicken mince
1 tsp	- Green chilli (chopped)
1 tsp	- Green coriander (chopped)
2 tsp	- Dry fruits (coarsely chopped)
To taste	- Salt
A pinch	- Kasoori methi powder
A pinch	- Garam masala
A pinch	- Turmeric powder
A pinch	- Saffron
3 tsp	- Processed cheese (grated)

Second Marination
½ cup	- Hung curd
To taste	- Salt
½ tsp	- Ginger garlic paste
½ tsp	- White pepper powder
2 tsp	- Cashewnut paste
A pinch	- Elaichi powder
½ tsp	- Green chilli (chopped)
1 tsp	- Green coriander (chopped)
1 no	- Egg white
1 tsp	- Cornflour

For basting - Clarified butter

METHOD

1. Clean, wash and slit chicken from shoulder bone and from lower side of the thigh and leg and make a hole with a finger, pat dry and keep aside.

First Marination
2. In a bowl mix salt, ginger garlic paste, white pepper, malt vinegar and apply this to the chicken pieces, rub well and keep aside for at least 1 hour.

Stuffing
3. Heat oil in a pan, add chopped onions and saute it then add chicken mince, green chilli, green coriander, salt, dry fruits, kasoori methi, garam masala, turmeric, saffron and cook it till chicken is done and water evaporates. Keep aside for cooling and then add cheese, mix it well.
4. Stuff the chicken with this mixture from the shoulder bone and from lower part of leg and thigh, make 3 incisions on both breast and leg ensuring it does not pierce meat to avoid the stuffing come out.

Second Marination
5. In a bowl whisk hung curd add salt, ginger garlic paste, white pepper powder, cashewnut paste, elaichi powder, green chilli, green coriander, egg white, corn flour and mix it well.
6. Put stuffed chicken into this marinade, coat well and keep aside for at least 2 hours.

Cooking
7. Take a skewer and skew chicken from centre of the legs to the centre of the breast. Keep a tray underneath to collect drippings.
8. Roast in a moderately hot tandoor for 10-12 minutes.
9. Remove and hang skewer for (2 –3 minutes) so that excess moisture drains out completely, baste with clarified butter and further roast it for 3-4 minutes or till tender.
10. Serve hot with choice of a salad and chutney.

Seekh-E-Noorani

SOFT AND DELICIOUS EGG WHITE COATED CHICKEN MINCE SKEWER

Cooking time 7-8 minutes Serves 1-2

INGREDIENTS

2 tbsp	- Processed cheese (grated)
200 gm	- Chicken mince
1 tsp	- Ginger garlic paste
½ tsp	- Green chilli (chopped)
1 tsp	- Fresh coriander (chopped)
A pinch	- Royal cumin seeds
2 tsp	- Cream
To taste	- Salt
½ tsp	- White pepper powder
A pinch	- Elaichi javitri powder
For coating	- Boiled egg white (grated)
For basting	- Clarified butter

METHOD

1. In a deep tray mash processed cheese, put chicken mince, add all the remaining ingredients in the order listed, rub well and keep aside for at least half an hour.
2. Divide the mixture into 4 equal portions and make balls.

Cooking

1. Spread the mixture on the skewer using a wet hand along the length of the skewer in a cylindrical shape, coat with grated boiled egg and make each kebab 4-5 inches long.
2. Roast in a moderately hot tandoor or over charcoal grill for 5-6 minutes.
3. Remove and baste with clarified butter and further roast for 1-2 minutes or till tender.

Murg Badshahi

CHICKEN DRUMSTICKS KEBAB FLAVOURED WITH CARDAMOM AND MACE

Cooking time 10-12 minutes Serves 1-2

INGREDIENTS

(250-275 gm) 4pc - Chicken drumsticks

First Marination

To taste	- Salt
1/3 tsp	- White pepper powder
½ tsp	- Ginger garlic paste

Second Marination

4 tbsp	- Hung curd
To taste	- Salt
½ tsp	- Ginger garlic paste
2 tsp	- Cashenut paste
2 tsp	- Cream
2 tsp	- Egg white
A pinch	- Elaichi javitri pwder
A pinch	- Shahi jeera (black cumin)
½ tsp	- Cornflour
For basting	- Clarified butter

METHOD

1. Clean, wash and make 3 incisions on chicken drumsticks with a sharp knife, pat dry and keep aside.

First Marination

2. In a bowl mix salt, white pepper, ginger garlic paste, apply this to chicken drumsticks, rub well and keep aside for at least 45 minutes.

Second Marination

3. In a bowl whisk hung curd, add salt, ginger garlic paste, cashew nut paste, cream, egg white, elaichi javitri powder, shahi jeera, corn flour and mix well.
4. Put the chicken drumsticks into this marinade, coat well and keep aside for at least 2 hours.

Cooking

5. Take a skewer and skew chicken drumstick horizontally leaving a gap of at least one inch between the legs. Keep a tray underneath to collect drippings.
6. Roast in a moderately hot tandoor or over a charcoal grill for 7-8 minutes.
7. Remove and hang skewer for (1 –2 minutes) so that excess moisture drains out completely, baste with clarified butter and further roast it for 2-3 minutes.
8. Serve hot with choice of a salad and chutney.

Malika -E- Hussn

ANOTHER DELICATE CHICKEN KEBAB STEEPED IN NUT PASTE, FLAVOURED WITH CARDAMOM AND MACE

Cooking time 10-12 minutes Serves 1-2

INGREDIENTS

2no. (200 – 225 gm) - Chicken breast (with shoulder bone)

First Marination
To taste	- Salt
½ tsp	- Ginger garlic paste
½ tsp	- White pepper powder

Stuffing
2 tsp	- Refined oil
2 tsp	- Onion (chopped)
75 gm	- Chicken mince
1 tsp	- Green coriander (chopped)
1 tsp	- Green chilli (chopped)
1 tsp	- Ginger (chopped)
To taste	- Salt
A pinch	- Amchur powder
A pinch	- Garam masala

Second Marination
4 tbsp	- Almond, Cashewnut and Chaar magaz paste
To taste	- Salt
1 no	- Egg
½ tsp	- White pepper powder
1 tsp	- Cornflour
A pinch	- Elaichi javitri powder
1 tsp	- Lemon juice

For basting - Clarified butter

METHOD

1. Clean, wash and slit chicken from shoulder and make a hole, pat dry and keep aside.

First Marination
2. In a bowl mix salt, ginger garlic paste, white pepper powder, apply this to the chicken pieces, rub well and keep aside for at least 45 minutes.

Stuffing
3. Heat oil in a pan, add chopped onions and saute it, then add chicken mince, green coriander, green chilli, ginger, salt, amchur powder, garam masala and cook it till chicken is done and moisture gets evaporates. Keep aside for cooling.
4. Stuff the chicken from the shoulder bone and make 3 incisions in each breast ensuring it does not pierce chicken mince to avoid stuffing bursting out.

Second Marination
5. In a bowl put almond, cashewnut, chaar magaz paste, add salt, egg, white pepper, corn flour, elaichi, javitri powder, lemon juice and mix it well.
6. Put stuffed chicken breast into this marinade, coat well and keep aside for at least 1 hour.

Cooking
7. Take a skewer and skew marinated chicken breast from shoulder. Keep a tray underneath to collect drippings.
8. Roast in a moderately hot tandoor or over a charcoal grill for 6 – 7 minutes.
9. Remove and hang skewer for (1 –2 minutes) so that excess moisture drains out completely. Baste with clarified butter and further roast it for 2-3 minutes or till tender.
10. Serve hot with choice of a salad and chutney.

Bharwan Gulmohar Tangri

CHICKEN DRUMSTICKS STUFFED WITH DELICIOUS AND RICH CHICKEN M,INCE
Cooking time 10-12 minutes Serves 1-2

INGREDIENTS

4 no. (250-275 gm) Chicken drumsticks

First Marination
To taste	- Salt
½ tsp	- Ginger garlic paste
½ tsp	- White pepper powder
1 tsp	- Vinegar

Stuffing
2 tsp	- Refined oil
½ tsp	- Ginger garlic paste
75 gm	- Chicken mince
To taste	- Salt
½ tsp	- White pepper powder
1 tsp	- Green chilli (chopped)
1 tsp	- Green coriander (chopped)

Second Marination
75 gm	- Processed cheese (grated)
1 no	- Egg white
½ tsp	- Ginger/garlic paste
4 tsp	- Cream
2 tsp	- Chaar magaz paste
To taste	- Salt
½ tsp	- White pepper
1 tsp	- Green chilli(chopped)
2 tsp	- Brown onion paste

For basting - Clarified butter

METHOD

1. Clean, wash and cut chicken leg, pat dry and keep aside.

First Marination

2. In a bowl mix salt, ginger garlic paste, white pepper, vinegar and apply this to chicken pieces, rub well and keep aside for at least 45 minutes.

Stuffing

3. Heat oil in a pan, add ginger garlic paste and saute it for a while, then add chicken mince, salt, white pepper powder, green chilli, cook till chicken is done and mixture becomes completely dry, keep aside for cooling and add coriander to it.
4. From the joint cut side with the help of thumb, make a hole, along the above of each drumstick. Stuff each chicken leg with this mixture and give three incisions behind the drumsticks, ensure that chicken is not pierced deep to avoid bursting of stuffing.

Second Marination

5. In a deep tray mash cheese, add egg white, ginger garlic paste, cream, char magaz paste, salt, white pepper, green chilli, onion paste and mix well to smooth consistency .
6. Put chicken drumsticks into this marinade, coat well and keep aside for at least 1 hour.

Cooking

7. Take a skewer and skew chicken legs horizontally leaving a gap of at least an inch between each leg.
8. Roast in a moderate hot tandoor or over a charcoal grill for 6-7 minutes. Remove and hang skewer so that the excess moisture drains out completely (1-2 minutes).
9. Baste with clarified butter and further roast for 2--3 minutes or till tender.
10. Serve hot with choice of a salad and chutney.

Murg Chilgoja Kebab

CHICKEN MINCE AND PINENUTS KEBAB INFUSED WITH CARDAMOM AND DRY GINGER
Cooking time 8-10 minutes Serves 1-2

INGREDIENTS

2 tbsp	- Processed cheese (grated)
200 gm	- Chicken mince
2 tbsp	- Roasted peanuts (roasted and crushed)
1 tsp	- Ginger garlic paste
½ tsp	- Green chilli (chopped seed less)
1tsp	- Green coriander (chopped)
½ tsp	- White pepper
1tsp	- Cream
½ tsp	- Green cardamom powder
½ tsp	- Dry ginger powder
To taste	- Salt

For basting - Clarified butter

METHOD

1. In a deep tray, mash processed cheese, put chicken mince, add all the remaining ingredients in the order listed, rub well and keep aside for at least half an hour.
2. Divide the mixture into 4 equal portions and make balls.

Cooking

3. Spread the mixture on the skewer using a wet hand along the length of the skewer in a cylindrical shape, one inch apart and make each kebab 4-5 inches long.
4. Roast in a moderately hot tandoor or over charcoal grill for 6 – 7 minutes.
5. Baste with clarified butter and further roast for 2-3 minutes or till tender

Bharwan Murg Tangri

THIS DELICIOUS KEBAB OF CHICKEN DRUMSTICK STUFFED WITH ENRICHED CHICKEN MINCE INFUSED WITH SAFFRON AND CARDAMOM

Cooking time 10-12 minutes Serves 1-2

INGREDIENTS

250 - 275 gm (4 no) - Chicken drumstick

First Marination
½ tsp	- Ginger garlic paste
1 tsp	- Lemon juice
To taste	- Salt
A pinch	- White pepper powder

Stuffing
2 tsp	- Refined oil
2 tsp	- Cashewnut (chopped)
75 gm	- Chicken mince
To taste	- Salt
A pinch	- White pepper powder
½ tsp	- Green chilli (chopped)
A pinch	- Saffron
1 tsp	- Fresh coriander (chopped)

Second Marination
5 tsp	- Processed cheese (grated)
1 no	- Egg white
½ tsp	- Ginger garlic paste
5 tsp	- Cream
To taste	- Salt
½ tsp	- White pepper powder
A pinch	- Elachi powder
½ tsp	- Green chilli (chopped)
1 tsp	- Cornflour

For basting - Clarified butter

METHOD

1. Clean, wash the chicken drumstick, pat dry and keep aside.

First Marination
2. In a bowl mix ginger garlic paste, lemon juice, salt, white pepper powder, apply this to chicken drumstick, rub well and keep aside for at least 45 minutes.

Stuffing
3. Heat oil in a pan, add cashewnuts, chicken mince and sauté till meat turns white. Add salt, white pepper powder, green chilli chopped, saffron. Cook till moisture evaporates and mixture becomes completely dry, keep aside for cooling and add coriander to it.
4. From the joint cut side with help of thumb, make a hole along the above of each tangri. Stuff each tangri with this mixture and make three incisions behind the tangri, ensure that chicken is not pierced deep to avoid bursting of stuffing.

Second Marination
5. In a deep tray mash grated cheese, egg white, ginger garlic paste and mix with the palm gradually. Pour cream, salt, white pepper powder, elaichi, green chilli, corn flour and further mix so that it becomes a smooth paste.
6. Put the chicken tangri into this marinade, coat well and keep aside for at least 1 hour.

Cooking
7. Take a skewer and skew chicken drumsticks horizontally leaving a gap of at least an inch between each leg.
8. Roast in a moderate hot tandoor or over a charcoal grill for 7-8 minutes. Remove and hang skewer so that the excess moisture drains out completely.(I-2 minutes)
9. Baste with clarified butter and further roast for 2-3 minutes or till tender.
10. Serve hot with choice of a salad and chutney.

Til Wali Tangri

A CREAMY CHICKEN DRUMSTICKS INFUSED WITH CARDAMOM POWDER AND ENRICHED WITH SESAME

Cooking time 10-12 minutes Serves 1-2

INGREDIENTS

250 - 275 gm (4 no) - Chicken drumsticks

First Marination
½ tsp	- Ginger garlic paste
To taste	- Salt
2 tsp	- Lemon juice
½ tsp	- White pepper powder

Second Marination
2 tbsp	- Processed cheese (grated)
1 no	- Egg white
2 tbsp	- Cream
2 tsp	- Hung curd
To taste	- Salt
1/3 tsp	- White pepper powder
4 tsp	- Sesame paste
1 tsp	- Cornflour
A pinch	- Elaichi powder
½ tsp	- Green chilli (chopped)
1 tsp	- Green coriander (chopped)
2 tsp	- Til white (roasted)

For basting - Clarified butter

METHOD

1. Clean, wash and make 3 incisions on chicken drumsticks with the help of a knife, pat dry and keep aside.

First Marination

2. In a bowl mix ginger garlic paste, salt, lemon juice, and white pepper powder, apply this to the chicken, rub well and keep aside for at least 45 minutes.

Second Marination

3. In a deep tray mash processed cheese, rub it well, add egg white rub it again, then add cream, hung curd, salt, white pepper, sesame paste, corn flour, elaichi powder, green chilli, green coriiander and sesame, mix well to smooth consistency.
4. Put chicken drumsticks into this marinade, coat well and keep aside for at least 2 hour.

Cooking

5. Take a skewer and skew the marinated chicken leg horizontally leaving a gap of an inch between. Keep a tray underneath to collect drippings.
6. Roast in a tandoor at a moderate temperature for 7-8 minutes.
7. Remove and hang the skewer upright to let the excess moisture drain out completely(1-2 minutes).
8. Baste with clarified butter and further roast for 2- 3 minutes.
9. Serve hot with choice of a salad and chutney.

Tandoori Murg Zaffrani

A SAFFRON FLAVOURED SOFT AND JUICY RICH CHICKEN KEBAB

Cooking time 10-12 minutes Serves 1-2

INGREDIENTS

(200-225 gm) 2 pcs - Chicken leg (boneless)

First marination
1 tsp	- Ginger garlic paste
½ tsp	- Yellow chilli powder
1tsp	- Lemon juice
To taste	- Salt

Second marination
2 tbsp	- Hung curd
2 tbsp	- Almonds and cashewnut paste
2 tbsp	- Cream
2 tsp	- Brown onion paste
½ tsp	- Garam masala
½ tsp	- Yellow chilli powder
A pinch	- Elaichi javitri powder
To taste	- Salt
¼ tsp	- Saffron

For basting - Clarified butter

METHOD

1. Clean, wash and cut each chicken leg into 3 pieces, pat dry and keep aside.

First marination

2. In a bowl mix ginger garlic paste, yellow chilli powder, lemon juice, salt, apply this to chicken, rub well and keep aside for at least 45 minutes.

Second marination

3. In a bowl whisk hung curd add almonds and cashewnut paste and all other ingredients listed above and mix well.
4. Squeeze excess moisture from the marinated chicken pieces, put marinade into this and keep aside for at least 1 hour.

Cooking

5. Take a skewer and skew marinated chicken pieces one by one, keep a tray underneath to collect drippings.
6. Roast in a moderately hot tandoor or over a charcoal grill for 7-8 minutes.
3. Remove and baste with clarified butter and roast for another 3-4 minutes.
7. Serve hot with choice of a salad and chutney.

Tandoori Pankhari Kebab

A UNIQUE CONCOCTION OF SPICY CHICKEN WINGS

Cooking time 6-8 minutes Serves 1-2

INGREDIENTS

(200-225 gm) 6 pcs-Murg pankhari
(chicken wings with shoulder from a large broiler)

First Marination

½ tsp	- Ginger garlic paste
To taste	- Salt
½ tsp	- Red chilli paste
1 tsp	- Lemon juice

Second Marination

4 tsp	- Hung curd
½ tsp	- Ginger garlic paste
To taste	- Salt
½ tsp	- Red chilli paste
1 tsp	- Lemon juice
½ tsp	- Garam masala
½ tsp	- Kasoori methi powder
2 tsp	- Refined oil

For basting - Clarified butter

METHOD

1. Wash, and clean chicken wings, pat dry and keep aside.

First Marination

2. In a bowl mix ginger garlic paste, salt, red chilli paste and lemon juice. Apply this to chicken wings, rub well and keep aside for at least 45 minutes.

Second Marination

3. In a bowl whisk hung curd, add ginger garlic paste, salt, red chilli paste, lemon juice, garam masala, kasoori methi, oil and mix well.
4. Put chicken pieces into this marinade coat, well and keep aside for at least 1 hour.

Cooking

5. Take a skewer and skew marinated wings one by one, leaving a gap of an inch between wings.
6. Roast in a moderate tandoor or over a charcoal grill for 4-5 minutes.
7. Remove and baste with clarified butter and again roast for 1-2 minutes.
8. Serve hot with choice of a salad and chutney.

Murg Kalmi Kebab

THIS SUPER KEBAB MADE OF CHICKEN LEG (THIGH) TRIMMED LIKE A WRITING PEN, ENHANCED WITH SYMPHONY OF SPICES AND HERBS

Cooking time 10-12 minutes Serves 1-2

INGREDIENTS

(325-350 gm) 4 no - Chicken leg (thigh only)

First Marination

½ tsp	- Ginger garlic paste
½ tsp	- Lemon juice
To taste	- Salt

Second Marination

3 tbsp	- Hung curd
½ tsp	- Ginger garlic paste
2 tbsp	- Cashewnut paste
1 tbsp	- Cream
1 no	- Egg white
½ tsp	- Green chilli (chopped)
1 tsp	- Fresh coriander (chopped)
A pinch	- Shahi jeera (black cumin)
½ tsp	- Garam masala
½ tsp	- Yellow chilli powder
½ tsp	- Dry rose petal powder
To taste	- Salt

For basting - Clarified butter

METHOD

1. Wash, clean and cut the thigh from one side and open it across the bone without disjoining from other side, pat dry and keep aside.

First Marination

2. In a bowl mix ginger garlic paste, lemon juice and salt, apply this to chicken, rub well and keep aside for at least 45 minutes.

Second Marination

3. In a bowl whisk hung curd and add ginger garlic paste, cashewnut paste, and all other ingredients listed above, mix well.
4. Put the chicken into this marinade, coat well and keep aside for at least 1 hour.

Cooking

5. Take a skewer and skew marinated chicken thigh, keep a tray underneath to collect drippings.
6. Roast in a moderately hot tandoor or over a charcoal grill for 6-7 minutes.
7. Remove and hang skewer (1-2 minutes), baste with clarified butter and further roast for 2-3 minutes.
8. Serve hot with choice of a salad and chutney.

Harra Tandoori Pankhari

SUCCULENT CHICKEN WINGS MARINATED WITH GREEN PASTE AND DELICATELY CHAR-GRILLED

Cooking time 6-8 minutes Serves 1-2

INGREDIENTS

(200-225 gm) 6 pcs-Murg pankhari
(chicke wings with shoulder from large broiler)

First Marination

½ tsp	- Ginger garlic paste
To taste	- Salt
1/3 tsp	- Yellow chilli powder
1 tsp	- Lemon juice

Second Marination

4 tsp	- Hung curd
½ tsp	- Ginger garlic paste
To taste	- Salt
1/3 tsp	- Yellow chilli powder
1 tsp	- Lemon juice
½ tsp	- Garam masala
½ tsp	- Kasoori methi powder
2 tsp	- Mint (chopped)
1 tsp	- Garlic (chopped)
1 tsp	- Spinach puree
2 tsp	- Refined oil

For basting - Clarified butter

METHOD

1. Wash, cut and clean chicken wings and shoulder, pat dry and keep aside.

First Marination

2. In a bowl take ginger garlic paste, salt, yellow chilli powder and lemon juice. Dip chicken pankhari, rub well and keep aside for at least 45 minutes.

Second Marination

3. In a bowl whisk hung curd, add ginger garlic paste, salt, yellow chilli powder, lemon juice, garam masala, kasoori methi, mint, spinach puree, oil and mix well.
4. Put the chicken pieces into this marinade and keep aside for at least 1 hour.

Cooking

5. Take a skewer and skew marinated pankhari pieces one by one, leaving a gap of an inch beetween wings.
6. Roast in a moderate tandoor or over a charcoal grill for 4-5 minutes.
7. Remove and baste with clarified butter and further roast for 1-2 minutes.
8. Serve hot with choice of a salad and chutney.

Chatpate Tandoori Gurdey

SPICY AND APPETIZING KEBAB MADE WITH LAMB SWEET BREAD AND DELICATELY CHAR-GRILLED

Cooking time 6-8 minutes Serves 1-2

INGREDIENTS

5 pcs (200-225grm) Gurdey (Sweet Bread)

First marination

To taste	- Salt
½ tsp	- Ginger garlic paste
½ tsp	- Red chilli paste
1tsp	- Lemon juice

Second marination

4 tbsp	- Hung curd
To taste	- Salt
½ tsp	- Ginger garlic paste
½ tsp	- Red chilli paste
1/3 tsp	- Kastoori methi powder
1/3 tsp	- Garam masala
1 tsp	- Refined Oil

For basting - Clarified butter

METHOD

1. Clean, wash and pat dry gurdey and keep aside.

First marination

2. In a bowl mix salt, ginger garlic paste, red chilli paste, lemon juice and apply this to gurdey rub well and keep aside for at least 30 minutes.

Second marination

3. Whisk hung curd in a bowl add salt, ginger garlic paste, red chilli, kasoori methi, garam masala, oil and mix well.
4. Put gurdey into this marinade coat well and keep aside for at least 1 hour.

Cooking

5. Take a skewer and skew the marinated gurdey pieces, keep a tray underneath to collect drippings.
6. Roast in a moderately hot tandoor or over a charcoal grill for 5-6 minutes.
7. Remove and baste with clarified butter and further roast for 1-2 minutes or till tender.
8. Serve hot with a choice of a salad and chutney.

Haryali Murg Tangri

SUCCULENT CHICKEN DRUMSTICKS MARINATED WITH GREEN PASTE AND POUNDED YELLOW CHILLI

Cooking time 10-12 minutes Serves 1-2

INGREDIENTS

(250-275 gm) 4 no - Chicken drumstick

First Marination
To taste	- Salt
½ tsp	- Ginger garlic paste
1/3 tsp	- Yellow chilli powder
1 tsp	- Lemon Juice

Green paste
10 gm	- Mint leaves
50 gm	- Fresh coriander leaves
3 no	- Green chilli
03 gm	- Ginger (whole)
1 tsp	- Lemon juice
To taste	- Salt

Second Marination
½ tsp	- Hung curd
To taste	- Salt
½ tsp	- Ginger garlic paste
2 tsp	- Lemon juice
½ tsp	- Garam masala
1/3 tsp	- Yellow chilli powder
2 tsp	- Mustard oil

For basting - Clarified butter

METHOD

1. Clean, wash and make 3 incisions on chicken drumstick with the help of a knife, pat dry and keep aside

Green Paste
2. In a food processor put mint leaves, coriander, green chilli and make a fine paste. Transfer it to a bowl.

First Marination
3. In a bowl mix, ginger garlic paste, lemon juice, salt and yellow chilli, apply this to the chicken drumstick and keep aside for at least 45 minutes.

Second Marination
4. In a bowl whisk hung curd and add (4 tsp) green paste, salt, ginger garlic paste, lemon juice, garam masala, yellow chilli powder, musard oil and mix well.
5. Put the chicken pieces into this marinade, coat well and keep aside for at least 1 hour.

Cooking
6. Take a skewer and skew the marinated chicken pieces. Keep a tray underneath to collect drippings.
7. Roast in a moderately hot tandoor or over a charcoal grill for 6-7 minutes.
8. Remove and hang the skewer to let excess moisture drain out completely (1-2 minutes). Baste with clarified butter and roast for another 2-3 minutes or till tender.
9. Transfer cooked chicken on to a plate.
10. Serve hot with choice of a salad and chutney.

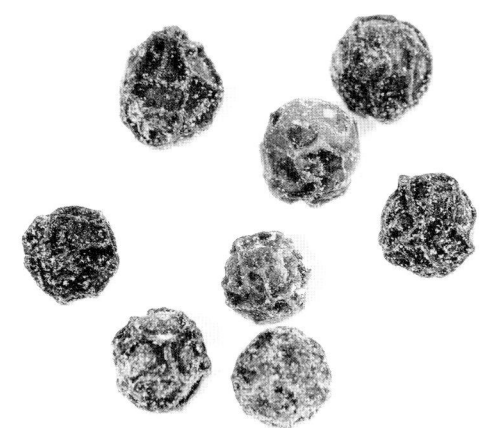

Tandoori Khatta Murg

HOT AND SOUR CHICKEN BREAST KEBAB STUFFED WITH APPETIZING CHEESE INFUSED WITH CINNAMON

Cooking time 10-12 minutes Serves 1-2

INGREDIENTS

200-225 gm (2 no) - Chicken breast (with shoulder bone)

First Marination
½ tsp	- Ginger garlic paste
1 tsp	- Lemon juice
To taste	- Salt

Stuffing
50 gm	- Processed cheese (grated)
1 tsp	- Ginger (chopped)
½ tsp	- Green chilli (chopped)
1 tsp	- Mint (chopped)
A pinch	- Dalchini powder
½ tsp	- Amchur powder
¼ tsp	- White pepper powder
To taste	- Salt

Second Marination
4 tbsp	- Hung curd
1 tbsp	- Almond paste
1 tbsp	- Cream
1 tsp	- Ginger garlic paste
½ tsp	- White pepper powder
1 tsp	- Amchur powder
To taste	- Salt

For basting - Clarified butter

METHOD

1. Clean and with tip of a knife make deep slit along the bone of chicken breast from the centre to make a hole taking care not to penetrate from the opposite side, pat dry and keep aside.

First Marination
2. In a bowl mix ginger garlic paste, lemon juice, salt and apply this to chicken breast, rub well and keep aside for at least 1 hour.

Stuffing
3. In a deep tray mash grated cheese and add all the remaining ingredients listed above and mix well. Divide the mixture into 2 parts and stuff mixture in each breast and seal with the tip of knife, ensuring that the flesh is not pierced.

Second Marination
4. In a bowl, whisk hung curd, add almond paste and all the remaining ingredients listed above and mix it well.
5. Put the chicken breast into this marinade, coat well and keep aside for at least 1 hour.

Cooking
6. Take a skewer and skew marinated chicken breast leaving a gap of at least an inch between each breast. Keep a tray underneath to collect drippings.
7. Roast in a moderate hot tandoor or oven for 7-8 minutes.
8. Remove and baste with clarified butter and further roast for 3-4 minutes or till tender.
9. Serve hot with choice of a salad and chutney.

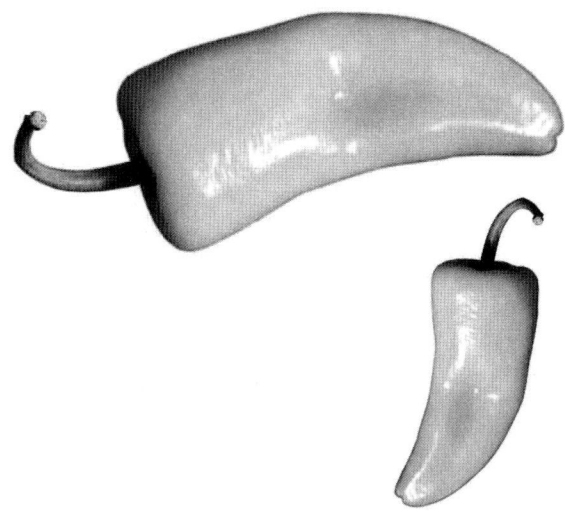

Bhatti Da Murg Pindiwala

LEGS OF CHICKEN MARINATED WITH SYMPHONY OF SPICES INCLUDING THE RARELY USED MAGGA, FIRST COOKED IN THE CLAY OVEN THEN FINISHED ON OPEN FIRE GRILL

Cooking time 14-15 minutes Serves 1-2

INGREDIENTS

(300-325 gm) 2no - Chicken leg (with bone)

First Marination
1 tsp	- Ginger garlic paste
1 tsp	- Kashmiri red chilli powder
1 tsp	- Lemon juice
To taste	- Salt

Second Marination
4 tbsp	- Hung curd
½ tsp	- Ginger garlic paste
½ tsp	- Jeera powder
½ tsp	- Dhania powder
½ tsp	- Black pepper crushed
½ tsp	- Kashmiri red chilli powder
A pinch	- Dalchini powder
A pinch	- Elaichi javitri powder
¼ tsp	- Clove powder
¼ tsp	- Nutmeg powder

For basting - Clarified butter

METHOD

1. Clean, wash and make 3 incisions on chicken leg with the help of a knife, pat dry and keep aside.

First Marination
2. In bowl mix ginger garlic paste paste, salt, lemon juice, and Kashmiri red chilli powder, apply this to chicken, rub well and keep aside for 45 minutes.

Second Marination
3. In a bowl whisk hung curd and add ginger garlic paste and all other ingredients listed above and mix well.
4. Put the chicken into this marinade, coat well and keep aside for 1 hour.

Cooking
5. Take a skewer and skew the marinated chicken pieces. Keep a tray underneath to collect drippings.
6. Roast in a moderately hot tandoor or over a charcoal grill for 8-9 minutes.
7. Remove and hang the skewer to let excess moisture drain out completely (2-3 minutes). Baste with clarified butter and roast for another 2-3 minutes.
8. Transfer cooked chicken on to a plate.
9. Serve hot with choice of salad and chutney.

Murg-a-Pa

JUICY WHOLE CHICKEN LEG INFUSED WITH CINNAMON AND CRUSHED BLACK PEPPER CORN

Cooking time 14-15 minutes Serves 1-2

INGREDIENTS

300-325 gm (2no) - Chicken legs (on bone)

First Marination
1 tsp	- Ginger garlic paste
½ tsp	- Red chilli paste
To taste	- Salt
1tsp	- Vinegar

Second Marination
4 tbsp	- Hung curd
1 tsp	- Ginger garlic paste
½ tsp	- Red chilli paste
To taste	- Salt
½ tsp	- White pepper powder
½ tsp	- Garam masala
1/3 tsp	- Cinnamon powder
½ tsp	- Cardamom (crushed)
½ tsp	- Black pepper corn (crushed)
1tsp	- Lemon juice
2 tsp	- Refined oil

For basting - Clarified butter

METHOD

1. Clean, wash and make 3 incisions on both sides of chicken leg, pat dry and keep aside.

First Marination
2. In a bowl mix ginger garlic paste, salt, red chilli paste, vinegar and apply this to chicken pieces, rub well and keep aside for at least 1 hour.

Second Marination
3. In a bowl whisk hung curd, add all the remaining ingredients listed in the order above, mix well.
4. Put the chicken pieces into this marinade, coat well and keep aside for at least 2 hours.

Cooking
5. Take a skewer and skew marinated chicken pieces along the skewer lengthwise. Keep a tray underneath to collect drippings.
6. Roast in a tandoor or over charcoal grill at a moderate temperature for 9-10 minutes.
7. Remove and hang the skewer so that the excess moisture drains out completely (1-2 minutes). Baste with clarified butter and further roast for 2-3 minutes or till tender.
8. Serve hot along with choice of a salad and chutney.

Murg Ke Paarchey

PICATTA OF CHICKEN MILDLY SPICED WITH CONDIMENTS AND COOKED ON GRIDDLE

Cooking time 8-10 minutes Serves 1-2

INGREDIENTS

225-250 gm (2 no) - Chicken breast

First Marination
1tsp	- Ginger garlic paste
1tsp	- Lemon juice
To taste	- Salt

Second Marination
4 no	- Cloves
3 no	- Green cardamom
2 tbsp	- Chironji
1 flower	- Javitri
6 no	- Black peppercorn
2 no	- Black cardamom
2 tbsp	- Coconut powder
30 gm	- Rosted cashewnut
2 tbsp	- Roasted channa powder
3 tbsp	- Cream
1 gm	- Saffron
A drop	- kewra water/ittre
To taste	- Salt

For frying - Refined oil

METHOD

1. Clean, wash and make 3 incisions on each chicken breast, pat dry and keep aside.

First Marination

2. In a bowl mix ginger garlic paste paste, salt, lemon juice, apply this to chicken breast, rub well and keep aside for at least 45 minutes.

Second Marination

3. In a non stick pan, roast cloves, green cardamom, chironji, javitri, black pepper corn, black cardamom, coconut powder stirring till it emits its aroma.
4. Put all these ingredients with roasted cashewnut, channa powder and water in a blender to make paste, remove and keep aside.
5. Transfer to a bowl, add cream, kewra water, saffron, apply this to chicken breast and keep aside for at least 1 hour.

Cooking

6. Heat oil on a pan or griddle, add the coated chicken breast and shallow fry on over medium heat on both sides till chicken is cooked.
7. Serve hot with choice of salad and chutney.

Murg Hazarvi Kebab

ANOTHER CREATION OF CHICKEN BONELESS STEEPED IN A SMOOTH CHEESE AND ALMOND MARINADE WITH FLORAL AROMA AND SUBTLE SPICES

Cooking time 10-12 minutes Serves 1 – 2

INGREDIENTS

(225-250 gm) 3no-Chicken breast (bone less)

First Marination
1tsp	- Ginger garlic paste
1tsp	- Lemon juice
½ tsp	- White pepper powder
To taste	- Salt

Second Marination
2 tbsp	- Processed cheese (grated)
1 no	- Egg white
2 tbsp	- Cream
1 tbsp	- Almond paste
½ tsp	- Green chilli(chopped)
1 tsp	- Fresh coriander (chopped)
A pinch	- Elaichi javitri powder
½ tsp	- Nutmeg powder
To taste	- Salt

For basting - Clarified butter

METHOD

1. Clean, wash and cut the chicken breast into 2 pieces, pat dry and keep aside.

First Marination

2. In a bowl mix ginger garlic paste, lemon juice, white pepper powder, salt, apply this to chicken, rub well and keep aside for at least half an hour.

Second Marination

3. In a deep tray mash grated cheese, add egg white and mix it gradually with your palm. Pour cream and further mix it, so that it becomes a smooth paste, add all other ingredients listed above and mix well.
4. Put the chicken pieces into this marinade and keep aside for at least 1 hour.

Cooking

5. Take a skewer and skew marinated chicken pieces, keep a tray underneath to collect drippings.
6. Roast in a moderately hot tandoor or over a charcoal grill for 8-9 minutes.
7. Remove and baste with clarified butter and roast for another 2-3 minutes.
8. Serve hot with choice of a salad and chutney.

Murg Pasanda Kebab

PICCATA OF CHICKEN BREAST WRAPPED IN SAFFRON FLAVOURED DRY FRUITS FILLING
Cooking time 8-10 minutes Serves 1-2

INGREDIENTS

200-225 gm (4pcs) - Chicken breast boneless

First Marination
To taste	- Salt
½ tsp	- Ginger garlic paste
1/3 tsp	- White pepper powder
1 tsp	- Lemon juice

Stuffing
50 gm	- Khoya (grated)
A pinch	- Saffron
1 tbsp	- Dry fruits (chopped)
1 tsp	- Coconut powder

Second Marination
4 tsp	- Processed Cheese (grated)
2 tsp	- Egg White
½ tsp	- Ginger garlic paste
4 tbsp	- Cream
To taste	- Salt
½ tsp	- White pepper Powder
½ tsp	- Green chilli (chopped)
A pinch	- Elaichi powder
A pinch	- Shahi jeera

For basting - Clarified butter

METHOD

1. Clean and cut each breast in pasanda shape slit the chicken from the centre and make a hole, pat dry and keep aside.

First Marination
2. In a bowl mix salt, ginger garlic paste, white pepper powder, lemon juice, rub well and apply this to chicken breast and keep aside for at least 45 minutes.

Stuffing
3. In a bowl mix khoya, saffron, dry fruits, coconut powder, mix well and divide in two equal parts.
4. Stuff each breast with portion of stuffing and seal with back of knife.

Second Marination
5. In a deep tray mash grated cheese, egg white, ginger garlic paste and mix gradually with your palm, pour cream and mix further so that it becomes a smooth paste. Add salt, white pepper, green chilli, green coriander, elaichi powder, shahi jeera and mix well.
6. Put stuffed chicken breast into this marinade, coat well and keep aside for at least 1 hour.

Cooking
7. Take a skewer and skew the marinated stuffed chicken breast.
8. Roast in a moderately hot tandoor for 6-7 minutes.
9. Remove and baste with clarified butter and further roast for 2-3 minutes or till tender.
10. Serve hot with choice of a salad and chutney.

Kalmi Shirazi

TENDER CHICKEN LEG (THIGH) STEEPED IN A CARDAMOM FLAVOURED MARINADE AND CAREFULLY ROASTED

Cooking time 10-12 minutes **Serves** 1-2

INGREDIENTS

325-350 gm (4no) - Chicken thigh

First Marination
½ tsp	- Ginger garlic paste
½ tsp	- White pepper powder
To taste	- Salt

Second Marination
2 tsp	- Refined oil
4 tsp	- Besan (gram flour)
1 no	- Egg
2 tbsp	- Cream
½ tsp	- Ginger garlic paste
To taste	- Salt
1/3 tsp	- White pepper powder
A pinch	- Elaichi powder

For basting - Clarified butter

METHOD

1. Wash, clean and cut chicken thigh from one side and open it across the bone without disjoining from other side, pat dry and keep aside.

First Marination

2. In a bowl mix ginger garlic paste, white pepper, salt and apply this to chicken, rub well and keep aside for at least 45 minutes,.

Second Marination

3. Heat oil in a pan, add besan cook it on slow fire for a while till raw smell goes off, keep aside for cooling.
4. In a bowl put besan, egg, cream, ginger garlic paste, salt, white pepper, elaichi powder and mix well. Put the chicken into this marinade, coat well and keep aside for at least 1 hour.

Cooking

5. Take a skewer and skew the marinated chicken pieces. Keep a tray underneath to collect drippings.
6. Roast in a moderately hot tandoor or over a charcoal grill for 6-7 minutes.
7. Remove and hang the skewer to let excess moisture drain out completely (1-2 minutes). Baste with clarified butter and roast for another 2-3 minutes.
8. Transfer cooked chicken on to a plate.
9. Serve hot with choice of salad and chutney.

Gazab Ka Seena (for recipe turn to page no: 69)

Rajasthani Murg Burra (for recipe turn to page no: 73)

Murg Badshahi (for recipe turn to page no: 80)

Bharwan Murg Tangri (for recipe turn to page no: 83)

Lagan Ka Teetar (for recipe turn to page no: 105)

Khatta Meetha Tandoori Duck (for recipe turn to page no: 101)

Tandoori Bater Kali Mirch

FARM QUAILS WITH PREDOMINANT FLAVOUR OF BLACK PEPPER CORN
Cooking time 10-12 minutes Serves 1-2

INGREDIENTS

2 no (125 gm) each Quail (skin less)

First Marination
01 tsp	- Ginger/garlic paste
01 tsp	- Black pepper powder
10 ml	- Lemon juice
To taste	- Salt

Second Marination
03 tbsp	- Processed cheese
01 no	- Egg white
02 tbsp	- Hung curd
1 ½ tbsp	- Cash nut paste
1 ½ tbsp	- Watermelon seeds paste
½ tsp	- Ginger garlic paste
60 ml	- Cream
½ tsp	- Black pepper powder
½ tsp	- Black pepper (crushed)
02 no	- Green chilli (chopped & seeds less)
½ tsp	- Green coriander (chopped)

For basting - Clarified butter

METHOD

1. Clean, give two insercions with a sharp knife on leg & breast of quails, pat dry & keep aside.

First Marination

2. In a bowl mix ginger garlic paste, salt and black pepper powder and lemon juice, apply this to quails rub well and keep aside for atleast 45 minutes.

Second Marination

3. In a deep tray put grated cheese and egg white, ginger /garlic paste and rub it well to make a smooth paste, add cream and remaining ingredients listed above and mix well.
4. Put the marinated quails into this mixture, coat well and keep aside for atleast 1 hour.

Cooking

5. Take a skewer & skew marinated quails, keep a tray underneath to collect drippings.
6. Roast in a moderately hot tandoor or over a charcoal grill for 6-7 minutes.
7. Remove and hang skewer (1-2 minutes) baste with clarified butter and further roast for 3-4 minutes or until tender.
8. Serve hot with choice of salad and chutney.

Khatta Meetha Tandoori Duck

SWEET & SOUR DUCK DELICACY
Cooking time 10-12 minutes Serves 1-2

INGREDIENTS

2 pcs (250 - 225gm) Duck, breast (boneless) with skin

First Marination
02 tsp	- Ginger/garlic paste
02 tbsp	- Malt vinegar
01 tsp	- Yellow chilli powder
To taste	- Salt

Second Marination
120 gm	- Mascarpone cheese
01 no	- Egg white
1 tbs	- Tamarind pulp
02 tbsp	- Hung curd
01 tbsp	- Raw mango pulp
1 ½ tbsp	- Honey
1 tsp	- Black salt
½ tsp	- Cinnamon powder
½ tsp	- Kasoori methi powder
½ tsp	- Garam masala powder
A pinch	- Royal cumin seeds
01 tbsp	- Corn flour

For basting - Clarified butter

METHOD

Cut and clean duck leg and breast, wash, pat dry and keep aside.

First Marination
In a bowl mix ginger garlic paste, malt vinegar, salt, yellow chilli powder and apply this to duck, rub well and keep aside for at least 45 minutes.

Second Marination

1. In a deep tray put mascarpone cheese, egg white, hung curd and mix well to make a smooth paste, add cream, add all remaining ingredients listed above and mix well.
2. Put the marinated duck in to this mixture, coat well and keep aside for atleast 1 hour:

Cooking

1. Take a skewer & skew marinated duck pieces. keep a tray underneath to collect drippings.
2. Roast in a moderately hot tandoor or over a charcoal grill for 6-7 minutes.
3. Remove and hang skewer (1-2 minutes) baste with clarified butter and further roast for 3-4 minutes or until tender.
4. Serve hot with choice of a salad and chutney.

Murg Tikka Kandhari

CHICKEN CHUNKS MARINATED IN A BLEND OF FRESH POMEGRANATE AND SYMPHONY OF EXOTIC SPICES KABUL & KANDHAR ARE POPULAR FOR THEIR MEAT DELICACIES

Cooking time 10-12 minutes Serves 1- 2

INGREDIENTS

200-225 gm (2 pcs) Chicken Leg (boneless)

First Marination
½ tsp	- Ginger garlic Paste
To taste	- Salt
2 tsp	- Anar Juice (pomegranate)
1 tsp	- Lemon Juice

Second Marination
4 tbsp	- Hung Curd
½ tsp	- Ginger garlic Paste
To taste	- Salt
½ tsp	- Red Chilli Paste
½ tsp	- Raw Mango Powder
2 tsp	- Anar juice
3 tsp	- Pomegranate seeds (crushed)
1 tsp	- Refined Oil

For basting - Clarified butter

METHOD

1. Clean, wash and cut each chicken leg into 3 pieces each (large cube) pat dry and keep aside.

First Marination

2. In a bowl mix ginger/garlic paste, salt, anar juice, lemon juice, apply this to chicken pieces, rub well and keep aside for at least 30 minutes.

Second Marination

3. In a bowl whisk hung curd add the ingredients in order listed above and mix well
4. Squeeze extra moisture, put chicken pieces into this marinade, coat well and keep aside for at least 1 hour.

Cooking

5. Take a skewer & skew marinated chicken pieces, keeping a tray underneath to collect dripping.
6. Roast in a moderately hot tandoor or over a charcoal grill for 7-8 minutes until half done.
7. Remove and baste with clarified butter and further roast for 3-4 minutes or until tender.
8. Serve hot with choice of a salad and chutney.

Murg Anmol Tikka

ABSOLUTELY SOFT CHICKEN KEBAB RESERVED IN A NON YOGHURT MARINADE WHICH IS RICH IN TASTE AND FLAVOUR

Cooking time 8-10 minutes Serves 1-2

INGREDIENTS

200-225 gm (3 no) Chicken Breast (Boneless)

First Marination
1 tsp	- Ginger Garlic Paste
To taste	- Salt
½ tsp	- White Pepper Powder
2 tbsp	- Refined Oil
1 tsp	- Garlic (Chopped)
1 tbsp	- Onion (Chopped)
2 tbsp	- Gram Flour

Second Marination
3 tbsp	- Cashewnut Paste
1 tbsp	- Cream
½ tsp	- Ginger Garlic Paste
To taste	- Salt
½ tsp	- White Pepper Powder

For basting - Clarified Butter

METHOD

1. Clean and wash each chicken breast and cut into 2 pieces, pat dry and keep aside.

First Marination
2. In a bowl mix ginger paste, salt, white pepper powder and apply this to chicken pieces, rub well and keep aside for atleast 45 minutes.
3. Heat oil in a pan, add garlic, chopped onion and sauté, add gram flour and slightly saute so that it does not change its colour. Leave it for cooling.

Second Marination
4. In a bowl take cashewnut paste, roasted gram flour mixture, cream, ginger garlic paste, salt and white pepper powder and mix well.
5. Put the marinated chicken into this mixture, coat well and keep aside for atleast 1 hour.

Cooking
6. Take a skewer and skew the marinated chicken pieces. Keep a tray underneath to collect drippings.
7. Roast in a moderately hot tandoor or over a charcoal grill for 6-7 minutes until half done.
8. Remove and baste with clarified butter during cooking and further roast for 2-3 minutes or until tender.
9. Serve hot with choice of a salad and chutney.

Lahsuni Murg Tikka

CHICKEN MORSELS MARINATED WITH SPICES AND FRESH GARLIC IN ABUNDANCE
Cooking time 8-10 minutes Serves 1-2

INGREDIENTS

2 pcs (225-250) Chicken leg boneless

First Marination
01 tbsp	- Garlic paste
1/3 tsp	- Yellow chilli powder
To taste	- Salt

Second Marination
01 tbsp	- Besan
20 ml	- Cream
01 tsp	- Refind oil
To taste	- Salt

METHOD

Clean and wash chicken leg into 3 pcs each, pat dry and keep aside.

First Marination
In a bowl mix garlic paste, yellow chilli paste, salt and apply this to chicken piceces, rub well and keep aside for at least 45 minutes

Second Marination
1. In a bowl whisk besan and cream, refined oil add salt mix well.
2. Put the chicken pieces into this marinade, coat well and keep aside for at least 1 hour.

Cooking
1. Take a skewer and skew marinated chicken pieces one by one keeping a distance in between. Keep a tray underneath to collect drippings.
2. Roast in moderately hot tandoor or over a charcoal grill for 6-8 minutes.
3. Remove and let extra moisture drain out completely (1-2 minutes)
4. Baste with clarified butter and further roast for 3-4 minutes or until tender.
5. Serve hot with choice of a salad and chutney

Lagan Ka Teetar

IN THE AWADH OF THE PAST, ONE SPORT POPULAR AMONG THE NAWAB WAS HUNTING. THE MEAT OF QUAILS & PARTRIDGE WAS CONSIDERED A DELICACY. THIS UNIQUE KEBAB OF PARTRIDGES MADE IN TRUE AWADHI STYLE IN A LAGAN (A ROUND & SHALLOW COPPER UTENCIL WITH A SLIGHTLY CONCAVE BOTTOM

Cooking time 3-4 minutes Serves 1-2

INGREDIENTS

02 no Partridges (skinless) (100 gm each)

First Marination
½ tsp	- Ginger Garlic paste
½ tsp	- Yellow chilly powder
To Taste	- Salt

Second Marination
05 Tbsp	- Hung curd
02 Tbsp	- Brown onion paste
½ Tsp	- Ginger garlic paste
01 Tsp	- Yellow chilli powder
½ Tsp	- Nutmeg powder
½ Tsp	- Stone flower powder
½ Tsp	- Kebab chinn powder
A pinch	- Saffron thread
To Taste	- Salt
100 Gm	- Clarified butter (desi ghee)
04 no	- Clove whole
02 no	- Green cardamoms (whole)
02 no	- Black cardamoms (whole)
05 no	- Black pepper (whole)
06 no	- Dry rose leaves
01 tsp	- Chopped coriander

METHOD

1. Cut, clean and wash Teetar, pat dry and keep aside.

First Marination
2. In a bowl mix ginger/garlic paste, yellow chilly powder, salt apply this to Teetar, rub well and keep aside for atleast 1 hour.

Second Marination
3. Whisk hung curd, add all remaining ingredients listed above and mix well expect whole masala.
4. Put the marinated partridges to this mixture, coat well and keep aside for atleast 1 ½ hour.

Cooking
5. Put clarified butter in a lagan (a flat copper vessel), add whole garam masala, when masala start to cracked, put the marinated quails, put little water/stock and keep it on charcoal for slow cooking. Cover with a lid and put charcoal on top. Keep stirring in between. When partridges are tender, masala is cooked and oil floats on top, add chopped coriander.
6. Serve hot with a choice of a salad and chutney.

Sea Food

Man is thought to have caught, prepared and eaten fresh and marine-water fish much before he domesticated animals. Today fish is an important part of most kitchens of the world. There are large varieties of edible sea and fresh-water fish that are known and available in India. Sole, Mali, Surmai, Pomfret, Bekti, Singhara, White Salmon, Rohu are the ones used most often in Indian food preparations.

Fish being the low in fat and high in water content and is very delicate. For best results in cooking of fish follow the given tips:

1. Use absolutely fresh fish.
2. Cooking time should be kept to minimum as the fish gets dry when over cooked.
3. Temperature should remain low while cooking fish to give the right texture.
4. Basting should be done a couple of times to keep the fish moist.
5. Cooking time is allotted by the type of cut and size being used.
6. Deodorizing and skewing the fish in the correct way are the most important features.

The type of cuts used for tandoori cooking are:-

Whole Fish	-	Medium sized fish Pomfret (300-325 gms) Or Trout (250 – 275gms).
Tikka	-	2-2 ½ inch boneless pieces.
Mince	-	Fresh mince can be made by taking thick fillets of fish.
Lobster	-	A rare delicacy – fresh lobster tails Usually 100-125 gms each are recommended.
Fresh Prawns	-	Medium size prawn tails approx. (75 – 90 gms) each with tail.

Prawn Tails

Squid Fish

Sole Steak

Fish Mince

Sole Fish Tikka

Machhli Ke Shammi Kebab (for recipe turn to page no: 117)

Sarson wali Machhli (for recipe turn to page no: 117)

Jugal Bandi Seekh (for recipe turn to page no: 127)

Malika-e-Dariya (for recipe turn to page no: 123)

Tandoori Ajwaini Lobster (for recipe turn to page no: 125)

Afghani Fish Tikka (for recipe turn to page no: 122)

Machhli ke Shammi Kebab

ADAPTION OF FAMOUS LUCKNOWI KEBAB MADE WITH FISH

Cooking time 2-3 minutes Serves 1-2

INGREDIENTS

25 gm	- Channa dal (pre soaked in water)
200 gm	- Fish fillet (sole)
2 no	- Big cardamom
2 no	- Small cardamom
3-4 no	- Cloves
2 no	- Whole red chilli
To taste	- Salt
3 no	- Garlic (whole)
5 gm	- Ginger (whole)
½ tsp	- Garam masala
½ tsp	- Yellow chilli powder
½ tsp	- Turmeric powder
½ tsp	- Green chilli (chopped)
a pinch	- Ajwain
1 no	- Egg white

Stuffing

3 tsp	- onion (chopped)
½ tsp	- Green chilli(chopped)
3 tsp	- Roasted peanuts (chopped)

For frying - Refined oil

METHOD

1. Boil channa dal for about 30 minutes then put fish fillet and add all the whole condiments, boil for atleast 15 minutes.
2. Remove condiments and make a fine paste.
3. In a bowl mix green chilli, ajwain, egg white, apply this to the above paste and mix well.
4. Divide the mixture into 6 equal balls. Flatten each ball between wet palm, place a stuffing in center, fold, again flatten in shape of medallion (tikki) and keep aside.

Cooking

5. Heat oil and deep fry shammi until golden brown and crisp. Remove & drain excess of oil.
6. Serve hot with choice of a salad and chutney.

Sarson Wali Machhli

DELICIOUS FISH TIKKA INFUSED WITH FRESHLY CRUSHED MUSTARD GRAINS

Cookingtime 5-7 minutes Serves 1-2

INGREDIENTS

225-250 gm-Fish Fillet (Sole) (6 Pcs)

First Marination

½ tsp	- Ginger Garlic Paste
To taste	- Salt
½ tsp	- Yellow Chilli Powder
1 tsp	- Lemon Juice
1 tsp	- Mustard Oil
1 tsp	- Mustard Grain (Crushed)

Second Marination

4 tbsp	- Hung Curd (Low fat)
½ tsp	- Ginger Garlic Paste
2 tsp	- Mustard Oil
To taste	- Salt
½ tsp	- Yellow Chilli Powder
½ tsp	- Garam masala
1 tsp	- Lemon Juice
1 tsp	- Mustard paste

For basting - Clarified butter

METHOD

1. Clean and cut large cubes of fish (1½" X 1½"), wash, pat dry and keep aside.

First Marination

2. In a bowl mix ginger, garlic paste, salt, yellow chilli powder, lemon juice. Heat mustard oil in a pan, add crushed mustard grain, when it starts crackling immediately transfer it to the bowl. Apply this to fish cubes, rub well and keep aside for atleast ½ hours.

Second Marination

3. In a bowl whisk hung curd, add all the remaining ingredients in the order listed.
4. Squeeze excess moisture from the fish and put cubes into the second marinade, coat well and keep atleast for 1hour.

Cooking

5. Take a skewer and skew marinated fish pieces one by one an inch apart. Apply remaining marinade on fish.
6. Roast in a tandoor or over a charcoal grill at a moderate temperature for 5–7 minutes, baste with clarified butter during cooking.
7. Serve hot with choice of a salad and chutney.

Khatti Meethi Machhli

SWEET AND SOUR FISH TIKKA

Cooking time 5-7 minutes **Serves** 1-2

INGREDIENTS

225-250 gm Sole fish fillet (6 pcs)

First Marination

½ tsp	- Ginger Garlic Paste
To taste	- Salt
½ tsp	- Yellow Chilli powder
1 tsp	- Lemon juice
3 tbsp	- Mango chutney

Second Marination

4 tbsp	- Hung curd
½ tsp	- Garam Masala
½ tsp	- Ginger Garlic Paste
1 tsp	- Yellow Chilli powde
To taste	- Salt
A pinch	- Turmeric
½ tsp	- Roasted jeera powder
1 tsp	- Mustard Oil
½ tsp	- Black salt powder

For basting - Clarified butter

METHOD

1. Clean and cut large cubes of fish (1 ½ " X 1 ½ "), wash, pat dry and Keep aside.

First Marination

2. In a bowl mix ginger garlic paste, salt, yellow chilli powder, lemon juice, apply this to fish cubes, rub well and keep aside for atleast ½ hour.
3. Make a fine paste of mango chutney.

Second Marination

4. In a bowl whisk hung curd, add mango chutney and all the remaining ingredients in order listed above, mix well.
5. Remove extra moisture from the marinated fish and put into this marinade, coat well and keep aside for atleast 1 hour.

Cooking

6. Take a skewer and skew the marinated fish pieces one by one keeping an inch gap in between. Apply remaining marinade on fish.
7. Roast in a tandoor or over charcoal grill at a moderate temperature for 5-7 minutes. Baste with clarified butter during cooking.
8. Serve hot with choice of a salad and chutney.

Dalchini Machhli Tikka

A LUSCIOUS FISH TIKKA INFUSED WITH CINNAMON

Cooking time 5-7 minutes **Serves** 1-2

INGREDIENTS

225-250 gm - Sole fish fillet (6 pcs)

First Marination

To taste	- Salt
½ tsp	- Ginger Garlic paste
½ tsp	- Yellowchillipowder
1 tsp	- Lemon juice

Second Marination

4 tbsp	- Hung curd
To taste	- Salt
½ tsp	- Ginger Garlic paste
½ tsp	- Yellow chilli powder
1 tsp	- Lemon juice
1 tsp	- Dal chini powder
A pinch	- Turmeric powder
1 tsp	- Mustard oil

For basting - Clarified butter
Dam percerem, conem tes! Sentiem. Abem sernihicum arivivat.Ex me

METHOD

1. Clean, cut large cubes of fish (1 ½ " X 1 ½), wash,pat dry and keep aside.

First Marination

2. In a bowl mix salt, ginger garlic paste, yellow chilli powder, lemon juice and apply this to the fish, rub well and keep aside for at least ½ hour.

Second Marination

3. In a bowl whisk hung curd, add all the remaining ingredients in order listed, mix well.
4. Remove extra moisture from the fish and put in the above marinade, coat well and keep aside for at least 2 hour.

Cooking

5. Take a skewer and skew the marinated fish pieces one by one an inch apart.
6. Roast in a moderately hot tandoor or over a charcoal grill for 5-7 minutes, baste with clarified butter during cooking.
7. Transfer on to a plate and serve hot with choice of a salad and chutney.

Goanese Mahi Kebab

EXOTIC FISH TIKKA PREPARED WITH GOAN SPICES
Cooking time 5-7 minutes Serves 1-2

INGREDIENTS

225 – 250 gm - Sole fish fillet (6 pcs)

First Marination
½ tsp	- Ginger Garlic paste
To taste	- Salt
½ tsp	- Red chilli paste
1 tsp	- Lemon juice
1 tsp	- Vinegar

Second Marination
4 tbsp	- Hung curd
½ tsp	- Ginger Garlic paste
To taste	- Salt
1 tsp	- Red chilli paste
½ tsp	- Red chilli crushed
4 tsp	- Tamarind pulp
2 tbsp	- Coconut oil
A pinch	- Turmeric powder
2 tsp	- Coconut powder

For basting - Clarified butter

METHOD

1. Clean, wash and cut large cubes of fish (1 ½ X 1 ½). Wash, pat dry and keep aside.

First Marination

2. In a bowl mix ginger garlic paste, salt, red chilli paste, lemon juice and vinegar.
3. Apply this mixture to fish cubes, rub well and keep aside for atleast ½ hour.

Second Marination

4. In a bowl whisk hung curd, add all the remaining ingredients listed in order above.
5. Squeeze excess moisture from the fish and put the cubes into this marinade. Coat well and keep aside for atleast 1 hour.

Cooking

6. Take a skewer and skew the marinated fish pieces one by one an inch apart. Apply remaining marinade on the fish pieces.
7. Roast in a tandoor or over charcoal grill at a moderate temperature for 5-7 minutes, baste with clarified butter during cooking.
8. Serve hot with choice of a salad and chutney.

Tandoori Khusk Machhli

CRUNCHY FISH KEBAB ENHANCED WITH POPPY SEEDS
Cooking time 5-7 minutes Serves 1-2

INGREDIENTS

225-250 gm - Sole fish fillet (6 pcs)

First Marination
½ tsp	- Ginger Garlic paste
2 tsp	- Vinegar
To taste	- Salt
½ tsp	- Ajwain
½ tsp	- Red chilli crushed

Second Marination
2 tbsp	- Hung curd
To taste	- Salt
½ tsp	- Ginger Garlic paste
3 tbsp	- Khus khus paste
1 tsp	- Yellow chilli powder
A pinch	- Turmeric powder

For basting - Clarified butter

METHOD

1. Clean, cut large cube of fish (1 ½ X 1 ½) wash, pat dry and keep aside.

First Marination

2. In a bowl mix ginger Garlic paste, vinegar, salt, ajwain, red chilli crushed and apply this to fish pieces, rub well and keep aside for at least ½ hour.

Second Marination

3. In a bowl whisk hung curd, add all the remaining ingredients listed in order above and mix well.
4. Remove extra moisture from fish and put it in the above marinade, coat well and keep aside for at least 1 ½ hour.

Cooking

5. Take a skewer and skew the marinated fish pieces one by one an inch apart. Apply remaining marinade on the fish pieces.
6. Roast in a tandoor at a moderate temperature for 5-7 minutes, baste with clarified butter during cooking.
7. Serve hot with choice of a salad and chutney.

Amchur Machhli Ke Tikke

AN APPETIZING FISH KEBAB WITH EXTRA TOUCH OF DRY MANGO POWDER

Cooking time 5-7 minutes Serves 1-2

INGREDIENTS

225-250 gm - Sole Fish fillet (6 pcs)

First Marination
½ tsp	- Ginger Garlic paste
To taste	- Salt
½ tsp	- Yellow chilly powder
2 tsp	- Lemon juice

Second Marination
4 tbsp	- Hung curd
To taste	- Salt
½ tsp	- Yellow chilli powder
2 tsp	- Amchur powder
2 tsp	- Mustard oil
1 tsp	- Tamarind pulp
For basting	- Clarified butter

METHOD

1. Clean, cut large cubes of fish pieces (1 ½ X 1 ½), wash, pat dry and keep aside.

First Marination

2. In a bowl mix ginger garlic paste, salt and yellow chilli powder and apply this to the fish pieces, rub well and keep aside for at least ½ hour.

Second Marination

3. In a bowl whisk hung curd and add all the remaining ingredients in order listed above and mix well.
4. Remove excess moisture from the marinated fish and mix with the above marinade, coat well and keep aside for atleast ½ hour.

Cooking

5. Take a skewer and skew the marinated fish pieces one by one an inch apart. Apply remaining marinade on fish.
6. Roast in a moderately hot tandoor or over charcoal grill for 5-7 minutes, baste with clarified butter during cooking.
7. Serve hot with choice of a salad and chutney.

Tandoori Methi Machhi

DELICATE FISH TIKKA WITH FRESH FENUGREEK ROASTED IN CLAY OVEN

Cooking time 5-7 minutes Serves 1-2

INGREDIENTS

225-250 gm Fish fillet
(sole, rahu or singhara) (6pcs)

First marination
½ tsp	- Ginger Garlic paste
To taste	- Salt
½ tsp	- Yellow chilli powder
1 tsp	- Lemon juice

Second Marination
4 tbsp	- Hung curd
½ tsp	- Ginger Garlic paste
4 tsp	- Kasoori methi (chopped)
To taste	- Salt
½ tsp	- Yellow chilli powder
1 tsp	- Kasoori methi powder
1 tsp	- Lemon juice
½ tsp	- Garam masala
For basting	- Clarified butter

METHOD

1. Clean, cut large cubes of fish (1 ½" X 1 ½"), wash, pat dry and keep aside

First Marination

2. In a bowl mix ginger garlic paste, salt, yellow chilli powder, lemon juice and apply this to fish pieces, rub well and keep aside for atleast ½ hour.

Second Marination

3. In a bowl whisk hung curd, add all the remaining ingredients in the order listed and mix well.
4. Squeeze excess moisture from the marinated fish and put into this marinade, coat well and keep aside for atleast 1-2 hour.

Cooking

5. Take a skewer and skew the marinated fish pieces, apply remaining marinade on fish.
6. Roast in a moderately hot tandoor for 5-7 minutes, baste with clarified butter during cooking.
7. Serve hot with choice of a salad and chutney.

Haryali Machhi Tikka

A DELICIOUS AND SPICY FISH KEBAB DIPPED IN GREEN PASTE AND GRILLED OVER CHARCOAL

Cooking time 5-7 minutes **Serves** 1-2

INGREDIENTS

225-250 gm - Fish fillet (6 pcs)

First Marination
To taste	- Salt
1 tsp	- Lemon juice
½ tsp	- Ginger Garlic paste

Second Marination
2 tbsp	- Hung curd
2 tbsp	- Green paste
½ tsp	- Ginger Garlic paste
1 tsp	- Yellow chilli powder
½ tsp	- Kasoori methi powder
2 tsp	- Spinach paste
½ tsp	- Garam masala
1 tsp	- Lemon juice
To taste	- Salt

For basting - Clarified butter

METHOD

1. Trim and cut fish into tikka (large cubes) (1½" x 1½"). Wash, pat dry and keep aside.

First Marination

2. In a bowl mix salt, lemon juice, ginger garlic paste, apply this to fish pieces, rub well and keep aside for ½ hour.

Second Marination

3. In a bowl whisk hung curd, add green paste, ginger garlic paste, yellow chilli powder, kasoori methi powder, Spinach paste paste, salt, lemon juice, garam masala and oil. Mix well.
4. Squeeze excess moisture from the fish and put cubes in this marinade, coat well and keep aside for atleast 1 hour.

Cooking

5. Take a skewer and skew the marinated fish pieces. Apply remaining marinade on fish.
6. Roast in a moderately hot tandoor or over charcoal grill for 5–7 minutes, baste with clarified butter during cooking.
7. Serve hot with choice of a salad and chutney.

Mahi Tikka AJWAINI

CARUM SEED FLAVOURED FISH KEBAB DELICATELY ROASTED

Cooking time 5-7 minutes **Serves** 1-2

INGREDIENTS

225-250gm - Fish fillet (sole) (06 pcs)

First Marination
1 tsp	- Lemon juice
½ tsp	- Ginger Garlic paste
To taste	- Salt
1 tsp	- Yellow chilli powder
1 tsp	- Ajwain
½ tsp	- Turmeric powder

Second Marination
4 tbsp	- Hung Curd
½ tsp	- Garam masala powder
2 tsp	- Mustard oil
To taste	- Salt
1 tsp	- Yellow Chilli powder
½ tsp	- Ginger Garlic Paste
1 tsp	- Lemon Juice
½ tsp	- Kasoori methi powder

For basting - Clarified butter

METHOD

1. Trim and cut fish fillet into tikka (large cubes) (1 ½" X 1 ½"), wash, pat dry and keep aside.

First Marination

2. In a bowl mix lemon juice, ginger garlic paste, salt, yellow chilli powder, ajwain, turmeric powder and apply this to fish cubes and keep aside for atleast 30 minutes.

Second Marination

3. In a bowl whisk hung curd, add all the remaining ingredients listed in order, mix well.
4. Put marinated fish cubes after removing excess moisture, in this marinade, coat well and keep aside for atleast1 hours.

Cooking

5. Take a skewer and skew the marinated fish pieces one by one an inch apart, coating with remaining marinade.
6. Roast in a moderately hot tandoor or over a charcoal grill for 5 – 7 minutes, baste with clarified butter during cooking.
7. Transfer to a plate and serve hot with choice of a salad and chutney.

Afghani Fish Tikka

A CREAMY KEBAB MADE FROM FISH MARINATED WITH MILD SPICES

Cooking time 5-7 minutes Serves 1-2

INGREDIENTS

225-250 gm - Fish fillet (sole) (6 pcs)

First Marination
½ tsp	- Ginger Garlic paste
1 tsp	- Lemon juice
To taste	- Salt
½ tsp	- Shahi jeera

Second Marination
60 gm	- Processed cheese
4 tbsp	- Cream
1 no	- Egg (white)
2 tsp	- Cashewnut paste
1 tsp	- Coconut milk powder
½ tsp	- White pepper
To taste	- Salt
For basting	- Clarified butter

METHOD

1. Clean, cut large cubes of fish (1 ½" X 1 ½"), wash, pat dry and keep aside.

First Marination

2. In a bowl mix ginger garlic paste, lemon juice, salt, shahi jeera and apply this to fish pieces and keep aside for atleast 30 minutes.

Second Marination

3. In a tray mash cheese with the help of a wet hand and add cream, egg white, cashewnut paste, coconut milk powder, white pepper, salt and mix well to smooth consistency.
4. Put marinated fish pieces after removing excess moisture, in this mixture. Coat well and keep aside for atleast 1 hours.

Cooking

5. Take a skewer and skew the marinated fish pieces one by one an inch apart, coating with remaining marinade.
6. Roast in a moderately hot tandoor or over a charcoal grill for 5-7 minutes, baste with clarified butter during cooking.
7. Transfer to a plate and serve hot with choice of a salad and chutney.

Mahi Dill Se

FISH CHUNKS INFUSED WITH DILL LEAVES

Cooking time 4-5 minutes Serves 1-2

INGRIDENTS:

200-225 gm - Pink salmon (fillet) 5pcs

First Marination
1/3 tsp	- Ginger Garlic paste
1/3 tsp	- Red chilli paste
1 tsp	- Balsamic vinegar
To taste	- Salt

Second Marination
1 tbsp	- Mustard oil
1 tsp	- Gram flour (besan)
2 tbsp	- Hung curd
1 tsp	- Fennel powder (saunf)
1 tsp	- Fresh dill leaves (chopped)
1 tsp	- Dill leaves (paste)
½ tsp	- Red chilly paste
1tsp	- Lemon juice
For basting	- Clarified butter

METHOD

1. Clean-cut cubes of fish (1 ½"x1 ½"), wash, pat dry and keep aside.

First Marination

2. In a bowl mix ginger garlic paste, red chilli paste, vinegar, salt. Apply this mixture to fish cubes, rub well and keep aside for half an hour.

Second Marination

3. In a bowl put mustard oil and gram flour (besan), mix well with palm, add all the remaining ingredients in the listed order.
4. Squeeze excess moisture from the fish and put cubes into second marinade, rub well and keep for 1-2 hours.

Cooking

5. Take a skewer and skew marinated fish pieces one by one, an inch apart and apply remaining marinated fish.
6. Roast in tandoor or over a charcoal grill at a moderate temperature for 3-4 minutes.
7. Remove and hang skewer so that the excess moisture can drain out completely (2-3 minutes).
8. Baste with clarified butter and further roast.
9. Serve hot with choice of salad and chutney.

Kastoori Mahi TIKKA

AN EGG COATED VARIATION OF FISH KEBAB, SPICED WITH WHITE PEPPER

Cooking Time 6-8 Minutes   Serves 1-2

INGREDIENTS

6 pcs (225-250gm) - Fish fillet (sole)

First marination

1tsp	- Ginger Garlic paste
2 tsp	- Lemon juice
½ tsp	- White papper powder
To taste	- Salt

Second marination

1 no	- Egg white
2tbsp	- Processed cheese(grated)
½ tsp	- White pepper powder
½ cup	- Cream
½ tsp	- Green chilli(chopped)
½ tsp	- Green coriander(chopped)
To taste	- Salt
2 no	- Egg white (for coating)

METHOD

1. Clean, cut the fish into cubes (1 ½"x1 ½"). Wash, pat dry and keep aside.

First marination

2. In a bowl mix ginger garlic paste, lemon juice, white papper, salt, apply this to fish pieces and keep aside for atleast 30 minutes.

Second marination

3. In a tray mash grated cheese, rub it with your plam, add egg white, cream, mix it gradually so that it gets blended well and smooth in consistency.
4. Add green chilli, green coriander, salt and mix well. Put sole fish cubes into this marinade, rub well and keep aside for atleast 1hour.

Cooking

1. Take a skewer and skew marinated fish pieces one by one an inch apart and apply remaining marinade on fish.
5. Roast in a tandoor at moderate temperature for 5-6 minutes, baste with clarified butter during butter.

Coating

6. In a bowl whisk egg white until froth, apply egg white on fish and further roast for 1-2 minutes.
7. Serve hot along with choice of salad and chutney.

Malika-e-Dariya

A SIMPLE YET SPECTACULAR NORWEGIAN PINK SALMON INFUSED WITH SPICES

Cooking time 5-7 minutes Serves 1-2

INGREDIENTS

225-250 gm - Pink salmon fillet (6pcs)

First marination

1 tsp	- Ginger Garlic paste
To taste	- Salt
1 tsp	- Lemon juice

Second marination

4 tbsp	- Hung curd
½ tsp	- Kasoori methi powder
1 tsp	- Amchur powder
1 tsp	- Fresh dill (chopped)
1 tsp	- Saunf (Aniseed)
1 tsp	- Mustard oil
1 tbsp	- Cream
2 tsp	- Cheese
To taste	- Salt

For basting - Clarified butter

METHOD

1. Clean, cut fish into (1 ½" X 1 ½") cubes. Wash, pat dry and keep aside.

First marination

2. In a bowl mix ginger garlic paste, salt, lemon juice, apply this to fish pieces, rub well and keep aside for atleast 1 hour.

Second marination

3. In a bowl whisk hung curd, add all the remaining ingredients listed in order above and mix well.
4. Squeeze excess moisture from the marinated fish pieces and put them into the second marinade, coat well and keep aside for atleast ½ hour.

Cooking

5. Take a skewer and skew marinated fish pieces one by one keeping an inch apart.
6. Roast it in a moderately hot tandoor or over a charcoal grill for 5 - 7 minutes, baste with clarified butter during cooking.
7. Serve hot along with the choice of a salad and chutney.

Lahori Mahi Kebab

DELICIOUS FISH TIKKA PREPARED IN LAHORI STYLE
Cooking time 5-7 minutes Serves 1-2

INGREDIENTS

225-250 gm - Boneless fish cubes (surmai, sole)

First Marination
1 tsp	- Ginger Garlic paste
1 tsp	- Lemon juice
½ tsp	- Yellow chilli powde
½ tsp	- Red chilli powder
To taste	- Lahori salt

Second Marination
2 tbsp	- Hung curd
½ tsp	- Ajwain
2 tsp	- Mustard oil
To taste	- Lahori salt

Paste
	- Curry leaves
2 tsp	- Green chilli
	- Coriander

For basting - Clarified butter

METHOD

1. Clean, wash fish cubes, pat dry and keep aside.

First Marination
2. In a bowl mix ginger garlic paste, lemon juice, yellow chilli powder, red chilli powder, lahori salt apply this to fish cubes, rub well and keep aside for atleast ½ hour.
3. In a food processor put curry leaves, green chilli, coriander and make a fine paste.

Second Marination
4. In a bowl whisk hung curd add ajwain, mustard oil, lahori salt, green paste, mix well. Put marinated fish cubes into this marinade, coat well and keep aside for atleast 2 hours.

Cooking
5. Take a skewer and skew marinated fish pieces one by one keeping an inch apart.
6. Roast it in a moderately hot tandoor or over a charcoal grill for 5-7 minutes, baste with clarified butter during cooking.
7. Serve hot along with the choice of a salad and chutney.

Malabari Mahi Tikka

AN EXCITING FISH KEBAB PREPARED WITH SPICES OF MALABAR
Cooking time 5-7 minutes Serves 1-2

INGREDIENTS

225-250 gm - Fish fillet (sole, surmai) (6 pcs)

First marination
1 tsp	- To taste - Salt
1 tsp	- Ginger Garlic paste
1 tsp	- Lemonjuice
3 tbsp	- Red chilli paste

Second marination
2 tsp	- Hung curd
1 tsp	- Coconut powder
2 tsp	- Coconut milk
1 tsp	- Coconut oil
2 tsp	- Green chilli paste
1 tsp	- Garam masala
To taste	- Salt
10 no	- Fried curry leaves

For basting - Clarified butter

METHOD

1. Clean, cut fish into cubes (1 ½"x1 ½") wash, pat dry and keep aside.

First marination
2. In a bowl mix salt, ginger garlic paste, lemon juice, red chilli paste and apply this to fish pieces, rub well and keep aside for ½ hour.

Second marination
3. In a bowl whisk hung curd, add coconut powder, coconut milk, coconut oil, green chilli paste, garam masala, salt, mix well.
4. Squeeze excess moisture from marinated fish pieces, put them into the above marinade, coat well. Sprinkle crushed fried curry leaves on top and keep aside for 2 hours.

Cooking
5. Take a skewer and skew marinated fish pieces one by one keeping an inch apart.
6. Roast it in a moderately hot tandoor or over a charcoal grill for 5 – 7 minutes, baste with clarified butter during cooking.
7. Serve hot along with the choice of a salad and chutney.

Tandoori Achari Machhli

AN UNUSUAL AND COLOURFUL FISH TIKKA MARINATED WITH PICKLE SPICES AND ROASTED IN CLAY OVEN

Cooking time 5-7 minutes Serves 1-2

INGREDIENTS

225-250 gm - Sole fish fillet (6pcs)

First Marination
1 tsp	- Ginger Garlic paste
½ tsp	- Yellow chilli powder
1 tsp	- Lemon juice
to taste	- Salt
1 tsp	- Mustard oil

Second Marination
04 tsp	- Hung curd
1 tsp	- Roasted gram flour
1 tsp	- Achar paste (pickle paste)
½ tsp	- Yellow chilli powder
To taste	- Salt
For basting	- Clarified butter

Tempering
2 tsp	- Mustard oil
1 tsp	- Garlic chopped
2 tsp	- Methi dana, kalonji, saunf, mustard seeds (Achar Masala)
5 no	- Curry leaves
For basting	- Clarified butter

METHOD

1. Clean, cut large cubes of fish (1½" x 1½"), wash, pat dry and keep aside.

First Marination

2. In a bowl mix ginger garlic paste, yellow chilli powder, lemon juice, salt, mustard oil, apply this to fish cubes, rub well and keep aside for atleast ½ hours.

Second Marination

3. In a bowl whisk hung curd, add all the remaining ingredients in the listed order, mix well.
4. Squeeze excess moisture from the fish and put cubes into the second marinade, coat well.
5. Heat oil in pan add garlic chopped, achar masala, curry leaves, when it starts cracking immediately add to marinade and keep aside for 1 hour.

Cooking

6. Taking a skewer and skew marinated fish pieces one by one an inch apart. Apply remaining marinade on fish.
7. Roast in a tandoor at a moderate temperature for 5-7 minutes, baste with clarified butter during cooking.
8. Serve hot with choice of a salad and chutney.

Tandoori Ajwaini Lobster

CARUM SEED FLAVOURED LOBSTER TAILS ROASTED IN CLAY OVEN

Cooking time 8-10 minutes Serves 1-2

INGREDIENTS

300-325 gm - Lobster (tail) 2 pcs

First Marination
To taste	- Salt
½ tsp	- Yellow chilli powde
1 ½ tsp	- Lemon juice
½ tsp	- Ginger Garlic paste

Second Marination
4 tbsp	- Hung curd
To taste	- Salt
½ tsp	- Ginger Garlic paste
½ tsp	- Yellow chilli powder
A pinch	- Turmeric powder
2 tsp	- Mustard oil
½ tsp	- Ajwain
For basting	- Clarified butter

METHOD

1. Deshell, devein the lobster retaining its tail, wash pat dry and keep aside.

First Marination

2. In a bowl mix salt, yellow chilli powder, lemon juice, ginger garlic paste and apply this to the lobster, rub well and keep aside for at least half an hour.

Second Marination

3. In a bowl whisk hung curd, add all the remaining ingredients listed in the order above, mix well.
4. Squeeze excess moisture from lobster tail and put in this mixture, coat well and keep for at least 1 hour.

Cooking

5. Take a skewer and skew marinated lobster from tail to head on both sides. Apply the remaining mixture on them.
6. Roast in a tandoor or over a charcoal grill at moderate temperature for 8-10 minutes, baste with clarified butter during cooking.
7. Serve hot along with choice of a salad and chutney.

Tandoori Kalyera Lobster

SOUTHERN SPICED LOBSTER

Cooking time 8-10 minutes Serves 1-2

INGREDIENTS

300-325 gm - Lobster tail (2 pcs)

First Marination
To taste	- Salt
½ tsp	- Ginger Garlic paste
2 tsp	- Turmeric powder
A pinch	- Lemon juice

Second Marination
4 tbsp	- Hung curd
To taste	- Salt
½ tsp	- Ginger Garlic paste
½ tsp	- Curry powder
1 tsp	- Coconut powder
A pinch	- Turmeric powder
2 tsp	- Coconut oil
½ tsp	- Mustard seeds
5 no	- Curry leaves

For basting - Clarified butter

METHOD

1. Deshell, devein the lobster retaining its tail, wash, pat dry and keep aside.

First Marination

2. In a bowl mix salt, ginger garlic paste, turmeric powder, lemon juice and apply this to the lobster, rub well and keep aside for at least half an hour.

Second Marination

3. In a bowl whisk hung curd, add all the remaining ingredients in the order listed above and mix well.
4. Heat coconut oil in a pan, put mustard seeds, curry leaves when it starts crackling immediately add in the marinade.
5. Squeeze excess moisture from lobster tail and dip in the above mixture, coat well and keep aside for at least 1 ½ hours.

Cooking

6. Take a skewer and skew marinated lobster from tail to head, apply remaining mixture on them.
7. Roast in a tandoor at a moderate temperature for 8 – 10 minutes, baste with clarified butter during cooking.
8. Serve hot along with the choice of a salad and chutney.

Samundari Manthan

A DELICIOUS MIX SEA FOOD KEBAB

Cooking time 4-6 minutes Serves 1-2

INGREDIENTS

60 gm	- Sole (mince)
50 gm	- Prawn meat (Chopped)
50 gm	- Crab (mince)
To taste	- Salt
1 tsp	- Ginger Garlic paste
½ tsp	- Yellow chilli powder
4 tbsp	- Processed cheese (grated)
½ tsp	- Green chilli
a pinch	- Turmeric powder
1 tsp	- Lemon juice
1 tsp	- Green coriander (chopped)
1 tsp	- Refined oil
½ tsp	- Mint (chopped)

For basting - Clarified butter

METHOD

1. In a bowl mix sole mince, chopped prawn and crab mince with all the ingredients listed in order, mix well to smooth consistency and keep aside for atleast 45 minutes to 1 hour.
2. Divide this mixture into 4 equal parts and make balls.

Cooking

3. Take a skewer, apply this mixture on skewer in a cylindrical shape, roast in a moderately hot tandoor or over a charcoal grill for 4-6 minutes, baste with clarified butter during cooking.
4. Serve hot with choice of a salad and chutney.

Jugal Bandi Seekh

PREFECT BLEND OF FISH AND PRAWN INFUSED WITH CLASSIC SPICES

Cooking time 4-6 minutes Serves 1-2

INGREDIENTS

100 gm	- Fish mince (sole)
100 gm	- Prawns (chopped)
4 tsp	- Processed cheese (grated)
½ tsp	- Ginger Garlic paste
To taste	- Salt
1 tsp	- Coriander (chopped)
½ tsp	- Green chilli (chopped)
½ tsp	- Yellow chilli powder
½ tsp	- Curry powder
1 tsp	- Coconut powder
½ tsp	- Roasted jeera powder
10 no	- Fried curry leaves (crushed)
For basting	- Clarified butter

METHOD

1. In a deep tray, mash grated cheese, add fish mince, chopped prawn and all the remaining ingredients in the order listed, mix well to smooth consistency and keep it aside for at least half an hour.
2. Divide the mixture into 4-6 equal parts.

Cooking

3. Take a skewer, apply this mixture on the skewer in a cylindrical shape, one inch apart making each kebab 4 inches long, spread evenly and roast in a moderately hot tandoor or over a charcoal grill for 4-6 minutes, baste with clarified butter during cooking.
4. Serve hot with choice of a salad and chutney.

Tandoori Machhli Seekh

A DELICIOUS YET LIGHT FISH MINCE SKEWER

Cooking time 4-6 minutes Serves 1-2

INGREDIENTS

4 tsp	- Processed cheese (grated)
200 gm	- Fish mince (fine)
1 tsp	- Ginger Garlic paste
To taste	- Salt
½ tsp	- Green chilli (chopped)
1 tsp	- Coriander (chopped)
½ tsp	- Yellow mirch powder
A pinch	- Kutti red chilli
A pinch	- Turmeric powder
½ tsp	- Garam masala
For basting	- Clarified butter

METHOD

1. In a deep tray mash grated cheese, add fish mince and all the remaining ingredients listed in the order above, mix well, keep aside for at least 1 hour.
2. Divide the mixture into 4 equal parts.

Cooking

3. Spread this mixture individually on the skewer using a wet hand by pressing each portion along the length of the skewer in a cylindrical shape, one inch apart making each kebab 4 inches long, spread evenly.
4. Roast in a tandoor at moderate temperature for 4-6 minutes, baste with clarified butter during cooking.
5. Serve hot along with choice of a salad and chutney.

Methi Machhli Seekh

FISH MINCE BLENDED WITH FRESH FENUGREEK

Cooking time 4-6 minutes Serves 1-2

INGREDIENTS

200 gm	- Fish mince (Sole)
4 tsp	- Processed cheese (grated)
1/3 tsp	- White pepper
To taste	- Salt
1 tsp	- Ginger Garlic paste
1 tsp	- Green coriander(chopped)
½ tsp	- Green chilli (chopped)
1 ½ tsp	- Fresh methi (chopped)
A pinch	- Ajwain
½ tsp	- Roasted jeera powder
For basting	- Clarified butter

METHOD

1. Squeeze excess moisture of mince and keep aside.
2. In a deep tray mash processed cheese with palm. Add fish mince and all the remaining ingredients listed in order, mix well to smooth consistency and keep aside for at least half an hour.
3. Divide the mixture into 4 equal parts.

Cooking

4. Spread this mixture individually on the skewer using a wet hand by pressing each portion along the length of the skewer in a cylindrical shape, one inch apart and making each kebab 4 inches long. Spread evenly.
5. Roast in a moderately hot tandoor or over a charcoal grill for 4-6 minutes, baste it with clarified butter during cooking.
6. Serve hot with choice of a salad and chutney.

Tandoori Paatrani Machhli

DELICIOUS FISH KEBAB ROLLED IN BANANA LEAF AND ROASTED IN CLAY OVEN. IT IS A PARSI DELICACY

Cooking time 5-7 minutes Serves 1-2

INGREDIENTS

225-250 gm-Sole fish slices (5-6 no)

To taste	- Salt
½ tsp	- Yellow chilli powder
4 tsp	- Green paste
½ tsp	- Garam masala
1 tsp	- Lemon juice
6 no	- Banana leaf

METHOD

1. Pat dry sole fish slice and keep aside.
2. In a bowl mix salt, yellow chilli powder, green paste, garam masala, lemon juice and apply this to fish slice, rub well and keep aside for at least half an hour.
3. Wrap each sole fish slice in a banana leaf and then wrap in a silver foil.

Cooking

4. Take a skewer and skew each piece and cook at a moderate temperature in tandoor for 5-7 minutes.
5. Serve hot without removing silver foil and banana leaf with choice of a salad and chutney.

Tandoori Pomfret

ALL TIME FAVOURITE WHOLE POMFRET DELICACY

Cooking time 12-15 minutes Serves 1-2

INGREDIENTS

1 no (300-325 gm) Pomfret fish

First Marination
To taste	- Salt
½ tsp	- Ginger Garlic paste
1 tsp	- Lemon juice
½ tsp	- Yellow chilli powder
A pinch	- Ajwain

Second Marination
4 tbsp	- Hung curd
To taste	- Salt
½ tsp	- Ginger Garlic paste
½ tsp	- Yellow chilli powder
1 tsp	- Lemon juice
A pinch	- Turmeric powder
2 tsp	- Mustard oil
2 tsp	- Roasted besan

For basting - Clarified butter

METHOD

1. Clean, slightly trim fins, tails wash and make incisions 3-4 on both sides, pat dry and keep aside.

First Marination

2. In a bowl mix salt, ginger garlic paste, lemon juice, yellow chilli powder and ajwain, apply this to pomfret, rub well and keep aside for at least half an hour.

Second Marination

3. In a bowl whisk hung curd, add all the remaining ingredients in the order listed and mix well.
4. Squeeze excess moisture from the pomfret and dip in above marination, coat well and keep aside for at least 1 hour.

Cooking

5. Take a skewer and skew marinated pomfret from tail to head. Apply the remaining marinade. Roast in a moderately hot tandoor for 12-15 minutes, baste with clarified butter during cooking.
6. Remove, serve hot with choice of a salad and chutney.

Amritsari Machhi

RED, HOT AND SPICY FISH PREPARED IN TYPICAL AMRITSARI STYLE

Cooking time 12-15 minutes Serves 1-2

INGREDIENTS

300-325 gm - Pomfret (1no)

First Marination
½ tsp	- Ginger Garlic paste
To taste	- Salt
½ tsp	- Red chilli powder
2 tsp	- Lemon juice

Second Marination
100 gm	- Besan
½ tsp	- Ginger Garlic paste
½ tsp	- Ajwain
To taste	- Salt
1 tsp	- Red chilli paste
1 tsp	- Lemon juice
1 no	- Egg
1 tsp	- Corn flour

For frying - Refined oil

METHOD

1. Clean and cut fish in large chunks. Wash and pat dry with kitchen paper.

First Marination

2. In a bowl mix ginger garlic paste, salt, red chilli powder and lemon juice. Apply this to fish, rub well and keep aside for at least half an hour.

Second Marination

3. In a bowl take besan add all the remaining ingredients listed in order, mix well. Add water for making batter and keep aside for at least 15 minutes.
4. Put the fish into the marinade, coat well and keep aside for at least 1 hour.

Cooking

5. Heat oil in a non-stick kadai.
6. Put pieces of fish one by one and fry them to golden brown at moderate temperature. Drain excess of oil
7. Serve hot with white radish salad and Mint chutney.

Puddine Wali Tandoori Pomfret

REFRESHING FRESH MINT FLAVOURED WHOLE POMFRET ROASTED IN CLAY OVEN
Cooking time 12-15 minutes **Serves** 1-2

INGREDIENTS

300-325 gm - Pomfret

First Marination

½ tsp	- Ginger Garlic paste
To taste	- Salt
½ tsp	- Yellow chilli powder
1 tsp	- Lemon juice
A pinch	- Ajwain

Second Marination

4 tbsp	- Hung curd
To taste	- Salt
½ tsp	- Yellow chilli powder
1 tsp	- Garam masala
½ tsp	- Kasoori methi powder
1 tsp	- Lemon juice
½ tsp	- Ginger Garlic paste
1 tsp	- Mint powder
2 tsp	- Refined oil
½ tsp	- Fresh Garlic (chopped)
3 tsp	- Fresh mint (chopped)

For basting - Clarified butter

METHOD

1. Wash, clean and cut pomfret and make three incisions with knife on both sides of fish.

First Marination

2. In a bowl mix ginger garlic paste, salt, yellow chilli powder, lemon juice and ajwain. Apply this to fish, rub well and keep aside for at least 1 hour.

Second Marination

3. In a bowl whisk hung curd and add all the remaining ingredients listed in the order, mix well.
4. In a pan heat oil and sauté garlic, then add mint and sauté, add this to the above mixture in a bowl and mix well.
5. Put fish into this marinade, coat well and keep aside for at least 1 hour.

Cooking

6. Take a skewer, skew marinated pomfret from tail to head 2 inches apart. Apply the remaining marinade. Roast in a tandoor at a moderate temperature for 12-15 minutes, baste with clarified butter during cooking.
7. Serve hot with choice of a salad and chutney.

Samunder Ki Rani

ANOTHER DELICACY OF TRADITIONAL WHOLE POMFRET
Cooking time 12-15 minutes **Serves** 1-2

INGREDIENTS

1 no. 300-325 gm - Pomfret fish

First Marination

To taste	- Salt
½ tsp	- Ginger-Garlic paste
2 tsp	- Lemon juice
½ tsp	- Yellow chilli powder
½ tsp	- Mustard powder
1tsp	- Mustard oil

Second Marination

4 tbsp	- Hung curd
To taste	- Salt
½ tsp	- Ginger/Garlic paste
1 ts	- Lemon juice
1tsp	- Mustard oil
½ tsp	- Yellow chilli powder
½ tsp	- Garam masala
½ tsp	- Mustard powder
A pinch	- Turmeric powder
1 tsp	- Kasoori methi powder

For basting - Clarified butter

METHOD

1. Clean, slightly trim fins, tails, wash and make 3-4 incisions on both sides. Pat dry and keep aside.

First Marination

2. In a bowl mix salt, ginger garlic paste, lemon juice, yellow chilli powder, mustard powder, mustard oil, apply this to the pomfret, rub well and keep it for at least half an hours.

Second Marination

3. In a bowl whisk hung curd, add all the remaining ingredients in the order listed and mix well.
4. Squeeze excess moisture from the pomfret and dip it in the above marination. Rub well and keep aside for at least 2 hours.

Cooking

5. Take a skewer, skew marinated pomfret from tail to head 2 inches apart. Apply the remaining marination on top.
6. Roast it in a moderately hot tandoor for 12-15 minutes, baste with clarified butter during cooking.
7. Serve hot along with choice of a salad and chutney.

Ajwaini Tandoori Pomfret

CARUM SEED FLAVOURED, TASTY AND ATTRACTIVE WHOLE POMFRET ROASTED IN CLAY OVEN

Cooking time 12-15 minutes Serves 1-2

INGREDIENTS

300-325 gms Pomfret fish

First Marination
To taste	- Salt
½ tsp	- Ginger Garlic paste
1 tsp	- Lemon juice
½ tsp	- Yellow chilli powder

Second Marination
4 tbsp	- Hung curd
To taste	- Salt
½ tsp	- Ginger Garlic paste
1 tsp	- Lemon juice
½ tsp	- Yellow chilli powder
A pinch	- Turmeric powder
½ tsp	- Ajwain
2 tsp	- Mustard oil
½ tsp	- Ajwain powder
2 tsp	- Roasted besan

Foe basting - Clarified butter

METHOD

1. Clean, slightly trim fins, tail, wash and make 3-4 incisions on both sides of the fish, pat dry and keep aside.

First Marination

2. In a bowl mix salt, ginger garlic paste, lemon juice, yellow chilli powder and apply this to the fish, rub well and keep aside for at least half an hour.

Second Marination

3. In a bowl whisk hung curd, add all the remaining ingredients listed in order and mix well.
4. Squeeze excess moisture from the pomfret and dip in the above marinade. Coat well and keep aside for at least 1½ hours.

Cooking

5. Take a skewer and skew the marinated pomfret from tail to head. Apply the remaining marinade.
6. Roast in a tandoor at a moderate temperature for 12-15 minutes, baste with clarified butter during cooking.
7. Serve hot with choice of a salad and chutney.

Haryali Tandoori Pomfret

A REFRESHING WHOLE POMFRET DIPPED IN GREEN PASTE AND ROASTED IN CLAY OVEN

Cooking time 12-15 minutes Serves 1-2

INGREDIENTS

300-325 gm - Pomfret fish

First Marination
To taste	- Salt
½ tsp	- Ginger/Garlic paste
2 tsp	- Lemon juice
1/3 tsp	- Yellow chilli powder

Second Marination
50 gm	- Green coriander (chopped)
25 gm	- Mint leaves
5 gm	- Ginger
5 gm	- Garlic
1 no	- Green chilli
4 tbsp	- Hung curd
To taste	- Salt
½ tsp	- Garam masala
1 tsp	- Lemon juice
1 tsp	- Refined oil
½ tsp	- Kasoori methi powder

For basting - Clarified butter

METHOD

1. Clean, slightly trim fins, tail. Wash and make incisions (3-4) on both sides of the fish, pat dry and keep aside

First Marination

2. In a bowl mix salt, ginger garlic paste, lemon juice, yellow chilli powder and apply this to pomfret, rub well and keep aside for at least half an hour
3. In a food processor make a fine paste of green coriander, mint, ginger, garlic and green chilli.

Second Marination

4. In a bowl whisk hung curd, add all the remaining ingredients in the order listed and mix well. Add the green paste (5 tsp), mix well.
5. Squeeze excess moisture from the pomfret and dip it in the above marinade. Coat well and keep aside for at least 1 ½ hour.

Cooking

6. Take a skewer, skew marinated pomfret from tail to head. Apply the remaining marinade and roast it in a tandoor at a moderate temperature for 12-15 minutes, baste with clarified butter during cooking.
7. Serve hot with choice of a salad and chutney.

Lobster of The Raj

NOURISHING AND SATISFYING LOBSTER MARINATED WITH SPICES OF THE RAJ TIMES

Cooking time 8-10 minutes Serves 1-2

INGREDIENTS

300-325 gm - Lobster Tail (2 pcs)

First Marination
½ tsp	- Ginger Garlic paste
To taste	- Salt
2 tsp	- Lemon juice
1 tsp	- Oil
1 tsp	- Paprika powder

Second Marination
4 tbsp	- Hung curd
To taste	- Salt
½ tsp	- Ginger Garlic paste
1 tsp	- Curry powder
½ tsp	- Roasted cumin powder
A pinch	- Turmeric powder
For basting	- Clarified butter

METHOD

1. Deshell, devein the lobster, retaining its tail, wash, pat dry and keep aside.

First Marination

2. In a bowl mix ginger garlic paste, salt, lemon juice, oil, Paprika powder and apply this to lobster tails, rub well and keep aside for at least half an hour.

Second Marination

3. In a bowl whisk hung curd, add all the remaining ingredients in the order listed and mix well.
4. Squeeze excess moisture from lobster tail and dip in the above mixture. Coat well and keep it for at least 1 hour.

Cooking

5. Take a skewer, skew marinated lobster from tail to head. Apply the remaining marinade and roast it in a tandoor at a moderate temperature for 8-10 minutes, baste with clarified butter during cooking.
6. Serve hot with choice of a salad and chutney.

Tandoori Haryali Lobster

A JOY TO THE EYE AS WELL AS TO THE PALATE DELICIOUS LOBSTER COATED WITH GREEN PASTE

Cooking time 8-10 minutes Serves 1-2

INGREDIENTS

300-325 gm - Lobster Tail (2 No)

First Marination
½ tsp	- Ginger Garlic paste
To taste	- Salt
1 tsp	- Lemon juice

Green paste
50 gm	- Green coriander
25 gm	- Mint
5 gm	- Ginger
5 gm	- Garlic
2 no	- Green chilli

Second Marination
3 tbsp	- Hung curd
½ tsp	- Ginger Garlic paste
To taste	- Salt
1 tsp	- Garam masala
1 tsp	- Lemon juice
A pinch	- Turmeric powder
½ tsp	- Yellow chilli powder
2 tsp	- Spinach paste
For basting	- Clarified butter

METHOD

1. Deshell, devein the lobster retaining its tail. Wash, pat dry and keep aside.

First Marination

2. In a bowl mix ginger garlic paste, lemon juice, and salt and apply this to lobster, rub well. Keep aside for at least half an hour.

Green paste

3. In a food processor, put coriander, mint, ginger, garlic, chilli and make fine paste remove and keep aside.

Second Marination

4. In a bowl whisk hung curd, add 4tsp green paste and add all the remaining ingredients and mix well.
5. Remove excess moisture from lobster and coat well in the above mixture and keep aside for at least half an hour.

Cooking

6. Take a skewer and skew marinated lobster from tail to head on both sides. Apply the remaining mixture.
7. Roast in tandoor at a moderate temperature for 8-10 minutes or till tender.
8. Baste with clarified butter during cooking.
9. Serve hot along with choice of a salad and chutney.

Jhinga Adraki

GINGER FLAVOURED KEBAB MADE FROM KING PRAWNS
Cooking time 6-8 minutes Serves 1-2

INGREDIENTS

250-275 gm - Prawns (headless) (6 pcs)

First Marination
To taste	- Salt
1 tsp	- Lemon juice
½ tsp	- Yellow chilli powder
½ tsp	- Ginger Garlic paste
2 tsp	- Ginger juice

Second Marination
3 tbsp	- Hung curd
To taste	- Salt
½ tsp	- Yellow chilli powder
1 tsp	- Ginger powder
1 tsp	- Ginger (chopped)
1 tsp	- Lemon juice
2 tsp	- Mustard oil
2 tsp	- Turmeric powder

For basting - Clarified butter

METHOD

1. De-shell prawns retaining the end tail. De-vein, wash, pat dry and keep aside.

First Marination
2. In a bowl mix salt, lemon juice, yellow chilli powder, ginger garlic paste, ginger juice and apply this to the prawns tail and keep aside for at least 1 ½ hours.

Second Marination
3. In a bowl whisk hung curd, add salt, yellow chilli powder, ginger powder, chopped ginger, lemon juice and mix well.
4. Heat mustard oil in a pan (at smoking point). Add turmeric, immediately add this to the mixture. Cover the bowl with a lid for 2 minutes Mix well.
5. Put prawns in this marinade, mix well and keep aside for half an hour.

Cooking
6. Take a skewer and skew marinated prawns from tail to head on both sides. Apply the remaining mixture on them.
7. Roast in a tandoor or over a charcoal grill at a moderate temperature for 6-8 minutes, baste with clarified butter during cooking.
8. Serve hot along with choice of a salad and chutney.

Zameen Ki Machhi

UNUSUAL FISH KEBAB WRAPPED IN BANANA LEAF COOKED ON STONE IN EARTH
Cooking time 30-40 minutes Serves 1-2

INGREDIENTS

1no. (350 gms) - Pomfret fish

2 tbsp	- Hung curd
1 tsp	- Ginger Garlic paste
2 tbsp	- Green paste
A pinch	- Black cumin
½ tsp	- Black pepper (crushed)
1 tsp	- Lemon juice
To taste	- Salt
1 tsp	- Refined oil
1 no	- Banana leaf

METHOD

1. Clean, wash pomfret, pat dry, make 2-3 incisions on both sides of the fish and keep aside.

Marination
2. In a bowl, whisk hung curd, add ginger garlic paste, green paste, black cumin, black pepper, lemon juice, salt, oil and mix well.
3. Coat the fish with this marinade.
4. Place the fish on a banana leaf large enough to cover the fish and fold it completely from all the sides. Cover it with silver foil seal from all the sides and keep aside for one hour.

Cooking
5. Dig a small pit in the earth about 8-10" deep and large enough to take the covered fish.
6. Arrange a layer of hot red stone in the pit, put a very fine layer of fine earth over the red stone to make even surface.
7. Place the wrapped fish over the layer of earth, cover the fish with another very thin earth then layer of red hot stones.
8. Let the pomfret cook in the heat of the stone from both sides.
9. The fish should be ready in about 30-40 minutes.
10. When cooked, remove the silver foil and place banana wrapped fish on a platter.
11. Serve hot with lachha and lemon wedge.

Tandoori Chilli Prawns Chinese Style

SPICY PRAWNS INFUSED WITH CHINESE SPICES AND ROASTED IN CLAY OVEN
Cooking time 6-8 minutes Serves 1-2

INGREDIENTS

250-275 gm - Prawns tails (with shell) (6 pcs)

First Marination
To taste	- Salt
½ tsp	- Ginger Garlic paste
1 tsp	- Lemon juice

Second Marination
½ tsp	- Soya sauce
4 tbsp	- Hung curd
To taste	- Salt
½ tsp	- Ginger Garlic paste
1 tsp	- Soya sauce
1 tsp	- Lemon juice
1 tsp	- Red chilli paste
2 tsp	- Corn flour

For basting - Clarified butter

METHOD

1. De-shell, de-vein, clean and wash the prawns retaining the tail. Pat dry and keep aside.

First Marination

2. In a bowl mix salt, ginger garlic paste, soya sauce, lemon juice and apply this to the prawns, rub well and keep aside for at least 45 minutes.

Second Marination

3. In a bowl whisk hung curd, add all the remaining ingredients listed in order above and mix well.
4. Squeeze excess moisture from the prawns and put them into this marinade. Coat well and keep aside for at least 1½ hours.

Cooking

5. Take a skewer and skew marinated prawns from tail to head on both sides. Apply the remaining mixture on them.
6. Roast in tandoor at a moderate temperature for 6 – 8 minutes, baste with clarified butter during cooking.
7. Serve hot along with choice of a salad and chutney.

Kasoori Jhinga

EXCITING PRAWNS WITH EXTRA TOUCH OF DRY FENUGREEK
Cooking time 6-8 minutes Serves 1-2

INGREDIENTS

250-275 gm - Prawn (headless) (6 pcs)

First Marination
½ tsp	- Ginger Garlic paste
To taste	- Salt
½ tsp	- Yellow chilli powder
1 tsp	- Lemon juice

Second Marination
25 gm	- Green coriander (chopped)
10 gm	- Fresh mint
4 no	- Green chilli
5 gm	- Ginger
4 clove	- Garlic
50 gm	- Kasoori methi
2 tbsp	- Hung curd
½ tsp	- Garam masala
½ tsp	- Ginger Garlic paste
To taste	- Salt
½ tsp	- Yellow chilli powder
1 tsp	- Lemon juice
2 tsp	- Refined oil

For basting - Clarified butter

METHOD

1. De-shell prawn retaining end tail, de-vein, wash pat dry and keep aside.

First Marination

2. In a bowl mix ginger garlic paste, salt, yellow chilli powder, lemon juice, and apply this to prawns, rub well and keep aside for at least half an hour.
3. In a processor put coriander, mint, green chilli, ginger, garlic, Kasoori methi and make a fine paste.

Second Marination

4. In a bowl whisk hung curd, add 4 tsp of green paste, garam masala, ginger garlic paste, salt, yellow chilli powder, lemon juice, oil and mix well.
5. Squeeze extra moisture from prawns and put them into this mariande. Coat well and keep aside for at least 1 hour.

Cooking

6. Take a skewer and skew the marinated prawns one by one keeping an inch gap in between. Apply remaining marinade on prawns.
7. Roast in a tandoor or over charcoal grill at a moderate temperature for 6 – 8 minutes, baste with clarified butter during cooking.
8. Serve hot with choice of a salad and chutney.

Aatish-E- Jhinga

HOT AND SPICY PRAWNS CHARCOAL GRILLED
Cooking time 6-8 minutes Serves 1-2

INGREDIENTS

250-275 gm - Prawns headless (6pcs)

First Marination
To taste	- Salt
½ tsp	- Ginger Garlic paste
1 tsp	- Red chilli paste
1 tsp	- Lemon juice

Second Marination
3 tbs	- Hung curd
To taste	- Salt
½ tsp	- Ginger Garlic paste
½ tsp	- Red chilli paste
1/3 tsp	- Garam masala
1/3 tsp	- Ajwain
½ tsp	- Black pepper powder
1 tsp	- Lemon juice
1 tsp	- Mustard Oil

For basting - Clarified butter

METHOD
1. De-shell prawns retaining the end tail, de-vein, wash, pat dry and keep aside.

First Marination
2. In a bowl mix salt, ginger garlic paste, red chilli paste, lemon juice and apply this to prawns, rub well and keep aside for at least half an hour.

Second Marination
3. In a bowl whisk hung curd and all the remaining ingredients in the order listed, mix well.
4. Remove extra moisture from the prawn tail and put this into the above marinade, coat well and keep aside for at least 45 minutes.

Cooking
5. Take a skewer and skew marinated prawns from tail to head on both sides. Apply the remaining marinade on them.
6. Roast in a tandoor or over a charcoal grill at a moderate temperature for 6-8 minutes, baste with clarified butter during cooking.
7. Serve hot along with choice of a salad and chutney.

Tandoori Achari Jhinga

ITS SUCCULENT PRAWNS MARINATED WITH TRADITIONAL PICKLING SPICES AND ROASTED IN CLAY OVEN
Cooking time 6-8 minutes Serves 1-2

INGREDIENTS

250-275 gm - Prawn headless (6 pcs)

First Marination
½ tsp	- Ginger Garlic paste
To taste	- Salt
½ tsp	- Yellow chilli powder
1 tsp	- Lemon juice

Second Marination
3 tbsp	- Hung curd
½ tsp	- Ginger Garlic paste
To taste	- Salt
½ tsp	- Yellow chilli powder
2 tsp	- Achar masala
1 tsp	- Lemon juice
½ tsp	- Garam masala
2 tsp	- Mustard oil
1 tsp	- Kalonji, Sauf, Ajwain
¼ tsp	- Jeera whole
½ tsp	- Mustard seeds

For basting - Clarified butter

METHOD
1. De-shell, prawns retaining the end tail, de-vein, wash, pat dry and keep aside.

First Marination
2. In a bowl mix ginger garlic paste, salt, yellow chilli powder, lemon juice and apply this to prawns, rub well and keep aside for at least 1 hour.

Second Marination
3. In a bowl whisk hung curd add ginger garlic paste, salt, yellow chilli powder, lemon juice and garam masala. Mix well.
4. Heat mustard oil in a pan (till smoking point) add kalonji, sauf, ajwain, jeera whole, mustard seeds when it starts crackling immediately add this to the mixture & mix well.
5. Squeeze excess moisture from prawns and put them in this marinade, mix well and keep aside for at least 1½ hours.

Cooking
6. Take a skewer and skew marinated prawns from tail to head on both sides. Apply the remaining mixture on them.
7. Roast in a moderate tandoor for 6-8 minutes, baste with clarified butter during cooking.
8. Serve hot with choice of a salad and chutney.

Jhinga Haldi Mirch

EXCITING PRAWN DELICACY FLAVOURED WITH TURMERIC POWDER AND YELLOW CHILLI

Cooking time 6-8 minutes **Serves** 1-2

INGREDIENTS

250-275 gm - Prawn headless (6 pcs)

First Marination

To taste	- Salt
½ tsp	- Ginger Garlic paste
½ tsp	- Yelow chilli powder
½ tsp	- Lemon juice

Second Marination

A pinch	- Turmeric powder
1 tsp	- Mustard oil
3 tbsp	- Hung curd
To taste	- Salt
½ tsp	- Ginger Garlic paste
½ tsp	- Yellow chilli powder
½ tsp	- Lemon juice
A pinch	- Turmeric powder
½ tsp	- Garam masala
1 tsp	- Mustard oil

For basting - Clarified butter

METHOD

1. De-shell prawns retaining the end tail, de-vein, wash, pat dry and keep aside.

First Marination

2. In a bowl mix salt, ginger garlic paste, yellow chilli powder, lemon juice, turmeric and apply this to the prawns tail and keep aside for at least 1½ hours.

Second Marination

3. In a bowl whisk hung curd, add all the remaining ingredients in the order listed and mix well.
4. Remove extra moisture from the prawns and put them in the marinade, coat well keep aside for at least 2 hours.

Cooking

5. Take a skewer and skew marinated prawns from tail to head on both sides. Apply remaining marinade on them.
6. Roast in a tandoor or over a charcoal grill at a moderate temperature for 6–8 minutes, baste with clarified butter during cooking.
7. Serve hot along with choice of a salad and chutney.

Ajwain Aur Lahsun Wale Jhinge

CARUM SEED FLAVOURED JUICY PRAWNS DONE TO PERFECTION IN A CREAMY GARLIC MARINATION

Cooking time 6-8 minutes **Serves** 1-2

INGREDIENTS

250-275 gm - Prawns (headless) (6pcs)

First Marination

To taste	- Salt
1 tsp	- Garlic paste
1 tsp	- Lemon juice
1/3 tsp	- Ajwain
½ tsp	- Yellow chilli powder

Second Marination

3 tbsp	- Hung curd
To taste	- Salt
1 tsp	- Garlic paste
1 tsp	- Lemon juice
½ tsp	- Yellow chilli powder
1/3 tsp	- Ajwain
A pinch	- Turmeric powder
1 tsp	- Roasted besan
1 tsp	- Mustard oil

For basting - Clarified butter

METHOD

1. Remove the shell of prawns retaining end tail, de-vein, wash, pat dry and keep aside.

First Marination

2. In a bowl mix salt, garlic paste, lemon juice, ajwain, yellow chilli powder and apply this to prawns, rub well and keep aside for at least half an hour.

Second Marination

3. In a bowl whisk hung curd, add remaining ingredients listed and mix well.
4. Remove extra moisture from marinated prawns & put them into this marinade, coat well and keep aside for atleast 1 hour.

Cooking

5. Take a skewer and skew the marinated prawns one by one keeping an inch gap in between. Apply remaining marinade on prawns.
6. Roast in a tandoor or over charcoal grill at a moderate temperature for 6-8 minutes, baste with clarified butter during cooking.
7. Serve hot with choice of a salad and chutney.

Haryali Tandoori Jhinga

EXTREMELY SOFT PRAWNS MARINATED WITH MINT AND CORIANDER PASTE

Cooking time 6-8 minutes Serves 1-2

INGREDIENTS

250-275 gm - Prawns headless (6 pcs)

First Marination
½ tsp	- Ginger Garlic paste
½ tsp	- Yellow chilli powder
To taste	- Salt
½ tsp	- Lemon juice

Second Marination
50 gm	- Green coriander (chopped)
25 gm	- Mint
2 no	- Green chilli (chopped)
5 gm	- Ginger
5 gm	- Garlic
3 tbsp	- Hung curd
½ tsp	- Garam masala
½ tsp	- Ginger Garlic paste
To taste	- Salt
½ tsp	- Yellow chilli powder
1 tsp	- Lemon juice
1 tsp	- Refined oil

For basting - Clarified butter

METHOD

1. Remove the shell of prawns retaining end tail, de-vein, wash, pat dry and keep aside.

First Marination

2. In a bowl mix ginger garlic paste, yellow chilli powder, salt, lemon juice and apply this to prawns, rub well and keep aside for at least half an hour.
3. Green paste:
   In a processor put coriander, mint, green chilli, ginger, garlic make fine paste and keep aside.

Second Marination

4. In a bowl whisk hung curd and add 4 tsp of green paste. Add all the remaining ingredients listed above and mix well.
5. Remove excess moistures, from marinated prawns and put them into this marinade, coat well and keep aside for at least 1 hour.

Cooking

6. Take a skewer and skew the marinated prawns one by one keeping an inch gap in between. Apply remaining marinade on prawn.
7. Roast in a tandoor at a moderate temperature for 6-8 minutes, baste with clarified butter during cooking.
8. Serve hot with choice of a salad and chutney.

Anmol Tandoori Jhinga

ORIENTAL PRAWN KEBAB WITH LEMON AND CHILLI

Cooking time 5-6 minutes Serves 1-2

INGRIDENTS:

5 pieces-King prawns tail (55-60gms each)

1 tsp	- Balsamic vinegar
3 no	- Garlic (crushed)
½ tbsp	- Lemon grass (chopped)
1 tbsp	- Olive oil
2 tbsp	- Green onion (chopped)
1 tbsp	- Sweet chilly sauce
To taste	- Salt

For Chilly Lime Sauce
50gm	- Sugar
1/3 cup	- Water
1 ½ tsp	- Lime rind
2 no	- Red Thai chilli (chopped)
2 tbsp	- Sweet chilli sauce
2 tbsp	- Lime juice
To taste	- Black salt

For basting - Clarified butter

METHOD

1. De-shell, de-vein prawns retaining tails, wash, put dry and keep aside.

Marination

2. In a bowl put balsamic vinegar, garlic, lemon grass, olive oil, green onion, sweet chilly sauce, salt and prawns. Rub well and keep aside for 2hours.

Lime & chilli sauce

3. Put sugar and water in a small saucepan, stir until sugar dissolves completely in water. Put other ingredients in the order listed except lemon juice. Cook 3-4 Minutes, add lemon juice and cool.

Cooking

4. Take a skewer and skew marinated prawns from tail to head on both sides. Apply remaining mixture on them.
5. Roast in a moderate temperature in tandoor for 3-4 minutes.
6. Baste with melted butter and further roast for 2-3 minutes.
7. Serve hot with lemon and chilli sauce.

Tandoori Jhinga Goanese Style

DELICACY OF KING PRAWNS FLAVOURED WITH GOAN SPICES AND HERBS

Cooking time 6-8 minutes Serves 1-2

INGREDIENTS

250-275 gm - Headless prawns (6 pcs)

First Marination
½ tsp	- Ginger Garlic paste
To taste	- Salt
2 tsp	- Lemon juice
½ tsp	- Red chilli paste

Second Marination
2 tbsp	- Hung curd
2 tsp	- Coconut cream
To taste	- Salt
1 tsp	- Lemon juice
½ tsp	- Ginger Garlic paste
½ tsp	- Red chilli paste
2 tsp	- Tamarind pulp
1 tsp	- Refined oil
2 tsp	- Coconut powder

For basting - Clarified butter

METHOD

1. De-shell, prawn retaining the tail, and de-vein, wash, pat dry and keep aside.

First Marination

2. In a bowl mix ginger garlic paste, salt, lemon juice and red chilli paste. Apply this to prawns, rub well and keep aside for at least half an hour.

Second Marination

3. In a bowl whisk hung curd, add all the remaining ingredients listed in the order above and mix well.
4. Remove excess moisture of prawns, add the marinade and keep aside for at least half an hour.

Cooking

5. Take a skewer and skew marinated prawns from tail to head on both sides. Apply remaining marinade on them.
6. Roast in a tandoor at a moderate temperature for 6 – 8 minutes, baste with clarified butter during cooking.
7. Serve hot along with choice of a salad and chutney.

Tandoori Jhinga Shashlik

A DELICIOUS AND COLOURFUL PRAWNS SKEWERED WITH BELL PEPPERS

Cooking time 6-8 minutes Serves 1-2

INGREDIENTS

250-275 gms - Headless prawns (6 pcs)

1 no	- Red capsicum (small)
1 no	- Yellow capsicum (small)
1 no	- Green capsicum (small)
1 no	- Onion (small)

First Marination
½ tsp	- Ginger Garlic paste
To taste	- Salt
1 tsp	- Lemon juice
½ tsp	- Yellow chilli powder

Second Marination
4 tbsp	- Hung curd
To taste	- Salt
½ tsp	- Yellow chilli powder
½ tsp	- Ginger Garlic paste
2 tsp	- Lemon juice
A pinch	- Ajwain
A pinch	- Turmeric powder
2 tsp	- Mustard oil
1 tsp	- Garam masala
1 tsp	- Roasted besan
½ tsp	- Kasoori methi powder

For basting - Clarified butter

METHOD

1. De-shell prawns retaining the end tail, de-vein, wash, pat dry and keep aside.
2. Peel onion, deseed capsicum & cut large cubes of onion, red, yellow and green capsicum

First Marination

3. In a bowl mix ginger garlic paste, salt, lemon juice, yellow chilli powder and apply this to prawns, rub well and keep aside for at least half an hour.

Second Marination

4. In a bowl whisk hung curd and add all the remaining ingredients listed in order and mix well.
5. Squeeze excess moisture from prawns, put them into this marinade, coat well and keep aside for atleast 1 ½ hours.

Cooking

6. Take a skewer and skew the marinated prawns from tail to head and capsicum, onion alternatively. Apply remaining marinade on top.
7. Roast in a moderately hot tandoor for 6-8 minutes, baste with clarified butter during cooking.
8. Serve hot along with choice of a salad and chutney.

Surkh Lal Tandoori Jhinga

DEEP RED AND SPICY PRAWNS ROASTED IN CLAY OVEN

Cooking time 6-8 minutes Serves 1-2

INGREDIENTS

250-275 gm - Headless prawns (6 pcs)

First Marination
To taste	- Salt
½ tsp	- Ginger Garlic paste
½ tsp	- Red chilli paste
1 tsp	- Lemon juice

Second Marination
4 tbsp	- Hung curd
To taste	- Salt
½ tsp	- Ginger Garlic paste
½ tsp	- Red chilli paste
1 tsp	- Lemon juice
1/3 tsp	- Garam masala
A pinch	- Kasoori methi powde
1 tsp	- Refined oil

For basting - Clarified butter

METHOD

1. De-shell prawn retaining end tail, de-vein, wash, pat dry and keep aside.

First Marination

2. In a bowl mix salt, ginger garlic paste, red chilli paste, lemon juice and apply this to prawns, rub well and keep aside for atleast ½ hour.

Second Marination

3. In a bowl whisk hung curd and mix all the ingredients in the order listed. Put prawns into this marinade, coat well and keep aside for at least 1 hour.

Cooking

4. Take a skewer and skew marinated prawns from tail to head. Apply the remaining marinade on them.
5. Roast in a tandoor at a moderate temperature for 6-8 minutes, baste with clarified butter during cooking.
6. Serve hot along with choice of a salad and chutney.

Tandoori Lemon Chilli Prawns

KING PRAWNS MARINATED WITH ORIENTAL SPICES AND ROASTED IN CLAY OVEN

Cooking time 6-8 minutes Serves 1-2

INGREDIENTS

250-275 gm - Headless prawns (6 pcs)

1 tsp	- Ginger Garlic paste
1 tsp	- Chinese red chilli paste
1 tsp	- Lemon juice
1½ tsp	- Soya sauce
1 tsp	- Ginger (chopped)
1 tsp	- Garlic (chopped)
2 tsp	- Corn flour
To taste	- Salt

For basting - Sesame oil

METHOD

1. Clean and wash prawns with shell, pat dry and keep aside.

Marination

2. In a bowl mix ginger garlic paste, red chilli paste, lemon juice, soy sauce, ginger chopped, garlic chopped, corn flour, salt and mix well.
3. Squeeze excess moisture from the prawns and put them into this marinade, coat well and keep aside for at least 1 ½ hours.

Cooking

4. Take a skewer and skew marinated prawns from tail to head on both sides. Apply the remaining mixture on them.
5. Roast in tandoor at a moderate temperature for 6-8 minutes, baste with sesame oil during cooking.
6. Serve hot along with choice of a salad and chutney.

Nashila Tandoori Jhinga

A SIMPLE YET SPECTACULAR PRAWNS FLAVOURED WITH BRANDY AND ROASTED IN CLAY OVEN

Cooking time 6-8 minutes Serves 1-2

INGREDIENTS

250-275 gm - Prawns headless (6 pcs)

First Marination
½ tsp	- Yellow chilli powder
1 tsp	- Ginger Garlic paste
To taste	- Salt
1 tsp	- Lemon juice

Second Marination
50 gm	- Coriander leaves
25 gm	- Mint leaves
5 gm	- Ginger
5 gm	- Garlic
2 no	- Green chillies
4 tbsp	- Hung curd
To taste	- Salt
½ tsp	- Garam masala
A pinch	- Kasoori methi powder
2 tsp	- Refined oil
1 tsp	- Lemon juice
20 ml	- Brandy/Rhum
1 tsp	- Roasted besan

For basting - Clarified butter

METHOD

1. De-shell prawns retaining end tail, de-vein, wash, pat dry and keep aside.

First Marination

2. In a bowl mix yellow chilli powder, ginger garlic paste, salt, lemon juice and apply this to prawns, rub well and keep aside for at least 1 hour.
3. In a food processor, put coriander leaves, mint leaves, ginger, garlic and green chillies and make a fine paste, keep aside.

Second Marination

4. In a bowl whisk hung curd, add green paste (4 tsp) and add all the ingredients in the order listed. Put prawn tails into this marinade, coat well and keep aside for atleast 1 hour.

Cooking

5. Take a skewer and skew marinated prawns from tail to head from both sides. Apply the remaining mixture on them.
6. Roast in a tandoor at a moderate temperature for 6-8 minutes, baste with clarified butter during cooking.
7. Serve hot along with choice of a salad and chutney.

Kolmi Na Kebab (Parsi)

A SUCCULENT KEBAB MADE FROM PRAWN MINCE IN PARSI STYLE

Cooking time 2- 3 minutes Serves 1– 2

INGREDIENTS

200 gm - Prawn Meat (minced)

½ tsp	- Green chilli (chopped)
2 tsp	- Onion (chopped)
1 tsp	- Garlic (chopped)
1 tsp	- Fresh coriander leaves (chopped)
1/3 tsp	- Turmeric powder
30-40 gm	- Potatoes (boiled)
To taste	- Salt
1/3 tsp	- White pepper powder
2 tbsp	- Breadcrumbs
A pinch	- Ajwain
1 no	- Egg white

For frying - Refined oil

METHOD

1. Put prawn mince in a deep tray and add all the remaining ingredients in the order listed except egg. Rub well and keep aside for half an hour.
2. Divide the mixture into 8-10 parts & make balls and whisk white of egg untill fluffy, dip prawn balls.

Cooking

3. Heat oil in a kadhai and deep fry prawn balls to a golden brown colour on medium heat or till cooked.
4. Serve hot with choice of a salad and chutney.

Tandoori Machhli Seekh (for recipe turn to page no: 127)

Puddine Wali Tandoori Pomfret (for recipe turn to page no: 130)

Haryali Tandoori Jhinga (for recipe turn to page no: 137)

Mahi Mussallam (for recipe turn to page no: 145)

Jhinga Mahi jugalbandi (for recipe turn to page no: 151)

Samundari Sher (for recipe turn to page no: 153)

Tandoori Mahi Bharwan (for recipe turn to page no: 154)

Mahi Mussallam

THIS MAGNIFICENT TROUT FISH KEBAB IS STUFFED WITH EXOTIC PRAWN MINCE AND COOKED IN AWADH STYLE

Cooking time 8-10 minutes Serves 1-2

INGREDIENTS

1 no (325-350 gm) - Trout fish

First Marination
1 tsp	- Ginger Garlic paste
½ tsp	- Red chilli paste
1 tsp	- Lemon juice
A pinch	- Turmeric powder
To taste	- Salt

Stuffing
100 gms	- Shrimps (chopped)
½ tsp	- Green chilli (chopped)
1 tsp	- Fresh coriander (chopped)
1 tsp	- Desiccated coconut
½ tsp	- Crushed black pepper
To taste	- Salt

Second Marination
4 tbsp	- Hung curd
1 tsp	- Ginger Garlic paste
½ tsp	- Red chilli paste
1 tsp	- Roasted besan
½ tsp	- Garam masala
½ tsp	- Dalchini powder
To taste	- Salt
2 tsp	- Mustard oil

For basting - Clarified butter

METHOD

1. Clean and wash trout, make 3-4 incisions on both sides of the fish, pat dry and keep aside.

First Marination
2. In a bowl mix ginger garlic paste, red chilli paste, lemon juice, turmeric, salt, apply this to fish, rub well and keep aside for at least 1½ hours.

Stuffing
3. In a pan, heat oil add chopped ginger, chopped shrimps cook it for a while, add green chilli chopped, desiccated coconut, black pepper powder and salt and mix it well.
4. Stuff this mixture in the belly part of the trout and tie the fish with toothpicks.

Second Marination
5. In a bowl whisk hung curd, add all the remaining ingredients listed above, mix well. Put trout in this marinade, coat well and keep aside for at least 1 hour.

Cooking
6. Take a skewer and skew the marinated trout from mouth upward towards tail.
7. Roast in a moderately hot temperature in tandoor for 7-8 minutes.
8. Remove and baste with clarified butter and further roast for 1-2 minutes.
9. Serve hot with choice of a salad and chutney.

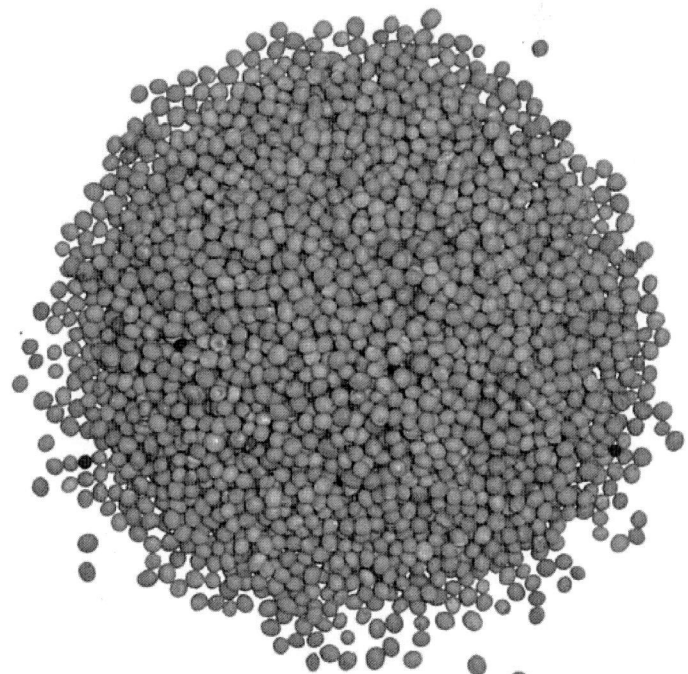

Adraki Mahi Shashlik

GINGER FLAVOURED FISH TIKKA SKEWERED WITH BELL PEPPERS ON BAMBOO STICKS

Cooking time 3-4 minutes Serves 1-2

INGREDIENTS

225-250 gm-Firm fish fillet (surmai or sole) (6 pcs)

First Marination
1 tsp	- Ginger paste
½ tsp	- Yellow chilli powder
To taste	- Salt
2 tsp	- Lemon juice

Second Marination
1 tsp	- Ginger (chopped)
½ tsp	- Garlic (chopped)
1 no	- Egg white
1 tsp	- Light soya sauce
4 pcs	- Pineapple chunk (canned)
12 pcs	- Onion (large dice 1"/1")
2 pcs	- Red and yellow capsicum (large dice 1"/1")

For frying
4 tsp	- Refined oil

METHOD

1. Clean, cut cubes of fish (1 ½" X 1 ½"), wash, pat dry and keep aside.

First Marination

2. In a bowl mix ginger paste, yellow chilli powder, salt, lemon juice, apply this to fish, rub well and keep aside for at least half an Hour.

Second Marination

3. In a bowl mix ginger and chopped garlic, egg white, soya sauce, put marinated fish pieces, onion, capsicum and pineapple, mix well and keep aside for at least 1 hour.

Cooking

4. Take a wooden skewer (5 "), skew two fish pieces, onion, capsicum alternatively with pineapple (total four skewers).
5. Heat oil in a pan or griddle plate, fry shashliks for 3-4 minutes on medium heat ensuring dark golden brown colour.
6. When cooked remove on an absorbent paper to drain excess fat.
7. Arrange on a plate and serve with choice of a salad and chutney.

Crab Aur Jhinga Kebab

A PERFECT MATCH OF CRAB AND PRAWNS

Cooking time 4-6 minutes Serves 1-2

INGREDIENTS

4 tsp	- Processed cheese (grated)
125 gm	- Crabmeat (coarsely chopped)
75 gm	- Prawn meat (coarsely chopped)
1 tsp	- Ginger Garlic paste
½ tsp	- Green chilli (chopped)
1 tsp	- Green coriander (chopped)
½ tsp	- White pepper powder
A pinch	- Elaichi powder
½ tsp	- Ginger powder
½ tsp	- Anardana crushed
For basting	- Clarified butter

METHOD

1. In a flat tray mash processed cheese, add crabmeat, prawn mince, ginger garlic paste, all the ingredients listed above, mix well and keep aside for 1 hour.

Cooking

2. Divide mixture into four equal parts, take skewer, apply mixture in a cylindrical shape (4-5 inches). Make smooth texture by using wet palm.
3. Roast in a tandoor or a charcoal grill at a moderate temperature for 4-6 minutes, baste with clarified butter during cooking.
4. Serve hot with choice of a salad and chutney.

Jhinga Mahi jugalbandi

BEAUTIFUL AND DELICATE MELANGE OF KING PRAWNS AND FISH

Cooking time 10-12 minutes Serves 1-2

INGREDIENTS

2no (200 gm) - Sole fish fillet
4no (175 - 200 gm) - Prawn tail (large size)

First Marination
1 tsp	- Ginger Garlic paste
1 tsp	- Lemon juice
½ tsp	- Yellow chilli powder
A pinch	- Turmeric powder
To taste	- Salt

First Marination
4 tbsp	- Hung curd
½ tsp	- Ginger Garlic paste
½ tsp	- Yellow chilli powder
½ tsp	- Garam masala
½ tsp	- Kasoori methi powder
A pinch	- Ajwain
To taste	- Salt
1 tbsp	- Mustard oil

For basting - Clarified butter

METHOD

1. Clean, de-vien prawns, cut the sole fish fillet into flat pieces (5"x2"x 5cm), wash, pat dry and keep aside.

First Marination

2. In a bowl mix ginger garlic paste, yellow chilli powder, lemon juice, turmeric powder, salt and apply this to fish and prawns both, rub well and keep aside for at least 1 ½ hours.
3. Spread fish fillet on flat surface, place the two prawns face to face, roll, seal it with wooden toothpicks.

Second Marination

4. In a bowl, whisk hung curd, ginger garlic paste and all other remaining ingredients listed above, mix well.
5. Put fish in this marinade, coat well and keep aside for at least 1 hour.

Cooking

6. Take a skewer and skew the fish pieces horizontally and carefully.
7. Roast in a moderately hot tandoor for 10-12 minutes, baste with clarified butter during cooking.
8. Remove toothpicks and serve with choice of a salad and chutney.

Machhli Tawa Kebab

ANOTHER VARIATION OF POMFRET FISH COOKED ON A GRIDDLE

Cooking time 4-5 minutes Serves 1-2

INGREDIENTS

200-225 gm - Pomfret fillet

1 tsp	- Ginger Garlic paste
½ tsp	- Ajwain
½ tsp	- Green chilli (chopped)
½ tsp	- Green coriander (chopped)
To taste	- Salt
½ tsp	- White pepper powder
For binding	- Bread crumbs
½ tsp	- Kutti red chilli
1 no	- Egg white

For frying - Refined oil

METHOD

1. In a food processor put pomfret fish fillet and make fine mince.
2. In a tray take pomfret mince, add the remaining ingredients, listed in order, mix thoroughly with the help of palm, ensuring all ingredients are mixed well and it forms a smooth texture. Keep aside for at least 1 hour.
3. Divide this mixture in equal 4-5 parts and make balls. Flatten each ball between the palms into thick round patties.

Cooking

4. Heat oil on a tawa/griddle and shallow fry the patties on a medium heat till a crisp layer is formed on both the sides.
5. Remove to absorbant paper to drain the excess fat. Serve hot with a choice of salad and chutney.

Lajawab Tandoori Mahi Tikka

AN IMPRESSIVE FISH KEBAB MARINATED WITH EXOTIC SPICES

Cooking time 5-7 minutes **Serves** 1-2

INGREDIENTS

225-250 gm - Fish fillet (sole) (6 pcs)

Green Paste
2 no	- Green chilli
50 gm	- Coriander leaves
25 gm	- Mint leaves
10 no	- Curry leaves
5 gm	- Anardana
15 gm	- Onion (sliced)

Marination
2 tbsp	- Hung curd
1 tsp	- Ginger Garlic paste
2 tsp	- Peanut paste
To taste	- Salt
½ tsp	- Dalchini powder
½ tsp	- Crushed black pepper powder
½ tsp	- Anardana (crushed)
1 tsp	- Ginger (chopped)
1 tsp	- Roasted gram flour
2 tsp	- Lemon juice
2 tsp	- Refined oil

For basting - Clarified butter

PREPARATION

1. Take fish fillet, cut it in cubes (1½ x 1½) wash and pat dry.

Green Paste

2. In a food processor put green chilli, coriander leaves, mint leaves, curry leaves, anardana and onion, make into a smooth paste and keep aside.

Marination

3. In a bowl whisk hung curd, add ginger garlic paste, peanut paste, salt, dalchini powder, crushed black pepper powder, crushed anardana, chopped ginger, roasted gram flour, lemon juice, add 4 tsp of green paste and refined oil. Mix well.
4. Put fish pieces into this marinade, coat well and keep aside for at least 1-1 ½ hour.

Cooking

5. Take a skewer, skew marinated fish and roast in a moderately hot tandoor for 5-7 minutes, baste with clarified butter during cooking.
6. Serve hot on to a plate with a choice of a salad and chutney.

Jhinga Samrat

AN UNUSUAL RECIPE OF TANDOORI PRAWN FROM THE ROYAL KITCHEN

Cooking time 6-8 minutes **Serves** 1-2

INGREDIENTS

250-275 gm - Prawn tails (6 pcs)

4 tbsp	- Hung curd
1 tbsp	- Cream
1 no	- Egg yolk
1 tsp	- Ginger Garlic paste
½ tsp	- Green chilli paste
1 tsp	- Soya sauce
2 tsp	- Besan (roasted)
To taste	- Salt
½ tsp	- Red chilli powder
A pinch	- Turmeric powder
½ tsp	- Onion seed (kalounji)
2 tsp	- Mustard oil

For basting - Clarified butter

METHOD

1. De-shell prawn retaining its tail, de-vein, wash, pat dry and keep aside.

Marination

2. In a bowl, whisk hung curd, add cream, egg, ginger garlic paste, green chilli paste, soya sauce, roasted besan, salt, red chilli powder, turmeric powder, onion seed and mustard oil. Mix well.
3. Put prawns into this marinade, coat well and keep aside for at least 1½ hours.

Cooking

4. Take a skewer and skew marinated prawns and roast in a moderately hot tandoor or over charcoal grill, baste with clarified butter during cooking.
5. Serve hot with choice of a salad and chutney.

Mahi Tikka Noorani

ANOTHER VARIATION OF FISH KEBAB MARINATED WITH EXOTIC GREEN PASTE

Cooking time 5-7 minutes Serves 1-2

INGREDIENTS

225-250 - Fish cubes (boneless) (6 pcs)

First Marination
1 tsp	- Ginger Garlic paste
½ tsp	- Ajwain
To taste	- Salt
½ tsp	- Yellow chilli powder
2 tsp	- Lemon juice
2 tsp	- Mustard oil

Green Paste
25 gm	- Mint leaves
50 gm	- Coriander leaves
2 no	- Green chilli
5 gm	- Peeled Garlic
5 gm	- Ginger

Second Marination
4 tbsp	- Hung curd
To taste	- Salt
1/3 tsp	- Yellow chilli powder

For basting - Clarified butter

METHOD

1. Clean, wash and cut the fish fillet in shape (size 1 ½ # 1 ½).

First Marination

2. Apply ginger garlic paste, ajwain, salt, yellow chilli, lemon juice and mustard oil to the fish and keep aside.

Green Paste

3. In a food processor grind mint leaves, coriander leaves, green chilli, peeled garlic, ginger to a paste.

Second Marination

4. In a bowl, whisk hung curd, add 4 tsp of green paste, salt and yellow chilli and mix well.
5. Put fish pieces into this marinade, coat well and keep aside for at least 1 hour.

Cooking

6. Take a skewer and skew marinated fish and roast in a clay oven or charcoal grill, baste with clarified butter during cooking.
7. Serve hot with a choice of a salad and chutney.

Samundari Sher

KING LOBSTER WITH AN EXOTIC AND DIFFERENT MARINATION-A FANTASTIC DELICACY OF SEA LION

Cooking time 8-10 minutes Serves 1-2

INGREDIENTS

300-325 gm - Lobster tail (2 pcs)

First Marination
To taste	- Salt
½ tsp	- Kashmiri red chilli powder
1 ½ tsp	- Lemon juice
½ tsp	- Ginger Garlic paste
4 tbsp	- Hung curd
½ tsp	- Ginger Garlic paste

Second Marination
3 tbsp	- Hung curd
1 no	- Egg
To taste	- Salt
½ tsp	- Kashmiri red chilli powder
½ tsp	- Garam masala
A pinch	- Ajwain
1/3 tsp	- Kalonji
A pinch	- Turmeric powder
1 tsp	- Raw mango powder
¼ tsp	- Mustard powder
1 tsp	- Roasted besan
2 tsp	- Mustard oil

For basting - Clarified butter

METHOD

1. De-shell, de-vein the lobster retaining its tail, wash, pat dry and keep aside.

First Marination

2. In a bowl mix salt, red chilli powder, lemon juice, ginger garlic paste and apply this to the lobster, rub well and keep aside for at least half an hour.

Second Marination

3. In a bowl whisk hung curd, add all the remaining ingredients listed in the order above, mix well.
4. Squeeze excess moisture from lobster tail and put in the above mixture, coat well and keep for at least 1 hour.

Cooking

5. Take a skewer and skew marinated lobster from tail to head on both sides. Apply the remaining mixture on them.
6. Roast in a tandoor or over charcoal grill at moderate temperature for 8-10 minutes, baste with clarified butter during cooking.
7. Serve hot along with choice of a salad and chutney.

Tandoori Mahi Bharwan

FILLET OF FISH ROLLED WITH DELICIOUS FISH MINCE & DELICATELY ROASTED

Cooking time 8-10 minutes **Serves** 1-2

INGREDIENTS

02 no (90 gm) Sole Fish fillet (long)

First Marination
½ tsp	- Ginger/garlic paste
½ tsp	- White pepper powder
01 tsp	- Lemon juice
To taste	- Salt

Stuffing
80gm	- Fine Fish mince (Red snapper)
A pinch	- Ajwain
A pinch	- Turmeric powder
½ tsp	- Yellow chilli powder
1/3 tsp	- Ginger (chopped)
1/3 tsp	- Green coriander (chopped)
½ tsp	- Processed cheese (grated)

Second Marination
01 tbsp	- Processed cheese (grated)
1 ½ tbsp	- Hung curd
01 tsp	- Ginger/garlic paste
½ tsp	- White pepper powder
01 tsp	- Egg white
To taste	- Salt
For basting	- Clarified butter

METHOD

1. Clean cut the fish fillet into flat piece (5"into 2" into 5 cm), wash, pat dry and keep aside.

First Marination

2. In a bowl mix ginger/garlic paste, white pepper powder, lemon juice, salt and apply this to fish fillet rub well and keep aside for atleast 1 ½ hours.

Stuffing

3. In a pan, heat oil add ajwain, chopped ginger, fish mince cook it for a while add turmeric powder, yellow chilli powder, processed cheese, chopped green coriander. Remove & keep aside to cool.
4. Divide stuffing into equal parts, spread fish fillets on flat surface, place the stuffing on the center of each fish fillet, roll, and seal it with a wooden toothpick.

Second Marination

5. In a bowl mash processed cheese, whisk hung curd add, ginger / garlic paste, white pepper powder, egg white, salt and mix well.
6. Put fish in this marinade, coat well and keep aside for atleast 1hour.

Cooking

7. Take a skewer and skew the fish pieces horizontal & carefully.
8. Roast in a moderately hot tandoor or over charcoal grill for 8-10 minutes, baste with clarified butter during cooking.
9. Remove toothpick and serve with choice of salad and chutney.

Salmon Ali Shaan

BEAUTIFUL KEBAB OF PINK SALMON FLAVOURED WITH BASIL

Cooking time 5-7 minutes **Serves** 1-2

INGREDIENTS

225-250 gm (6 pcs) Pink salmon fillet

First Marination
½ tsp	- Ginger garlic paste
1 tbsp	- Basil paste
1 tsp	- Basil (chopped)
1 tsp	- Lemon juice
To taste	- Salt

Second Marination
3 tbsp	- Hung curd
½ tsp	- Yellow chilli powder
½ tsp	- Roasted besan
1 tsp	- Lemon juice
1 tsp	- Musterd oil
To taste	- Salt
For basting	- Clarified butter

METHOD

1. Clean, wash and cut large cubes of fish (1 ½" X 1 ½") pat dry and keep aside.

First Marination

2. In a bowl mix ginger garlic paste, basil paste, chopped basil, lemon juice, salt apply this to fish cubes, rub well and keep aside for atleast half an hour.

Second Marination

3. In a bowl whisk hung curd, add all the remaining ingredients in the listed order, mix well.
4. Squeeze excess moisture from the fish and put it into the second marinade, coat well and keep aside

Cooking

5. Take a skewer and skew marinated fish pieces one by one an inch apart. Apply remaining marinade on fish.
6. Roast in a tandoor or over a charcoal grill at a moderate temperature for 5-7 minutes. Baste with clarified butter during cooking.
7. Serve hot with choice of a salad and chutney.

Lamb

Lamb kebabs in particular are delicious. Tender, lean meat from the hind quarter, usually referred to as a prime cut, is the best for kebabs. In addition to the two basic cuts, tikka and kebabs, that are common to poultry. Lamb has a number of other cuts that play an important role for tandoori food.

Lamb boti lamb (1 ½" thickness, 100-110 gms)	-	Chunks of lamb with bone in the leg of
Raan	-	Leg of kid lamb weight = 800-900gms
Rib Chops	-	A chop is half an inch thick pieces of meat with two bones.
Pasanday	-	Flattened pieces of lamb, 4-5 inches long and ½ inch thick from hind leg of lamb. They are beaten and scored on one side in criss-cross pattern to facilitate tenderizing.
Tikka	-	2 inch cubes of lean meat from the hind leg of lamb.
Mince	-	Meat from the hind leg of lamb, free from fat and gristle minced.

NOTE:- Before marinating, lamb meat should always be washed and drained well with a kitchen towel and then placed into marinade. Always use meat from a young animal as the meat is tender & soft.

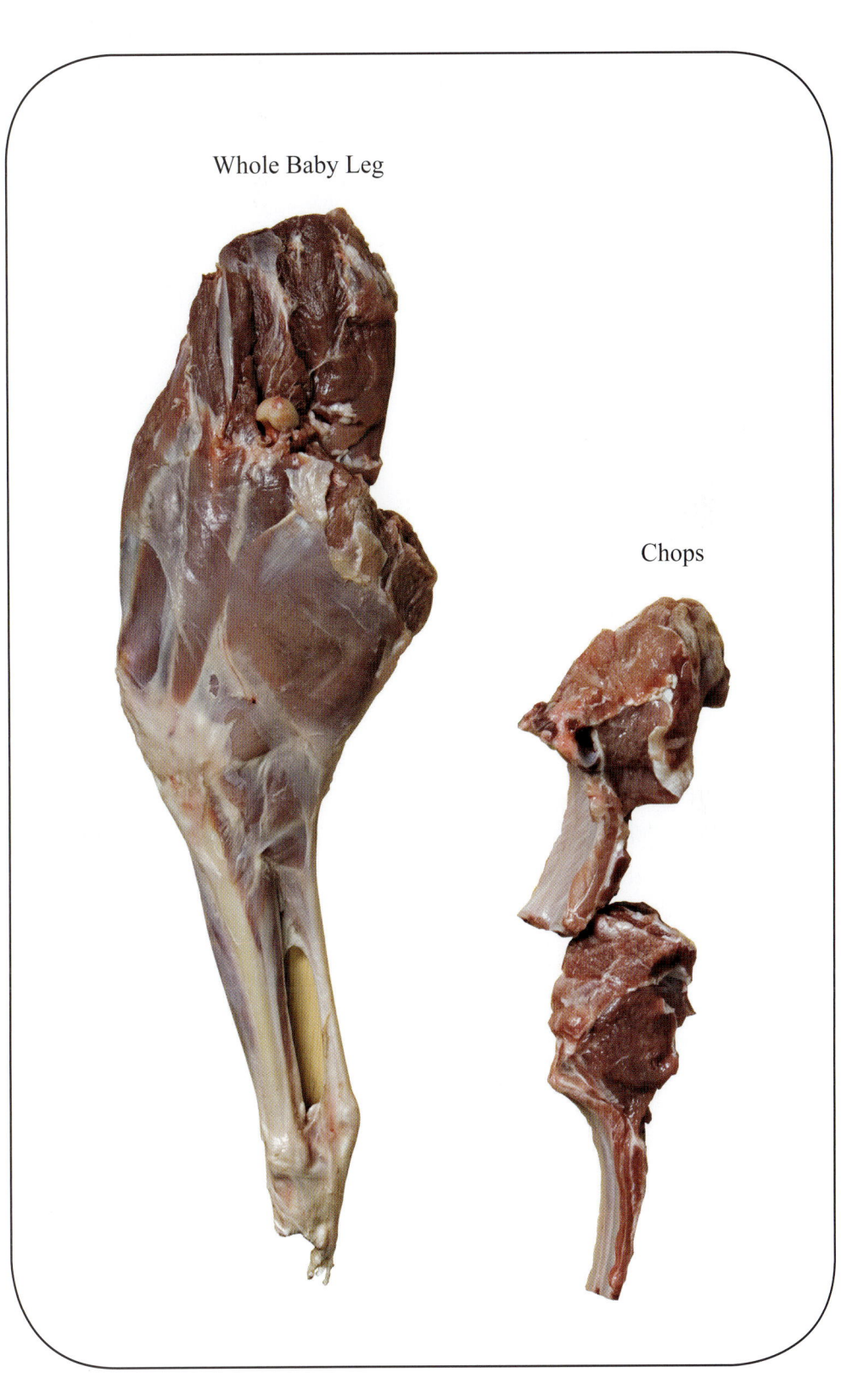

Burra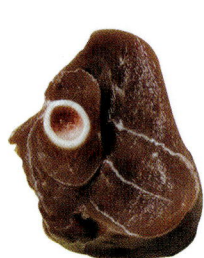

Tikka / Boti

Pasanda

Lamb Mince

Sangam Seekh Kebab (for recipe turn to page no: 165)

Shalimar Raan (for recipe turn to page no: 175)

Pathar Ka Gosht (for recipe turn to page no: 194)

Bhyankar Tandoori Champen (for recipe turn to page no: 170)

Adrak Ke Panje (for recipe turn to page no: 171)

Sunheri Tandoori Anda (for recipe turn to page no: 182)

Jahangiri Seekh Kebab

A BEFITTING TRIBUTE TO AWADH'S GOURMET RECIPE PREPARED WITH LAMB

Cooking time 8-10 minutes Serves 1-2

INGREDIENTS

2 tbsp	- Processed cheese (grated)
200 gm	- Lamb mince
1 tsp	- Ginger garlic paste
To taste	- Salt
½ tsp	- Garam masala
1 tsp	- Green chilli (chopped)
1 tsp	- Green coriander (chopped)
A pinch	- Turmeric powder
1 tsp	- Cumin seeds
2 tsp	- Desi ghee
2 tsp	- Onion chopped)
2 tsp	- Tomato (chopped)
2 tsp	- Capsicum (chopped)
1 tsp	- Fresh coriander (chopped)
For basting	- Clarified butter

METHOD

1. In a deep tray, mash processed cheese, put Lamb mince, add all the remaining ingredients in the order listed, rub well and keep aside for at least half an hour.
2. Divide the mixture into 4 equal portions and make balls.

Cooking

3. Spread the mixture on the skewer using a wet hand along the length of the skewer in a cylindrical shape, one inch apart and make each kebab 4-5 inches long.
4. Roast in a moderately hot tandoor or over charcoal grill for 6-7 minutes.
5. Baste with clarified butter and further roast for 2-3 minutes or till tender.
6. Remove the lamb from skewer and cut into 1 inch pieces.
7. Heat oil in a pan, saute onion, add tomatoes and capsicum for a while till it softens, put in lamb pieces, toss and sprinkle fresh coriander.
8. Serve hot with choice of a salad and chutney.

Sangam Seekh Kebab

AN UNUSUAL KEBAB MADE OF LAMB AND CHICKEN BEAUTIFULLY PRESENTED

Cooking time 8-10 minutes Serves 1-2

INGREDIENTS

Lamb Mince

2 tbsp	- Processed cheese (grated)
1 tsp	- Ginger garlic paste
To taste	- Salt
100 gm	- Lamb mince
½ tsp	- Red chilli paste
½ tsp	- Ginger (chopped)
½ tsp	- Green chilli (chopped)
1/3 tsp	- Garam masala
1 tsp	- Green coriander (chopped)

Chicken Mince

2 tbsp	- Processed cheese (grated)
100 gm	- Chicken mince
A pinch	- Shahi jeera (black cumin)
½ tsp	- Ginger garlic paste
A pinch	- Elaichi powder
A pinch	- White pepper powder
To taste	- Salt
½ tsp	- Green chilli (chopped)
1 tsp	- Green coriander (chopped)
For basting	- Clarified butter

METHOD

Lamb Mince

1. In a deep tray mash processed cheese, add lamb mince and all the remaining ingredients, mix well with palm and keep aside for at least 30 minutes.

Chicken Mince

2. In a deep tray mash processed cheese, add chicken mince and all the ingredients, mix with palm and keep aside for at least 30 minutes.

Cooking

3. Divide both the marinated mince into four equal parts and make balls.
4. Mix each ball of chicken with mutton and spread mince on the skewer by pressing each ball along the length of the skewer in a cylindrical shape one inch apart, making each kebab 4 inches long.
5. Roast in a moderately hot tandoor or over charcoal grill for 6-7 minutes.
6. Baste with clarified butter and further roast for 2-3 minutes or till tender.
7. Serve hot with choice of a salad and chutney

Seekh Patialashahi

A LAMB DELICACY FROM THE SPLENDID KITCHEN OF THE ROYAL HOUSE OF PATIALA

Cooking time 8-10 minutes Serves 1-2

INGREDIENTS

2 tbsp	- Processed cheese (grated)
200 gm	- Lamb mince
½ tsp	- Garlic (chopped)
½ tsp	- Red chilli paste
1 tsp	- Ginger (chopped)
1 tsp	- Green chilli (chopped)
1 tsp	- Mint (chopped)
To taste	- Salt
½ tsp	- Garam masala
A pinch	- Kasoori methi powder
A pinch	- Shahi jeera
For basting	- Clarified butter

METHOD

1. In a deep tray mash processed cheese, add lamb mince, garlic chopped, red chilli paste and all other ingredients listed in the order above. Mix well with palm and keep aside for at least 1 hour.

Cooking

2. Divide mince mixture into 4 equal parts and make balls.
3. Spread the mixture on the skewer using a wet hand along the length of the skewer in a cylindrical shape, one inch apart and make each kebab 4 inches long.
4. Roast in a moderately hot tandoor or over a charcoal grill for 6 – 7 minutes.
5. Baste with clarified butter and further roast for 2-3 minutes or till tender.
6. Serve hot with choice of a salad and chutney.

Malai Seekh Kebab

ABSOLUTELY SOFT LAMB MINCE KEBAB INFUSED WITH DRY FENUGREEK

Cooking time 8-10 minutes Serves 1-2

INGREDIENTS

2 tbsp	- Processed cheese (grated)
1 tsp	- Ginger garlic paste
200 gm	- Lamb mince
½ tsp	- Red chilli paste
To taste	- Salt
½ tsp	- Green chilli (chopped)
1 tsp	- Coriander (chopped)
½ tsp	- Ginger (chopped)
1/3 tsp	- Garam masala
A pinch	- Kasooori methi powder
5 tsp	- Processed cheese (grated)
4 tsp	- Cream
For basting	- Clarified butter

METHOD

1. Take lamb mince in a deep tray and all the above ingredients and mix well with palm and keep aside for at least half an hour.
2. Divide the dough into 4 equal portions and make balls.

Cooking

3. Take a skewer and apply mixture along it with a moist palm to press each ball along the length of the skewer in a cylindrical shape and making each ball 4 inches long.
4. Roast in a moderately hot tandoor or over a charcoal grill for 6 – 7 minutes.
5. Baste with clarified butter and further roast for 2-3 minutes.
6. Transfer it on to a plate.
7. In a bowl mix processed cheese and cream to form a smooth paste and transfer to a piping bag (used for making pastries).
8. Stuff the cheese mixtures inside the seekh kebab.
9. Serve hot with choice of a salad and chutney.

Lucknowi Seekh Kebab

ANOTHER VARIATION OF LAMB MINCE KEBAB PREPARED WITH LUCKNOWI SPICES AND CONDIMENTS

Cooking time 8-10 minutes Serves 1-2

INGREDIENTS

4 tsp	- Processed cheese (grated)
1 tsp	- Ginger garlic paste
200 gm	- Lamb mince
To taste	- Salt
½ tsp	- Deghi mirch powder
A pinch	- Kasoori methi powder
½ tsp	- Ginger (chopped)
1 tsp	- Green coriander (chopped)
½ tsp	- Lucknowi masala
A drop	- Attar (essence)
2no	- Cloves
1 tsp	- Desi ghee
For basting	- Clarified butter

METHOD

1. In a deep tray mash processed cheese, add ginger garlic paste, lamb mince and all other ingredients listed above, mix well and keep aside for at least half an hour, transfer to a bowl.
2. Put one small bowl in the centre of lamb mince, place one piece of burning charcoal. On top of it put 2 pieces of cloves, 1 tsp of desi ghee and cover it with a lid for 2-3 minutes (to give smoke flavour).
3. Divide mixture into 4 equal portions and make balls.

Cooking

4. Spread the mixture on the skewer using a wet hand along the length of the skewer in a cylindrical shape, one inch apart and make each kebab 4 inches long.
5. Roast in a moderately hot tandoor or over a charcoal grill for 6-7 minutes.
6. Baste with clarified butter and further roast for 2-3 minutes.
7. Serve hot with choice of a salad and chutney.

Khusk Seekh Kebab

CRUNCHY, LAMB MINCE KEBAB PREPARED WITH SELECT SPICES AND COATED WITH CORNFLAKES

Cooking time 8-10 minutes Serves 1-2

INGREDIENTS

4 tsp	- Processed cheese (grated)
1 tsp	- Ginger garlic paste
200 gm	- Lamb mince
To taste	- Salt
½ tsp	- Red chilli paste
½ tsp	- Garam masala
½ tsp	- Kasoori methi powder
1 tsp	- Green coriander (chopped)
1 tsp	- Mint (chopped)
1 tsp	- Ginger (chopped)
1 tsp	- Green chilli (chopped)
Batter	
4 tbsp	- Cornflour
as required	- water
For coating	- Cornflakes (crushed)
For basting	- Clarified butter
For frying	- Refined oil

METHOD

1. Take processed cheese in a deep tray, rub it well with the help of your palm, add all the remaining ingredients in the order listed, mix well to smooth consistency and keep aside for at least 1 hour.
2. Divide the mixture into 4 equal parts and make balls.

Cooking

3. Take a skewer and apply each ball using a wet hand along the length of the skewer in a cylindrical shape, one inch apart and making each kebab 4 inches long.
4. Roast in a moderately hot tandoor or over charcoal grill for 6-7 minutes. Baste it with clarified butter and further roast for 2-3 minutes and keep to cool.
5. Make thin batter with corn flour and water, dip each kebab into the batter, roll in crushed cornflakes and deep fry till crisp.
6. Serve hot with choice of a salad and chutney.

Kebab-e-Gulmarg

KASHMIRI SKEWERED LAMB SEEKH KEBAB

Cooking time 8-10 minutes **Serves** 1-2

INGREDIENTS

200 gm	-	Lamb mince
1 tsp	-	Red chilli powder
To taste	-	Salt
1/3 tsp	-	Black cardamom
½ no	-	Egg
½ tsp	-	Black cumin seeds
A pinch	-	Saffron
1 tsp	-	Green coriander (chopped)
½ tsp	-	Dry mint powder
For basting	-	Clarified butter

METHOD

1. In a tray put lamb mince, add red chilli powder, salt and mix well with the help of your palm. Keep in a refrigerator for at least 1 hour.
2. Pass through the refrigerated meat once again in a mincing machine.
3. Add cardomon powder, egg (beaten) cumin seeds, saffron, coriander, dry mint and mix well.
4. Divide the mixture into 4-5 equal size portions.

Cooking

5. Take a skewer and apply each ball using a wet hand along the length of the skewer in a cylindrical shape, one inch apart and making each kebab 4 – 5 inches long.
6. Roast in a moderately hot tandoor or over charcoal grill for 6 – 7 minutes. Baste it with clarified butter and further roast for 2 – 3 minutes or till done.
7. Serve hot with choice of salad and walnut chutney.

Dum Ke Awadhi Kebab

THIS DELICACY OF AWADH; THE LAMB MINCE IS SMOKED BEFORE THE KEBAB IS ROASTED

Cooking time 3-4 minutes **Serves** 1-2

INGREDIENTS

200 gm	-	Lamb mince
½ tsp	-	Ginger garic paste
2 tsp	-	Brown onion paste
2 tsp	-	Chironji paste
½ tsp	-	Yellow chilli powder
1/3 tsp	-	Soda
½ tsp	-	Ginger garlic paste
½ tsp	-	Lucknowi garam masala
A pinch	-	Elaichi powder
A pinch	-	Saffron
½ tsp	-	Maida
2 no	-	Cloves
For smoke (Dum)	-	Desi ghee
For cooking	-	Desi ghee

METHOD

1. In a deep tray take lamb mince and add all the ingredients in the order listed, mix well to smooth consistency and transfer to a bowl.
2. Put one small bowl in the centre of lamb mince, place one piece of burning charcoal, put 2 pieces of laung and put a tsp of desi ghee and cover it with a lid for at least 4-5 minutes (to give smoking flavour).
3. Divide the mixture into 4-6 portions and make balls.

Cooking

4. Press each ball between your palm to give it a medallion (tikki) shape.
5. Heat ghee in a lagan or thick-bottomed pan and shallow fry for 3-4 minute till golden brown.
6. Serve hot with choice of a salad and chutney.

Kasoori Seekh Kebab

DRIED FENUGREEK FLAVOURED LAMB SEEKH KEBAB

Cooking time 8-10 minutes Serves 1-2

INGREDIENTS

2 tbsp gm	- Processed cheese (grated)
½ tsp	- Ginger garlic paste
200 gm	- Lamb mince
To taste	- Salt
½ tsp	- Red chilli paste
1 tsp	- Kasoori methi powder
½ tsp	- Garam masala
½ tsp	- Ginger (chopped)
1 tsp	- Green coriander (chopped)
1 tsp	- Green chilli (chopped)
3 tsp	- Mint (chopped)
For basting	- Clarified butter

METHOD

1. Mash processed cheese in a deep tray, add ginger garilc paste, lamb mince and remaining ingredients in the order listed and mix well. Keep aside for at least half an hour.
2. Divide the mixture into 4 equal parts and make balls.

Cooking

3. Take a skewer and apply each ball on to the skewer using a wet hand along the length of the skewer in cylindrical shape, an inch apart making each kebab 4 inches long.
4. Roast in a moderately hot tandoor or over a charcoal grill for 6-7 minutes.
5. Baste with clarified butter and further cook for 2 – 3 minutes.
6. Transfer on to a plate and serve hot with choice of a salad and chutney.

Lagan Ke Gosht Kebab

A DELICACY OF LAMB NAPPED IN A RICH MASALA AND COOKED ON DUM IN A SPECIAL POT

Cooking time 24-26 minutes Serves 1-2

INGREDIENTS

225-250 gm (6 pcs) - Boneless lamb boti

First Marination

2 tsp	- Raw papaya paste
To taste	- Salt
½ tsp	- Ginger garlic paste
4 tbsp	- Hung curd
½ tsp	- Ginger garlic paste

Second Marination

2 tbsp	- Hung curd
3 tsp	- Paste (Nariyal, chironji, khus khus, Badam)
½ tsp	- Yellow chilli powder
To taste	- Salt
A pinch	- Turmeric powder
A pinch	- Dalchini powder
A pinch	- Elaichi powder
3 tsp	- Brown onion paste
2 tsp	- Lemon juice
2 tsp	- Mustard oil
A pinch	- Saffron
1tsp	- Green coriander (chopped)

METHOD

1. Cut, clean and wash lamb boti, pat dry and keep aside.

First Marination

2. In a bowl mix papaya paste, salt, ginger garlic paste, apply this to lamb, rub well and keep aside for at least 1 hour.

Second Marination

3. In a bowl whisk hung curd, add paste and all other remaining ingredients listed above except green coriander and mix well.
4. Put the marinated lamb boti into this mixture, coat well and keep aside for at least 1 ½ hours.

Cooking

5. Put mustard oil into the lagan, add the lamb pieces, sprinkle saffron, apply a little water/stock and keep it on tandoor for slow cooking. Cover for 20-25 minutes.
6. Keep stirring in between.
7. When the lamb is tender, masala is cooked and oil floats on top, add chopped coriander and lime juice.
8. Serve hot with choice of a salad and chutney.

Dhania Wali Tandoori Champen

LAMB CHOPS WITH A DIFFERENCE DONE TO PERFECTION IN CLAY OVEN WITH FRESH CORIANDER

Cooking time 15-16 minutes Serves 1-2

INGREDIENTS

400-450 gm (5 pcs) - Lamb chops

First Marination
To taste	- Salt
½ tsp	- Ginger garlic paste
2 tsp	- Raw papaya paste
2 tsp	- Lemon juice
½ tsp	- Yellow chilli powder

Second Marination
4 tbsp	- Hung curd
To taste	- Salt
½ tsp	- Ginger garlic paste
1 tsp	- Lemon juice
½ tsp	- Yellow chilli powder
1 tsp	- Whole coriander (crushed)
1 tsp	- Ginger (julienne)
A pinch	- Turmeric powder
1 tsp	- Coriander powder
1/3 tsp	- Garam masala
2 tsp	- Refined oil

For basting - Clarified butter

METHOD

1. Cut, clean and wash lamb chops, make incisions/marks with a knife, pat dry and keep aside.

First Marination

2. In a bowl mix salt, ginger garlic paste, raw papaya paste, lemon juice, yellow chilli powder, apply this to lamb chops and keep aside for at least 1 hour.

Second Marination

3. In a bowl whisk hung curd, add all the remaining ingredients listed above and mix well.
4. Squeeze excess of moisture from the chops and put them into the marinade, coat well and keep aside for at least 2 hours.

Cooking

5. In a skewer, skew marinated chops one by one leaving a gap of an inch. Roast in a moderately hot tandoor for about 10-12 minutes.
6. Remove and hang so that excess moisture drains out completely (2 minutes)
7. Baste with clarified butter and further roast for 2-3 minutes or till tender.
8. Serve hot along with choice of a salad and chutney.

Bhyankar Tandoori Champen

ABSOLUTELY HOT AND SPICY LAMB CHOPS WITH POUNDED RED CHILLI IN ABUNDANCE AND ROASTED IN CLAY OVEN

Cooking time 15-16 minutes Serves 1-2

INGREDIENTS

400-450 gm (5 pcs) - Lamb chops

First Marination
To taste	- Salt
½ tsp	- Ginger garlic paste
2 tsp	- Raw papaya paste
1 tsp	- Red chilli paste

Second Marination
4 tbsp	- Hung curd
To taste	- Salt
½ tsp	- Ginger garlic paste
1 tsp	- Red chilli paste
½ tsp	- Garam masala
1/3 tsp	- Kasoori methi powder
2 tsp	- Lemon juice
1 tsp	- Kutti red chilli
2 tsp	- Refined oil

For basting - Clarified butter

METHOD

1. Cut, clean and wash lamb chops, make incisions/marks with a knike, pat dry and keep aside.

First Marination

2. In a bowl mix salt, ginger garlic paste, raw papaya paste, red chilli paste, apply this to chops, rub well and keep aside for at least 1 hours.

Second Marination

3. In a bowl whisk hung curd and add all the remaining ingredients listed above, mix well.
4. Remove extra moisture from chops and dip in the above marinade, coat well and keep aside for at least 2 hours.

Cooking

5. In a skewer, skew marinated chops one by one leaving a gap of an inch. Roast in a moderately hot tandoor for about 10-12 minutes.
6. Remove and hang so that excess moisture drains out completely (2 minutes).
7. Baste with clarified butter and further roast for 2-3 minutes or till tender.
8. Serve hot along with choice of a salad and chutney.

Methi Seekh Kebab

A DELICACY OF LAMB MINCE AND FRESH FENUGREEK

Cooking time 8-10 minutes Serves 1-2

INGREDIENTS

2 tbsp	- Processed cheese (grated)
200 gm	- Lamb mince
To taste	- Salt
1/3 tsp	- Red chilli paste
1/3 tsp	- Ginger garlic paste
A pinch	- Kasoori methi powder
1/3 tsp	- Garam masala
1 tsp	- Green coriander (chopped)
4 tsp	- Fresh methi (chopped)
1 tsp	- Cream
For basting	- Clarified butter

METHOD

1. In a deep tray mash processed cheese, add lamb mince, and all the remaining ingredients listed above, mix well with the help of palm. Keep aside for at least half an hour.
2. Divide mince mixture into 4 equal parts and make balls.

Cooking

3. Spread this mixture on the skewer using a wet palm to press each ball along the length of the skewer in a cylindrical shape an inch apart and making each kebab 4 inches. long.
4. Roast in a moderate hot tandoor or over a charcoal grill for 6-7 minutes, baste with clarified butter and further roast for 2-3 minutes.
5. Transfer on to a plate and serve hot with choice of a salad and chutney.

Adrak Ke Panje

A RARE DELICACY OF LAMB CHOPS WITH EXTRA TOUCH OF GINGER

Cooking time 14-16 minutes Serves 1-2

INGREDIENTS

400-450 gm (5 pcs) - Lamb chops

First Marination

To taste	- Salt
½ tsp	- Ginger garlic paste
½ tsp	- Red chilli paste
2 tsp	- Raw papaya paste

Second Marination

4 tbsp	- Hung curd
To taste	- Salt
½ tsp	- Red chilli paste
1/3 tsp	- Kasoori methi powder
1/3 tsp	- Garam masala
2 tsp	- Lemon juice
1 tsp	- Ginger (chopped)
A pinch	- Turmeric powder
2 tsp	- Refined oil
For basting	- Clarified butter

METHOD

1. Wash lamb chops, make incision marks with a knife, pat dry and keep aside.

First Marination

2. In a bowl mix salt, ginger garlic paste, red chilli paste, raw papaya paste, apply this to mutton pieces, rub well and keep aside for at least 1 hour.

Second Marination

3. In a bowl whisk hung curd, add all the remaining ingredients in the order listed and mix well.
4. Remove excess moisture from the marinated chops and put them into this marinade, coat well and keep aside for at least 2 hours.

Cooking

5. Take a skewer and skew the marinated lamb chops along the bone so that it does not fall.
6. Roast it in a tandoor or grill over charcoal at a moderate temperature for 10-12 minutes.
7. Hang the skewer to let the excess moisture drain out completely for about 2 minutes.
8. Baste with clarified butter and further roast for 2-3 minutes or till tender.
9. Serve hot along with choice of a salad and chutney.

Hyderabadi Seekh Kebab

ANOTHER EXAMPLE OF LAMB MINCE KEBAB

Cooking time 8-10 minutes Serves 1-2

INGREDIENTS

25 gm	- Processed cheese (grated)
200 gm	- Lamb mince
To taste	- Salt
½ tsp	- Ginger garlic paste
1 tsp	- Red chilli paste
1 tsp	- Green coriander (chopped)
½ tsp	- Green chilli (chopped)
½ tsp	- Ginger (chopped)
1/3 tsp	- Kasoori methi powder
1/3 tsp	- Garam masala
1 tsp	- Mint (chopped)
½ tsp	- Crushed black pepper
For basting	- Clarified butter

METHOD

1. In a deep tray mash processed cheese, add lamb mince, add all the ingredients listed above, mix well with the help of your palm. Keep aside for at least half an hour.
2. Divide mince mixture into 4 equal portions and make balls.

Cooking

3. Spread this mixture on the skewer using a wet palm to press each ball along the length of the skewer in a cylindrical shape an inch apart. Make each kebab 4 inches long.
4. Roast in a moderate hot tandoor or over a charcoal grill for 6-7 minutes. Baste it with clarified butter and further roast for 2-3 minutes or till tender.
5. Transfer on to a plate and serve hot with choice of a salad and chutney

Champ-E- Charminar

A DELICACY OF SUCCULENT LAMB CHOPS MARINATED WITH SPICES FROM HYDERABAD AND ROASTED

Cooking time 14-16 minutes Serves 1-2

INGREDIENTS

400-450 gm (5 pcs) - Lamb chops

First Marination

To taste	- Salt
½ tsp	- Ginger garlic paste
1 tsp	- Red philli powder
4 tsp	- Raw papaya paste

Second Marination

4 tbsp	- Hung curd
½ tsp	- Ginger garlic paste
½ tsp	- Garam masala
A pinch	- Kasoori methi powder
To taste	- Salt
1 tsp	- Kutti red chilli
1 tsp	- Mustard oil
For basting	- Clarified butter

METHOD

1. Clean, cut and wash lamb chops, make incisions/marks with a knife, pat dry and keep aside.

First Marination

2. In a bowl mix salt, ginger garlic paste, red chilli powder, raw papaya, lemon juice and apply this to lamb chops, rub well and keep aside for at least 1 hour.

Second Marination

3. In a bowl whisk hung curd and add all the remaining ingredients listed above and mix well.
4. Remove excess moisture from lamb chops and put them into this marinade, coat well and keep aside for at least 2 hours.

Cooking

5. Take a skewer and skew the marinated chops one by one leaving a gap of an inch. Roast in a moderately hot tandoor or over a charcoal grill for 10-11 minutes.
6. Hang the skewer to let the excess moisture drain out (2 minutes)
7. Baste with clarified butter and roast for another 2-3 minutes.
8. Serve hot with choice of a salad and chutney.

Hussaini Seekh Kebab

RICH KEBAB MADE OF LAMB MINCE SOMEWHAT DIFFERENT IN AWADHI STYLE

Cooking time 8-10 minutes **Serves** 1-2

INGREDIENTS

2 tbsp	- Proccessed chesse (grated)
200 gm	- Lamb mince
½ tsp	- Ginger garlic paste
½ tsp	- Roast cumin seeds (freshly)
½ tsp	- Whole coriander (crushed)
To taste	- Salt
1/3 tsp	- Black pepper (ground)
1 tsp	- Lemon juice
½ tsp	- Green chilli (chopped)
½ tsp	- Red chilli powder
1 tsp	- Green corriander (chopped)

For basting - Clarified butter

Toppings

1 tsp	- Butter (melted)
2 tbsp	- Cream
2 tbsp	- cashewnut (broken)

METHOD

1. In a deep tray mash processed cheese, add lamb mince, rub well, add the remaining ingredients and mix thoroughly and keep aside for at least one hour.
2. Divide the mixture into 4 equal portions and make balls.

Cooking

3. Spread this mixture on the skewer using a wet hand to press each ball along the length of the skewer in a cylindrical shape, 1 inch apart and making each kebab 4 inch long.
4. Roast in moderately hot tandoor or over charcoal grill for 6-7 minutes.
5. Baste with clarified butter and further roast for 2-3 minutes.
6. Remove from skewer, cut seekh kebab each into 3 or 4 piece and arrange on a serving platter.
7. Heat oil, fry chopped cashewnut for a while, add cream, salt and pour this creamy mixture on top of seekh kebab. Serve hot.

Raan-E- Patialashahi

A CLASSIC CULINARY TRIBUTE TO GREAT CITY OF PATIALA, IS A LEG OF LAMB WITH EXQUISITE MARINATION

Cooking time 1hour-1: 10 minutes **Serves** 1-2

INGREDIENTS

800-900 gm (1 no) - Leg of baby lamb

First Marination

3 tbsp	- Raw papaya paste
1 tsp	- Red chilli paste
4 no	- Black pepper
1 tsp	- Ginger garlic paste
½ no	- Nutmeg (grated)
2 no	- Cloves (crushed)
2 no	- Black cardamom (crushed)
2 no	- Green cardamom (crushed)
To taste	- Salt

Second Marination

1 cup	- Hung curd
1 tsp	- Ginger garlic paste
1 tsp	- Red chilli paste
½ tsp	- Turmeric powder
2 tbsp	- Lemon juice
¼ cup	- Refined oil
½ tsp	- Garam masala
1/3 tsp	- Kasoori methi powder

For basting - Clarified butter

METHOD

1. Clean and remove the blade bone of the leg, make incisions on both sides of the leg, wash, pat dry and keep aside.

First Marination

2. In a bowl mix raw papaya paste, red chilli paste, black pepper, ginger garlic paste, green cardamom, clove, nutmeg, black cardamom, salt, apply this to lamb leg, rub well and keep aside for at least 1-2 hours.

Second Marination

3. Whisk hung curd in a bowl and put the remaining ingredients in the order listed, mix well. Remove extra moisture from the marinated raan and put it in this marinade. Coat well and keep aside for at least 2-3 hours.

Cooking

4. Take a thick-bottomed pan tray and place the lamb leg along with entire marinade.
5. In a preheated oven (180°C), roast lamb leg till ¾ cooked (one hour) and remove.
6. Cut lamb leg into 3-4 pieces along the bone.
7. Take a skewer and skew cut lamb leg pieces and further roast in a moderately hot tandoor for 6-8 minutes.
8. Baste with clarified butter and further roast for 3-4 minutes or till tender.
9. Cut dices/cubes as desired, arrange on a platter and serve hot along with choice of a salad and chutney.

Keema Goli Kebab

JUICY LAMB DUMPLINGS INFUSED WITH CINNAMON

Cooking time 3-4 minutes Serves 1-2

INGREDIENTS

2 tbsp	- Processed cheese (grated)
200 gm	- Lamb mince
To taste	- Salt
½ tsp	- Ginger garlic paste
½ tsp	- Roasted jeera powder
A pinch	- Cinnamon powder
1 tsp	- Green coriander (chopped)
½ tsp	- Green chilli (chopped)
1 tsp	- Ginger (chopped)
½ tsp	- Red chilli paste

For cooking - Refined oil

METHOD

1. In a deep tray mash processed cheese, rub it well, add lamb mince and the remaining ingredients listed above, mix well with the help of your palm. Keep aside for at least 1 hour.
2. Divide mince mixture into 10-12 equal parts and make balls.

Cooking

3. Heat oil in a pan and place meat dumplings on it and cover with a lid and cook on slow heat for 3-4 minutes. Stir occasionally till it gets cooked to golden brown colour.
4. Serve hot with choice of a salad and chutney.

Nawabi Pasande

A LAMB PICATTA COOKED ON SLOW FIRE FROM THE KITCHEN'S OF ROYAL KINGS

Cooking time 14-16 minutes Serves 1-2

INGREDIENTS

200-225 gm (4 no) - Lamb chunk

First Marination

2 tsp	- Raw papaya paste
To taste	- Salt
½ tsp	- Red chilli paste
½ tsp	- Ginger garlic paste
4 tsp	- Fresh mint (chopped)

Second Marination

4 tbsp	- Hung curd
To taste	- Salt
2 tsp	- Cream
½ tsp	- Ginger garlic paste
2 tsp	- Cashew nut paste
1 tsp	- Cornflour
1 tsp	- Green chilli (chopped)
1 tsp	- Green coriander (chopped)
A pinch	- Shahi jeera

For Cooking - Refined oil

METHOD

1. Cut lamb chunk into slices 4 no of 50 gm each, wash, pat dry and keep aside.

First Marination

2. In a bowl mix raw papaya paste, salt, red chilli paste, ginger garlic paste, apply this to lamb pieces, rub well and keep aside for at least 1 hour.

Stuffing

3. Stuff chopped mint between lamb slices by making an incisions with a sharp knike.

Second Marination

4. In a bowl whisk hung curd, add all the ingredients listed above. Mix well.
5. Put marinated lamb pasanda into this marinade, coat well and keep aside for at least 2 hours.

Cooking

6. Heat oil in thick bottom pan, put marinated lamb pasanda and cook on slow fire for 14-15 minutes or till tender.
7. Serve hot with choice of a salad and chutney.

Kebab-E-Baluchistan

DELICIOUS LAMB KEBAB FROM THE CITY OF BALUCHISTAN

Cooking time 8-10 minutes **Serves** 1-2

INGREDIENTS

200 gm	- Lamb mince
As required	- Water
2-3tsp	- Makkai atta
To taste	- Salt
1tsp	- Green chilli (chopped)
40 gm	- Onion (roughly chopped)
1tsp	- Kutti red chilli
1tsp	- Crushed dhania whole
1/3tsp	- Soda sweet
For basting	- Clarified butter

METHOD

1. In a bowl, put lamb mince, add water to soften the mince, then add all the remaining ingredients listed in order, rub well with palm, keep aside for at least 1 hour.
2. Divide the mixture into 4 equal portions and make balls

Cooking

3. Spread this mixture on the skewer using wet hand, press each ball along the length of the skewer in a cylindrical shape.
4. Roast in moderately hot tandoor or over charcoal grill for 6-7 minutes.
5. Baste with clarified butter and further roast for 2-3 minutes or till tender.
6. Serve hot along with a choice of a salad and chutney

Shalimar Raan

A ROYAL PREPARATION OF BABY LAMB LEG PREPARED WITH CONDIMENTS AND HERBS

Cooking time 1hour-1: 10 minutes **Serves** 1-2

INGREDIENTS

800-900 gm (1no) - Leg of baby lamb

First Marination

3 tbsp	- Raw papaya paste
2 tsp	- Red chilli paste
2-3 no	- Black pepper
1 tsp	- Ginger garlic paste
½ no	- Grated nutmeg
2 no	- Cloves (crushed)
2 no	- Black cardamom (crushed)
2 no	- Green cardamom (crushed)
2 tsp	- Ginger garlic paste

Second Marination

4 tbsp	- Hung curd
30 ml	- Refined oil
1 tsp	- Garam masala
1 tsp	- Red chilli paste
3 tsp	- Mint leaves (chopped)
2 tsp	- Coriander leaves (chopped)
To taste	- Salt
½ tsp	- Kasoori methi powder
For basting	- Clarified butter

METHOD

1. Clean and remove the blade bone of the leg, making incisions on both sides, wash, pat dry and keep aside.

First Marination

2. In a bowl mix raw papaya paste, red chilli paste, black pepper, ginger garlic paste, green cardamom, clove, nutmeg, black cardamom, apply this to raan, rub well and keep aside for 1-2 hours.

Second Marination

3. Whisk hung curd in a bowl and put the remaining ingredients in the order listed, mix well.
4. Remove extra moisture from the marinated raan and put it in this marinade. Coat well and keep aside for at least 2-3 hours.

Cooking

5. Take a thick bottomed pan tray and place the raan along with entire marinade.
6. In a preheated oven (180°C), roast raan till ¾ cooked (one hour) and remove.
7. Cut raan into 3-4 pieces along the bone.
8. Take a skewer and skew raan pieces and further roast in a moderately hot tandoor for 6-8 minutes.
9. Baste with clarified butter and further roast for 3-4 minutes or till tender.
10. Cut cubes of meat pieces, arrange on a platter and serve hot along with choice of a salad and chutney.

Gosht Elaichi Pasanda

CARDAMOM FLAVOURED LAMB PICATTA COOKED IN LUCKNOWI STYLE

Cooking time 10-12 minutes Serves 1-2

INGREDIENTS

225-250 gm (1 no) - Lamb chunk

First Marination
2 tsp	- Raw papaya paste
To taste	- Salt
½ tsp	- Red chilli paste
½ tsp	- Ginger garlic paste
1/3 tsp	- Elaichi powder

Second Marination
3 tsp	- Processed cheese (grated)
½ tsp	- Ginger garlic paste
4 tsp	- Cream
1/3 tsp	- White pepper powder
To taste	- Salt
3 tbsp	- Hung curd
½ tsp	- Green chilli (chopped)
1 tsp	- Fresh coriander (chopped)
1 tsp	- Cashewnut paste
½ tsp	- Elaichi powder
1 tsp	- Cornflour

For basting - Clarified butter

METHOD

1. Cut lamb chunk into thick slices 4 no of 50 gm each, pat dry and keep aside.

First Marination
2. In a bowl mix raw papaya paste, salt, red chilli paste, ginger garlic paste, elaichi powder, apply this to lamb pieces, rub well and keep aside for at least 1 hour.

Second Marination
3. In a deep tray, take grated cheese, mash it with the palm, add all the ingredients listed above and mix well till smooth.
4. Put marinated lamb pieces, add ½ tsp of elaichi powder on top with this above marinade, coat well and keep aside for at least 1 hour.

Cooking
5. Take a skewer, skew marinated lamb one by one. Roast in a moderately hot tandoor or over a charcoal grill for 8-9 minutes.
6. Remove and baste with clarified butter and roast for another 2-3 minutes.
7. Serve hot with choice of a salad and chutney or till tender.

Lahsuni Burra Kebab

SUCCULENT KEBAB OF LAMB SHANKS COOKED TO PERFECTION WITH GARLIC IN ABUNDANCE

Cooking time 15-16 minutes Serves 1-2

INGREDIENTS

400-425 gm - Lamb shanks (from leg 4 pcs.)

First Marination
½ tsp	- Garlic paste
2 tsp	- Raw papaya paste
1/3 tsp	- Red chilli powder
To taste	- Salt

Second Marination
4 tbsp	- Hung curd
To taste	- Salt
½ tsp	- Garlic paste
½ tsp	- Red chilli powder
2 tsp	- Lemon juice
½ tsp	- Garam masala
A pinch	- Kasoori methi powder
2 tsp	- Fresh mint (chapped)
1 tsp	- Fresh garlic (chopped)
1 tsp	- Refined oil

For basting - Clarified butter

METHOD

1. Trim, wash and pat dry lamb shanks and keep aside.

First Marination
2. In a bowl mix garlic paste, raw papaya paste, red chilli powder, salt, apply this to lamb shanks, rub well and keep aside for at least 1 hour.

Second Marination
3. In a bowl whisk hung curd and add all the remaining ingredients listed above. Mix well. Put lamb shanks into this marinade, coat well and keep aside for at least 1 ½ hours.

Cooking
4. Take a skewer, skew marinated lamb one by one. Roast in a moderately hot tandoor or over a charcoal grill for 10-12 minutes.
5. Remove and hang so that the excess moisture drains out (1-2 minutes).
6. Baste with clarified butter and roast for another 2-3 minutes or till tender.
7. Serve hot with choice of a salad and chutney.

Majedar Tandoori Champen

AN EXOTIC AND COLOURFUL LAMB CHOPS ROASTED IN CLAY OVEN

Cooking time 14-16 minutes Serves 1-2

INGREDIENTS

400-450 gm (5 pcs.) - Lamb chops

First Marination
To taste	- Salt
½ tsp	- Ginger garlic paste
½ tsp	- Red chilli paste
2 tsp	- Raw papaya paste

Second Marination
3 tbsp	- Hung curd
To taste	- Salt
½ tsp	- Ginger garlic paste
½ tsp	- Red chilli paste
2 tsp	- Methi (chopped)
1/3 tsp	- Garam masala
1/3 tsp	- Kasoori methi powder
A pinch	- Elaichi powder
A pinch	- Shahi jeera

For basting - Clarified butter

METHOD

1. Clean, cut and wash lamb chop, make incisions/marks with a knife, pat dry and keep aside.

First Marination

2. In a bowl mix salt, ginger garlic paste, red chilli powder, raw papaya paste and apply this to lamb chops, rub well and keep aside for at least 1 hour.

Second Marination

3. In a bowl whisk hung curd and add all the ingredients listed and mix well, put marinated chops into this marinade, coat well and keep aside for at least 1 hour.

Cooking

4. In a skewer leaving a gap of an inch skew the marinated chops one by one. Roast in a moderately hot tandoor or over a charcoal grill for 10-12 minutes.
5. Remove and hang so that the excess moisture drains out (1-2 minutes).
6. Baste with clarified butter and roast for another 3-4 minutes.
7. Serve hot with choice of a salad and chutney.

Gosht Puddina Champen

A DELICACY OF FRESH MINT FLAVOURED LAMB CHOPS

Cooking time 14-16 minutes Serves 1-2

INGREDIENTS

400-450 gm (5 no) - Lamb chops

First Marination
To taste	- Salt
½ tsp	- Ginger garlic paste
½ tsp	- Green chilli paste
2 tsp	- Raw papaya paste
4 tsp	- Green paste

Second Marination
3 tbsp	- Hung curd
To taste	- Salt
½ tsp	- Ginger garlic paste
½ tsp	- Green chilli paste
1 tsp	- Fresh mint (chopped)
1/3 tsp	- Garam masala
2 tsp	- Lemon juice
1 tsp	- Green chilli (chopped)
1/3 tsp	- Kasoori methi powder

For basting - Clarified butter

METHOD

1. Clean, cut and wash lamb chops. Make incisions/marks with a knife, pat dry and keep aside.

First Marination

2. In a bowl mix salt, ginger garlic paste, green chilli paste, raw papaya, apply this to lamb chops, rub well and keep aside for at least 1 hour.

Second Marination

3. In a bowl whisk hung curd and add all the ingredients listed and mix well, put lamb chops into this marinade, coat well and keep aside for at least 1 hour.

Cooking

4. In a skewer leaving a gap of an inch skew the marinated chops one by one. Roast in a moderately hot tandoor or over a charcoal grill for 10-12 minutes.
5. Remove and hang so that the excess moisture drains out (1-2 minutes)
6. Baste with clarified butter and roast for another 2-3 minutes or till tender.
7. Serve hot with choice of a salad and chutney.

Kabuli Gosht Tikka

ANOTHER FANTASY OF LAMB KEBAB FROM THE CITY OF KABUL

Cooking time 10-12 minutes Serves 1-2

INGREDIENTS

225-250 gm (6 pcs) - Lamb boneless cubes (40 gm)

First Marination
3 tsp	- Raw papaya paste
½ tsp	- Ginger garlic paste
To taste	- Salt
1 tsp	- Lemon juice

Second Marination
2 tsp	- Processed cheese (grated)
½ tsp	- Ginger garlic paste
½ tsp	- Red chilli paste
2 tsp	- Cream
To taste	- Salt
4 tbsp	- Hung curd
½ tsp	- Kalonji and saunf powder
2 tsp	- Mustard oil

For basting - Clarified butter

METHOD

1. Clean, wash, pat dry lamb pieces and keep aside.

First Marination

2. In a bowl mix ginger garlic paste, lemon juice, salt, raw papaya paste and apply this to lamb pieces, rub well and keep aside for at least one hour.

Second Marination

3. In a bowl, mash grated cheese, hung curd and add all the remaining ingredients in the order listed, mix well.
4. Remove excess moisture from the marinated lamb pieces and put them in the above marinade, coat well and keep aside for at least 2-3 hours.

Cooking

5. Take a skewer and skew the marinated pieces an inch apart along the skewer.
6. Roast in a charcoal grill at a moderate temperature for 8-9 minutes.
7. Baste with clarified butter and further roast for 2-3 minutes or till tender.
8. Serve hot with choice of a salad and chutney.

Raan-E-Gulistan

THIS MAGNIFICENT KEBAB IS PREPARED WITH LAMB SHANKS (NALLI) ENCLOSED WITH LAMB MINCE AND ROASTED

Cooking time 1-1: 10 minutes Serves 1–2

INGREDIENTS

(250-275 gm) 2 no - Lamb shanks (from leg 4"-5"leg bone)

Marination
½ tsp	- Ginger garlic paste
½ tsp	- Red chilli paste
To taste	- Salt
As required	- Water
2 no	- Small cardamom
2 no	- Big cardamom
1 no	- Bayleaf
3 no	- Clove
1 stick	- Cinnamon
4no	- Black pepper corn
A pinch	- Nutmeg powder
2 tbsp	- Refined oil
To taste	- Salt

The Mince
100 gm	- Lamb mince
3 tsp	- Processed cheese (grated)
½ tsp	- Ginger garlic paste
1/3tsp	- Red chilli paste
½ tsp	- Green chilli (chopped)
1 tsp	- Fresh coriander (chopped)
1 tsp	- Mint (chopped)
½ tsp	- Garam masala
To taste	- Salt

For basting - Clarified butter

METHOD

1. Clean, wash lamb shanks, pat dry and keep aside.

Marination

2. In a bowl take ginger garlic paste, red chilli paste, salt, mix well and apply this to lamb shanks, rub well and keep aside for at least 1 hour.
3. In thick bottomed pan place mutton shanks, crushed small cardamom, big cardamom, bayleaf, cinnamon, cloves, black pepper corn, nutmeg powder, salt, oil, cover with enough water.
4. In a preheated oven, braise lamb shanks till cooked for at least 1 hour. Remove and discard liquid.

The Mince

5. In a deep tray, mash processed cheese, add ginger garlic paste, lamb mince, all other ingredients listed above and mix well to smooth consistency and keep aside for 1 hour.
6. Divide the mixture into two equal parts and make balls.

Cooking

7. Using a wet palm spread the mixture to cover the lamb shanks, pressing firmly to make a drumstick shape, keep to refrigerate for half an hour.
8. Take a skewer and skew each piece placing from bottom to top.
9. Roast in a tandoor or over a charcoal grill at a moderate temperature for at least 5-6 minutes, baste with clarified butter and further roast for 2-3 minutes or till tender.
10. Serve hot with choice of a salad and chutney.

Lamb Kufta Kebab

ANOTHER VARIATION OF LAMB MINCE KEBAB PREPARED IN ARABIC STYLE

Cooking time 3-4 minutes Serves 1-2

INGREDIENTS

200 gm	- Lamb mince
To taste	- Salt
1 tsp	- Onion (chopped)
½ tsp	- Garlic (chopped)
1 tsp	- Fresh coriander (chopped)
1 tsp	- Whole coriander (crushed)
1 tsp	- Red chilli paste
1 tsp	- Roasted channa powder
1 tsp	- Olive oil
3 tsp	- Pine nuts (chopped)

For frying - Refined oil

METHOD

1. In a bowl put lamb mince, add salt, chopped onions, garlic, fresh coriander (chopped) whole coriander crushed, red chilli paste, roasted channa and olive oil, mix it well and keep aside for at least half an hour.
2. Divide the mixture into 5-6 equal parts.
3. Apply oil on your palm and roll each ball in round shape.
4. Press each ball between your palms and stuff it with pine nuts and make a medallion (tikki) shape.

Cooking

5. Heat oil in a non-stick pan, place kebab and shallow fry till golden brown on both sides.
6. Serve hot with choice of a salad and chutney.

Turkish Boti Kebab

AN ADAPTATION OF TURKISH KEBAB INFUSED WITH INDIAN SPICES

Cooking time 10-12 minutes Serves 1-2

INGREDIENTS

225-250 gm (6 pcs) Lamb boneles cubes (40 gm)

First Marination
To taste	- Salt
½ tsp	- Ginger garlic paste
1/3 tsp	- Red chilli powder
3 tsp	- Raw papaya paste

Second Marination
5 tbsp	- Hung curd
To taste	- Salt
2 tsp	- Lemon juice
1/3 tsp	- Red chilli powder
½ tsp	- Black pepper crushed
2 tsp	- Refined oil
1 tsp	- Ginger (chopped)
1 tsp	- Onion paste

For basting - Clarified butter

METHOD

1. Clean, wash and pat dry lamb pieces.

First Marination
2. In a bowl mix salt, ginger garlic paste, red chilli powder, raw papaya paste and apply this to lamb boti, rub well and keep aside for at least 2 hours.

Second Marination
3. In a bowl whisk hung curd and add all the remaining ingredients in the order listed. Mix well.
4. Remove excess moisture from the marinated lamb pieces and put them in the above marinade, coat well and keep aside for at least 2-3 hours.

Cooking
5. Take a skewer and skew marinated pieces one inch apart along the skewer.
6. Roast in a charcoal grill at a moderate temperature for 8 – 9 minutes.
7. Baste with clarified butter and further roast for 2-3 minutes or till tender.
8. Serve hot with choice of a salad and chutney.

Chatpate Narial Gosht Ke Tikke

SUCCULENT LAMB MORSELS FLAVOURED WITH ORIENTAL SPICES

Cooking time 12-15 minutes Serves 1-2

INGREDIENTS

225-250 gm (6pcs) - Lamb boti (boneless)

1 tsp	- Raw papaya paste
1 tsp	- Onion (chopped)
1 tsp	- Garlic (chopped)
1 tsp	- Ginger (chopped)
1 tsp	- Tamarind paste
2 tbsp	- Coconut milk
1 tsp	- Soya sauce
1 tsp	- Brown sugar
½ tsp	- Crushed black pepper
To taste	- Salt

For basting - Clarified butter

METHOD

1. Clean, wash lamb cubes, pat dry and keep aside.

Marination
2. In a bowl combine all the ingredients listed above, put lamb cubes in this marinade, mix well and keep aside for 3-4 hours.

Cooking
3. Take a skewer, skew marinated lamb one by one. Roast in a moderately hot tandoor or over a charcoal grill for 10-12 minutes.
4. Baste with clarified butter and roast for another 3-4 minutes or till tender.
5. Serve hot with choice of a salad and chutney.

Tandoori Raseeli Botian

AN ABSOLUTELY JUICY AND EXOTIC KEBAB MADE WITH LAMB MORSELS, ROASTED IN CLAY OVEN

Cooking time 12-14 minutes Serves 1-2

INGREDIENTS

(220-250 gm) 6 pcs - Lamb cubes

First Marination
1 tbsp	- Raw papaya paste
1/3 tsp	- Kashmiri red chilli powder
½ tsp	- Ginger garlic paste
1 tsp	- Malt vinegar
To taste	- Salt

Second Marination
2 tbsp	- Hung curd
1 tbsp	- Cream
1/3 tsp	- Garam masala
1 tsp	- Mustard oil
½ tsp	- Jeera powder
To taste	- Salt

For basting - Clarified butter

METHOD

1. Wash and pat dry lamb cubes.

First Marination

2. In a bowl mix, raw papaya paste, Kashmiri red chilli powder, ginger garlic paste, malt vinegar and salt. Apply this to lamb cubes and mix, rub well and keep aside for at least 1-2 hours.

Second Marination

3. In a bowl whisk hung curd add all the remaining ingredients in the order listed, mix well.
4. Put lamb cubes into this marinade, coat well and keep aside for at least 2 hours.

Cooking

5. Take a skewer and skew marinated lamb pieces an inch apart along the skewer.
6. Roast in a tandoor or over a charcoal grill at a moderate temperature for 12-14 minutes, baste with clarified butter during cooking.
7. Serve hot with choice of a salad and chutney.

Gosht Puddina Champen

SUCCULENT LAMB CHOPS WITH FRESH MINT IN ABUNDANCE

Cooking time 14-16 minutes Serves 1-2

INGREDIENTS

400-450 gm (5 pcs) - Lamb chops

First Marination
To taste	- Salt
½ tsp	- Ginger garlic paste
2 tsp	- Raw papaya paste
2 tsp	- Lemon juice

Green Paste
50 gm	- Fresh mint leaves
25 gm	- Fresh coriander leaves
3 no	- Green chilli
5 no	- Curry leaves

Second Marination
4 tbsp	- Hung curd
1 tbsp	- Cream
1 tbsp	- Cashewnut paste
To taste	- Salt
½ tsp	- Yellow chilli powder
½ tsp	- Garam masala
1 tsp	- Lemon juice
2 tsp	- Refined oil

For basting - Clarified butter

METHOD

1. Cut, clean, wash lamb chops, make incisions/marks with a knife, pat dry and keep aside.

First Marination

2. In a bowl mix salt, ginger garlic paste, raw papaya paste, lemon juice, apply this to lamb chops and keep aside for at least 1 hour.

Green Paste

3. In a food processor, grind mint leaves, coriander leaves, green chilli, curry leaves to a smooth paste.

Second Marination

4. In a bowl whisk hung curd, add all the remaining ingredients listed above, add green paste and mix well.
5. Squeeze excess of moisture from the chops and put them into this marinade, coat well and keep aside for at least 2 hours.

Cooking

6. In a skewer, skew marinated chops one by one leaving a gap of an inch. Roast in a moderately hot tandoor for about 10-12 minutes.
7. Remove and hang so that excess moisture drains out completely (2 minutes).
8. Baste with clarified butter and further roast for 2-3 minutes or till tender.
9. Serve hot along with choice of a salad and chutney.

Kebab-e-Mehfil

JUICY LAMB MINCE KEBAB ENHANCED WITH DIFFERENT INGREDIENTS BEST AS A COCKTAIL SNACK

Cooking time 3-4 minutes Serves 1-2

INGREDIENTS

200 gm	- Lamb mince
1/3 tsp	- White jeera (cumin seeds)
To taste	- Salt
½ tsp	- Green chilli (chopped)
1 tsp	- Coriander green (chopped)
½ tsp	- Ginger garlic paste
1 tsp	- Red chilli powder
A pinch	- Turmeric powder
1 tsp	- Corn flour
1 no	- Egg white
For frying	- Refined oil

METHOD

1. Put lamb mince in a deep tray, add all the ingredients in the order listed, mix well and keep aside for at least 1 hour.
2. Divide the mixture into 4-5 equal portions and make balls and flatten it to a medallion (tikki) shape between your palms.

Cooking

3. Heat oil in a pan and place lamb patties and cover it for 3-4 minutes, turning occasionally till it gets cooked to a golden brown colour on both sides.
4. Serve hot with choice of a salad and chutney.

Sunheri Tandoori Anda

AN IMPRESSIVE AND ELEGANT KEBAB MADE OF BOILED EGG AND LAMB MINCE THE GOLDEN WAY

Cooking time 8-10 minutes Serves 1–2

INGREDIENTS

2 no	- Eggs (hard boiled)
200 gm	- Lamb mince
½ tsp	- Ginger garlic paste
2 tbsp	- Processed cheese (grated)
1 tsp	- Roasted channa powder
1 tsp	- Onion (chopped)
½ tsp	- Ginger (chopped)
½ tsp	- Green chilli (chopped)
1 tsp	- Fresh coriander (chopped)
To taste	- Salt
½ tsp	- Kashmiri red chilli powder
½ tsp	- Garam masala
1 tsp	- Gram flour (roasted)
2 tsp	- Cornflour
For basting	- Clarified butter
½ tsp	- Chaat masala

METHOD

1. Shell hard boil eggs, and keep aside.
2. In a bowl take lamb mince, add the remaining ingredients in the order listed, rub well and keep aside for 1 hour.
3. Divide this into 2 equal portions and make balls.
4. Flatten each ball on a wet palm. Placed a boiled egg on the flattened mince and cover it with mince. Seal, shape it with a moist/oily hand and keep it in a freezer for at least 2 hours.

Cooking

5. Take a skewer and skew each egg one inch apart. Roast in a moderate hot tandoor or over grill for 8 – 10 minutes.
6. Baste with clarified butter. Remove and cut each egg into half. Sprinkle chaat masala.
7. Serve hot with choice of a salad and chutney.

Sunheri Boti Kebab

ANOTHER VARIATION OF LAMB CHUNKS SPICED WITH CRUSHED BLACK PEPPER CORN AND SPECIAL BLEND OF SPICES

Cooking time 10-12 minutes Serves 1-2

INGREDIENTS

225-250 gm (6 pcs) - Lamb boneless cubes (40 gm each)

First Marination
To taste	- Salt
½ tsp	- Ginger garlic paste
½ tsp	- Red chilli powder
2 tsp	- Raw papaya

Second Marination
3 tbsp	- Hung curd
To taste	- Salt
½ tsp	- Ginger garlic paste
1 tsp	- Garlic (chopped)
½ tsp	- Red chilli powder
½ tsp	- Crushed black pepper
1 nop	- Egg
1 tsp	- Green chilli (chopped)
1/3 tsp	- Garam masala
A pinch	- Turmeric powder

For basting - Clarified butter

METHOD

1. Trim, wash, pat dry lamb pieces and keep aside.

First Marination

2. In a bowl mix salt, ginger garlic paste, red chilli powder, raw papaya paste and apply this to lamb pieces, rub well and keep aside for at least 1 hour.

Second Marination

3. In a bowl whisk hung curd, add all the remaining ingredients listed above. Mix well.
4. Squeeze extra moisture from marinated lamb pieces and put them into this marinade, coat well and keep aside for at least 2-3 hours.

Cooking

5. Take a skewer and skew marinated pieces one by one an inch apart along the skewer.
6. Roast in a tandoor or over a charcoal grill at a moderate temperature for 8-9 minutes.
7. Baste with clarified butter and further roast for 2-3 minutes or till tender.
8. Serve hot along with choice of a salad and chutney.

Lahori Seekh Kebab

YET ANOTHER EXAMPLE OF LAMB KEBAB PREPARED IN TRUE LAHORI WAY

Cooking time 8-10 minutes Serves 1-2

INGREDIENTS

200 gm	- Lamb mince
As required	- Water
10-15 gm	- Makkai atta
To taste	- Salt
1 tsp	- Green chilli chopped
4 tsp	- Onion (roughly chopped)
1 tsp	- Green coriander (chopped)
1tsp	- Kutti red chilli
1tsp	- Jeera whole
2 tsp	- Crushed dhania whole
1/3tsp	- Soda sweet

For basting - Clarified butter

METHOD

1. In a deep bowl, take lamb mince, put water to soften the mince, then add all the remaining ingredients, rub with your palm, keep aside for at least 1 hour.
2. Divide the mixture into 4 equal portions and make balls

Cooking

3. Spread this mixture on the skewer using wet hand, press each ball along the length of the skewer in a cylindrical shape.
4. Roast in moderately hot tandoor or over charcoal grill for 6-7 minutes.
5. Baste with clarified butter and further roast for 2-3 minutes or till tender.
6. Serve hot along with a choice of a salad and chutney.

Lajawab Gosht Ke Tikke

SUCCULENT EXOTIC LAMB MORSELS INFUSED WITH DRIED FENUGREEK AND HOMEGROUND SPICES, ROASTED IN CLAY OVEN

Cooking time 10-12 minutes Serves 1-2

INGREDIENTS

225-250 (6 pcs) - Lamb boneless (40 gm) each

First Marination
To taste	- Salt
½ tsp	- Ginger garlic paste
½ tsp	- Red chilli paste
2 tsp	- Raw papaya paste
1/3 tsp	- Garam masala

Second Marination
3 tbsp	- Hung curd
½ tsp	- Ginger garlic paste
To taste	- Salt
1/3 tsp	- Kasoori methi powder
1/3 tsp	- Garam masala
2 tsp	- Lemon juice

For basting - Clarified butter

METHOD

1. Trim, wash, pat dry lamb pieces and keep aside.

First Marination

2. In a bowl mix salt, ginger garlic paste, red chilli paste, raw papaya paste, garam masala and apply this to lamb pieces, rub well and keep aside for at least 1 hour.

Second Marination

3. In a bowl whisk hung curd, add all the remaining ingredients listed above. Mix well.
4. Squeeze extra moisture from marinated lamb pieces and put them into this marinade, coat well and keep aside for at least 2-3 hours.

Cooking

5. Take a skewer and skew marinated pieces one by one an inch apart along the skewer
6. Roast in a tandoor or over a charcoal grill at a moderate temperature for 8-9 minutes.
7. Baste with clarified butter and further roast for 2-3 minutes or till tender.
8. Serve hot along with choice of a salad and chutney.

Lajawab Methi Tikka

AS WITH ALMOST EVERY DELICACY LAMB GOES WELL WITH FRESH FENUGREEK

Cooking time 10-12 minutes Serves 1-2

INGREDIENTS

225-250 gm (6 pcs) Lamb boneless cubes (40 gm)

First Marination
To taste	- Salt
½ tsp	- Ginger garlic paste
3 tsp	- Raw papaya paste
½ tsp	- Red chilli paste

Second Marination
4 tbsp	- Hung curd
To taste	- Salt
½ tsp	- Ginger garlic paste
A pinch	- Kasoori methi powder
1/3 tsp	- Garam masala
1 tsp	- Lemon juice
3 tsp	- Methi (chopped)
1 tsp	- Kutti red chilli
2 tsp	- Mustard oil

For basting - Clarified butter

METHOD

1. Clean, wash and pat dry lamb pieces.

First Marination

2. In a bowl mix salt, ginger garlic paste, red chilli paste, raw papaya juice and apply this to lamb boti, rub well and keep aside for at least one hour.

Second Marination

3. In a bowl whisk hung curd, add the remaining ingredients in the order listed and mix well.
4. Remove excess moisture from the marinated lamb pieces and put them in the above marinade, coat well and keep aside for at least 2-3 hours.

Cooking

1. Take a skewer and skew marinated pieces one inch apart along the skewer.
2. Roast in a charcoal grill at a moderate temperature for 8-9 minutes.
3. Baste with clarified butter and further roast for 2-3 minutes or till tender.
4. Serve hot with choice of a salad and chutney.

Kasoori Gosht Tikka

THE TENDER LAMB KEBAB MADE FROM LAMB CHUNKS INFUSED WITH DRY FENUGREEK POWDER

Cooking time 10-12 minutes Serves 1-2

INGREDIENTS

225-250 gm (6 pcs) - Lamb boneless cubes (40 gm each)

First Marination
To taste	- Salt
½ tsp	- Ginger garlic paste
½ tsp	- Red chilli powder
2 tsp	- Raw papaya paste

Second Marination
3 tbsp	- Hung curd
To taste	- Salt
½ tsp	- Ginger garlic paste
1 tsp	- Kasoori methi powder
2 tsp	- Lemon juice
½ tsp	- Coriander powder
A pinch	- Saffron
For basting	- Clarified butter

METHOD

1. Trim, wash, pat dry lamb pieces and keep aside.

First Marination

2. In a bowl mix salt, ginger garlic paste, red chilli powder, raw papaya paste and apply this to lamb pieces, rub well and keep aside for at least 1 hour.

Second Marination

3. In a bowl whisk hung curd, add all the remaining ingredients listed above. Mix well.
4. Squeeze extra moisture from marinated lamb pieces and put them into this marinade, coat well and keep aside for at least 2-3 hours.

Cooking

5. Take a skewer and skew marinated pieces one by one an inch apart along the skewer.
6. Roast in a tandoor or over a charcoal grill at a moderate temperature for 8-9 minutes.
7. Baste with clarified butter and further roast for 2-3 minutes or till tender.
8. Serve hot along with choice of a salad and chutney.

Lamb Chilgoja Seekh

JUICY LAMB MINCE & PINENUTS KEBAB

Cooking time 8-10 minutes Serves 1-2

INGREDIENTS

2 tbsp	- Processed cheese (grated)
200 gm	- Lamb mince
2 tbsp	- Roasted peanuts (roasted and crushed)
½ tsp	- Red chilli paste
1 tsp	- Ginger garlic paste
½ tsp	- Green chilli (chopped)
1 tsp	- Green coriander (chopped)
½ tsp	- Garam masala
½ tsp	- Kasoori methi powder
To taste	- Salt
For basting	- Clarified butter

METHOD

1. In a deep tray, mash processed cheese, put lamb mince, add all the remaining ingredients in the order listed, rub well and keep aside for at least half an hour.
2. Divide the mixture into 4 equal portions and make balls.

Cooking

3. Spread the mixture on the skewer using a wet hand along the length of the skewer in a cylindrical shape, one inch apart and make each kebab 4-5 inches long.
4. Roast in a moderately hot tandoor or over charcoal grill for 6-7 minutes.
5. Baste with clarified butter and further roast for 2-3 minutes or till tender
6. Serve hot along with choice of salad and chutney.

Akbari Seekh Kebab

PERFECT COMBINATION OF LAMB AND CHICKEN FLAVOURED WITH CURRY LEAVES AND DELICATELY ROASTED

Cooking time 8-10 minutes Serves 1-2

INGREDIENTS

2 tbsp	- Processed cheese (grated)
100 gm	- Lamb mince
100 gm	- Chicken mince
1 tsp	- Onion (chopped)
1 tsp	- Coriander (chopped)
½ tsp	- Ginger garlic paste
½ tsp	- Green chilli (chopped)
1 tsp	- Cashewnuts (chopped)
To taste	- Salt
½ tsp	- Red chilli powder
1/3 tsp	- Garam masala
1 no	- Egg
Few no	- Curry leaves (chopped)

For basting - Clarified butter

METHOD

1. In a tray, mash processed cheese, add the remaining ingredients in the order listed above, mix well till smooth. Keep aside for at least 1 hour.
2. Divide this mixture into 4-5 parts.

Cooking

3. Spread the mixture on the skewer using a wet hand along the length of the skewer in a cylindrical shape, one inch apart and make each kebab 4 inches long.
4. Roast in a moderately hot tandoor or over charcoal grill for 6-7 minutes.
5. Baste with clarified butter and further roast for 2-3 minutes or till tender.
6. Serve hot with choice of a salad and chutney.

Gosht Boti Kaliyan

SUCCULENT KEBAB MADE OF LAMB CHUNKS SPICED WITH ROYAL CUMIN AND FLAVOURED WITH SAFFRON

Cooking time 10-12 minutes Serves 1-2

INGREDIENTS

225-250 gm (6 pcs) - Lamb boneless cubes (40 gm each)

First Marination

To taste	- Salt
½ tsp	- Ginger garlic paste
2 tsp	- Raw papaya paste
½ tsp	- Red chilli paste

Second Marination

4 tbsp	- Hung curd
A pinch	- Saffron
To taste	- Salt
½ tsp	- Ginger garlic paste
1/3 tsp	- Garam masala
1/3 tsp	- Kasoori methi powder
½ tsp	- Red chilli paste
1/3 tsp	- Black salt
1/3 tsp	- Shahi jeera (royal cumin)
1 tsp	- Green coriander (chopped)

For basting - Clarified butter

METHOD

1. Trim, wash, pat dry lamb pieces and keep aside.

First Marination

2. In a bowl mix salt, ginger garlic paste, red chilli paste, raw papaya paste, and apply this to lamb pieces, rub well and keep aside for at least 1 hour.

Second Marination

3. In a bowl whisk hung curd, add all the remaining ingredients listed above, mix well.
4. Squeeze extra moisture from marinated lamb pieces and put them into this marinade, coat well and keep aside for at least 2-3 hours.

Cooking

5. Take a skewer and skew marinated pieces one by one an inch apart along the skewer.
6. Roast in a tandoor or over a charcoal grill at a moderate temperature for 8-9 minutes.
7. Baste with clarified butter and further roast for 2-3 minutes or till tender.
8. Serve hot along with choice of a salad and chutney.

Hyderabadi Kaleji Kebab

THIS IS A DELECTABLE KEBAB MADE WITH LAMB LIVER TASTEFULLY PREPARED IN HYDERABADI STYLE

Cooking time 6-8 minutes Serves 1-2

INGREDIENTS

200-225 gm (5-6 pcs) Lamb liver (large cubes)

Marination
2 tbsp	- Hung curd
1 tsp	- Ginger garlic paste
1/3 tsp	- Garam masala
½ tsp	- Coriander powder
½ tsp	- Red chilli powder
To taste	- Salt
1 tsp	- Lemon juice
1 tsp	- Refined oil
2 tbsp	- Green paste

For basting - Clarified butter

METHOD

1. Trim, wash, lamb liver, pat dry and keep aside.

Marination

2. In a bowl whisk hung curd, add all the remaining ingredients listed above. Mix well.
3. Squeeze extra moisture from lamb liver and put them into this marinade, coat well and keep aside for at least 2-3 hours.

Cooking

4. Take a skewer and skew marinated pieces one by one an inch apart along the skewer.
5. Roast in a tandoor or over a charcoal grill at a moderate temperature for 5-6 minutes.
6. Baste with clarified butter and further roast for 1-2 minutes or till tender.
7. Serve hot along with choice of a salad and chutney.

Peshawari Boti Kebab

A PIQUANT LAMB CHUNKS KEBAB INFUSED WITH CRUSHED BLACK PEPPER

Cooking time 12-15 minutes Serves 1-2

INGREDIENTS

225-250 gm (6 pcs) Lamb cubes (boneless) (40 gm each)

First Marination
½ tsp	- Ginger garlic paste
To taste	- Salt
3 tsp	- Raw papaya paste
½ tsp	- Red chilli paste

Second Marination
4 tbsp	- Hung curd
To taste	- Salt
½ tsp	- Ginger garlic paste
1/3 tsp	- Garam masala
1 tsp	- White vinegar
½ tsp	- Red chilli paste
A pinch	- Kasoori methi powder
1 tsp	- Roasted channa powder
1 tsp	- Black pepper (crushed)
1 tsp	- Refined oil

METHOD

1. Clean, wash and pat dry lamb boti.

First Marination

2. In a bowl mix ginger garlic paste, raw papaya paste and apply this to lamb boti, rub well and keep aside for at least 1-2 hours.

Second Marination

3. Whisk hung curd in a bowl, add all the remaining ingredients in the order listed. Mix well.
4. Remove extra moisture from the marinated lamb boti and put them into this marinade, coat well and keep aside for at least 2 hours.

Cooking

5. Heat oil in a pan/lagan and add lamb boti. Cover and cook on slow fire (12-15 minutes).
6. Keep changing side from time to time and cook to a golden brown.
7. Serve hot with choice of a salad and chutney.

Rajasthani Boti Kebab

THIS LAMB DELIGHT IS COOKED WITH POUNDED SPICES TO STIMULATE THE PALATE

Cooking time 10-12 minutes Serves 1-2

INGREDIENTS

225-250 gm (6 pcs) - Lamb boti (40 gm each)

First Marination
To taste	- Salt
½ tsp	- Ginger garlic paste
½ tsp	- Red chilli paste
3 tsp	- Raw papaya paste
1 tsp	- Vinegar

Second Marination
3 tbsp	- Hung curd
½ tsp	- Ginger garlic paste
½ tsp	- Red chilli paste
1/3 tsp	- Garam masala
1/3 tsp	- Kasoori methi powder
To taste	- Salt
½ tsp	- Cinnamon powder
2 tsp	- Refined oil

For basting - Clarified butter

METHOD

1. Clean, wash and pat dry lamb pieces.

First Marination

2. In a bowl mix salt, ginger garlic paste, red chilli paste, raw papaya paste, vinegar and apply this to lamb boti, rub well and keep aside for at least half an hour.

Second Marination

3. In a bowl whisk hung curd, add the remaining ingredients in the order listed and mix well.
4. Remove excess moisture from the marinated lamb pieces, put them in this marinate, coat well and keep aside for at least 2-3 hours.

Cooking

5. Take a skewer and skew marinated pieces one inch apart along the skewer.
6. Roast in a moderately hot tandoor or over a charcoal grill for 6-8 minutes.
7. Baste with clarified butter and further roast for 2-3 minutes or till tender.
8. Serve hot with choice of a salad and chutney.

Gosht Dalcha Kebab

YET ANOTHER DELICIOUS HYDERABADI LAMB AND LENTIL KEBAB

Cooking time 10-12 minutes Serves 1-2

INGREDIENTS

225-250 gm (6 pcs) - Lamb boti (40 gm each)

First Marination
To taste	- Salt
½ tsp	- Ginger garlic paste
½ tsp	- Yellow chilli powder
1 tsp	- Vinegar
3 tsp	- Raw papaya paste
25 gm	- Boiled channa dal

Second Marination
2 tbsp	- Hung curd
½ tsp	- Ginger garlic paste
1/3 tsp	- Yellow chilli powder
To taste	- Salt
A pinch	- Turmeric powder
A pinch	- Nutmeg powder
2 tsp	- Refined oil

For basting - Clarified butter

METHOD

1. Clean, and wash lamb pieces, pat dry and keep aside.

First Marination

2. In a bowl mix salt, ginger garlic paste, yellow chilli powder, vinegar, raw papaya paste, apply this to lamb pieces, rub well and keep aside for at least half an hour.
3. In a food processor put boiled channa dal and make a fine paste.

Second Marination

4. In a bowl whisk hung curd, and add the remaining ingredients in the order listed. Mix well, add 3 tsp of the channa dal paste and mix well.
5. Remove excess moisture from the marinated lamb pieces and put them in this marinade, coat well and keep aside for at least 2 hours.

Cooking

6. Take a skewer and skew marinated pieces one inch apart along the skewer.
7. Roast in a moderately hot tandoor or over a charcoal grill for 8-9 minutes.
8. Baste with clarified butter and further roast for 2-3 minutes or till tender.
9. Serve hot with choice of a salad and chutney.

Multani Seekh Kebab

A JUICY LAMB MINCE KEBAB FROM THE CITY OF MULTAN

Cooking time 8-10 minutes Serves 1-2

INGREDIENTS

200 gm	- Lamb mince
2 tsp	- Processed cheese (grated)
25 gm	- Khoya (grated)
25 gm	- Chenna paneer (grated)
1 tsp	- Ginger garlic paste
½ tsp	- Red chilli paste
½ tsp	- Green chilli (chopped)
1 tsp	- Fresh coriander (chopped)
1 tsp	- Fresh mint (chopped)
½ tsp	- Garam masala
To taste	- Salt
For basting	- Clarified butter

METHOD

1. In a deep tray mash processed cheese, khoya and chenna paneer, add lamb mince and add all the ingredients in the order listed above, mix well with palm, keep the mixture aside for at least 1 hour.
2. Divide the mixture into 4 equal balls.

Cooking

3. Spread this mixture individually on the skewer using wet hand by pressing each portion along the length of the skewer in a cylindrical shape, one inch apart making each kebab 4 inches long, spread evenly.
4. Roast in a moderately hot tandoor or over a charcoal grill for 6-7 minutes.
5. Baste with clarified butter and further roast for 2-3 minutes.
6. Serve hot along with choice of a salad and chutney.

Joshiley Boti Kebab

HOT AND SPICY SUCCULENT LAMB KEBAB

Cooking time 10-12 minutes Serves 1-2

INGREDIENTS

225-250 gm (6 pcs) - Lamb boneless (40 gm each)

First Marination

To taste	- Salt
3 tsp	- Raw papaya paste
½ tsp	- Ginger garlic paste
½ tsp	- Red chilli paste
1 tsp	- White vinegar

Second Marination

4 tbsp	- Hung curd
To taste	- Salt
½ tsp	- Ginger garlic paste
1/3 tsp	- Garam masala
1/3 tsp	- Kasoori methi powder
2 tsp	- Lemon juice
2 tsp	- Mustard oil
For basting	- Clarified butter

METHOD

1. Wash, pat dry lamb pieces and keep aside.

First Marination

2. In a bowl mix salt, raw papaya paste, ginger garlic paste, red chilli paste and vinegar. Apply this to lamb boti, rub well and keep aside for at least one hour.

Second Marination

3. In a bowl whisk hung curd and add all the remaining ingredients in the order listed, mix well.
4. Remove excess moisture from the marinated lamb pieces and put them in this marinade, coat well and keep aside for at least 2-3 hours.

Cooking

5. Take a skewer and skew marinated pieces one by one an inch apart along the skewer
6. Roast in a tandoor or over a charcoal grill at a moderate temperature for 8-9 minutes.
7. Baste with clarified butter and further roast for 2-3 minutes or till tender.
8. Serve hot along with choice of a salad and chutney.

Gosht Kashmiri Tikke

A DELICACY OF LAMB PREPARED WITH KASHMIRI SPICES

Cooking time 10-12 minutes Serves 1-2

INGREDIENTS

225-225 gm (8 pcs) - Lamb boneless (30 gm)

First Marination
½ tsp	- Ginger garlic paste
To taste	- Salt
2 tsp	- Lemon juice
2 tsp	- Raw papaya juice

Second Marination
5 tsp	- Hung curd
½ tsp	- Ginger garlic paste
To taste	- Salt
1 tsp	- Lemon juice
2 tsp	- Aniseed powder
1/3 tsp	- Kasoori methi powder
A pinch	- Saffron
2 tsp	- Refined oil

For basting - Clarified butter

METHOD

1. Wash and pat dry lamb pieces and keep aside.

First Marination

2. In a bowl mix ginger garlic paste, salt, lemon juice, raw papaya juice and apply this to lamb pieces, rub well and keep aside for at least 1 hour.

Second Marination

3. In a bowl whisk hung curd, add the remaining ingredients in the order listed and mix well.
4. Remove the excess moisture from the marinated lamb pieces and put them in the above marinade, coat well and keep aside for at least 1 hour.

Cooking

5. Take a skewer and skew the marinated lamb pieces one inch apart along the skewer.
6. Roast in a charcoal grill at a moderate temperature for 8-9 minutes.
7. Baste with clarified butter and further roast for 2-3 minutes.
8. Serve hot along with choice of a salad and chutney.

Lazeez Dohra Kebab

DOUBLE COOKED LAMB KEBAB

Cooking time 12-15 minutes Serves 1-2

INGREDIENTS

(225-250) 6 pcs - Lamb cube (boneless)

First Marination
1 tsp	- Ginger garlic paste
2 tsp	- Raw papaya paste
To taste	- Salt

Second Marination
4 tbsp	- Hung curd
1 tbsp	- Almonds paste
1 tsp	- Red chilli powder
½ tsp	- Black pepper powder
½ tsp	- Clove powder
2 tsp	- Malt vinegar
1 tsp	- Lemon juice
To taste	- Salt

For basting - Clarified butter

2 tsp	- Deshi Ghee
2 tsp	- Chopped onion
2 tbsp	- Fresh cream
5 no	- Fresh mint leaves
½ tsp	- Roasted cumin powder

METHOD

1. Clean, wash lamb cubes, pat dry and keep aside.

First Marination

2. In a bowl mix ginger garlic paste, raw papaya paste, salt and apply this to lamb cubes, rub well and keep aside at least for 1 ½ hours.

Second Marination

3. In a bowl whisk hung curd and add all other ingredients listed in the order above. Mix well, put lamb cubes in this marinade, coat well and keep aside for at least 1 ½ hours.

Cooking

4. Take a skewer, skew marinated lamb pieces one by one. Roast in a moderately hot tandoor or over a charcoal grill for 10-12 minutes.
5. Baste with clarified butter and roast for another 3-4 minutes or till tender.
6. Remove lamb pieces from the skewer and arrange on a serving platter.
7. Heat desi ghee in a pan, put chopped onion, sauté it, add fresh cream, mint leaves, roasted cumin powder and cook it for a while and immediately pour on lamb pieces.
8. Serve hot with choice of a salad and chutney.

Boti Keema Kebab

UNIQUE KEBAB MADE WITH LAMB MORSELS COATED WITH LAMB MINCE AND ROASTED

Cooking time 14-16 minutes **Serves 2-3**

INGREDIENTS

(225-250 gm) 6 pcs - Boneless lamb cubes

Marination

2 tsp	- Raw papaya paste
½ tsp	- Ginger garlic paste
To taste	- Salt
1 tsp	- White vinegar
1 tsp	- Red chilli paste
1tsp	- Oil
2 tbsp	- Processed cheese (grated)
200 gm	- Lamb mince
To taste	- Salt
½ tsp	- Garam masala
½ tsp	- Kasoori methi powder
½ tsp	- Green chilli (chopped)
½ tsp	- Green coriander (chopped)

For basting - Clarified butter

METHOD

1. Wash and pat dry lamb cubes and keep aside.

Marination

2. In a bowl take raw papaya paste, ginger garlic paste, salt, white vinegar, red chilli paste, oil, lamb boti, rub well and keep aside for at least 1-2 hours.
3. In a deep tray mash grated cheese, add lamb mince and the all remaining ingredients listed in order, mix well till thoroughly blended and forms smooth consistency. Divide into 5 equal parts and make balls.

Cooking

4. Take skewer and skew marinated lamb pieces one by one an inch apart along the skewer.
5. Roast in a tandoor or over a charcoal grill at a moderate temperature for 8-10 minutes keep aside for cooling on the skewer itself.
6. Take mutton mince, apply on each lamb boti using a moist palm giving an oval shape.
7. Roast in moderately hot tandoor or over charcoal grill for about 5-6 minutes till done, baste with clarified butter during cooking.
8. Serve hot with choice of a salad and chutney.

Gilawat Ke Kebab

PRIDE OF INDIA – A FAMOUS LAMB KEBEB FROM THE CITY OF LUCKNOW, SO SOFT THAT IT MELTS IN THE MOUTH

Cooking time 4-6 minutes **Serves 1-2**

INGREDIENTS

200 gm	- Lamb mince (twice minced)
1 tsp	- Onion (fine chopped)
1/3 tsp	- Ginger (fine chopped)
1 tsp	- Raw papaya paste
1 tbsp	- Roasted channa powder
1 tsp	- Brown onion paste
To taste	- Salt
1tsp	- Roasted almond (chopped)
1tsp	- Hung curd
½ tsp	- Cream
½ tsp	- Galouti masala
1/3 tsp	- Saffron
1 tbsp	- Warm milk

Smoking

2 no	- Cloves
For smoking	- Desi ghee

For cooking - Desi ghee

METHOD

1. Crush saffron threads with back of spoon, soak in warm milk for 10 minutes.
2. Put mince in a bowl, add remaining ingredients listed in order, mix well to smooth consistency and keep it aside for at least 1 hour.

Smoking

3. Take a small bowl (katori), place in the middle of the mixture bowl, put 2 pieces of burning charcoal, cloves and pour desi ghee, immediately cover with lid and keep aside for 3-5 minutes.
4. Divide this mixture into 4-5 equal parts and make balls, apply a little melted ghee on your palm and flatten the mince balls into round patties or medallion shape (tikki).

Cooking

5. Heat ghee on a pan or griddle, place kebab and shallow fry over low heat till both side are evenly brown.
6. Serve hot with choice of a salad and chutney.

Dum Keema Kebab

JUICY LAMB MINCE KEBAB MADE WITH LUCKNOWI SPICES AND COOKED ON SLOW FIRE ON LAGAN

Cooking time 6-8 minutes Serves 1-2

INGREDIENTS

50 gm	- Cheese (grated)
200 gm	- Lamb mince
1 tsp	- Ginger garlic paste
½ tsp	- Raw Papaya paste
2 tsp	- Brown onion paste
1 no	- Egg white
½ tsp	- Green chilli (chopped)
1 tsp	- Fresh coriander (chopped)
½ tsp	- Kebabchini powder
½ tsp	- Yellow chilli powder
To taste	- Salt
For cooking	- Desi ghee

METHOD

1. In a deep tray, mash grated cheese, add lamb mince, ginger garlic paste and all the remaining ingredients listed in order, mix well to smooth consistency and keep aside for at least 2 hours.
2. Divide lamb mixture into 4-5 balls, press each ball between your palm and give shape of a medallion (tikki).

Cooking

3. In a thick bottom pan (lagan), heat desi ghee, place kebab and cook on slow fire till lamb is cooked.
4. Serve hot with choice of a salad and chutney.

Patiala Seekh

SEEKH OF KID MINCE, SPICED WITH CARDAMOM, CLOVES, CINNAMON, ENRICHED WITH TOASTED ALMOND, CASHEWNUTS

Cooking time 8-10 minutes Serves 1-2

INGREDIENTS

2 tbsp	- Processed cheese (grated)
200 gm	- Lamb mince
1 tsp	- Ginger garlic paste
½ tsp	- Red chilli paste
To taste	- Salt
½ tsp	- Garam masala
1 tsp	- Green chilli (chopped)
1 tsp	- Green corriander (chopped)
1 tsp	- kalonji, saunf
For basting	- Clarified butter
For coating	
2 tsp	- Almond and cashewnut (chopped)
1 tbsp	- Onion, bell pepper (fine chopped)

METHOD

1. In a deep tray, mash processed cheese, put lamb mince, add all the remaining ingredients in the order listed, rub well and keep aside for at least half an hour.
2. Divide the mixture into 4 equal portions and make balls.

Cooking

3. Spread the mixture on the skewer using a wet hand along the length of the skewer in a cylindrical shape one inch apart, coat with almonds, cashewnut, bell pepper, onion and make each kebab 4-5 inches long.
4. Roast in a moderately hot tandoor or over charcoal grill for 6-7 minutes.
5. Baste with clarified butter and further roast for 2-3 minutes or till tender.
6. Serve hot with choice of a salad and chutney.

Gosht Kebab Wajid Ali

A BEFITTING TRIBUTE TO AWADH'S BEST KNOWN GOURMET, NAWAB WAJID ALI SHAH, THIS DELICACY OF SAFFRON FLAVOURED LAMB CHUNKS IS DONE IN A RICH ALMOND-BASED MARINADE

Cooking time 24-26 minutes Serves 1-2

INGREDIENTS

225-250 gm (6 pcs) Boneless Lamb (40 gm)

First Marination
3 tsp	- Raw papaya paste
To taste	- Salt
½ tsp	- Ginger garlic paste

Second Marination
5 tbsp	- Hung curd
3 tsp	- Chironji paste
3 tsp	- Dry coconut paste
3 tsp	- Almond paste
To taste	- Salt
½ tsp	- Ginger garlic paste
½ tsp	- Red chilli paste
A pinch	- Cinnamon powder
A pinch	- Elachi powder
2 tsp	- Brown onion paste
2 tsp	- Pure ghee
A pinch	- Saffron
2 tsp	- Lemon juice

METHOD

1. Clean, wash lamb pieces, pat dry and keep aside.

First Marination
2. In a bowl mix papaya paste, salt, ginger garlic paste and apply this to lamb pieces, rub well and keep aside for at least one hour.

Second Marination
3. In a bowl whisk hung curd, add all the remaining ingredients in the order listed and mix well.
4. Put the marinated lamb boti into this marinade, coat well and keep aside for at least 2 hours.

Cooking
5. Heat pure ghee in a lagan, put the lamb pieces in and add a little water/stock and keep it on tandoor for cooking, cover it.
6. Keep stirring in between.
7. When lamb is tender, masala is cooked and ghee floats on top, add lime juice, sprinkle saffron on it.
8. Serve hot with choice of a salad and chutney.

Dum Ka Kebab

BAKED KEBAB CAKES

Baking time 10-12 minutes Serves 1-2

INGREDIENTS

2 tbsp	- Processed cheese (grated)
200 gm	- Lamb mince
1 tsp	- Ginger garlic paste
2 tsp	- Chopped onion
1 tsp	- Fresh coriander (chopped)
½ tsp	- Green chilli (chopped)
1 no	- Egg
½ tsp	- Yellow chilli powder
A pinch	- Shahi jeera (royal cumin)
To taste	- Salt
1 tbsp	- Oil
1 tbsp	- Watermelon seeds
2 tbsp	- Cashewnut (chopped)
2 tsp	- Almonds (chopped)
1 no	- Boiled egg
2 no	- Silver leaves (chandi varq)

METHOD

1. In a deep tray, mash grated cheese add ginger garlic paste, lamb mince, chopped onion, fresh coriander, green chilli, beaten egg, yellow chilli powder, shahi jeera, salt and mix well to smooth consistency and keep aside.

Cooking
2. Fry the watermelon seeds, almonds and cashewnuts and spread on absorbent paper and keep aside.
3. Brush a baking dish (rectangular shape) with oil, spread mince on baking dish
4. Brush the top layer of the mince with oil, sprinkle the watermelon seeds, almonds, cashewnuts on the kebab, bake it till the lamb is cooked and turn golden brown colour.
5. Cut the lamb into, square or rectangular pieces of 2 ½" –2 ½"size, grate boiled egg on kebab.
6. Spread silver leaves on the kebab.
7. Serve hot with choice of a salad and chutney.

Seekh–Pa

A SIMPLE YET DELICIOUS LAMB MINCE KEBAB, WHICH IS FILLED WITH CREAMY CHEESE AFTER BEING ROASTED

Cooking time 8-10 minutes **Serves** 1–2

INGREDIENTS

200 gm	- Lamb mince
2 tbs	- Processed cheese (grated)
1 tsp	- Ginger garlic paste
½ tsp	- Red chilli paste
½ tsp	- Green chilli (chopped)
1 tsp	- Fresh coriander (chopped)
1 tsp	- Fresh mint (chopped)
½ tsp	- Garam masala
To taste	- Salt

For basting - Clarified butter

4 tbsp	- Processed cheese (grated)
2 tsp	- Cream

METHOD

1. In a deep tray mash processed cheese, add lamb mince and add all the remaining ingredients in the order listed above, except grated cheese and cream, mix well with palm, keep the mixture aside for at least 1 hour.
2. Divide the mixture into 4 equal balls.

Cooking

3. Spread this mixture individually on the skewer using wet hand by pressing each portion along the length of the skewer in a cylindrical shape, one inch apart making each kebab 4 inches long, spread evenly.
4. Roast in a moderately hot tandoor or over a charcoal grill for 6-7 minutes.
5. Baste with clarified butter and further roast for 2-3 minutes, remove and keep aside.
6. Mash grated cheese, add cream and make a smooth paste.
7. Put cheese paste into a piping bag and fill each seekh kebab with this mixture in equal quantity.
8. Serve hot along with choice of a salad and chutney.

Pathar Ka Gosht

AN UNUSUAL LAMB KEBAB BARBEQUED ON A HEATED RED STONE SLAB

Cooking time 15-18 minutes **Serves** 1–2

INGREDIENTS

(225-250) 4 pcs - Lamb chunks (boneless)

1 tsp	- Ginger garlic paste
2 tsp	- Raw papaya paste
½ tsp	- Black pepper corn powder
2 tsp	- Brown onion paste
½ tsp	- Kebabchini powder (cassia buds)
To taste	- Salt

For cooking - Oil

METHOD

1. Clean, cut lamb chunks into flat pieces (2 ½ "x2"x1cm.)
2. Gently beat the pieces with hammer, pat dry and keep aside.

Marination

3. In a bowl, combine all the ingredients in the order listed above, put lamb pieces in this marinade, rub well and keep aside for at least 2 hours.

Cooking

4. Take a thick red stone slab (smooth surface) of 2 ½ 'x 1 ½ x 2". Wash the stone and place it on bricks on two sides to make a bridge.
5. Heat the stone well with hot charcoal underneath, put some oil on surface of stone.
6. When the stone is absolutely hot put marinated mutton pieces on it, turn them from time to time, keep basting occasionally with oil. Cook it for 15-18minutes or till tender
7. Serve hot with choice of a salad and chutney.

Tandoori Rogani Champen

AN IMPRESSIVE AND ELEGANT LAMB CHOPS MARINATED WITH RARELY USED KASHMIRI ROGAN AND SPECIAL BLEND OF POUNDED SPICES

Cooking time 15-16 minutes Serves 1-2

INGREDIENTS

400-450 (5 pcs) - Lamb chops

First Marination
To taste	- Salt
½ tsp	- Ginger garlic paste
3 tsp	- Raw papaya paste

Second Marination
4 tbsp	- Hung curd
½ tsp	- Ginger garlic paste
1 tsp	- Lemon juice
1 tbsp	- Rogan
½ tsp	- Garam masala
½ tsp	- Dhania powder
A pinch	- Kebab chini powder
To taste	- Salt

For basting - Clarified butter

METHOD

1. Clean, wash lamb chops, pat dry and keep aside.

First Marination

2. In a bowl mix salt, raw papaya paste, ginger garlic paste, apply this to lamb chops, rub well and keep aside for at least 1 hour.

Second Marination

3. In a bowl whisk hung curd, add all the remaining ingredients listed in order, mix well. Squeeze excess moisture from the marinated lamb chops and put them into this marinade, coat well and keep aside for at least 2-3 hours.

Cooking

4. Take a skewer, skew lamb chops one by one from the middle, in an upward position leaving a gap of one inch in between, coat the remaining marinade on top.
5. Roast in a moderately hot tandoor or over a charcoal grill for 13-14 minutes, remove extra moisture and completely drain out, then baste with clarified butter and further roast for 2-3 minutes.
6. Serve hot with choice of a salad and chutney.

Shahi Gosht Tikke

ROYAL LAMB CHUNKS KEBAB WITH DIFFERENT VARIATION OF AWADHI TOUCH

Cooking time 10-12 minutes Serves 1-2

INGREDIENTS

225-250 (6pcs)-Boneless lamb cube (40 gm each)

First Marination
1 tsp	- Ginger garlic paste
2 tsp	- Raw papaya paste
To taste	- Salt
1 tsp	- Vinegar
2 tbsp	- Cashewnut paste

Second Marination
2 tbsp	- Chenna paneer
2 tbsp	- Cream
½ tsp	- Ginger garlic paste
1 tsp	- Green chilli (chopped)
1 no	- Egg white
½ tsp	- Black pepper powder
½ tsp	- Elaichi javitri powder
1 tsp	- Lemon juice
To taste	- Salt
20 ml	- White wine
1 tbsp	- Refined oil

For basting - Clarified butter

METHOD

1. Wash and pat dry lamb pieces.

First Marination

2. In a bowl, take a raw papaya paste, ginger, garlic paste, red chilli paste, salt, vinegar and apply this to lamb boti, rub well and keep aside for at least 1-2 hours.

Second Marination

3. In a bowl mash chenna paneer and add the remaining ingredients in the order listed. Mix well.
4. Remove excess moisture from the marinated lamb pieces and put them in this marinade. Coat well and keep aside for 2-3 hours.

Cooking

5. Take a skewer and skew marinated pieces one inch apart along the skewer.
6. Roast in a tandoor or over a charcoal grill at a moderate temperature for 8-9 minutes.
7. Baste with clarified butter and further roast for 3-4 minutes.
8. Serve hot along with choice of a salad and chutney.

Joshiley Tandoori Pasliyan

THIS IS A DELECTABLE KEBAB MADE OF KID LAMB RACK FLAVOURED WITH KASOORI DRY FENUGREEK AND YELLOW CHILLI POWDER. IT IS A RARE DELICACY

Cooking time 15-16 minutes Serves 1-2

INGREDIENTS

400-450 gm (5 pcs) - Lamb chops

First Marination
To taste	- Salt
3 tsp	- Raw papaya paste
1 tsp	- Ginger garlic paste
½ tsp	- Red chilli paste

Second Marination
4 tbsp	- Hung curd
1 no	- Egg
1 tsp	- Garlic (chopped)
1 tsp	- Yellow chilli powder
A pinch	- Kebabchinni powder
½ tsp	- Kasoori methi powder
A pinch	- Turmeric powder
1 tsp	- Gram flour (roasted)
1 tbsp	- Refined oil

For basting - Clarified butter

METHOD

1. Clean, wash lamb chops, pat dry and keep aside.

First Marination

2. In a bowl mix salt, raw papaya paste, ginger garlic paste, red chilli paste, apply this to lamb chops, rub well and keep aside for at least 1 hour.

Second Marination

3. In a bowl wisk hung curd, add all the remaining ingredients listed in order, mix well. Squeeze excess moisture from the marinated lamb chops and put them into this marinade, coat well and keep aside for at least 2-3 hour.

Cooking

4. Take a skewer, skew lamb chops one by one piercing from the middle in an upward position leaving a gap of one inch in between, coat the remaining marinade on top.
5. Roast in a moderately hot tandoor or over a charcoal grill for 13-14 minutes. Hang the skewer to let excess moisture drain out completely, baste with clarified butter and further roast for 2-3 minutes.
6. Serve hot with choice of a salad and chutney.

Chatpate Tandoori Gurdey

SPICY AND APPETIZING KEBAB MADE WITH LAMB SWEET BREAD AND DELICATELY CHAR-GRILLED

Cooking time 6-8 minutes Serves 1-2

INGREDIENTS

(200-225gm) - 5 pcs Gurdey (Sweet Bread)

First Marination
To taste	- Salt
½ tsp	- Ginger/garlic paste
½ tsp	- Red chilli paste
1 tsp	- Lemon juice

Second Marination
4 tsp	- Hung curd
To taste	- Salt
½ tsp	- Ginger garlic paste
½ tsp	- Red chilli paste
1/3 tsp	- Kastoori methi powder
1/3 tsp	- Garam masala
1 tsp	- Refined oil

For basting - Clarified butter

METHOD

1. Clean, wash and pat dry gurdey and keep aside.

First Marination

2. In a bowl mix salt, ginger/garlic paste, red chilli paste, lemon juice and apply this to gurdey, rub well and keep aside for at least 30 minutes.

Second Marination

3. Whisk hung curd in a bowl, add salt, ginger garlic paste, red chilli paste, kasoori methi, garam masala, oil and mix well.
4. Put gurdey into this marinade, coat well and keep aside for at least 1 hour.

Cooking

5. Take a skewer and skew the marinated gurdey pieces, keep a tray underneath to collect drippings.
6. Roast in a moderately hot tandoor or over a charcoal grill for 5-6 minutes.
7. Remove and baste with clarified butter and further roast for 1-2 minutes or till tender.
8. Serve hot with choice of a salad and chutney.

Gilawat ke Kebab (for recipe turn to page no: 191)

Shikampuri Kebab (for recipe turn to page no: 201)

Chapli Kebab (for recipe turn to page no: 205)

Kakori Kebab (for recipe turn to page no: 206)

Purdah Nashin Kebab (for recipe turn to page no: 207)

Kashmiri Shammi Kebab

ANOTHER VERSION OF SHAMMI PREPARED WITH SPICES FROM VALLEY OF KASHMIR

Cooking time 2-3 minutes Serves 1-2

INGREDIENTS

250 gm	- Lamb chunk (small size)
50gm	- Channa dal
2 no	- Black cardamom
4 no	- Green cardamom
2 no	- Cinnamon sticks
½ tsp	- Kashmiri red chilli powder
½ tsp	- Turmeric powder
½ tsp	- Dry ginger powder
1tsp	- Ginger (chopped)
3-4no	- Garlic (cloves)
½ tsp	- Green chilli (chopped)
1 tsp	- Green coriander (chopped)
½ tsp	- Black cumin seeds
To taste	- Salt
For frying	- Refined oil

METHOD

1. In a pan take lamb chunks, channa dal, black cardamom, green cardamom, cinnamon sticks, red chilli powder, salt, turmeric powder, dry ginger powder, garlic, add water and cook all ingredients on slow fire till done and water evaporates.
2. Remove the pan from the heat and keep aside to cool. Discard the condiments. Pass the cooked mixture twice in a food processor and make a fine paste. Transfer this mixture to a bowl, add chopped green chilli, chopped green coriander, salt and mix well.

Cooking

3. Divide this mixture into 4 equal parts and make balls. Apply a little melted ghee in your palm and flatten the mince ball into a round medallion (tikki) shape.
4. Heat oil in a pan, deep fry till golden brown and crisp on both sides.
5. Serve hot along with choice of a salad and chutney.

Shikampuri Kebab

THIS IS AN ORIGINAL OF AWADH KEBAB WHICH IS STUFFED WITH TANGY FILLING AND FRIED TO PERFECTION

Cooking time 3-4 minutes Serves 1-2

INGREDIENTS

150 gm - Lamb chunk (from the leg)

30 gm	- Channa dal (split gram)
no	- Green chilli (whole)
2 no	- Black cardamom
2 no	- Bay leaves
1 no	- Cinnamon sticks
6 no	- Cloves
½ tsp	- Ginger garlic paste
½ tsp	- Yellow chilli powder
½ tsp	- Garam masala
½ tsp	- Fresh mint (chopped)
1 tsp	- Fresh coriander (chopped)
1 tbsp	- Lime juice
To taste	- Salt

Stuffing

½ tsp	- Onion (fine chopped)
½ tsp	- Ginger (fine chopped)
½ tsp	- Green chilli (fine chopped)
½ tsp	- Boiled spinach (fine chopped)
To taste	- Salt
For cooking	- Oil or desi ghee

METHOD

1. In a pan take lamb chunk, channa dal, green chilli, black cardamom, bay leaves, cinnamon sticks, cloves, add water and cook all ingredients on slow fire till done and water evaporates.
2. Remove whole condiments and cool.
3. In a food processor put the lamb and make a fine paste. Transfer paste to a bowl. Add ginger garlic paste, yellow chilli powder, garam masala, chopped mint, coriander, lemon juice, salt and mix well.
4. Divide this mixture into 4 equal parts.

Stuffing

5. In a bowl, mix chopped onion, ginger, green chilli, boiled spinach, salt and divide into 4 equal parts.
6. Press each ball between wet palms, place a filling, seal and flatten to give shape of medallion (tikki) and refrigerate for some time.

Cooking

7. Heat oil in a pan, place kebeb and shallow Fry till golden brown in colour on both sides and crisp.
8. Serve hot with choice of a salad and chutney.

Shahi Shikampuri Kebab

EGG COATED VERSION OF SHIKAMPURI KEBAB FROM CITY OF LUCKNOW

Cooking time 3-4 minutes **Serves** 1-2

INGREDIENTS

150 gm	- Lamb chunk (from leg)
30 gm	- Channa dal
2 no	- Green cardamom
2 no	- Black cardamom
2 no	- Bay leaves
1 no	- Cinnamon stick
6 no	- Cloves
2 no	- Fresh green chilli
½ tsp	- Ginger garlic paste
½ tsp	- Yellow chilly powder
½ tsp	- Garam masala
1 tsp	- Fresh coriander (chopped)
1 tsp	- Fresh mint (chopped)
1 tbsp	- Limejuice
To taste	- Salt
1 tbsp	- Hung curd (stuffing)
1 no	- Beaten egg (for coating)
For cooking	- Desi ghee or oil

METHOD

1. In a pan take lamb chunk, channa dal, green cardamom, black cardamom, bay leaves, cinnamon stick, cloves, green chilli. Add water and cook all ingredients on slow fire till done and water gets evaporates.
2. Remove whole condiments and cool.
3. In a processor add the lamb and channa dal and make fine paste. Transfer paste to a bowl, add ginger garlic paste, yellow chilli powder, garam masala, chopped coriander, mint, lemon juice, salt and mix well.
4. Divide the mixture into 4 equal parts. Take a portion of the paste and roll it into a ball between your palms. Flatten slightly and make an indentation in the centre of the meat, like a small cup. Fill this indentation with a small part of hung curd, seal carefully and make balls, flatten into round patties.

Cooking

5. In beaten egg dip shikampuri kebab into this and pan fry on medium hot ghee or oil till golden brown and crisp on both sides.
6. Serve hot with choice of a salad and chutney.

Tabakh Maaz

SUCCULENT BABY LAMB RIBS-A KASHMIRI DELICACY

Cooking time 1 ½-2 hours **Serves** 4-5

INGREDIENTS

1 kg-Rib cage (seperate membranes part of the ribs from the chops)

6 litre	- Water
3 tsp	- Garlic paste
To taste	- Salt
3 litre	- Cold water
To taste	- Salt
3 tsp	- Dry ginger powder
8-10	- Cloves
8-10	- Black cardamom
1 tsp	- Turmeric powder
500 gm	- Pure ghee

METHOD

1. Clean, wash and pat dry lamb rib cage
2. Bring the water to boil, add the lamb ribs, continue to boil, removing the scum that rises to surface. Repeat till the water is clear. Boil and cover till the lamb ribs are half cooked. Add garlic paste, mix and further cook for 10-15 minutes, add salt and boil covered continuously, till membrane between the ribs can be pierced with the thumb. Remove the pan from the heat and drain the water. Cool the ribs and then immerse in a pan of cold water. Wash thoroughly, and keep them aside, do not discard this water.
3. Cut the lamb ribs with a heavy, sharp knife into 8-10 equal rectangular pieces.
4. Boil the water in which the ribs were washed. Add the ribs, salt, dry ginger powder, cloves, black cardamom and turmeric powder. Mix well, let it boil till the bones can be extracted from the membrane easily. Remove the pan from the heat and take out the ribs, keep aside.
5. Heat pure ghee in frying pan, add ribs not overlapping each other and fry till ribs are golden brown, keep turning occasionally. Remove to absorbent paper.
6. Serve hot with walnut chutney.

Balti Muthi Kebab

MUTHI MEANS FIST IN URDU. THE LAMB MINCE IS SHAPED IN CLOSED FIST WITH FINGER MERLES IN THE FIST, HENCE THE NAME MUTHI. ALTERNATIVELY THE MINCE CAN BE SHAPED INTO ROUNDS OR LONG OVALS

Cooking time 3-4 minutes Serves 1-2

INGREDIENTS

200 gm	- Lamb mince
1 tsp	- Ginger garlic paste
½ tsp	- Ginger (chopped)
½ tsp	- Green chilli (chopped)
1 tsp	- Green coriander (chopped)
½ tsp	- Mint (chopped)
A pinch	- Nutmeg powder
½ tsp	- Garam masala
½ tsp	- Yellow chilli powder
To taste	- Salt
A pinch	- Elaichi powder
2 tsp	- Roasted channa powder
For frying	- Refined oil

METHOD

1. In a bowl put lamb mince, add all the above ingredients in the order listed. Mix well until thoroughly blended and form a smooth consistency.
2. Keep the mixture aside for atleast 45-60 minutes.
3. Divide the mixture into 6 equal parts/balls.

Cooking

4. Using a moist palm give a palm (muthi) shape to each mutton ball.
5. Heat oil in a pan and shallow fry until cooked golden brown and crisp on both sides.
6. Serve hot along with choice of a salad and chutney.

Champ-e- Gulistan

SAFFRON FLAVOURED TANDOORI LAMB CHOP - A DISTINCT KASHMIRI DELICACY - IT IS ALSO KNOWN AS KABARGAH

Cooking time 6-8 minutes Serves 1-2

INGREDIENTS

400-450 gm Lamb single bone chops (05 no)
(Three rib lamb chops, 2 bones removed)

For Boiling

01 lit	- Milk
1 cup	- Water
01 no	- Bay leaf
02 no	- Star anis
01 tsp	- Black pepper corn
05 no	- Green cardamom
04 no	- Cloves
01 tbsp	- Raw papaya paste
A pinch	- Saffron
To taste	- Salt

Batter

01 no	- Egg
03 tbsp	- Besan
01 tsp	- Red chilli powder
Ta taste	- Salt
1/3 tsp	- Soda metha
As required	- Water

Basting

01 tbsp	- Desi ghee
Saffron	- ¼ tsp

METHOD

1. Wash, pat dry lamb pieces and keep aside.
1. Cut, clean and wash mutton chops, give incisions/marks with a knife, pat dry and keep aside.
2. Bring milk & water to boil add all whole spices, lamb chops, raw papaya paste, saffron, salt. Cook till lamb is tender and the liquid has evaporated, remove chops from the pan and leave aside to cool.
3. To make batter in a bowl whisk egg, add besan, red chilli powder, salt, soda, water, mix well to thick & smooth consistency, put boiled lamb chops into this batter & coat well.

Cooking

4. Take a skewer, skew the lamb chops one by one and in a moderately hot tandoor or over a charcoal grill for 5-6 minutes, baste with clarified butter & further roast for of 2 minutes.
5. Serve hot with choice of a salad and walnut chutney.

Pasanda Kebab

AWADH IS A HOME TO VAST VARIETY OF KEBABS. THEY DIFFER IN SHAPE & SIZE, THE KIND OF MEAT USED OR THE METHOD OF COOKING INVOLVED. CONTRARY TO THE NOTION THAT KEBABS ARE EITHER BARBEQUED OR GRIDDLE FRIED THIS PARTICULAR PASANDA IS A 2 INCH SQUARE FLAT LAMB WHICH IS COOKED IN A BRASS VESSEL. COOKING ON SLOW FIRE WITH GHEE & SPICE INFUSES THE MEAT A SUBTTE AROMA & SOFT TEXTURE

Cooking time 15-18 minutes Serves 1-2

INGREDIENTS

First Marination
04 no (200 gm)	- Lamb chunks
01 tsp	- Ginger/garlic paste
1 ½ tbsp	- Raw papaya paste
½ tsp	- Yellow chilli powder
To taste	- Salt

Stuffing
80 gm	- Chicken mince
A pinch	- Cumin seeds (whole)
A pinch	- Saffron threads
01 tsp	- Coconut powder
½ tsp	- Fresh green coriander (chopped)
To taste	- Salt

Second Marination
½ cup	- Hung curd
4 tbsp	- Cashew nut paste
01 tsp	- Yellow chilli pwder
01 tsp	- Kebab chini powder
½ tsp	- Elachi/ javitri powder
½ tsp	- Garam masala
To taste	- Salt

METHOD

1. Clean, cut lamb chunks into flat pieces (2 ½ "into 2" into 1 cm)
2. Gently beat the pieces with hammer and give a slide cut in the center of the meat, pat dry and keep aside.

First Marination
3. In a bowl mix ginger/garlic paste, raw papaya paste, yellow chilli power, salt apply this to lamb pieces, rub well and keep aside for atleast 1 hour.

Stuffing
4. Heat oil in a pan add whole cumin seeds when they are crackle add chicken mince, coconut powder saffron threads, salt and chopped green coriander and cook until moisture gets evaporated. Remove & let it cool.
5. Divide cooked chicken mince into 4 equal parts, stuff each lamb piece with this mixture, seal the end part with knife & keep aside.

Second Marination
6. In a bowl, combine all the ingredients in order listed above, put stuffed lamb pieces in this marinade, coat well and keep aside for 2 hours.

Cooking
7. Take a skewer, skew marinated lamb one by one and roast in preheated tandoor or over lagan (pot) char grill for about 8-10 minutes.
8. Remove and hang so that the excess moisture drains out completely (1-2 minutes).
9. Baste with melted butter and further roast for about 3-5 minutes.
10. Remove and serve hot with choice of salad and chutney.

Chapli Kebab

CHAPLI KEBAB IS FAMOUS LAMB KEBAB FROM PESHAWAR 'CHAPLI' LITERALLY TRANSLATES INTO 'SLIPPER', SO NAMED DUE TO THE LARGE 18 – 20 CM (7 – 8 INCH) SIZE & LEATHERY APPEARANCE OF THE KEBAB. THE MAIZ IS AN IMPORTANT INGREDIENT IN THIS

Cooking time 3-4 minutes Serves 1-2

INGREDIENTS

200 gm	- Lamb Mince
As required	- Water
10-15 gm	- Makkai atta
To taste	- Salt
1 tsp	- Green Chilli (Chopped)
4 tsp	- Onion paste (rough)
1 tsp	- Kulli red chilli
1 tsp	- Green coriander (chopped)
1 tsp	- Jeera whole
1/3 tsp	- Soda sweet
2 tsp	- Dhania whole (crushed)
1 tsp	- Anardana (crushed)
For frying	- Refined oil

METHOD

1. In a deep bowl, put lamb mince add water to soften the mince, add all the remaining ingredients, rub well with your palm & keep aside.
2. Divide the mixture into 2 equal portions and make balls.

Cooking

3. Apply oil on palm and flatten each ball in a round shape or make a round flat shape with the help of polythene.
4. Heat oil in a non-stick pan and shallow fry until golden brown and crisp on both sides.
5. Serve hot along with choice of salad and chutney.

Kakori Kebab

THE KING OF LAMB KEBAB, SO SOFT THAT IT MELTS IN YOUR MOUTH. THIS FAMOUS KEBAB ORIGINATED FROM KAKORI, WHICH IS WELL SITUATED ON THE BANKS OF THIS GOMTI RIVER IN LUCKNOW

THE SEEKH HAS LONG BEEN CONSIDERED A PIECE DE RESISTANCE IN THE AWADHI CUISINE. THE SEEKH KEBAB, INTRODUCED IN THIS REGION BY THE MUGHALS, WAS ORIGINALLY PREPARED FROM BEEF MINCE ON SKEWERS AND COOKED ON CHARCOAL FIRE. BUT LATER INFLUENCES AND INNOVATIONS LED TO THE USE OF LAMB MINCE WHICH WAS PREFERRED FOR ITS SOFT TEXTURE. ONE BAWARCHI FROM KAKORI FOUND MUCH ACCLAIM FOR HIS EFFORTS IN THIS DIRECTION. KAKORI IS A SMALL HAMLET ON THE OUTSKIRTS OF LUCKNOW, IN THE LUCKNOW-MALIHABAD MANGO BELT.

AT ONE SUCH PARTY IN KAKORI, STUNG BY THE REMARK OF A BRITISH OFFICER REGARDING THE COARSE TEXTURE OF SEEKH KABAB, THE HOST, THE LATE NAWAB SYED MOHAMMAD HAIDER KAZMI SUMMONED HIS RAKABDARS, HAKIMS AND ATTARS THE VERY NEXT DAY AND ASKED THEM TO EVOLVE A MORE REFINED VARIETY OF THE SEEKH KABAB.

SINCE THEN THE SEEKH KABABS OF KAKORI BECAME FAMOUS BY WORD OF MOUTH AND EVEN TODAY, THOUGH COOKED ELSEWHERE, ARE KNOWN AS 'KAKORI KABABS'.

Cooking time 8-10 minutes Serves 1-2

INGREDIENTS

200 gm	- Lamb mince (Leg meat)
1 tsp	- Raw papaya paste
To taste	- Salt
½ tsp	- Garam masala
½ tsp	- Yellow chilli powder
01 tsp	- Brown onion paste
½ tsp	- Khus khus paste
½ tsp	- Ginger garlic paste
½ tsp	- Copra
For binding	- Roasted gram flour
1 tsp	- Refined flour
1 tsp	- Chironji paste
2 drop	- Itter
1 tsp	- Kakori masala
2-3no	- Cloves whole
1 tsp	- Desi ghee

METHOD

1. Take very fine mince of lamb in a bowl, add papaya paste, salt garam masala, yellow chilli powder and keep aside for atleast 1-1 ½ hour.
2. Put this mixture in a bowl, keep small bowl in the center, put a piece of burning coal in center, put two pieces of cloves and ½ tsp of ghee and cover with a lid for smoking. Keep aside for atleast 3-4 minutes, uncovered & transfer meat to another bowl.
3. Now add brown onion, khus khus, ginger garlic paste, copra and roasted gram flour, chironji paste, itter, kakori masala and blend well.
4. Divide the mixture into four equal portions and make balls.

Cooking

5. Take a skewer and apply the mixture along the skewer with moist hands, in a cylindrical shape. Roast over a charcoal grill at moderate heat for 8-10 minutes.
6. Serve hot with choice of a salad and chutney.

Purdah Nashin Kebab

IT IS AN INTERESTING VARIANCE OF POPULAR GALAWAT KE KEBAB LAMB MINCE PATTY CAMOUFLAGED WITH AN EGG COATED & DELICATELY FRIED IN A KARCHI (LADDLE).

Cooking time 15-18 minutes Serves 1-2

INGREDIENTS

200 gm	- Lamb mince
02 tsp	- Raw papaya paste
½ tsp	- Ginger garlic paste
½ tsp	- Red chilli paste
To taste	- Salt
3 tbsp	- Hung curd
02 tsp	- Brown onion paste
1 tsp	- Roasted channa powder
1 tsp	- Green coriander (chopped)
1 tsp	- Mint (chopped)
To taste	- Salt
A drop	- Kewra water
1/3 tsp	- Garam masala
1 tsp	- Desi ghee
2-3 no.	- Cloves
2 no	- Egg (without shell)
For frying	- Desi ghee

METHOD

1. In a deep tray take lamb mince, add papaya paste, ginger garlic paste, red chilli paste, salt and mix well. Keep aside for atleast ½ hour.
2. Whisk hung curd add other ingredients to lamb mince, mix it well. Give dhunger (smoking) to it with cloves, live charcoal and ghee, cover it for 10-15 minutes
3. Divide the mixture into 6-8 equal portions and make balls. Press between your palm giving it a shape of a medallion (tikki).

Cooking

4. Heat oil in a pan and deep fry lamb patties until golden brown. Remove excess of oil & keep aside.
5. Beat the eggs and add a pinch of salt.
6. Place a ladle on the flame and pour a tablespoon of ghee and put egg. When half set place one mince pattie in it and allow the egg to rise up on the sides and lamb patties gets envelope.
7. When set place a plate on the bowl of the ladle and turn it up side down and remove on a plate.
8. Repeat for the remaining patties.
9. Serve hot with choice of a salad and chutney.

Tunde Ke Kebab

FAMOUS & MOST DELICIOUS LUCKNOWI KEBAB MADE OF LAMB, IT MELTS IN MOUTH, COOKED ON MAHI TAWA (IS AN AWADH VERSION OF THE GRIDDLE)

Cooking time 2-3 minutes Serves 1-2

INGREDIENTS

200 gm	- Lamb mince (fine & without fat)
03 tbsp	- Raw papaya paste
01 tbsp	- Ginger/garlic paste
1 ½ tbsp	- Brown onion paste
1/3 tsp	- Red chilli powder
1/3 tsp	- Cinnamon powder
1/3 tsp	- Cumin seeds powder
1/3 tsp	- Black pepper powder
1/3 tsp	- Clove powder
2 ½ tbsp	- Roasted gram flour
To taste	- Salt
2 drops	- Eter or kewra
For shallow fry	- Desi ghee

METHOD

1. Wash, pat dry lamb pieces and keep aside.
2. Cut, clean and wash lamb chops, give incisions/marks with a knife, pat dry and keep aside.
3. Bring milk & water to boil add all whole spices, lamb chops, raw papaya paste, saffron, salt. Cook till lamb is tender and the liquid has evaporated, remove chops from the pan and leave aside to cool.
4. To make batter in a bowl whisk egg, add besan, red chilli powder, salt, soda, water, mix well to thick & smooth consistency, put boiled lamb chops into this batter & coat well.

Cooking

5. Take a skewer, skew the lamb chops one by one and in a moderately hot tandoor or over a charcoal grill for 5-6 minutes, baste with clarified butter & further roast for of 2 minutes.
6. Serve hot with choice of a salad and walnut chutney.

Maas Ke Sule

THIS IS THE QUINTESSENTIAL RAJPUT KEBAB GENERALLY MADE FROM GAME (VENSION WILD BOARD, QUAIL, PARTIDGE) LAMB & CHICKEN ETC

Cooking time 10-12 minutes Serves 1-2

INGREDIENTS

225-250 gm (4 pcs) Lamb boneless (60gm)

First Marination
To taste	- Salt
½ tsp	- Ginger garlic paste
3 tsp	- Raw papaya paste
1 tsp	- Vinegar
½ tsp	- Red chilli paste

Second Marination
5 tbsp	- Hung curd
4 tbs	- Brown onion paste
To taste	- Salt
1 tsp	- Red chilli paste
1/3 tsp	- Garam masala
1/3 tsp	- Kastoori methi powder
1 tsp	- Garlic paste
2 tsp	- Refined Oil
2 no	- Cloves
1 tsp	- Ghee
For basting	- Clarified butter

METHOD

1. Clean, slightly flatter lamb pieces with backside of a knife, pat dry and keep aside.

First Marination

2. In a bowl mix salt, ginger garlic paste, raw papaya paste, vinegar & red chilli paste and apply this to lamb pieces, rub well and keep aside for atleast 1 hour.

Second Marination

3. In a bowl whisk hung curd and add the remaining ingredients in order listed, mix well.
4. Put lamb pieces to the above marinade, coat well and keep aside for 3-4 hour.
5. Put marinated lamb pieces in a pot. Take a very small bowl (katari), keep along the lamb, put 2 pieces of burning charcoal, 2 pieces of cloves, pour ghee & immediately cover the pot with a lid for 2-3 minutes so that the smoke flavour penetrates into the lamb pieces.

Cooking

6. Take a skewer and skew the lamb pieces one inch apart along the skewer.
7. Roast in a moderately hot tandoor for 8-9 minutes.
8. Baste with clarified butter and roast for (2-3 minutes) or until tender
9. Serve hot along with choice of a salad and chutney.

Dori Ke Kebab

ABSOLUTELY SOFT LAMB KEBAB WHICH IS UNIQUE IN TASTE, TEXTURE & ITS TIED WITH A THREAD BEFORE COOKING AS IT TEXTURE IS VERY CREAMY. A SPECIALTY OF AWADH.

Cooking time 7-8 minutes Serves 1-2

INGREDIENTS

250 gm	- Lamb chunk (mince-fatless)
1 ½ tbsp	- Raw papaya (grated)
05 gm	- Ginger (whole)
05 gm	- Garlic (whole)
01 tbsp	- Black pepper (crushed)
01 tbsp	- Coriander powder
01 tsp	- Red chilli paste
01 TSP	- Green chilli (seeds less & chopped)
01 tbsp	- Fresh green coriander (chopped)
02 tbsp	- Hung curd
As desired	- Flour
To taste	- Salt

Thread for tying

METHOD

1. Trim the meat of excess fat. Pound lamb meat pieces with a meat mallet or "hamam dista" till reduced to pulp, add grated raw papaya, whole ginger, garlic & put in the blender to make a paste.
2. Put all the remaining ingredients listed above and mix well. Divide mixture into 4-5 portions. Take a thick skeswer & apply on it giving egg shape. Tie each piece with a thread & wrap around.

Cooking

3. Roast over a charcoal grill for 5-6 minutes.
4. Baste with melted butter and further roast for 2-3 minutes.
5. Serve hot along with choice of salad and chutney.

Vegetarian

VEGETABLE KEBABS

In the history of kebabs one finds that vegetarian kebabs were non-existent, with the exception of a few fried ones. Over the years Vegetarian kebabs or vegetarian barbecue have achieved a considerable significance. A large variety of vegetarian kebabs are listed in this book. These recipes are absolutely new, well tried and innovative.

One must keep in mind that vegetables when cooked in a tandoor, unlike meat retain most of their food value as the juices are sealed within by high temperature and limited cooking time.

Vegetables ideally recommended for barbecue are:-

Broccoli	-	Green cauliflower
Gobhi	-	Whole baby cauliflower
Aloo	-	Whole medium sized potato
Pyaz	-	Whole medium sized onion
Shimla Mirch	-	Whole medium sized capsicum
Karela	-	Whole medium sized bitter gourd
Tamater	-	Whole large tomato
Khumb	-	Whole fresh button mushroom
Kacha Kela	-	Raw banana
Arbi	-	Calocasia
Kathal	-	Jackfruit
Jimi kand	-	Yam
Lauki	-	White pumpkin
Bhutta	-	Baby corn
Nadru	-	Lotus stem
Parmal	-	Snake Guard

I have eliminated old myth that kebabs are generally non-vegetarian. Here we present large variety of vegetable kebabs.

Paneer (Cottage Cheese)

Lahsuni Paneer Tikka

GARLIC FLAVOURED COTTAGE CHEESE CHUNKS CHAR-GRILLED

Cooking time 5-6 minutes Serves 1-2

INGREDIENTS

200 gm (5 pcs.) - Cottage cheese

First Marination
To taste	- Salt
½ tsp	- White pepper powder
½ tsp	- Ginger garlic paste

Second Marination
4 tbsp	- Hung curd
2 tsp	- Cream
2 tsp	- Garlic paste
½ tsp	- Green chilli (chopped)
1 tsp	- Fresh coriander (chopped)
To taste	- Salt
½ tsp	- White pepper powder
1 tsp	- Refined oil
1 tsp	- Roasted besan

METHOD

1. Cut cottage cheese into square cubes (1 ½ " x 1 ½ ") pat dry and keep aside.

First Marination

2. In a bowl mix salt, white-pepper powder, ginger garlic paste, apply to cottage cheese and keep aside for at least half an hour.

Second Marination

3. Whisk hung curd in a bowl add cream, garlic paste, green chilli, coriander, salt, white pepper powder, refined oil and mix well.
4. Put marinated cottage cheese cubes into this marinade, coat well and keep aside for at least half an hours.

Cooking

5. Take a skewer and skew cottage cheese pieces one by one keeping a one inch gap in between each.
6. Roast/grill over charcoal or in a tandoor at a moderate temperature for 5-6 minutes.
7. Serve hot with choice of a salad and chutney.

Paneer Tikka Shashlik

EXOTIC KEBAB OF COTTAGE CHEESE SKEWERED WITH BELL PEPPERS

Cooking time 5-6 minutes Serves 1-2

INGREDIENTS

200 gm (5 pcs) - Cottage cheese

1 no(each)	- Red, yellow, green capsicums
1 no	- Onion
3no	- Pineapple chunks (canned)

First Marination
½ tsp	- Ginger garlic paste
½ tsp	- Yellow chilli powder
To taste	- Salt

Second Marination
4 tbsp	- Hung curd
To taste	- Salt
½ tsp	- Ginger garlic paste
½ tsp	- Garam masala
A pinch	- Kasoori methi powder
1 tsp	- Red chilli paste
2 tsp	- Refined oil

METHOD

1. Cut cottage cheese into large cubes (1 ½" x 1 ½"). Pat dry and keep aside.
2. Cut all capsicums, onion into large dices (1½" x 1½") 4 pieces each and keep aside.

First Marination

3. In a bowl mix ginger garlic paste, yellow chilli powder, salt and apply this to the cottage cheese, rub well and keep aside for at least half an hour.

Second Marination

4. In a bowl whisk hung curd and add all the remaining ingredients in the order listed and mix well.
5. Put cottage cheese, vegetables and pineapple pieces into this marinade, coat well and keep aside for at least 45 minutes.

Cooking

6. Take a skewer and skew marinated cottage cheese and vegetables alternatively.
7. Roast in a tandoor or over a charcoal grill at a moderate temperature for 5-6 minutes.
8. Serve hot with choice of a salad and chutney.

Tandoori Sikandari Paneer

A COTTAGE CHEESE DELICACY WITH BOUQUET OF AROMATIC SPICES

Cooking time 5-6 minutes Serves 1-2

INGREDIENTS

200 gm	- Cottage cheese (5 pcs.)
1 no	- Tomatoes
1 no	- Capsicum
1 no	- Onions

Marination

4 tbsp	- Hung curd
1 tsp	- Ginger garlic paste
To taste	- Salt
1 tsp	- Lemon juice
1 tsp	- Khoya (grated)
½ tsp	- Garam masala
2 tsp	- Refined Oil
½ tsp	- Kutti red chilli
A pinch	- Green elaichi powder
½ tsp	- Black pepper crushed

METHOD

1. Cut cottage cheese in to cubes (1 ½" x 1 ½") pat dry and keep aside.
2. Cut tomatoes, capsicum, and onions in square (i.e shashlik cut equal to cottage cheese cubes)

Marination

3. In a bowl whisk hung curd, add ginger garlic paste, red chilli paste, salt, lemon juice, khoya, garam masala, oil, kutti red chilli, green elaichi powder and black pepper and mix well, put cottage cheese and vegetables into this marinade, coat well and keep aside for at least 45 minutes.

Cooking

4. Take a skewer and skew cottage cheese and vegetables alternatively one by one and roast in a moderately hot tandoor for 5-6 minutes
5. Serve hot with choice of a salad and chutney.

Khatta Meetha Paneer Tikka

SOUR AND SWEET COTTAGE CHEESE TASTE FULLY PREPARED WITH RAW MANGO

Cooking time 5-6 minutes Serves 1-2

INGREDIENTS

200 gm - Cottage cheese (5pcs.)

First Marination

½ tsp	- Ginger garlic paste
¼ tsp	- Yellow chilli powder
To taste	- Salt

Paste

50 gm	- Fresh coriander leaves
4 no	- Green chillies
2 tbsp	- Mango chutney
½ no	- Small raw mango powder

Second Marination

1 tbsp	- Processed cheese (grated)
To taste	- Salt
¼ tsp	- Chaat masala
½ tsp	- Ginger garlic paste
1 tsp	- Lemon juice
2 tsp	- Cornflour
1 tsp	- Refined oil
2 tsp	- Roasted channa powder
½ tsp	- Black salt

METHOD

1. Cut cottage cheese in large cubes (1 ½ -1 ½ x1"). Pat dry and keep aside.

First Marination

2. In a bowl mix salt, yellow chilli powder, ginger gralic paste, apply this to cottage cheese and keep aside for at least half an hour.

Paste

3. In a food processor, put corriander leaves, green chilli, mango chutney and raw mango and make a fine paste.

Second Marination

4. In a bowl, mash grated cheese, add 4 tsp of above paste, all the remaining ingredients as listed and mix well.
5. Put the cottage cheese cubes in the mixture, coat well and keep aside for at least half an hour.

Cooking

6. Take a skewer, skew marinated cottage cheese cubes one by one leaving an inch gap between each piece.
7. Roast in a moderately hot tandoor or over charcoal grill for 5-6 minutes.
8. Serve hot with choice of a salad and chutney.

Paneer Ka Sula

THICK COTTAGE CHEESE PICATTAS COOKED IN RAJASTHANI STYLE

Cooking time 5-6 minutes Serves 1-2

INGREDIENTS

200 gm	- Cottage cheese

First Marination

½ tsp	- Ginger garlic paste
To taste	- Salt
½ tsp	- Red chilli paste

Second Marination

2 tbsp	- Hung curd
2 tbsp	- Brown onion paste
½ tsp	- Ginger garlic paste
½ tsp	- Red chilli paste
To taste	- Salt
2 tsp	- Lemon juice
2 tsp	- Refined oil
½ tsp	- Garam masala

For smoking

2 no	- Cloves
1 tsp	- Ghee (pure)

METHOD

1. Cut cottage cheese into flat pieces (Size 2"x1½ x 1.5 cm). Pat dry and keep aside.

First Marination

2. In a bowl mix ginger garlic paste, salt, red chilli paste, apply this to cottage cheese, and keep aside for at least half an hour.

Second Marination

3. In a bowl whisk hung curd, add brown onion paste, all the remaining ingredients listed above and mix well.
4. Remove extra moisture from cheese and put them into this marinade.
5. Give smoke flovour, take another small bowl place in centre of the marinated pieces, put a piece of burning charcoal, two pieces of cloves, pour one spoon of desi ghee and cover the bowl with lid 2-3 minutes and keep aside for at least half an hour.

Cooking

6. Take a skewer and skew the cottage cheese one by one keeping an inch gap in between.
7. Roast/grill over charcoal or in tandoor at a moderate temperature for 5-6 minutes
8. Serve hot with choice of a salad and chutney.

Lajawab Paneer Seekh

A DELECTABLE MINCE COTTAGE CHEESE SWKEWER FLAVOURED WITH SPICES

Cooking time 5-6 minutes Serves 1-2

INGREDIENTS

150 gm	- Cottage Cheese (grated)
50 gm	- Boiled potato (grated)
½ tsp	- Green chilli (chopped)
1 tsp	- Fresh coriander (chopped)
½ tsp	- White pepper powder
A pinch	- Shahi jeera
2 tsp	- Cornflour
4 tsp	- Dry breadcrumbs
2 tsp	- Cashewnut (chopped)
½ tsp	- Yellow chilli powder
A pinch	- Elaichi powder
To taste	- Salt
4 tsp	- Red, yellow, green bell pepper (chopped)

METHOD

1. In a bowl mix cottage cheese, potato and add all the remaining ingredients listed above except chopped capsicum, mix well to form a smooth dough.
2. Divide the mixture into 4 equal parts and make balls.

Cooking

3. Take a skewer and apply mixture along it with a moist palm in a cylindrical shape (4"-5").
4. Apply the chopped bell pepper on top.
5. Roast in a moderately hot tandoor or over a charcoal grill for 5-6 minutes.
6. Serve hot with choice of a salad and chutney.

Chandi Paneer Tikka

A TRIBUTE TO AWADH COTTAGE CHEESE KEBAB ROLLED IN SILVER LEAVES

Cooking time 5-6 minutes Serves 1-2

INGREDIENTS

200 gm	- Cottage cheese (5 pcs)

First Marination

½ tsp	- Ginger garlic paste
To taste	- Salt
½ tsp	- White pepper powder

Stuffing

2 tsp	- Khoya (grated)
2 tsp	- Cottage cheese (grated)
To taste	- Salt
A pinch	- Saffron

Second Marination

3 tsp	- Hung curd
3 tsp	- Cream
½ tsp	- Ginger garlic paste
To taste	- Salt
½ tsp	- White pepper powder
A pinch	- Elaichi javatri powder
For coating	- Chandi varq

METHOD

1. Cut cottage cheese into large cubes (1 ½" x 1 ½"). Further slice each cube from the centre without disjoining it, pat dry and keep aside.

First Marination

2. In a bowl mix ginger garlic paste, salt, white pepper and apply this to cottage cheese, and keep aside for at least half an hour.

Stuffing

3. In a bowl mix khoya, cottage cheese, other ingredients listed and mix well. Stuff this mixture into each cube of paneer, press and keep aside.

Second Marination

4. In a bowl whisk hung curd, add the remaining ingredients in the order listed and mix well.
5. Remove extra moisture from cottage cheese and put them in this marinade and keep aside.

Cooking

6. Take a skewer and skew the cottage cheese one by one keeping an inch gap in between.
7. Roast over charcoal grill or in tandoor at a moderate temperature for 5-6 minutes.
8. When cooked remove and roll each piece with chandi varq.
9. Serve hot with choice of a salad and chutney.

Tandoori Paneer Tikka Kalimirch

BLACK PEPPER CORN FLAVOURED COTTAGE CHEESE ROASTED IN CLAY OVEN

Cooking time 5-6 minutes Serves 1-2

INGREDIENTS

200 gm	- Cottage cheese (5 pcs.)
1 tbsp	- Boiled onion paste
1 tbsp	- Cream
1 tsp	- Ginger garlic paste
To taste	- Salt
1 tbsp	- Crushed black pepper
1 tsp	- Lemon rind
50 gm	- Roasted besan
1 tsp	- Cornflour
1 tsp	- Refined oil

METHOD

1. Cut cottage cheese into cubes (1 ½"x 1 ½"). Pat dry and keep aside.

Marination

2. In a bowl mix boiled onion paste, cream, ginger garlic paste, salt, crushed black pepper, lemon rind, roasted besan, corn flour and refined oil and mix well.
3. Put cottage cheese cubes into this marinade, coat well and keep aside for at least 2 hours.

Cooking

4. Take a skewer and skew the marinated cottage cheese.
5. Roast in a moderately hot tandoor or over charcal grill for 5-6 minutes.
6. Serve hot along with choice of a salad and chutney.

Harra Bharra Paneer Tikka

COTTAGE CHEESE CHUNKS STUFFED WITH EXOTIC GREEN FILLING MARINATED & CHARGRILLED

Cooking time 5-6 minutes **Serves** 1-2

INGREDIENTS

200 gm	- Cottage Cheese (5 pcs.)

First Marination

½ tsp	- Ginger garlic paste
To taste	- Salt
½ tsp	- Yellow chilli powder

Stuffing

2 tsp	- Green paste
½ tsp	- Green chilli (chopped)
1 tsp	- Green coriander (chopped)
1 tsp	- Lemon juice
1 tsp	- Roasted channa powder

Second Marination

2 tbsp	- Hung curd
½ tsp	- Garam masala
½ tsp	- Ginger garlic paste
To taste	- Salt
½ tsp	- Yellow chilli powder
½ tsp	- Kasoori methi powder
2 tsp	- Lemon juice
1 tbsp	- Roasted besan

METHOD

1. Cut cottage cheese into square cubes (1½ x 1½) and make a slit from the centre without disjoining. Pat dry and keep aside.

First Marination

2. In a bowl mix ginger garlic paste, salt, yellow chilli powder and apply this to cottage cheese, and keep aside for at least half an hour.

Stuffing

3. In a bowl mix green paste, green chilli, green coariander, lemon juice, roasted channa powder. Mix well and stuff this mixture in equal portions in each cottage cheese piece.

Second Marination

4. In a bowl whisk hung curd and add all the remaining ingredients listed above, mix well.
5. Squeeze extra moisture from cheese, put them into this marinade, coat well and keep aside for 30 minutes.

Cooking

6. Take a skewer and skew the paneer one by one keeping an inch gap in between.
7. Roast over charcoal grill or in tandoor at a moderate temperature for 5-6 minutes.
8. Serve hot with choice of a salad and chutney.

Tandoori Amchurwala Paneer

APPETIZING COTTAGE CHEESE KEBAB WITH EXTRA TOUCH OF DRY MANGO POWDER ROASTED IN CLAY OVEN

Cooking time 5-6 minutes **Serves** 1-2

INGREDIENTS

200 gm	- Cottage cheese (5 pcs)

First Marination

½ tsp	- Ginger garlic paste
½ tsp	- Yellow chilli powder
To taste	- Salt

Second Marination

4 tbsp	- Hung curd
To taste	- Salt
½ tsp	- Ginger garlic paste
½ tsp	- Yellow chilli powder
2tsp	- Amchur powder
1/3 tsp	- Garam masala
½ tsp	- Mango chutney paste

METHOD

1. Cut cottage cheese into cubes (size 1 ½ " x 1 ½ "). Pat dry and keep aside.

First Marination

2. In a bowl mix salt, yellow chilli powder, ginger garlic paste, apply this to cottage cheese pieces, and keep aside for at least half an hour.

Second Marination

3. In a bowl, whisk hung curd and add all the remaining ingredients, mix well.
4. Remove extra moisture from cottage cheese pieces and put them into this marinade, coat well and keep aside for at least half an hour.

Cooking

5. Take a skewer, skew marinated cottage cheese pieces one by one leaving an inch gap between each portion.
6. Roast in a moderately hot tandoor or over charcoal grill for 5-6 minutes.
7. Serve hot with choice of a salad and chutney.

Tandoori Til Wala Paneer

MILD AND DELICIOUS KEBAB MADE OF COTTAGE CHEESE AND SESAME

Cooking time 5-6 minutes Serves 1-2

INGREDIENTS

200 gm	- Cottage cheese (5 pcs)

First marination

To taste	- Salt
½ tsp	- Ginger garlic paste
½ tsp	- White pepper powder

Second marination

2 tbsp	- White til paste
2 tbsp	- Cashewnut paste
To taste	- Salt
½ tsp	- Ginger garlic paste
½ tsp	- White pepper powder
A pinch	- Elaichi powder
½ tsp	- Green chilli (chopped) seedless
1 tsp	- Green coriander (chopped)
2 tsp	- Til white (sesame seeds)
2 tsp	- Cream

METHOD

1. Cut cottage cheese into large cubes (1½ X 1½), pat dry and keep aside.

First marination

2. In a bowl mix salt, ginger garlic paste, white pepper powder and apply this to cottage cheese pieces and keep aside for at least half an hour.

Second marination

3. In a bowl mix white til paste and all the remaining ingredients In order listed, mix well.
4. Remove excess moisture from the cottage cheese and put in the marinade, mix well and keep aside for at least half an hour.

Cooking

5. Take a skewer and skew marinated cottage cheese cubes one by one leaving an inch gap between each.
6. Roast in a tandoor or over a charcoal grill at a moderate temperature for 5-6 minutes.
7. Serve hot with choice of a salad and chutney.

Saunphia Paneer Tikka

ANISEED FLAVOURED COTTAGE CHEESE CHUNKS DELICATELY COOKED OVER CHARCOAL

Cooking time 4-6 minutes Serves 1-2

INGREDIENTS

200 gm	- Cottage cheese(5 pcs)

First Marination

½ tsp	- Ginger garlic paste
To taste	- Salt
½ tsp	- White pepper powder
2 tsp	- Lemon juice

Second Marination

4 tbsp	- Hung curd
½ tsp	- Ginger garlic paste
1 tsp	- Aniseed powder (saunf)
A pinch	- Garam masala
To taste	- Salt
1/3 tsp	- White pepper powder
2 tsp	- Cream
2 tsp	- Refined oil
½ tsp	- Aniseed whole

METHOD

1. Cut cottage cheese in cubes (1 ½ " x 1 ½ "). Pat dry and keep aside.

First Marination

2. In a bowl mix ginger garlic paste, salt, white pepper powder, lemon juice and apply this to cottage cheese, mix well and keep aside for at least half an hour.

Second Marination

3. In a bowl whisk hung curd and add all the remaining ingredients in the order listed above.
4. Put marinated pieces of cottage cheese into this marinade, coat well and keep aside for at least half an hour.

Cooking

5. Take a skewer, skew marinated cottage cheese pieces one by one leaving an inch gap between each piece.
6. Roast in a moderately hot tandoor or over charcoal grill for 5-6 minutes.
7. Serve hot with choice of a salad and chutney.

Bharwan Paneer Tikka

STUFFED COTTAGE CHEESE KEBAB INFUSED WITH CARDAMOM
Cooking time 5-6 minutes Serves 1-2

INGREDIENTS

200 gm	- Cottage cheese (5 pcs.)

First Marination
½ tsp	- Ginger garlic paste
To taste	- Salt
½ tsp	- White pepper powder

Stuffing
4 tsp	- Khoya (grated)
A pinch	- Saffron
1 tsp	- Cashewnut (chopped)
1 tsp	- Raisins (chopped)
To taste	- Salt
½ tsp	- Green chillies (chopped)

Second Marination
2 tbsp	- Hung curd
To taste	- Salt
2 tsp	- Cream
½ tsp	- Ginger garlic paste
½ tsp	- White pepper powder
A pinch	- Elaichi powder
½ tsp	- Green chilli (chopped)
2 tbsp	- Cashewnut paste
1 tsp	- Roasted besan

METHOD

1. Cut cottage cheese into cubes (1 ½ " x 1 ½ ") and make a slit from the centre without disjoining, pat dry and keep aside.

First Marination
2. In a bowl mix ginger garlic, salt, white pepper powder and apply this to the cottage cheese, mix well and keep aside for at least half an hour.

Stuffing
3. In a bowl take khoya (grated), saffron, cashewnut chopped, salt, green chilli, mix well and divide into 5 equal parts.
4. Stuff each cottage cheese with this mixture press tight and keep aside.

Second Marination
5. In a bowl whisk hung curd and add all the remaining ingredients and mix well.
6. Remove extra moisture from the cottage cheese and put the cottage cheese pieces into this marinade, coat well and keep aside for at least half an hour.

Cooking
7. Take a skewer, skew marinated cottage cheese pieces one by one leaving an inch gap between each piece.
8. Roast in a moderately hot tandoor or over charcoal grill for 5-6 minutes.
9. Serve hot with choice of a salad and chutney.

Tandoori Ghungroo Paneer De

AN UNUSUAL PEARL SHAPED COTTAGE CHEESE KEBAB STUFFED WITH TUTTI FRUTTI
Cooking time 5-6 minutes Serves 1-2

INGREDIENTS

200 gm	- Cottage cheese (5 pcs)

First Marination
To taste	- Salt
½ tsp	- Ginger garlic paste
1/3 tsp	- White pepper

Stuffing
20 gm	- Tutti frutti (chopped)

Second Marination
4 tsp	- Processed cheese (grated)
3 tbs	- Cream
To taste	- Salt
½ tsp	- White pepper powder
½ tsp	- Ginger garlic paste
A pinch	- Elaichi powder
½ tsp	- Green chilli (chopped)
1 tsp	- Fresh coriander (chopped)
1 tsp	- Cornflour

METHOD

1. Cut cottage cheese in a small round shape, scoop it from centre.

First Marination
2. In a bowl mix ginger garlic paste, white pepper powder, salt and apply this to cottage cheese and keep aside. Stuff each cottage cheese with tutti frutti.

Second Marination
3. In a deep tray mash grated cheese, add the remaining ingredients in the order listed above and mix well.
4. Remove excess moisture from cottage cheese and put it in the above marinade, coat well and keep aside for at least half an hour.

Cooking
5. Take a skewer and skew the marinated cottage cheese, scooped part upside leaving a gap of an inch between.
6. Roast in a tandoor for 5-6 minutes.
7. Serve hot with choice of a salad and chutney.

Jaipuri Paneer Tikka

COTTAGE CHEESE CHUNKS MARINATED WITH HOME MADE JAIPURI SPICE BLEND

Cooking time 5-6 minutes Serves 1-2

INGREDIENTS

(200 gms)   - Cottage cheese 5 pcs

First Marination
½ tsp   - Ginger garlic paste
To taste   - Salt
½ tsp   - Yellow chilli powder
1 tsp   - Lemon juice

Second Marination
3 tsp   - Processed cheese (grated)
2 tbsp   - Hung curd
To taste   - Salt
½ tsp   - Ginger garlic paste
½ tsp   - Yellow chilli powder
A pinch   - Elachi javaitri powder
½ tsp   - Roasted jeera powder
2 tsp   - Roasted channa powder
1 tsp   - Kutti red chilli
2 tsp   - Mustard oil
1/3 tsp   - Ajwain

METHOD

1. Cut cottage cheese into large cubes (1 ½ " x 1 ½ "). Pat dry and keep aside.

First Marination
2. In a bowl mix ginger garlic paste, salt, yellow chilli powder, lemon juice and apply this to cottage cheese and keep aside for at least half an hour.

Second Marination
3. In a bowl mash processed cheese, add hung curd, add all the remaining ingredients except ajwain and mustard oil and mix well.
4. Heat oil in a pan, add ajwain, let it crackle and then put it into the marinade and mix well.
5. Put the marinated cottage cheese into the marinade, mix well and keep aside for at least half an hour.

Cooking
6. Take a skewer and skew marinated cottage cheese pieces leaving a gap of an inch between.
7. Roast in a tandoor or over charcoal grill at a moderate temperature for 5-6 minutes.
8. Serve hot with choice of a salad and chutney.

Makhmali Paneer Seekh

VELVETTY COTTAGE CHEESE MINCE KEBAB ENHANCED WITH SELECT SPICES

Cooking time 5-6 minutes Serves 1-2

INGREDIENTS

150 gm   - Cottage cheese (grated)
50 gm   - Boiled potatoes (grated)
1 tsp   - Green chilli (chopped)
1 tbsp   - Fresh coriander (chopped)
1 tsp   - Capsicum (chopped)
3 tsp   - Tomatoes (chopped seedless and cheese)
½ tsp   - Yellow chilli powder
2 tsp   - Roasted channa powder
1 tbsp   - Breadcrumbs
1 tsp   - Raisins (chopped)
1 tsp   - Clarified butter
To taste   - Salt
A pinch   - Saffron

METHOD

1. In a bowl mix grated cottage cheese and potato.
2. Add chopped green chillies, coriander, capsicum, tomatoes and mix well.
3. Add yellow chilli powder, channa powder, breadcrumbs, raisins, melted butter and salt. Sprinkle saffron in the end, mix well to form a smooth dough.
4. Divide the mixture into 4 equal parts and make balls.

Cooking
5. Take a skewer and apply the mixture along the skewer with moist hands, in a cylindrical shape. Roast in a moderate hot tandoor or over a charcoal grill for 5-6 minutes.
6. Serve hot with choice of a salad and chutney.

Tiranga Paneer Tikka

AN EYE- PLEASING TRI COLOUR DELICACY OF COTTAGE CHEESE
Cooking time 5-6 minutes Serves 1-2

INGREDIENTS

200 gm	- Cottage cheese (5 pcs)

Stuffing

1 tbsp	- Khoya (grated)
A pinch	- Saffron
To taste	- Salt
1 tbsp	- Cottage cheese (grated)
1 tbsp	- Green paste
1 tsp	- Beetroot paste

Marination

4 tbsp	- Hung curd
1 tsp	- Ginger garlic paste
1 tsp	- Fresh coriander (chopped)
½ tsp	- Green chilli (chopped)
1/3 tsp	- White pepper powder
A pinch	- Cardamom powder
1 tsp	- Lemon juice
To taste	- Salt

METHOD

1. Cut cottage cheese into cubes (1 ½" x 1 ½ "), slit each cube into 3 layers without disjoining, pat dry and keep aside

Stuffing (3 types of stuffing)

2. In a small bowl mix khoya, saffron, keep aside. In another bowl mash cottage cheese, add salt and green paste and in another bowl mash cottage cheese, salt, beetroot paste and keep aside.
3. With the help of a knife stuff each slice in this order, green paste in the first layer, red in the second layer and yellow in the third layer in equal portion.(sprinkle a pinch of salt before stuffing.)

Marination

4. In a bowl whisk hung curd, add all the remaining ingredients listed in the order above, mix well.
5. Put stuffed cottage cheese into this marinade, coat well and keep aside for at least half an hour.

Cooking

6. Take a skewer and skew marinated cottage cheese one by one leaving an inch gap between each portion.
7. Roast in a tandoor or over a charcoal grill at a moderate temperature for 5-6 minutes.
8. Serve hot with choice of a salad and chutney.

Noorani Paneer Seekh

A DELICACY OF COTTAGE CHEESE INFUSED WITH MILD SPICES
Cooking time 5-6 minutes Serves 1-2

INGREDIENTS

150 gm	- Cottage cheese (grated)
50 gm	- Boiled potatoes (grated)
3 tsp	- Onion (chopped)
½ tsp	- Green chilli (chopped)
6 no	- Fried crushed curry leaves
½ tsp	- Red chilli powder
A pinch	- Elaichi javitri powder
1 tsp	- Chaat masala
½ tsp	- Shahi jeera (black cumin)
2 tsp	- Cashewnut (chopped)
To taste	- Salt
For binding	- Breadcrumbs

METHOD

1. In a deep tray mix grated cottage cheese and boiled potato.
2. Add chopped onions, garlic, green chillies, curry leaves, add salt, red chilli powder, elaichi javitri powder, chaat masala shahi jeera , cashewnut, mix well.
3. Add breadcrumbs for binding and make a smooth dough and divide the mixture into 4 parts.

Cooking

4. Take a skewer and apply the mixture along the skewer with moist hands in a cylindrical shape (4"-5").
5. Roast in tandoor in a moderate temperature or over a charcoal grill for 5-6 minutes.
6. Serve hot with choice of a salad and chutney.

Lajawab Paneer Roll

THE PIECE DE RESISTANCE AMONG RECIPES IN THE ROAST COTTAGE CHEESE KEBAB ROLLS

Cooking time 5-6 minutes Serves 2

INGREDIENTS

(150 gm)	- Cottage cheese (sliced) 4pcs

Stuffing

40 gm	- Khoya (grated)
40 gm	- Cottage Cheese (grated)
2 tsp	- Bell pepper (chopped)
1 tsp	- Cashewnut (chopped)
1 tsp	- Raisins (chopped)
½ tsp	- Green chilli (chopped)
1 tsp	- Green coriander (chopped)

Marination

4 tsp	- Processed cheese (grated)
2 tbsp	- Hung curd
2 tbsp	- Cream
½ tsp	- White pepper powder
A pinch	- Elaichi powder
1 tsp	- Green coriander (chopped)
1 tsp	- Green chilli (chopped)
To taste	- Salt

METHOD

1. Take a block of cottage cheese, with a sharp knife cut thin slices (5"x2"x5 cm), pat dry and keep aside.

Stuffing

2. In a bowl mix all the ingredients listed in order and divide into four equal parts.
3. Spread each cottage cheese on flat surface, place filling, roll in the capsule shape, seal it with wooden toothpicks to prevent the stuffing from falling.

Marination

4. In a deep tray mash processed cheese, add hung curd and all other remaining ingredients listed in order and mix well.
5. Put stuffed cottage cheese into this marinade, coat well and keep aside for at least half an hour.

Cooking

6. Take a skewer and skew the cottage cheese pieces horizontally.
7. Roast in a moderately hot tandoor or over charcoal grill for 5-6 minutes to give golden colour.
8. Remove toothpicks and serve with choice of a salad and chutney.

Kandhari Paneer Tikka

A DELICACY OF COTTAGE CHEESE STUFFED WITH POMEGRANATE AND AROMATIC SPICES

Cooking time 5-6 minutes Serves 1-2

INGREDIENTS

200 gm	- Cottage cheese (5 pcs)

Stuffing

2 tsp	- Boiled potato (grated)
2 tsp	- Khoya (grated)
1 tsp	- Cashewnut (chopped)
1 tsp	- Raisins (chopped)
1 tsp	- Pista (chopped)

Marination

4 tbsp	- Hung curd
½ tsp	- Ginger garlic paste
½ tsp	- Red chilli paste
2 tsp	- Annar juice
1/3 tsp	- Kasoori methi powder
A pinch	- Garam masala
1 tsp	- Refined oil
1 tsp	- Anar dana crushed
A pinch	- Turmeric powder
1 tsp	- Roasted besan
To taste	- Salt

METHOD

1. Cut cottage cheese into large cubes (1 ½"x1 ½" cubes) and slit from centre till half, pat dry and keep aside.

Stuffing

2. In a small bowl mix boiled potato, khoya, chopped cashewnuts, raisins, pista, mix well and divide into five parts.
3. Fill this mixture with help of knife into each cottage cheese piece, close again and keep aside.

Marination

4. In a bowl whisk hung curd, add all the remaining ingredients listed in order and mix well.
5. Put the stuffed cottage cheese pieces in this marinade, coat well and keep aside for at least half an hour.

Cooking

6. Take a skewer and skew marinated cottage cheese leaving a gap of an inch between each piece.
7. Roast it in a tandoor or over a charcoal grill at a moderate temperature for 5-6 minutes.
8. Serve hot along with choice of a salad and chutney.

Tandoori Paneer Gulnar

AN EYE-PLEASING AND COLOURFUL COTTAGE CHEESE ROLLED WITH DRY FRUITS
Cooking time 5-6 minutes Serves 1-2

INGREDIENTS

150 gm - Sliced cottage cheese (4 no.)

Stuffing
1 tsp	- Refined oil
½ tsp	- Whole jeera
25 gm	- Boiled carrot (chopped)
25 gm	- Boiled beans (chopped)
25 gm	- Cottage cheese grated
½ tsp	- Ginger (chopped)
½ tsp	- Green chilli (chopped)
1 tsp	- Cashewnut (chopped)
1 tsp	- Raisins (chopped)
1 tsp	- Crushed anardana
1 tsp	- Honey
To taste	- Salt

Marination
4 tbsp	- Hung curd
To taste	- Salt
½ tsp	- Ginger garlic paste
A pinch	- Kasori methi powder
1/3 tsp	- Garam masala
1 tsp	- Refined oil
A pinch	- Ajwain
½ tsp	- Yellow chilli powder
1 tsp	- Roasted besan

METHOD

1. Take a block of cottage cheese, cut into thin slices (5"x2"x.5cm), pat dry and keep aside.

Stuffing
2. Heat oil in a pan, add jeera and let it crackle, add carrot, beans and saute, add cottage cheese and all remaining ingredients, add honey, salt, mix it and keep aside for cooling.
3. Divide this mixture into four equal parts.
4. Spread each of slice cottage cheese on flat surface, place filling, roll in the capsule shape, seal it with wooden toothpicks to prevent the stuffing from falling.

Marination
5. In a bowl whisk hung curd, add all the ingredients and mix well.
6. Put the stuffed cottage cheese pieces in this marinade coat well and keep aside for at least half an hour.

Cooking
7. Take a skewer and skew the marinated cottage cheese pieces, horizontally.
8. Roast in a moderately hot tandoor or over charcoal grill for 5-6 minutes.
9. Remove toothpicks and serve with choice of a salad and chutney.

Tandoori Paneer Pasanda

A DELICACY OF COTTAGE CHEESE PICATTA STUFFED WITH EXOTIC FILLING AND CHARGRILLED

Cooking time 5-6 minutes **Serves 1-2**

INGREDIENTS

200 gm - Cottage cheese (5 pcs)

Stuffing
30 gm	- Khoya (Grated)
2 tsp	- Raisins (Chopped)
1 tsp	- Fresh coriander (chopped)
2 tsp	- Processed cheese (grated)
To taste	- Salt

Marination
2 tsp	- Processed cheese (grated)
4 tbsp	- Hung curd
To taste	- Salt
½ tsp	- White pepper powder
A pinch	- Cinnamon powder
1 tsp	- Roasted besan
A pinch	- Shahi jeera
2 tsp	- Corn flour
½ tsp	- Yellow chilli (powder)
A pinch	- Saffron

METHOD

1. Cut cottage cheese into 2"x2"x1 cm flat pieces and slit from centre till half.
2. Pat dry cottage cheese and keep aside.

Stuffing

3. In a bowl mix khoya, raisins, salt, green coriander and processed cheese, divide this mixture into five parts.
4. Fill this mixture into each slice of cottage cheese with the help of a knife, close and keep aside.

Marination

5. In a bowl mash cheese, add hung curd and all remaining ingredients in the order listed above and mix well.
6. Remove extra moisture from cottage cheese and put it in this marinade, coat well and keep aside for at least half an hour.

Cooking

7. Take a skewer and skew the marinated cottage cheese leaving a gap of 1 inch.
8. Roast in a tandoor or over charcol grill for 5-6 minutes.
9. Serve hot along with choice of a salad and chutney.

Saunphia Dum Paneer

ANISEED FLAVOURED COTTAGE CHEESE COOKED ON SLOW HEAT

Cooking time 3-4 minutes **Serves 1-2**

INGREDIENTS

200 gm - Cottage cheese (5 pcs)

First Marination
To taste	- Salt
½ tsp	- White pepper power
½ tsp	- Ginger garlic paste

Second Marination
4 tbsp	- Hung curd
To taste	- Salt
½ tsp	- Ginger garlic paste
½ tsp	- White pepper powder
1 tsp	- Saunf powder
1 tsp	- Cream
2 tsp	- Cornflour
½ tsp	- Green chilli (chopped)
1 tsp	- Green coriander (chopped)
½ tsp	- Yellow chilli powder
A pinch	- Chaat masala

For Cooking - Refined oil

METHOD

1. Cut cottage cheese into round (2"x2") flat pieces (thickness - 5cm), pat dry and keep aside.

First Marination

2. In a bowl mix salt, white pepper powder and ginger garlic paste and keep aside for at least half an hour.

Second Marination

3. In a bowl whisk hung curd, add all the remaining ingredients listed above and mix well.
4. Remove excess moisture from cheese, put in this marinade, coat well and keep aside for at least 45 minutes.

Cooking

5. Heat oil in a non-stick pan or thick bottom pan and put marinated cottage cheese pieces, cover it with lid and cook on slow fire for 3-4 minutes or till golden brown.
6. Serve hot with choice of a salad and chutney

Tutti Frutti Paneer Seekh

COMBINATION OF TUTTI FRUTTI AND COTTAGE CHEESE DELICATELY CHAR - GRILLED IN CLAY OVEN

Cooking time 5-6 minutes Serves 1-2

INGREDIENTS

175 gm	- Cottage cheese (grated)
75 gm	- Boiled potato (grated)
1 tsp	- Green coriander (chopped)
½ tsp	- Ginger chopped (chopped)
½ tsp	- Green chilli (chopped)
½ tsp	- White pepper powder
A pinch	- Shahi jeera
2 tsp	- Cream
2 tsp	- Processed cheese (grated)
3 tsp	- Tutty frutty (chopped)
1 tsp	- Raisins (chopped)
To taste	- Salt
2 tsp	- Cornflour
For binding	- Breadcrumbs
A pinch	- Elaichi powder

METHOD

1. In a bowl mix grated cottage cheese, add all the remaining ingredients in the order listed. Mix well to a smooth mixture.
2. Divide this mixture into 4 equal parts and make balls.

Cooking

3. Apply each ball on a skewer with moist hand in a cylindrical shape and grill over charcoal or in a tandoor at a moderate temperature for 5-6 minutes.
4. Serve hot with choice of a salad and chutney.

Bharwan Tandoori Paneer

STUFFED COTTAGE CHEESE CHUNKS ROASTED IN CLAY OVEN

Cooking time 5-6 minutes Serves 1-2

INGREDIENTS

200 gm	- Cottage cheese (5 pcs.)

Stuffing

30 gm	- Cottage cheese (grated)
½ tsp	- Ginger (chopped)
½ tsp	- Green chilli (chopped)
½ tsp	- Mint (chopped)
1 tsp	- Bell pepper (chopped)
To taste	- Salt

Marination

4 tbsp	- Hung curd
To taste	- Salt
1 tsp	- White pepper powder
½ tsp	- Ginger garlic paste
1 tbsp	- Cream
A pinch	- Elaichi powder
A pinch	- Shahi jeera (black cumin)
2 tsp	- Cornflour

METHOD

1. Cut cottage cheese into cubes (1 ½"x 1 ½"), slit from centre till half, pat dry and keep aside.

Stuffing

2. In a bowl mix grated cottage cheese, ginger, green chilli, mint, salt and bell pepper, mix well.
3. Stuff this mixture in equal quantity into each cottage cheese cubes.

Second Marination

4. In a bowl whisk hung curd and add all the remaining ingredients listed above and mix well.
5. Put the stuffed cottage cheese into this marinade, coat well and keep aside for at least half an hour.

Cooking

6. Take a skewer and skew the marinated cheese cubes one by one, scooped side to be kept upside.
7. Roast in a moderately hot tandoor for 5-6 minutes.
8. Serve hot along with choice of a salad and chutney.

Paneer Tikka Shashlik (for recipe turn to page no: 212)

Lajawab Paneer Seekh (for recipe turn to page no: 214)

Tandoori Paneer Pasanda (for recipe turn to page no: 223)

Tandoori Ghungroo Paneer De (for recipe turn to page no: 218)

Tiranga Paneer Tikka (for recipe turn to page no: 220)

Tandoori Tamatar Ka Dolma (for recipe turn to page no: 242)

Jaipuri Bharwan Aloo (for recipe turn to page no: 243)

Tandoori Shimla Mirch (for recipe turn to page no: 239)

Gajab Ka Phool (for recipe turn to page no: 239)

Tandoori Phalon Ki Chaat (for recipe turn to page no: 243)

Mungphal Aur Paneer Kebab

UNUSUAL COMBINATION OF PEANUTS AND COTTAGE CHEESE

Cooking time 2-3 minutes Serves 1-2

INGREDIENTS

100 gm	- Peanuts (crushed)
50 gm	- Cottage Cheese (grated)
50 gm	- Boiled potato (grated)
To taste	- Salt
½ tsp	- Green chilli (chopped)
½ tsp	- Ginger (chopped)
1 tsp	- Fresh coriander (chopped)
¼ tsp	- Yellow chilli powder
For binding	- Breadcrumbs
2 tsp	- Corn flour
6 tsp	- Peanuts (coarsely chopped)
For frying	- Refined oil

METHOD

1. In a bowl mix crushed peanuts, cottage cheese, add all the ingredients in the order listed and mix well to form a smooth mixture.

2. Divide the mixture into 4-6 balls and flatten each ball between wet palms into medallion (tikki) shape, roll in chopped peanuts and keep in refrigerator for some time.

Cooking

3. Heat oil in a pan and deep fry tikki till golden brown and crisp on both sides. Drain excess of oil.

4. Serve hot with choice of a salad and chutney.

Doranga Paneer Tikka

STUFFED COTTAGE CHEESE CHUNKS WITH TWO KINDS OF MARINATION

Cooking time 5-6 minutes Serves 1-2

INGREDIENTS

200 gm	- Cottage cheese

Stuffing

1 tsp	- Garlic paste
To taste	- Salt
1/3 tsp	- Garam masala
¼ tsp	- Red chilli powder
2 tsp	- Anardana (crushed)
1 tsp	- Vinegar
1 tsp	- Mustard oil

First Marination

2 tbsp	- Hung curd
1 tbsp	- Cream
½ tsp	- Ginger garlic paste
To taste	- Salt
1/3 tsp	- Garam masala
½ tsp	- Red chilli powder
A pinch	- Turmeric powder
1 tsp	- Roasted gram flour
1 tsp	- Lemon juice
1 tsp	- Refined oil

Second Marination

2 tbsp	- Hung curd
1 tbsp	- Cream
½ tsp	- Ginger garlic paste
1 tbsp	- Green paste
To taste	- Salt
¼ tsp	- White pepper powder
A pinch	- Ajwain
1 tsp	- Roasted gram flour
1 tsp	- Lemon juice
1 tsp	- Refined oil

METHOD

1. Cut cottage cheese into 2 ½ inch thick slices, slit each piece halfway without disjoining it, pat dry and keep aside.

Stuffing

2. In a bowl mix garlic paste, salt, garam masala, red chilli powder, crushed anardana, vinegar, mustard oil and mix thoroughly.
3. Stuff this mixture into each slice of cottage cheese with the help of a knife, keep aside.

First Marination

4. In a bowl whisk hung curd, add cream, ginger garlic paste, salt, garam masala, red chilli powder, turmeric powder, roasted gram flour, lemon juice, oil and mix well. Put half of the stuffed cottage cheese slices into this marinade and keep aside for at least 1 hour.

Second Marination

5. In a bowl whisk hung curd, add cream, ginger garlic paste green paste, salt, white pepper powder, ajwain roasted gram flour, lemon juice, oil and mix well. Put the remaining stuffed cottage cheese slice into this marinade and keep aside for at least 1 hour.

Cooking

6. Take a skewer and skew marinated cottage cheese alternately with both the marination leaving an inch gap between each portion.
7. Roast in a tandoor or over a charcoal grill at a moderate temperature for 5-6 minutes.
8. Serve hot with choice of a salad and chutney.

Vegetables

Tandoori Shakar Kandi

A NEW IDEA FOR SWEET POTATO KEBAB FLAVOURED WITH APPETIZING SPICES

Cooking time 5-6 minutes Serves 1-2

INGREDIENTS

225 gm (05 no.) - Sweat potato (boiled)

Marination

3 tbsp	- Hung curd
To taste	- Salt
1 tsp	- Red chilli powder
½ tsp	- Ginger/garlic paste
½ tsp	- Kasoori methi powder
½ tsp	- Garam masala
½ tsp	- Black salt
2 tsp	- Lemon juice
1 tsp	- Refined oil
1 tsp	- Roasted besan
To sprinkle	- Chaat masala

METHOD

1. Remove the skin of sweet potatoes and ensure that sweet potatoes are ¾ cooked.
2. Cut sweet potatoes into a circular shape of about 1 ½ - 2 inches.

Marination

3. In a bowl whisk hung curd, add all the ingredients listed above and mix well.
4. Put sweet potatoes into this marinade, mix well and keep aside for at least 1 hour.

Cooking

5. Take a skewer and skew the sweet potatoes leaving a gap of an inch.
6. Roast in a tandoor at moderate temperature for 5-6 minutes.
7. Sprinkle chaat masala on top and serve hot with choice of a salad and chutney.

Shakar Kandi Seekh

ANOTHER VARIATION OF SWEET POTATO SPICED WITH AJWAIN

Cooking time 4-6 minutes Serves 1-2

INGREDIENTS

150 gm	- Boiled sweet potato (grated)
75 gm	- Boiled potato (grated)
½ tsp	- Green chilli (chopped)
1 tsp	- Fresh coriander (chopped)
½ tsp	- Ginger (chopped)
To taste	- Salt
½ tsp	- Yellow chilli powder
½ tsp	- Roasted jeera powder
A pinch	- Ajwain
2 tsp	- Cornflour
For binding	- Breadcrumbs

METHOD

1. In a bowl mash grated sweet potato and potato, add all the remaining ingredients listed above and mix well.
2. Divide this mixture into 4-5 equal parts and make balls.

Cooking

3. Take a skewer and apply each ball on it along the skewer with moist palm to give a cylindrical shape (4"-5").
4. Roast in a tandoor or over a charcoal grill at a moderate temperature for 4-6 minutes.
5. Serve hot with choice of a salad and chutney.

Jimikand Seekh Kebab

THIS DELIGHTFUL KEBAB MADE OF YAM INFUSED WITH FLAVOURFUL SPICES

Cooking time 5-6 minutes Serves 1-2

INGREDIENTS

125 gm	- Boiled Jimikand (grated)
50 gm	- Boiled potatoes (grated)
50 gm	- Cottage cheese (grated)
½ tsp	- Green chilli (chopped)
½ tsp	- Fresh coriander (chopped)
½ tsp	- Ginger (chopped)
To taste	- Salt
½ tsp	- Yellow chilli powder
A pinch	- Dalchini powder
A pinch	- Elaichi powder
½ tsp	- Red chilli (kutti)
½ tsp	- Roasted jeera powder
2 tsp	- Cornflour
For binding	- Breadcrumbs

METHOD

1. Squeeze extra moisture completely from jimikand, potatoes and cottage cheese, mash it and transfer to a bowl.
2. Add all the remaining ingredients listed above and mix well to smooth consistency.
3. Divide this mixture into 4-5 equal portion and make balls.

Cooking

4. Take a skewer and apply each portion on to it along the skewer with moist palm to give a cylindrical shape (4"-5").
5. Roast in a tandoor or over a charcoal grill at a moderate temperature for 5-6 minutes.
6. Serve hot with choice of a salad and chutney.

Bharwan Tandoori Tinda

A SPICY AND UNUSUAL CREATION OF ROUND GOURD STUFFED WITH EXOTIC FILLING

Cooking time 5-6 minutes Serves 1-2

INGREDIENTS

200 gm (4 no)	- Tinda (round gourd)
For frying	- Refined oil

Stuffing

50 gm	- Cottage cheese (grated)
40 gm	- Potato (grated)
To taste	- Salt
½ tsp	- Roasted jeera powder
½ tsp	- Green chilli (chopped)
1 tsp	- Green coriander (chopped)

Marination

4 tbsp	- Hung curd
To taste	- Salt
½ tsp	- Ginger garlic paste
½ tsp	- Red chilli paste
1/3 tsp	- Kasoori methi powder
½ tsp	- Garam masala

METHOD

1. Peel, scoop tinda to make a hole with help of a sharp knife, wash, pat dry and keep aside.
2. Fry tinda in oil on slow heat till tender/half cooked.

Stuffing

3. In a bowl take cottage cheese, potato, salt, jeera powder, green chilli, coriander and mix well.
4. Stuff each tinda with above filling and keep aside.

Marination

5. In a bowl whisk hung curd, add all the remaining ingredients listed above and mix well.
6. Remove extra moisture from tinda and put them into this marinade, coat well and keep aside for at least 1 hour.

Cooking

7. Take a skewer and skew the marinated tinda one by one.
8. Roast in a tandoor at a moderate temperature for 5-6 minutes.
9. Serve hot with choice of a salad and chutney

Seeta Phal Ke Shammi

THIS VERSION OF RED PUMPKIN MAKES A HIGHLY NUTRITIOUS KEBAB FOR ALL SEASONS

Cooking time 2-3 minutes Serves 1-2

INGREDIENTS

100 gm	- Boiled seeta phal (red pumpkin)
50 gm	- Potatoes (grated)
50 gm	- Cottage cheese (grated)
½ tsp	- Green chilli (chopped)
1 tsp Fresh	- Fresh coriander (chopped)
2 tsp	- Cornflour
A pinch	- Ajwain
½ tsp	- Yellow chilli powder
To taste	- Salt
4 tsp (for binding)	- Breadcrumbs
To taste	- Salt

Filling

2 tsp	- Onion (chopped)
2 tsp	- Processed cheese (grated)
½ tsp	- Green coriander (chopped)
½ tsp	- Green chilli (chopped)
½ tsp	- Crushed cashewnut (crushed)
½ tsp	- Pista (crushed)
A pinch	- Salt

For frying - Refined oil

METHOD

1. Squeeze moisture/water completely from seetaphal
2. In a flat tray mash seetaphal, add all the remaining ingredients listed above and mix well. Divide this mixture in 5-6 equal parts and make balls.

Filling

3. In a bowl take onions, cheese, coriander, green chilli, cashewnut, pista, salt, mix well and divide in 5-6 parts
4. Flatten each ball between palms, place filling, seal, again flatten to give shape of medallion (tikki) and refrigerate for some time.

Cooking

5. Heat oil in a pan and deep fry till golden brown and crisp. Remove to an absorbent paper to remove excess oil.
6. Serve hot with choice of a salad and chutney.

Tandoori Bharwan Parmal

SNAKE GOURD STUFFED WITH SPICY COTTAGE CHEESE FILLING STEEPED IN DRIED FENUGREEK FLAVOURED MARINADE

Cooking time 5-6 minutes Serves 1-2

INGREDIENTS

100 gm (4 no) - Parmal (snake gourd)

For frying - Refined oil

Stuffing

50 gm	- Potato (grated)
50 gm	- Cottage cheese (grated)
To taste	- Salt
½ tsp	- Yellow chilli powder
½ tsp	- Ginger (chopped)
½ tsp	- Green chilli (chopped)
1 tsp	- Fresh coriander (chopped)

Marination

4 tbsp	- Hung curd
½ tsp	- Ginger garlic paste
½ tsp	- Red chilli paste
To taste	- Salt
½ tsp	- Garam masala
½ tsp	- Kasoori methi powder
1 tsp	- Refined oil
½ tsp	- Chaat masala

METHOD

1. Peel the upper skin of parmal leaving a strip of the skin alternatively and fry it till half cooked, pat dry and keep aside.

Stuffing

2. In a bowl mix potatoes, cottage cheese grated, add the remaining ingredients and mix well.
3. Stuff each parmal with the stuffing.

Marination

4. In a bowl whisk hung curd, add all the remaining ingredients listed above and mix well, put the stuffed parmal into this marinade, coat well and keep aside for at least 1 hour.

Cooking

5. Take a skewer and skew marinated parmal horizontally.
6. Roast in a tandoor or charcoal grill at a moderate temperature for 5-6 minutes.
7. Sprinkle chat masala, serve hot along with choice of a salad and chutney.

Tandoori Shimla Mirch

CAPSICUM STUFFED WITH COTTAGE CHEESE, GREEN PEAS AND ENRICHED WITH DRY FRUITS AND ROASTED IN CLAY OVEN

Cooking time 8-10 minutes Serves 1-2

INGREDIENTS

2 no	- Capsicum large

Stuffing

1 tbsp	- Refined oil
1 tsp	- Cumin seeds
50 gm	- Cottage cheese cubes (small)
50 gm	- Boiled potatoes cubes (small)
20 gm	- Green peas (boiled)
2 tsp	- Roasted cashewnut
2 tsp	- Raisins
To taste	- Salt
A pinch	- Turmeric powder
1 tsp	- Red chilli powder
A pinch	- Kalonji
A pinch	- Saunf

METHOD

1. Cut the caps of capsicum, remove seeds, wash, pat dry and keep aside.

Stuffing

2. Heat oil in a non-stick pan, add cumin seeds and let it crackle. Add cottage cheese, potatoes cubes, green peas and add all the remaining ingredients listed above. Saute for 1-2 minutes and transfer this mixture in a bowl and allow it to cool.
3. Stuff each capsicum with this mixture and cover with the caps and tie individually each capsicum with kitchen string.

Cooking

4. Take a skewer and skew each capsicum leaving a gap of 1inch. On the bottom of the skewer, a piece of potato or half cut onion can be used to prevent them from slipping.
5. Roast in a tandoor at a moderate temperature for 8-10 minutes.
6. Serve hot with choice of a salad and chutney.

Gajab Ka Phool

BABY CAULIFLOWER STEEPED IN CARUM SEED FLAVOURED YOGHURT MARINADE AND BAKED IN TANDOOR

Cooking time 8-10 minutes Serves 1-2

INGREDIENTS

225-250 gm (1 no)	- Baby cauliflower
2 no	- Big cardamom
2 no	- Small cardamom
1 tsp	- Turmeric powder
To taste	- Salt

Marination

4 tbsp	- Hung curd
½ tsp	- Yellow chilli powder
To taste	- Salt
½ tsp	- Garam masala
A pinch	- Ajwain
½ tsp	- Ginger garlic paste
1 tsp	- Lemon juice
2 tsp	- Mustard oil
A pinch	- Turmeric powder

METHOD

1. Wash and clean cauliflower, in boiling water, add small and big cardamom, turmeric, salt then put in cauliflower and cook till ¼ done.
2. Remove and let water drain out.

Marination

3. In a bowl whisk hung curd and add all the remaining ingredients listed above except turmeric and oil and mix well. Heat mustard oil in a pan, add turmeric and immediately put in marinade.
4. Apply this marinade to cauliflower all around and keep aside for at least 30 minutes.

Cooking

5. Take a skewer and skew marinated cauliflower and roast it in a moderately hot tandoor for 8-10 minutes.
6. Serve hot with choice of a salad and chutney.

Vilayati Seekh Kebab

DELICATE SEEKH KEBEB CRAFTED FROM ENGLISH VEGETABLES AND GRILLED

Cooking time 5-6 minutes Serves 1-2

INGREDIENTS

100 gm	- Broccoli (boiled)
100 gm	- Baby corn (boiled)
40 gm	- Asparagus (boiled & chopped)
40 gm	- Artichokes (chopped)
40 gm	- Boiled potatoes (grated)
40 gm	- Cottage cheese (grated)
To taste	- Salt
½ tsp	- Yellow chilli powder
½ tsp	- Ginger (chopped)
1 tsp	- Fresh oriander (chopped)
1/2 tsp	- Green chilli (chopped)
½ tsp	- Garam masala
1 tsp	- Cornflour
For binding	- Bread crumbs

METHOD

1. Remove excess moisture from artichokes, babycorn, asparagus and brocolli by squeezing.
2. In a food processor, put these vegetables, make a fine mince and transfer it to a deep tray.
3. Add potatoes, Cottage cheese and remaining ingredients, mix well with the help of palm and keep aside for at least 1 hour.
4. Divide the mixture into 5 equal parts and make balls.

Cooking

5. Take a skewer and apply along on it in cylindrical shape (4"-5") with a moist palm.
6. Roast in a moderately hot tandoor or over a charcoal grill for 5-6 minutes.
7. Serve hot with a choice of a salad and chutney.

Mazedaar Broccoli Seekh

DELICIOUS KEBEB OF BROCCOLI MINCE AND ENRICHED WITH DRY FRUITS

Cooking time 5-6 minutes Serves 1-2

INGREDIENTS

100 gm	- Boiled broccoli (chopped)
50 gm	- Cottage cheese (grated)
50 gm	- Boiled potato (grated)
To taste	- Salt
½ tsp	- Yellow chilli powder
½ tsp	- Ginger (chopped)
½ tsp	- Garam masala
1 tsp	- Pistachio (chopped)
1 tsp	- Cashewnut (chopped)
1 tsp	- Almond (chopped)
1tsp	- Cornflour
For binding	- Breadcrumbs

METHOD

1. Remove extra moisture from broccoli by squeezing it and put it in a deep tray.
2. Add all the remaining ingredients in the order listed above and mix well, keep aside for at least half an hour.
3. Divide the mixture into 4 equal portions.

Cooking

4. Take a skewer, apply the mixture in a cylindrical shape with a moist palm, grill it over a charcoal grill or in a tandoor for 5-6 minutes.
5. Serve hot along with choice of a salad and chutney.

Shikampuri Subz Kebab

YET ANOTHER EXAMPLE OF FAMOUS, SUPERLATIVE KEBAB FROM SHIKAMPUR PREPARED WITH VEGETABLES AND LUCKNOWI SPICES

Cooking time 2-3 minutes Serves 1-2

INGREDIENTS

100 gm	- Boiled carrot and beans (chopped)
25 gm	- Boiled green peas (chopped)
40 gm	- Potatoes (grated)
40 gm	- Cottage cheese (grated)
To taste	- Salt
1/3 tsp	- Yellow chilli powder
1/3 tsp	- Garam masala
1 tsp	- Green coriander chopped
½ tsp	- Green chilli chopped
1 tsp	- Cornflour
½ tsp	- Lucknowi masala
For binding	- Breadcrumbs

Stuffing

2 tbsp	- Onion (chopped)
2 tsp	- Boiled potato (grated)
½ tsp	- Green chilli (chopped)
1 tsp	- Green coriander (chopped)
To taste	- Salt
½ tsp	- Chaat masala
½ tsp	- Roasted jeera powder

For frying - Refined oil

METHOD

1. Put carrot and beans, green peas in a deep tray, add potatoes, cottage cheese and all the remaining ingredients in order listed, mix well to a smooth consistency and keep aside for at least half an hour.
2. Divide the mixture into 5 equal parts and make balls.

Stuffing

3. In a bowl mix onion, green chilli, coriander, salt, chaat masala, grated potatoes, jeera. Divide the mixture into 5 equal parts.
4. Flatten each ball between wet palms, place stuffing, seal again. Flatten it to give shape of a medallion (tikki).

Cooking

5. Heat oil in a pan and shallow fry till golden brown colour appears on both sides. Remove to an absorbent paper to remove excess oil.
6. Serve hot with choice of a salad and chutney.

Parsi Subz Kebab

A UNIQUE VEGETABLE CREATION PREPARED IN TRUE PARSI STYLE

Cooking time 2-3 minutes Serves 1-2

INGREDIENTS

50 gm	- Boiled beans and carrots (chopped)
4 tsp	- Boiled mushroom (chopped)
100 gm	- Potatoes (grated)
4 tsp	- Onions (chopped)
½ tsp	- Ginger garlic paste
1 tsp	- Green coriander (chopped)
½ tsp	- Green chilli (chopped)
To taste	- Salt
½ tsp	- Roasted jeera powder
A pinch	- Turmeric powder
2 tsp	- Cornflour
For binding	- Breadcrumbs

For batter

40 gm	- Besan
To taste	- Salt
1/2 tsp	- Red chilli powder
½ tsp	- Ajwain

For frying - Refined oil

METHOD

1. Put vegetables in a deep tray, add all the ingredients in the order listed, mix well and keep aside for at least half an hour.
2. Divide the mixture into 5-6 equal portion and make balls and press between your wet palm, giving medallion (tikki) shape and keep in refrigerator.
3. Make a thin batter of besan, salt, red chilli powder and water (coating consistency).

Cooking

4. Heat oil in a kadhai, dip each tikki into the batter and deep fry to golden brown colour and crisp. Remove to an absorbent paper to remove excess oil.
5. Serve hot with choice of a salad and chutney.

Tandoori Tamatar Ka Dolma

AN UNUSUAL AND DELICIOUS KEBAB MADE OF STUFFED TAMOTOES
DELICATELY BAKED IN CLAY OVEN

Cooking time 6-8 minutes Serves 1-2

INGREDIENTS

4 no	- Tomatoes (medium)

Stuffing
1 tsp	- Refined oil
½ tsp	- Cumin seeds
2 tsp	- Onion (chopped)
4 tbsp	- Boiled potatoes (grated)
4 tbsp	- Cottage cheese (grated)
½ tsp	- Green chilli (chopped)
½ tsp	- Ginger (chopped)
2 tsp	- Coconut powder
To taste	- Salt
½ tsp	- Turmeric powder
½ tsp	- Yellow chilli powder

Marination
4 tbsp	- Hung curd
½ tsp	- Ginger garlic paste
To taste	- Salt
A pinch	- Ajwain
½ tsp	- Red chilli paste
2 tsp	- Channa powder

METHOD

1. Cut caps of the tomatoes, remove seeds, wash, pat dry and keep aside.

Stuffing

2. Heat oil in a non-stick pan, add cumin seeds, let it crackle, add chopped onion and all other ingredients, saute for 1-2 minutes and transfer it to a bowl and allow it to cool.
3. Stuff each tomato with this mixture. Cover with the caps and individually tie each tomato with a kitchen string.

Marination

4. Prepare marination by mixing hung curd and other ingredients listed.
5. Dip the tomatoes in the marinade and keep aside for at least half an hour.

Cooking

6. Take a skewer and skew the tomatoes leaving at least an inch gap.
7. Roast in a moderately hot tandoor for 6-8 minutes.
8. Serve hot with choice of a salad and chutney.

Tandoori Surkh Lal Aloo

HOT AND FIERY POTATO BASKET STUFFED WITH EXOTIC COTTAGE CHEESE,
PEANUTS AND HOME GROUND SPICES

Cooking time 5-6 minutes Serves 1-2

INGREDIENTS

2 no	- Potato large
For frying	- Refined oil

Stuffing
1 tsp	- Refined oil
½ tsp	- Shahi jeera
50gm	- Boiled potato (dices)
50 gm	- Cottage cheese (dices)
½ tsp	- Ginger (chopped)
½ tsp	- Green chilli (chopped)
1 tsp	- Fresh coriander (chopped)
To taste	- Salt
½ tsp	- Yellow chilli powder
A pinch	- Elaichi javitri powder
2 tbsp	- Peanut crushed

Marination
2 tbsp	- Hung curd
½ tsp	- Ginger garlic paste
½ tsp	- Red chilli paste
To taste	- Salt
½ tsp	- Garam masala
A pinch	- Ajwain
2 tsp	- Lemon juice
1 tsp	- Refined oil

METHOD

1. Peal, scoop potatoes, wash, pat dry and keep aside.
2. Heat oil in a pan and deep fry potatoes till half cooked, drain oil and keep aside.

Stuffing

3. In a pan heat 1 tsp of oil, add potato dices and other ingredients listed above and sauté for 1-2 minutes. Transfer to a bowl for cooling.
4. Fill each potato with this stuffing and keep aside.

Marination

5. In a bowl whisk hung curd and add all other ingredients listed above and mix well.
6. Put stuffed potatoes into this marinade. Coat well and keep aside for at least ½ hour.

Cooking

7. Take a skewer and skew marinated potatoes one by one an inch apart and roast in a tandoor at a moderate temperature for 5-6 minutes.
8. Serve hot with choice of a salad and chutney.

Jaipuri Bharwan Aloo

ANOTHER VERSION OF STUFFED POTATO COATED WITH SESAME
Cooking time 5-6 minutes Serves 1-2

INGREDIENTS

2 pcs	- Potato large
3 tbsp	- Cornflour
For coating	- Til white/onion seeds
For frying	- Refined oil

Stuffing
50 gm	- Boiled potato cubes
50 gm	- Cottage cheese cubes
20 gm	- Green peas
½ tsp	- Red chilli powder
½ tsp	- Garam masala
½ tsp	- Ginger (chopped)
½ tsp	- Green chilli (chopped)
1 tsp	- Green coriander (chopped)
1 tsp	- Cashewnut (chopped)
1 tsp	- Raisins
To taste	- Salt

METHOD

1. Peal, scoop potato in a barrel shape, wash, pat dry and keep aside.
2. Make batter of cornflour to coating consistency, dip each potato into this batter, coat with till seeds and deep fry on slow fire till half cooked, to light brown colour.
3. Keep fried potatoes on a piece of cloth (upside down) to remove excess oil.

Stuffing
4. In a bowl mix potato, cottage cheese and mix all the remaining ingredients listed above.
5. Stuff each potato with this mixture and keep aside.

Cooking
6. Take a skewer, skew each potato on upward portion and roast in clay oven for 5-6 minutes.
7. Slice and arrange it on a plate. Serve hot with choice of a salad and chutney.

Tandoori Phalon Ki Chaat

A COLOURFUL AND APPETIZING KEBAB MADE OF SELECTED FRUITS
Cooking time 4-5 minutes Serves 2-3

INGREDIENTS

2½ no	- Pineapple
½ no	- Apple
½ no	- Guava
½ no	- Tomato (seedless)
1 no	- Capsicum (seedless)
1 no	- Pears
½ no	- Cucumber

Marination
4 tbsp	- Hung curd
½ tsp	- Red chilli powder
To taste	- Salt
½ tsp	- Garam masala
½ tsp	- Kasoori methi powder
1 tsp	- Refined oil
1 tsp	- Chaat masala
1 tsp	- Lemon juice
½ tsp	- Jeera powder

METHOD

1. Wash, peel and cut pineapple in 1 inch cubes.
2. Wash apple, guava and pear, cut them (with skin) into 1 inch cubes and keep aside.
3. Wash and deseed tomato, capsicum and cut them into 1 inch (large cubes). Keep aside.

Marination
4. In a bowl whisk hung curd, add red chilli powder, salt, garam masala, kasoori methi powder, refined oil, chaat masala, lemon juice, jeera powder and apply this to each fruit along with tomato and capsicum. Rub well and keep in a refrigerator for at least 1-1 ½ hour.

Cooking
5. Take a skewer and skew marinated fruits alternatively, then roast them in a moderately hot tandoor for 4-5 minutes till tender.
6. Sprinkle chaat masala and serve hot with the choice of a salad and chutney.

Palak Bhutte Ki Seekh

SEEKH KEBEB OF SPINACH AND CORN KERNELS, PERFUMED WITH HOME GROUND SPICES
AND DRIED FENUFREEK

Cooking time 4-6 minutes Serves 1-2

INGREDIENTS

75 gm	- Boiled spinach (roughly chopped)
50 gm	- Boiled baby corn (chopped)
50 gm	- Corn niblets (boiled)
40 gm	- Potatoes (grated)
40 gm	- Cottage cheese (grated)
To taste	- Salt
½ tsp	- Yellow chilli powder
½ tsp	- Kasoori methi powder
½ tsp	- Garam masala
For binding	- Breadcrumbs

METHOD

1. Squeeze the extra moisture from palak, corn niblets (1/2 qty.) and put in a deep tray.
2. Add all the remaining ingredients in order listed, mix well with the help of your palm. Check seasoning and keep aside for at least half an hour.
3. Divide the mixture into 4 equal parts and make balls.

Cooking

4. Take a skewer and apply mixture along on it in cylindrical shape (4"-5") with a moist palm. Stick remaining corn on top of this mixture with moist palms.
5. Roast in a moderately hot tandoor or over a charcoal grill for 4-6 minutes.
6. Serve hot with a choice of a salad and chutney.

Dahi Ke Shammi

ABSOLUTELY SOFT KEBAB MADE WITH FRESH YOGHURT CHEESE, STUFFED
WITH DRY FRUITS AND FRESH MINT

Cooking time 2-3 minutes Serves 1-2

INGREDIENTS

225 gm	- Double hung curd
½ tsp	- Ginger (chopped)
2 tsp	- Coconut powder
½ tsp	- Green chilli (chopped)
1 tsp	- Green coriander (chopped)
1/3 tsp	- Garam masala
1/3 tsp	- White pepper powder
To taste	- Salt

Filling

20 gm	- Raisins (chopped)
3 tsp	- Cashewnut (chopped)
1 tsp	- Mint (chopped)
2 tsp	- Roasted channa powder
1/3 tsp	- Elaichi powder
For frying	- Refined oil

METHOD

1. Remove whey/moisture from the curd completely to look like a thick paste.
2. In a bowl take hung curd, add ginger, green chilli, coriander, garam masala, white pepper powder, salt, elaichi powder, roasted channa powder mix well and keep aside for at least half an hour.
3. Divide the mixture into 5 equal portions and make balls.

Filling

4. In a bowl mix raisins, cashewnuts, mint, channa powder, elaichi powder.
5. Flatten each ball between your wet palms, put a portion of filling in the middle, seal, flatten again into tikki (medallion) shape and keep in refrigerator for at least 1 hour.

Cooking

6. Heat oil in a non-stick pan and shallow fry till golden brown and crisp on both sides. Remove on absorbent paper to remove excess oil.
7. Serve hot with choice of a salad and chutney.

Til Ke Khaas Kebab

COMBINATION OF VEGETABLES DELIGHTFULLY SEASONED WITH SPECIAL BLEND OF SPICES COATED WITH SESAME AND CRISPY FRIED

Cooking time 2-3 minutes Serves 1-2

INGREDIENTS

50 gm	- Beans (Boiled)
50 gm	- Carrots (Boiled)
50 gm	- Green Peas (Boiled)
50 gm	- Potatoes (Boiled and grated)
For binding	- Bread crumbs
½ tsp	- Yellow chilli powder
1 tsp	- Cornflour
To taste	- Salt
½ tsp	- Garam masala
A pinch	- Elaichi javitri powder
For coating	- Sesame seed
For frying	- Refined oil

METHOD

1. Remove excess moisture from beans, carrots and peas by squeezing it.
2. Put them in a processor and make a coarse paste.
3. Put coarse paste in a bowl, add all the remaining ingredients in order listed and mix well till smooth.
4. Divide the mixture into 4-5 equal parts or according to desired size and make round balls. Press each ball between wet palms to give the shape of a medallion (tikki).
5. Dust each piece with sesame seeds ensuring that it sticks well all around.

Cooking

6. Heat oil in a pan/kadhai and deep fry till golden brown and crisp.
7. Serve hot along with choice of a salad and chutney.

Subz Galouti Kebab

THE FIRST FAMILY OF KEBAB PAYS TRIBUTE TO THE VEGETARIANS WITH THIS TENDER, MAHI TAWA-FRIED VEGETABLE KEBAB

Cooking time 4-6 minutes Serves 1-2

INGREDIENTS

75 gm	- Beans (boiled)
75 gm	- Carrots (boiled)
50 gm	- Cauliflower (boiled)
5 no	- Babycorn (boiled)
25 gm	- Green peas (boiled)
50 gm	- Boiled potato (grated)
1 tsp	- Yellow chilli powder
To taste	- Salt
½ tsp	- Garam masala
A pinch	- Elaichi javitri powder
1 tbsp	- Roasted channa powder
1 tsp	- Desi ghee
2 no	- Cloves
For cooking	- Desi ghee

METHOD

1. Squeeze water/moisture completely from vegetables.
2. In a processor put all boiled vegetables and make a fine mince. Transfer it to a bowl. Add yellow chilli powder, salt, garam masala, elaichi javitri powder, potatoes, channa powder and mix thoroughly.
3. Put this mixture in a large pot. In another small bowl put pieces of burning charcoal and place beside the vegetable mixture. Put cloves, pour ghee and cover the pot with a lid for 3-5 minutes so that it gets a smoking flavour.
4. Open the lid and remove the mixture.
5. Divide the mixture into 4 equal parts. Make small balls and press between your palm to give a round shape like a medallion (tikki).

Cooking

6. Heat desi ghee in a non-stick pan or griddle, place kebab and shallow fry on slow fire till golden brown on both sides.
7. Serve hot with choice of a salad and chutney.

Kadak Sabudana Tikka

CRISPY TAPOICA KEBAB-BEST DURING NAVRATRAS

Cooking time 2-3 minutes Serves 1-2

INGREDIENTS

50 gm	- Sabudana (soaked in water)
175 gms	- Boiled potatoes (grated)
To taste	- Salt (senda namak)
1 tsp	- Green chilli (chopped)
1 tsp	- Green corriander (chopped)
For binding	- Kuttu flour
50 gms	- Sabudana (for coating)
½ tsp	- Roasted jeera powder
For frying	- Refined oil

METHOD

1. In a bowl take soaked sabudana, grated potatoes and other ingredients, mix well and keep aside for at least half an hour.
2. Divide the mixture into 4-6 equal parts and make balls.

Cooking

3. Coat each ball with sabudana and then flatten between palms each ball to a round medallion (tikki) shape.
4. Heat oil in a pan or kadhai and deep fry till golden brown colour or crisp.
5. Serve hot with choice of a salad and chutney.

Khus Ke Khaas Kebab

A SIMPLE YET DELICIOUS BLEND OF VEGETABLES DUSTED WITH POPPY SEEDS AND FRIED TO CRISPNESS

Cooking time 2-3 minutes Serves 1-2

INGREDIENTS

50 gm	- Beans (boiled)
50 gm	- Carrots (boiled)
50 gm	- Green peas (boiled)
50 gm	- Boiled potatoes (grated)
½ tsp	- Yellow chilli powder
To taste	- Salt
½ tsp	- Garam masala
1 tsp	- Cornflour
For binding	- Breadcrumbs

Filling

1 tsp	- Cashewnut (chopped)
1 tsp	- Almond (chopped)
½ tsp	- Raisin (chopped)
For coating	- Poppy seeds

For frying - Refined oil

METHOD

1. Remove the excess moisture from beans, carrots and peas by squeezing.
2. Put vegetables in a processor and make a coarse paste.
3. Transfer coarse paste in a bowl and add all the ingredients as listed and mix well to smooth consistency.
4. Divide the mixture into 5-6 equal parts or according to desired shape and make round balls.

Filing

5. Take cashewnut, almond, raisins and mix well and divide in 5-6 equal parts.
6. Flatten each ball, place filling, seal and press each ball between your palms to give the shape of a medallion (tikki).
7. Dust each piece with the poppy seeds ensuring that it sticks well all around.

Cooking

8. Heat oil in a pan and deep fry till golden brown and crisp. Remove on absorbent paper to remove excess oil.
9. Serve hot along with choice of a salad and chutney.

Harra Tawa Kebab

A COMBINATION OF SEASONAL GREEN VEGETABLES FRESH HERBS AND COOKED ON GRIDDLE

Cooking time 3-4 minutes **Serves 1-2**

INGREDIENTS

100 gm	- Carrot, beans and peas (Boiled)
50 gm	- Boiled spinach (chopped)
40 gm	- Boiled potatoes (grated)
40 gm	- Cottage cheese (grated)
To taste	- Salt
½ tsp	- Green chilli (chopped)
1 tsp	- Green coriander (chopped)
1 tsp	- Cornflour
For binding	- Breadcrumbs
For frying	- Desi ghee

METHOD

1. Drain and squeeze water from vegetables with help of a cloth.
2. Put vegetables in a food processor, make a fine mince, transfer it to a bowl.
3. Add all the remaining ingredients and mix thoroughly.
4. Divide this mixture into 4-5 equal balls. Press each ball between your palm to give it a medallion (tikki) shape.

Cooking

5. Heat ghee on a griddle/non-stick pan, fry kebabs on a slow fire till crisp on both sides. Remove on a absorbent paper to remove excess oil.
6. Serve hot with choice of a salad and chutney.

Bharwan Aloo Tikki

A CRISP KEBAB MADE OF POTATO WITH FRESH MINT AND CASHEWNUT FILLING

Cooking time 2-3 minutes **Serves 1-2**

INGREDIENTS

150 gm	- Boiled potato (grated)
To taste	- Salt
½ tsp	- Garam masala
½ tsp	- Roasted jeera powder
½ tsp	- Turmeric powder
A pinch	- Ajwain
For binding	- Bread crumbs

Filling

2 tsp	- Desi ghee
2 tsp	- Onion (chopped)
½ tsp	- Ginger (chopped)
5 gm	- Cashewnut (chopped)
1 tsp	- Green coriander (chopped)
½ tsp	- Mint leaf (chopped)
4 tbs	- Cornflour
For coating	- White till (sesame seeds)
For frying	- Refined oil

METHOD

1. In a bowl mash grated potatoes, add all the ingredients, mix well and keep aside for half an hour.
2. Divide the mixture into 5-6 equal parts and make balls.

Filling

3. Heat ghee in a pan, sauté onion, ginger, add all the remaining ingredients listed above and cook till the moisture drains out, keep aside for cooling. Divide this into 5-6 equal parts.
4. Flatten each ball, place filling, seal, then press it in between your palms to give a medallion (tikki) shape.
5. Dip each tikki into cornflour batter and then coat it with white till and keep in refrigerator for some time.

Cooking

6. Heat oil in a pan and deep fry till golden brown on both sides. Remove on a absorbent paper to remove excess oil.
7. Serve hot with a choice of a salad and chutney.

Khasta Subz Kebab

VEGETABLE KEBAB COATED WITH CRUNCHY VERMICELLI
Cooking time 2-3 minutes Serves 1-2

INGREDIENTS

150 gm	- Boiled carrot and beans
25 gm	- Boiled green peas
25 gm	- Boiled potatoes
25 gm	- Cottage cheese (grated)
To taste	- Salt
½ tsp	- Yellow chilli powder
A pinch	- Garam masala
½ tsp	- Green chilli (chopped)
1 tsp	- Green coriander chopped
2 tsp	- Cashewnut
2 tsp	- Cornflour
3 tsp	- Bread crumbs
For coating	- Vermicelli (crushed)
For frying	- Refined oil

METHOD

1. Remove excess moisture from carrots, beans and peas by squeezing it.
2. Put them in a food processor and make a coarse mince and transfer it to bowl, add all the remaining ingredients in order listed, mix well and keep aside for at least half an hour
3. Divide the mixture into 5-6 equal parts and make balls. Press each ball between your palms to give a medallion (tikki) shape, keep in refrigerator for sometime.

Cooking

4. Heat oil in a kadhai and deep fry till golden brown and crisp. Remove on absorbent paper to remove excess oil.
5. Serve hot with choice of a salad and chutney.

Til Mill Seekh Kebab

A CREAMY COTTAGE CHEESE WITH SESAME AND POUNDED MIX SPICES
Cooking time 4-6 minutes Serves 1-2

INGREDIENTS

150 gm	- Cottage cheese (grated)
75 gm	- Boiled potatoes (grated)
To taste	- Salt
½ tsp	- White pepper powder
1 tsp	- Green coriander (chopped)
1 tsp	- Green chilli chopped
1/3 tsp	- Garam masala
4 tsp	- Til white (sesame)
2 tsp	- Cornflour
For binding	- Breadcrumbs

METHOD

1. In a deep tray mash cottage cheese and add all the ingredients in the order listed, mix well and keep aside for at least half an hour.
2. Divide the mixture into 4-6 equal portions and make balls.

Cooking

3. Take a skewer and apply the mixture along the skewer with moist hand in a cylindrical shape (4"-5"). Roast in a moderately hot tandoor or over a charcoal grill for 4-6 minutes.
4. Serve hot along with choice of a salad and chutney.

Tandoori Aloo Nazakat

POTATO BASKET STUFFED WITH EXOTIC CHEESE, DRYFRUITS AND SPICES, COOKED IN CLAY OVEN

Cooking time 5-6 minutes Serves 1-2

INGREDIENTS

2 no (300 gm)	- Potato (large)
4 tsp	- Cornflour
For coating	- Poppy seed
For frying	- Refined oil

Stuffing

1 tsp	- Refined oil
A pinch	- White jeera (cumin seeds)
A pinch	- Turmeric powder
50 gm	- Potato (small dices)
50 gm	- Cottage cheese (small dices)
To taste	- Salt
1/3 tsp	- Red chilli powder
½ tsp	- Green coriander (chopped)
2 tsp	- Red capsicum (chopped)
2 tsp	- Yellow capsicum (chopped)
2 tsp	- Green capsicum (chopped)
2 tsp	- Raisins
20 gm	- Green peas
2 tsp	- Cashewnut (crushed)
1 tsp	- Red chilli powder

METHOD

1. Peel potatoes, cut the top from one side, with a sharp knife make it hollow. Wash, par boil (1/4th cooked), pat dry and keep aside.
2. Pre-heat oil in a kadai. Make batter with cornflour and water. Dip potatoes into the batter, roll them in sesame seed and fry for a minute till sesame seed gets brown in colour and keep aside. Keep fried potatoes on a piece of cloth (upside down) to remove excess oil.

Stuffing

3. In a non-stick pan, heat oil, put jeera, turmeric, put all the ingredients in the order listed and mix well. Cook on slow fire for 1 minute.
4. Keep aside for cooling and divide this in equal parts.
5. Stuff each potato with filling up to rim and press tight with thumb.

Cooking

6. Take a skewer and skew each potato one by one leaving a gap of an inch.
7. Roast in a tandoor at a moderate temperature for 5-6 minutes till golden brown.
8. Serve hot along with choice of a salad and chutney.

Muttar Kaju Kebab

FRESH GREEN PEAS PATTIES, SEASONED AND PACKED WITH CASHEWNUTS HALVES

Cooking time 3-4 minutes Serves 1-2

INGREDIENTS

100 gm	- Boiled green peas (chopped)
50 gm	- Boiled potato (chopped)
50 gm	- Cottage cheese (grated)
50 gm	- Cashewnut (chopped)
½ tsp	- Green chilli (chopped)
½ tsp	- Ginger (chopped)
1 tsp	- Fresh coriander (chopped)
To taste	- Salt
½ tsp	- Yellow chilli powder
½ tsp	- Garam Masala
2 tsp	- Corn flour
4 tsp	- Bread crumbs
5 no	- Cashewnut
For frying	- Refined oil

METHOD

1. Remove excess moisture from green peas by squeezing it, put in a bowl and add all the remaining ingredients listed above, except cashewnut, mix well and keep aside for at least half an hour.
2. Divide this mixture into 4-5 equal parts and make balls.
3. Press each ball between your palms, to give shape of a medallion (tikki). Place one piece of cashewnut on top in centre.

Cooking

4. Heat oil in a non-stick pan and shallow fry till golden brown and crisp on both sides.
5. Serve hot with choice of a salad and chutney.

Harre Muttar Ki Seekh

GREEN PEAS SKEWER INFUSED WITH ROASTED CUMIN SEEDS
Cooking time 4-6 minutes Serves 1-2

INGREDIENTS

125 gm	- Boiled green peas (chopped)
40 gm	- Boiled potato (grated)
40 gm	- Cottage cheese (grated)
To taste	- Salt
1/3 tsp	- Garam masala
½ tsp	- Yellow chilli powder
½ tsp	- Roasted jeera powder
½ tsp	- Green chilli (chopped)
½ tsp	- Ginger (chopped)
1 tsp	- Fresh coriander (chopped)
For binding	- Breadcrumbs
1 tsp	- Cornflour

METHOD

1. In a bowl take green peas, potato, cottage cheese, add all the remaining ingredients in order listed, mix well and keep aside for at least half an hour.
2. Divide the mixture into 4 equal parts and make balls.

Cooking

3. Take a skewer, apply the mixture along it in a cylindrical shape with a moist palm along the skewer.
4. Roast it in a tandoor or grill over charcoal at a moderate temperature for 4-6 minutes.
5. Serve hot along with choice of a salad and chutney.

Til Ke Khaas Soya Kebab

DELICATE KEBEB CRAFTED FROM SOYABEAN, ROLLED IN SESAME AND CRISPY FRIED
Cooking time 2-3 minutes Serves 1-2

INGREDIENTS

100 gm	- Soyabean granules
50 gm	- Cottage cheese (grated)
50 gm	- Boiled potatoes
1 tsp	- Ginger (chopped)
1 tsp	- Green chilli (chopped)
1 tsp	- Fresh coriander (chopped)
To taste	- Salt
½ tsp	- Yellow chilli powder
½ tsp	- Turmeric powder
A pinch	- Elaichi javitri powder
For coating	- White sesame seed
For frying	- Refined oil

METHOD

1. Boil soyabean granules for a minute and drain water. Squeeze excess water from soyabean and transfer to a tray.
2. Add cottage cheese, potatoes, ginger, green chilli, coriander, salt, yellow chilli powder, turmeric powder, elaichi javitri powder and mix with palm till smooth.
3. Divide the mixture into 5-6 equal parts and make balls.
4. Press each ball with moist palm to give a shape of medallion (tikki) and role in sesame seed.

Cooking

5. Heat oil in a pan and pan fry till golden brown and crisp on both sides. Remove on absorbent paper to remove excess oil.
6. Serve hot with choice of a salad and chutney.

Khaas Soya Seekh

SKEWER OF SOYABEAN DONNING A COLOURFUL GRAB WITH SINGING FLAVOUR OF BELL PEPPER CREATING AN EXTRAORDINARY PLAY OF TASTE
Cooking time 4-6 minutes Serves 1-2

INGREDIENTS

150 gm	- Soya granules
40 gm	- Potatoes (boiled)
40 gm	- Cottage cheese (grated)
To taste	- Salt
½ tsp	- Yellow chilli powder
½ tsp	- Garam masala
1 tsp	- Green coriander (chopped)
½ tsp	- Green chilli (chopped)
4 tsp	- Red, yellow, green capsicum (chopped)
2 tsp	- Cornflour
For binding	- Breadcrumbs

METHOD

1. Boil soyabean granules for a minute and drain water. Squeeze excess water from soya bean and transfer to a tray, add all the ingredients in the order listed, mix well and keep aside for at least half an hour.
2. Divide the mixture into 4 equal parts and make balls.

Cooking

3. Take a skewer, apply mixture portion-wise in cylindrical shape using moist palm, coat with chpped bell pepper, grill over charcoal or roast in a tandoor at a moderate temperature for 4-6 minutes.
4. Serve hot along with choice of a salad and chutney.

Tandoori Achari Aloo

AN UNUSUAL KEBAB OF BABY POTATOES WITH PICKLE SPICES

Cooking time 4-6 minutes Serves 1-2

INGREDIENTS

200-225 gm Baby potatoes (8 no)

For frying   - Refined oil

Marination
4 tbsp	- Hung curd
To taste	- Salt
2 tsp	- Besan (roasted)
½ tsp	- Yellow chilli powder
2 tsp	- Achar paste
A pinch	- Turmeric powder
1 tsp	- Mustard oil
½ tsp	- Garam masala
A pinch	- Kasoori methi powder
1 tsp	- Kalounji, Methi daana, Mustard seeds, Saunf (aniseed)

METHOD

1. Peel, wash and fry potatoes in oil till ¾ cooked, remove to absorbent paper and keep aside.

Marination
2. In a bowl whisk hung curd add all the other ingredients in the order listed and mix well.
3. Heat oil in a pan, add saunf, kalounji, mustard seeds and methi, when it starts crackling, immediately add to marinade.
4. Put fried potatoes in the marinade and mix well. Keep aside for at least 1 hour.

Cooking
5. Take a skewer and skew marinated potatoes one by one an inch apart and roast in tandoor at moderate temperature for 4-6 minutes.
6. Serve hot with choice of a salad and chutney.

Achari Bharwan Khumb Shashlik

FRESH STUFFED KING MIUSHROOMS SKEWERED WITH CAPSICUM, ONION, TOMATO
DELICATELY STEEPED IN MARINADE WITH MUSTARD SEEDS, SPICES AND GRILLED

Cooking time 8-10 minutes Serves 1-2

INGREDIENTS

10-12 pieces - Mushrooms (large size)

Stuffing
25 gm	- Processed cheese (grated)
To taste	- Salt
1/3 tsp	- White pepper powder
1 tsp	- Green coriander (chopped)
½ tsp	- Green chilli (chopped)
2 tsp	- Refined oil
2 tsp	- Roasted besan
A pinch	- Turmeric powder
½ tsp	- Yellow chilli powder
To taste	- Salt
½ tsp	- Ginger garlic paste
4 tsp	- Cream
½ tsp	- Red chilli paste
½ tsp	- Garam masala
2 no	- Yellow capsicum dices (1" x 1")
2 no	- Green capsicum dices (1" x 1")
2 no	- Red capsicum dices (1" x 1")
2 no	- Onion dices (1" x 1")

METHOD

1. Cut stems of mushroom, boil for 1 minute or till 1/3 cooked drain water and keep for cool.

Stuffing
2. In a bowl mash processed cheese, add salt, white pepper powder, coriander, green chilli and mix well. Stuff this cheese mixture into mushrooms caps tightly and keep aside.

Marination
3. In a pan heat oil, add the roasted channa flour and cook for a while. Keep aside for cooling.
4. In a deep tray take cooked gram flour add all the remaining ingredients listed above and mix well.

Cooking
5. Take a skewer and skew mushrooms and vegetables alternately.
6. Apply marinade on skewed mushrooms, coat well and keep aside for at least half an hour.
7. Roast in a tandoor or charcoal grill at a moderate temperature for 8-10 minutes.
8. Serve hot along with choice of a salad and chutney.

Mewey Aur Mawey Ki Kakori

DELICATE SEEKH FOR THE VEGETARIAN CRAFTED FROM KHOYA AND PANEER BLENDED WITH ROASTED ALMONDS AND GRILLED.

Cooking time 4-6 minutes Serves 1-2

INGREDIENTS

75 gm	- Carrot (boiled)
75 gm	- Beans (boiled)
50 gm	- Peas (boiled)
½ tsp	- Green chilli (chopped)
½ tsp	- Ginger (chopped)
1 tsp	- Fresh coriander (chopped)
1 tsp	- Khoya (grated)
To taste	- Salt
½ tsp	- Garam masala
½ tsp	- Cashewnut (chopped)
½ tsp	- Raisins (chopped)
½ tsp	- Almond (chopped)
1-2 tsp	- Cornflour
For binding	- Breadcrumbs

METHOD

1. Squeeze excess moisture completely from vegetables.
2. In a processor, put all boiled vegetables and make a fine mince. Transfer it to a bowl, add all the remaining ingredients in the order listed and mix well.
3. Divide the mixture into 4 equal parts and make balls.

Cooking

4. Take a skewer, apply this mixture portion-wise along the skewer with a moist palm in a cylindrical shape (4"- 5").
5. Grill over a charcoal grill for 4-6 minutes.
6. Serve hot with choice of a salad and chutney.

Soya Shammi Kebab

ANOTHER VERSION OF LUCKNOWI SHAMMI KEBEB MADE OF SOYABEAN

Cooking time 2-3 minutes Serves 1-2

INGREDIENTS

125 gm	- Soya granules(boiled)
50 gm	- Boiled potato (grated)
50 gm	- Cottage cheese (grated)
To taste	- Salt
½ tsp	- Yellow chilli powder
1 tsp	- Green coriander (chopped)
½ tsp	- Green chilli (chopped)
½ tsp	- Garam masala
2 tsp	- Cornflour
2 tsp	- Breadcrumbs (for binding)

Filling

4 tsp	- Onion (chopped)
½ tsp	- Green chilli (chopped)
1 tsp	- Green coriander (chopped)
1 tsp	- Ginger (chopped)
To taste	- Salt
For frying	- Refined oil

METHOD

1. Squeeze excess water from soyabean and put it in a deep tray.
2. Add all the ingredients in the order listed mix well and keep aside for half an hour.
3. Divide the mixture into 6 equal parts and make balls.

Stuffing

1. Take onion, green chilli, coriander, salt, mix well and divide into six parts.
2. Flatten soyaball between wet palms, place filling, seal, make ball and flatten in the shape of medallion (tikki).

Cooking

3. Heat oil in a pan or kadhai fry shammi for 2-3 minutes till crispy.
4. Remove to an absorbent paper to remove excess oil.
5. Serve hot with choice of a salad and chutney.

Saunphia Soya Kebab

SOYABEAN SKEWER WITH EXTRA FLAVOUR OF ANISEED
Cooking time 4-6 minutes Serves 1-2

INGREDIENTS

25 gm	- Soya granules (boiled)
50 gm	- Boiled potato (grated)
50 gm	- Cottage cheese (grated)
To taste	- Salt
½ tsp	- Yellow chilli powder
A pinch	- Turmeric powder
1 tsp	- Green coriander (chopped)
½ tsp	- Green chilli (chopped)
2 tsp	- Saunf powder (aniseed)
½ tsp	- Aniseed
½ tsp	- Ginger (chopped)
1 tsp	- Cornflour
For binding	- Breadcrumbs

METHOD

1. Remove excess moisture from soya by squeezing and put it in a deep tray, add all the remaining ingredients listed above and mix well. Keep aside for at least half an hour.
2. Divide the mixture into 4 equal parts and make balls.

Cooking

1. Take a skewer, apply the mixture in cylindrical shape with moist palm, then grill it over a charcoal grill or roast in clay oven in moderate heat for 4-6 minutes.
2. Serve hot with choice of a salad and chutney.

Tandoori Lahsuni Broccoli

THIS MAGNIFICENT LOW CALORIE KEBAB OF FRESH BROCCOLI IS FLAVOURED WITH GARLIC IN ABUNDANCE
Cooking time 8-10 minutes Serves 1-2

INGREDIENTS

1 no (225-250 gm) - Broccoli (without stem)

Marination

2 tsp	Olive oil
1 tsp	- Garlic (chopped)
3-4 tsp	- Besan
To taste	- Salt
½ tsp	- Red chilli powder
1 tsp	- Ginger garlic paste
½ cup	- Low fat cream
1 tsp	- Garlic paste

METHOD

1. Remove stem, wash and boil broccoli with a little salt until half cooked remove and let it cool.

Marination

2. In a pan heat olive oil, put garlic chopped and sauté it, add besan to it and sauté for a while till it changes colour to light brown and keep aside for cooling.
3. In a deep tray take the above mixture and add the remaining ingredients and mix well.
4. Put the blanched broccoli into this marinade, coat well and keep aside for at least half an hour.

Cooking

5. Take a skewer and skew marinated broccoli.
6. Roast in a tandoor at a moderate temperature for 8-10 minutes.
7. Serve hot with choice of a salad and chutney.

Khaas Palak Seekh

A DELICIOUS AND NUTRITIOUS GREEN SPINACH KEBAB WITH POUNDED YELLOW CHILLI

Cooking time 4-6 minutes Serves 1-2

INGREDIENTS

150 gm	- Boiled spinach (chopped)
50 gm	- Boiled potato
50 gm	- Cottage cheese
To taste	- Salt
½ tsp	- Yellow chilli powder
½ tsp	- Green chilli (chopped)
½ tsp	- Garam masala
1 tsp	- Ginger (chopped)
2 tsp	- Corn flour
For binding	- Bread crumbs

METHOD

1. Squeeze excess moisture from spinach and put it in a deep tray, add all the remaining ingredients in the order listed above, mix well and keep aside for at least half an hour.
2. Divide the mixture into 4 equal parts and make balls.

Cooking

3. Take a skewer and apply the mixture along the skewer with moist hands in a cylindrical shape (4-5 inches). Roast in a moderately hot tandoor or over a charcoal grill for 4-6 minutes.
4. Serve hot along with choice of a salad and chutney.

Shahi Tandoori Gobhi

ROYAL KEBAB MADE OF BABY CAULIFLOWER WITH CUMIN SEEDS AND DRIED FENUGREEK

Cooking time 10-12 minutes Serves 1-2

INGREDIENTS

225-250 gm - Baby cauliflower (without stem)

A pinch	- Turmeric powder
½ tsp	- Salt

Marination

4 tbsp	- Hung curd
½ tsp	- Ginger garlic paste
1/3 tsp	- Yellow chilli powder
½ tsp	- Kasoori methi powder
2 tsp	- Roasted besan
½ tsp	- Black cumin
1/3 tsp	- Chat masala
To taste	- Salt
1/2 tsp	- Garam masala
2 tsp	- Mustard oil

METHOD

1. Parboil cauliflower with turmeric and salt, completely drain water and let it cool.

Marination

2. In a bowl whisk hung curd, add all the ingredients listed and mix well.
3. Remove excess moisture and put cauliflower into this marinade, coat well and keep aside for at least 1 hour.

Cooking

4. Take a skewer and skew marinated cauliflower.
5. Roast in a tandoor at a moderate temperature for 10-12 minutes
6. Serve hot with choice of a salad and chutney.

Vilayati Shammi Kebab

EXCITING VERSION OF SHAMMI MADE WITH ENGLISH VEGETABLES AND POUNDED LUCKNOWI MASALA

Cooking time 2-3 minutes **Serves 1-2**

INGREDIENTS

20 gm	- Baby corn (boiled)
20 gm	- Asparagus (boiled)
40 gm	- Broccoli (boiled)
20 gm	- Artichokes (boiled)
50 gm	- Potatoes (grated)
½ tsp	- Green chilli (chopped)
1 tsp	- Green coriander (chopped)
½ tsp	- Lucknowi masala
½ tsp	- Yellow chilli powder
To taste	- Salt
½ tsp	- Ginger (chopped)
2 tsp	- Cornflour
For binding	- Breadcrumbs
For Frying	- Refined oil

METHOD

1. Squeeze excess water/moisture from vegetables.
2. In a processor put boiled vegetables and make a fine mince transfer to bowl. Add all the remaining ingredients listed above, mix well and keep aside for at least half an hour.
3. Divide the mixture into 4-5 equal portions and make round balls. Press each ball between your palms to give a shape of a medallion (tikki).

Cooking

4. Heat oil in a pan and deep fry till golden brown and crisp. Remove on absorbent paper to remove excess oil.
5. Serve hot with choice of a salad and chutney.

Bharwan Subz Kebab

KEBAB OF FINELY MINCED OF VEGETABLES ENHANCED WITH SPICES AND STUFFED WITH MELTING CHEESE

Cooking time 2-3 minutes **Serves 1-2**

INGREDIENTS

100 gm - Boiled carrot, beans, greenpeas (chopped)

50 gm	- Potatoes (grated)
50 gm	- Cottage cheese (grated)
To taste	- Salt
1/3 tsp	- Garam masala
A pinch	- Kasoori methi powder
1/3 tsp	- Yellow chilli powder
A pinch	- Cinnamon powder
½ tsp	- Kutti red chilli
For binding	- Breadcrumbs
2 tsp	- Cornflour

For Filling

2 tsp	- Processed cheese (grated)
½ tsp	- Green chilli (chopped)
½ tsp	- Ginger (chopped)
1 tsp	- Mint (chopped)
1 tsp	- Onion (chopped)
A pinch	- Salt

For Frying - Refined oil

METHOD

1. Squeeze excess moisture from boiled carrots, beans, green peas and transfer to a bowl, add potato, cottage cheese, add all the remaining ingredients listed above and mix well to form smooth dough.
2. Divide the mixture into 6 equal parts and make balls.

Filling

3. In a bowl mix processed cheese, chilli, ginger, mint, onion, salt, mix well and divide into 6 parts.
4. Press each ball between your palms, place filling, and seal, press again to give a medallion (tikki) shape and keep in a refrigerator for some time.

Cooking

5. Heat oil in a pan and deep fry the kebabs till crisp and golden brown. Remove on absorbent paper to remove excess oil.
6. Serve hot with choice of a salad and chutney.

Aloo Makai Seekh

SEEKH KEBAB OF POTATO AND TENDER CORN
Cooking time 4-6 minutes Serves 1-2

INGREDIENTS

75 gm	- Boiled potatoes (grated)
75 gm	- Boiled babycorn (chopped)
50 gm	- Cottage cheese (grated)
2 tbsp	- Sweet corn niblets
½ tsp	- Green chilli (chopped)
1 tsp	- Green coriander (chopped)
1 tsp	- Ginger (chopped)
To taste	- Salt
½ tsp	- Yellow chilli powder
½ tsp	- Garam masala
For binding	- Breadcrumbs
2 tsp	- Cornflour

METHOD

1. In a bowl put all the ingredients, mix well to form smooth dough. Divide the mixture into 4 equal portions.

Cooking

2. Take a skewer and apply this mixture on it in a cylindrical shape (4-6 inches) using wet palm and grill over charcoal or tandoor for 4-6 minutes.
3. Serve hot with choice of a salad and chutney.

Tawa Bhutta Kebab

FRESH BABY CORN PATTY FLAVOURED WITH DRIED FENUGREEK, CARUM SEEDS AND COOKED ON GRIDDLE
Cooking time 2-3 minutes Serves 1-2

INGREDIENTS

200-225 gm	- Boiled baby corn
To taste	- Salt
1/2 tsp	- Kasoori methi powder
1/2 tsp	- Red chilli powder
A pinch	- Garam masala
1 no	- Egg white
A pinch	- Ajwain
1 tsp	- Roasted channa powder
½ tsp	- Ginger garlic paste
For binding	- Breadcrumbs
4 tsp	- Cornflour
For frying	- Refined oil

METHOD

1. Squeeze excess moisture from baby corn.
2. In a food processor put boiled baby corn and make fine mince and transfer it to a bowl, add all the remaining ingredients in the order listed, mix well and keep aside for at least ½ hour.
3. Divide mixture in 4-5 parts and make balls. Press each ball between your palms to give a medallion (tikki) shape. Keep in refrigerator for some time.

Cooking

4. Heat oil on a tawa or griddle and shallow fry tikki to golden brown colour and crisp on both sides.
5. Serve hot with choice of a salad and chutney.

Multani Khumb Ki Shaan

AN EYE-PLEASING AND COLOURFUL DELICACY OF STUFFED FRESH MUSHROOM SKEWERED WITH BELL PEPPERS

Cooking time 4-6 minutes Serves 1-2

INGREDIENTS

175-200 gm (12 no) - Boiled button mushroom with stem

{Red, yellow, green capsicum-for shashlik pieces} - 1 no. each.

Stuffing
30 gm	- Processed cheese
A pinch	- White pepper
½ tsp	- Green chilli (chopped)
1 tsp	- Green coriander (chopped)
1 tsp	- Corn flour
½ tsp	- Ginger (chopped)

Marination
4 tbsp	- Hung curd
To taste	- Salt
½ tsp	- Red chilli paste
1/2 tsp	- Kastoori methi powder
A pinch	- Garam masala
½ tsp	- Ginger garlic paste
1 tsp	- Lemon juice
2 tsp	- Mustard oil
1 tsp	- Roasted channa powder

METHOD

1. Remove the stem of mushroom, pat dry. Cut large cubes of capsicums (as per mushroom) and keep aside.

Stuffing

2. In a bowl mix processed cheese and all the ingredients in the order listed, mix well.
3. Stuff each mushroom with this stuffing and keep aside.

Marination

4. In a bowl whisk hung curd, add all the ingredients in the order listed, mix well.
5. Dip the stuffed mushroom in the above marinade and capsicum, keep aside for at least half an hour.

Cooking

6. Take a skewer and skew marinated mushroom and capsicums alternatively one by one, apply remaining marinade on them.
7. Roast in a tandoor or charcoal grill at moderate temperature for 4-6 minutes.
8. Serve hot with choice of a salad and chutney.

Bhutta Seekh Kebab

FRESH CORN SKEWER FLAVOURED WITH FRESH MINT AND POMEGRANATE

Cooking time 4-6 minutes Serves 1-2

INGREDIENTS

75 gm	- Boiled baby corn (chopped)
50 gm	- Sweet corn niblets
40 gm	- Boiled potato (grated)
40 gm	- Cottage cheese (grated)
To taste	- Salt
½ tsp	- Yellow chilli powder
½ tsp	- Garam masala
½ tsp	- Green chilli (chopped)
1 tsp	- Green coriander (chopped)
1 tsp	- Fresh mint (chopped)
½ tsp	- Anardana (crushed)
A pinch	- Turmeric powder
For binding	- Breadcrumbs
2 tsp	- Cornflour

METHOD

1. Squeeze excess moisture from baby corn, transfer to a deep tray, add sweet corn, and all the remaining ingredients in the order listed above, mix well and keep aside for at least half an hour.
2. Divide the mixture into 04 equal parts and make balls.

Cooking

3. Take a skewer and apply mixture on it with a moist palm along the length of the skewer in a cylindrical shape 1 inch apart, make each kebab 4-5 inches long.
4. Roast in a moderate temperature over charcoal grill or in tandoor for 4-6 minutes.
5. Serve hot with choice of a salad and chutney.

Broccoli Bhutta Ke Shammi

BROCCOLI AND CORN PATTIES STUFFED WITH CHEESE AND CRISPY FRIED

Cooking time 2-3 minutes Serves 1-2

INGREDIENTS

75 gm	- Boiled baby corn (chopped)
75 gm	- Boiled broccoli (chopped)
25 gms	- Boiled potato (grated)
25 gm	- Cottage cheese (grated)
1 tsp	- Green chilli (chopped)
½ tsp	- Ginger (chopped)
To taste	- Salt
1 tsp	- Fresh coriander (chopped)
½ tsp	- Dalchini powder
1/3 tsp	- Yellow chilli powder
1/3 tsp	- Garam Masala
For binding	- Breadcrumbs
1 tsp	- Cornflour

Stuffing

1 tsp	- Processed cheese (grated)
4 tsp	- Onions (chopped)
1 tsp	- Green chilli (chopped)
1/3 tsp	- Garam masala
To taste	- Salt
1/2 tsp	- Mint (chopped)
1/3 tsp	- Yellow chilli powder

For frying - Refined oil

METHOD

1. Remove excess moisture from the baby corn and broccoli by squeezing, transfer to a deep tray.
2. Add potatoes, cottage cheese and add all the remaining ingredients listed above, mix well and keep aside for at least 1 hour.
3. Divide the mixture into 5-6 equal parts, make balls.

Stuffing

4. In a bowl, mash processed cheese and the remaining ingredients, mix well and divide in 5-6 parts.
5. Flatten each ball between wet palm, place stuffing mixture, seal it, again press it in a medallion (tikki shape) and keep aside.

Cooking

6. Heat oil in a pan or griddle and deep fry till golden brown and crisp.
7. Serve hot along with choice of a salad and chutney.

Tandoori Baby Bhutta

KING SIZE BABY CORN INFUSED WITH POUNDED RED CHILLI AND COOKED IN CLAY OVEN

Cooking time 3-4 minutes Serves 1-2

INGREDIENTS

200 gm (12 no.)	- Baby corn (large size)
A pinch	- Turmeric powder
To taste	- Salt

Marination

4 tbsp	- Hung curd
To taste	- Salt
½ tsp	- Ginger garlic paste
½ tsp	- Red chilli paste
½ tsp	- Kasoori methi powder
½ tsp	- Garam masala
1 tsp	- Refined oil
1 tsp	- Lemon juice
1 tsp	- Roasted besan
½ tsp	- Yellow chilli powder

METHOD

1. Parboil baby corn with turmeric and salt. Drain water and keep aside for cooling.

Marination

2. In a bowl whisk hung curd, add all the remaining ingredients in the order listed, mix well.
3. Remove excess moisture from the baby corn and mix in the above marinade, coat well and keep aside for at least half an hour.

Cooking

4. Take a skewer and skew babycorn leaving a gap of 1 inch between each piece.
5. Roast in a tandoor at a moderate temperature for 3-4 minutes.
6. Serve hot with choice of a salad and chutney.

Navrattan Seekh Kebab

SOFT KEBAB FROM NINE SELECTED FRUITS AND VEGETABLES ENHANCED WITH HOME GROUND SPICES
Cooking time 4-6 minutes Serves 1-2

INGREDIENTS

25 gm	- Baby corn (chopped)
25 gm	- Boiled beans (chopped)
25 gm	- Boiled carrots (chopped)
25 gm	- Boiled green peas (chopped)
25 gm	- Apple (chopped)
25 gm	- Pineapple (chopped)
25 gm	- Cherry (de-seeded)
25 gm	- Potatoes (grated)
25 gm	- Cottage cheese (grated)
To taste	- Salt
½ tsp	- Yellow chilli powder
½ tsp	- Green chilli (chopped)
½ tsp	- Ginger (chopped)
1 tsp	- Fresh coriander (chopped)
For binding	- Breadcrumbs
2 tsp	- Cornflour
½ tsp	- Garam masala
1 tsp	- Almond (chopped)

METHOD

1. In a bowl mix chopped carrots, beans, green peas, baby corn, apple, pineapple, cherry, grated potatoes and cottage cheese, add all the remaining ingredients listed above and mix well and keep aside for half an hour.

Cooking

2. Divide the mixture into 4-5 equal portions and make balls.
3. Spread this mixture on the skewer, using a wet palm to press each ball along the length of the skewer in a cylindrical shape, one inch apart, making each kebab 4-5 inches long.
4. Roast in a moderately hot tandoor or in an oven or charcoal grill for 4-6 minutes.
5. Transfer it on to a plate and serve hot along with choice of a salad and chutney.

Makkai Khumb Ki Kakori

THIS SUPERLATIVE VERSION OF FAMOUS LUCKNOWI KEBAB IS MADE WITH CORN AND MUSHROOM
Cooking time 4-6 minutes Serves 1-2

INGREDIENTS

60 gm	- Boiled mushroom
60 gm	- Boiled sweet corn
30 gm	- Boiled potato (grated)
30 gm	- Cottage cheese (grated)
½ tsp	- Green chilli (chopped)
½ tsp	- Ginger (chopped)
To taste	- Salt
½ tsp	- Yellow chilli powder
½ tsp	- Garam masala
2 tsp	- Cornflour
A pinch	- Luknowi masala
Few drops	- Ittre (kewra)
For binding	- Breadcrumbs

METHOD

1. Squeeze extra moisture completely from sweet corn and mushroom.
2. In a processor, put mushroom, sweet corn, make a fine mince and transfer to a bowl, add all the remaining ingredients listed above and mix well.
3. Divide the mixture into 4 equal parts and make balls.

Cooking

4. Take a skewer and apply the mixture in a cylindrical shape with a moist palm and grill over charcoal for 4-6 minutes.
5. Serve hot with choice of a salad and chutney.

Lazawab Tandoori Gobhi

A MOUTH WATERING DELICATE BABY CAULIFLOWER INFUSED WITH
CINNAMON AND BAKED IN TANDOOR

Cooking time 10-12 minutes Serves 1-2

INGREDIENTS

225-250 gm	- Baby cauliflower (without stem)
2 no	- Black peppercorn
1 no	- Black ardamom
2 no	- Green cardamom
1 no	- Cinnamon stick
2 no	- Clove
A pinch	- Turmeric powder
To taste	- Salt

Marination

5 tbsp	- Hung curd
To taste	- Salt
½ tsp	- Red chilli paste
½ tsp	- Ginger garlic paste
2 tsp	- Lemon juice
1 ½ tsp	- Mustard oil
A pinch	- Cinnamon powder
A pinch	- Shahi jeera (black cumin)
1 tsp	- Roasted besan

METHOD

1. Remove stem without disjoining the cauliflower.
2. Parboil cauliflower with black peppercorn, black cardamom (big), green cardamom, cinnamon stick and clove, turmeric, salt. Drain water and keep aside for cooling.

Marination

3. In a bowl whisk hung curd and all the remaining ingredients in the order listed above and mix well. Apply this to the cauliflower, coat well and leave for at least 1 hour.

Cooking

4. Take a skewer and skew cauliflower.
5. Roast in a tandoor at moderate temperature for 10-12 minutes.
6. Serve hot with choice of a salad and chutney.

Tandoori Dhingri Shashlik

ANOTHER CREATION OF FRESH MUSHROOM SKEWERED WITH BELL PEPPERS

Cooking time 8-10 minutes Serves 1-2

INGREDIENTS

200-225 gm	- Mushroom (boiled) 12 pcs
3 no	- Red, yellow, green capsicum (For shashlik)

Stuffing

20 gm	- Boiled potato (grated)
20 gm	- Boiled mushroom (chopped)
20 gm	- Cottage cheese (grated)
½ tsp	- Green coriander (chopped)
1 tsp	- Green chilli (chopped)
½ tsp	- Ginger (chopped)

Marination

4 tbsp	- Hung curd
To taste	- Salt
½ tsp	- Ginger garlic paste
½ tsp	- Red chilli paste
½ tsp	- Kasoori methi powder
½ tsp	- Garam masala
1 tsp	- Lemon juice
2 tsp	- Mustard oil

METHOD

1. Remove stem of mushroom, pat dry and keep aside. Cut capsicum into large dices.

Stuffing

2. In a bowl put potato, mushroom, cottage cheese, green coriander, green chilli, ginger and salt mix well.
3. Stuff each mushroom with the stuffing and keep aside.

Marination

4. In a bowl whisk hung curd, add all the remaining ingredients in the order listed, mix well.
5. Remove extra moisture from the mushroom and dip in the above marinade, coat well and keep aside for at least half an hour.

Cooking

6. Take a skewer and skew mushroom and capsicum alternatively one by one keeping a tray underneath to collect drippings.
7. Roast in a tandoor at a moderate temperature for 8-10 minutes till golden brown.
8. Serve hot with choice of a salad and chutney.

Subz Kakori Kebab

FINELY MINCED VEGETABLES WITH SUBTLE SPICES. UNIQUE DELICACY
FROM THE ROYAL STATE OF AWADH

Cooking time 4-5 minutes Serves 1-2

INGREDIENTS

75 gm	- Boiled carrot and beans
25 gm	- Boiled green peas
25 gm	- Boiled mushroom
25 gm	- Boiled potatoes (grated)
To taste	- Salt
½ tsp	- Yellow chilli powder
½ tsp	- Lucknowi masala
¼ tsp	- Green chilli (chopped)
1 tsp	- Green coriander (chopped)
½ tsp	- Ginger and garlic paste
A pinch	- Cinnamon powder
2 tsp	- Roasted channa powder
A pinch	- Saffron
2 drops	- Kewra/attar
1 tsp	- Desi ghee
For binding	- Breadcrumbs

METHOD

1. Squeeze excess moisture from the vegetables.
2. In a food processor put boiled vegetables, make a fine mince and transfer it to a bowl, add all the remaining ingredients in the order listed above and mix thoroughly and keep aside for at least 1 hour.
3. Divide the mixture into 4-5 equal parts and make balls.

Cooking

4. Take a skewer and apply mixture along on it with a moist palm in a cylindrical shape.
5. Roast at a moderate temperature over a charcoal grill for 4-5 minutes.
6. Serve hot with choice of a salad and chutney.

Shahi Khumb Galouti

THE LEGENDARY KEBAB PREPARED WITH FRESH MUSHROOM LUCKNOWI SPICES
AND COOKED ON A GRIDDLE

Cooking time 4-6 minutes Serves 1-2

INGREDIENTS

150 gm	- Boiled mushrooms
25 gm	- Boiled potato
25 gm	- Cottage cheese (grated)
½ tsp	- Yellow chilli powder
½ tsp	- Javitri and nutmeg powder
½ tsp	- Ginger garlic paste
To taste	- Salt
2 drops	- Kewra (Ittre)
½ tsp	- Luknowi masala
½ tsp	- Dalchini powder
3 tsp	- Roasted channa powder
1 tsp	- Desi ghee (for smoking)
3-4 no	- Clove
For cooking	- Desi ghee

METHOD

1. Squeeze extra moisture from boiled mushroom.
2. In a food processor finely mince mushroom and transfer to a bowl.
3. Add all the remaining ingredients listed above, mix well till smooth consistency.
4. Take a small bowl (katori), place in the middle of the mixture bowl, put 2 pieces of burning charcoal, cloves and pour desi ghee, immediately cover with lid and keep aside for 2-3 minutes.
5. Divide this mixture into 5-6 parts. Press each ball between your palm to give a medallion (tikki) shape.

Cooking

6. Heat desi ghee in a non-stick pan or griddle, place the kebab and shallow fry it on slow fire till golden brown on both sides.
7. Serve hot with choice of a salad and chutney.

Tandoori Lahsun Wali Gobhi

WHOLE BABY CAULIFLOWER MARINATED WITH EXTRA TOUCH OF GARLIC

Cooking time 10-12 minutes Serves 1-2

INGREDIENTS

225-250 gm - Cauliflower (without stem)

To taste	- Salt
½ tsp	- Turmeric powder
½ tsp	- Garlic paste
2 tsp	- Mustard oil
2 tsp	- Besan
To taste	- Salt
½ tsp	- Yellow chilli powder
2 tsp	- Garlic paste
½ tsp	- Kasoori methi powder
½ tsp	- Garam masala
4 tsp	- Cream
4 tbsp	- Hung curd

METHOD

1. Parboil cauliflower with salt, turmeric powder and garlic paste. Drain water and allow it to cool.

Marination

2. Heat oil in a pan, add besan and sauté till golden brown, remove and cool.
3. In a bowl take besan and add all the remaining ingredients, mix well. Apply this marinade to cauliflower all around and keep aside for at least half an hour.

Cooking

4. Take a skewer and skew cauliflower leaving a gap.
5. Roast in a tandoor at moderate temperature for 10-12 minutes.
6. Serve hot with choice of a salad and chutney.

Tandoori Adraki Gobhi

WHOLE CAULIFLOWER CHAR-GRILLED WITH EXTRA TOUCH OF GINGER AND MIX SPICES

Cooking time 10-12 minutes Serves 1-2

INGREDIENTS

225-250 gm - Baby cauliflower (1 no)

½ tsp	- Turmeric powder
To taste	- Salt

Marination

4 tbsp	- Hung curd
To taste	- Salt
½ tsp	- Yellow chilli powder
2 tsp	- Ginger paste
½ tsp	- Garam masala
A pinch	- Kasoori methi powder
1/3 tsp	- Turmeric powder
2 tsp	- Mustard oil
1 tbsp	- Cream
1 tsp	- Ginger (chopped)
½ tsp	- Red chilli paste

METHOD

1. Parboil cauliflower in salt and turmeric. Drain water and let it cool.

Marination

2. In a bowl whisk hung curd, add all the remaining ingredients in the order listed above. Mix well and apply this to cauliflower, coat well and keep aside for at least half an hour.

Cooking

3. Take a skewer and skew cauliflower.
4. Roast in a tandoor at a moderate temperature for 10-12 minutes.
5. Serve hot with choice of a salad and chutney with ginger julienne.

Lauki Ki Seekh

AN UNUSUAL CREATION OF BOTTLE GOURD PREPARED DELICATELY ON A SKEWER

Cooking time 4-6 minutes Serves 1-2

INGREDIENTS

150 gm	- Grated lauki (bottle gourd)
50 gm	- Boiled potatoes (grated)
50 gm	- Cottage cheese (grated)
½ tsp	- Ginger (chopped)
½ tsp	- Green chilli (chopped)
1 tsp	- Fresh coriander (chopped)
To taste	- Salt
½ tsp	- Yellow chilli powder
½ tsp	- Garam masala
½ tsp	- Roasted jeera powder
3-4 tsp	- Cornflour
For binding	- Breadcrumbs

METHOD

1. In a bowl take grated lauki, add all the ingredients listed above and mix well till it binds together and is smooth.
2. Divide this mixture into 4 equal parts and make balls.

Cooking

3. Take a skewer and apply mixture along on it in a cylindrical shape (4") with moist palm.
4. Roast in a tandoor or over a charcoal grill at a moderate temperature for 4-6 minutes.
5. Serve hot with choice of a salad and chutney.

Kathal Aur Kacche Kele Ke Kebab

AN IMPRESSIVE COMBINATION OF JACKFRUIT AND RAW BANANA, FLAVOURED WITH POUNDED RED CHILLI

Cooking time 2-3 minutes Serves 1-2

INGREDIENTS

100 gm	- Boiled jack fruit (without skin)
50 gm	- Boiled raw banana (grated)
50 gm	- Boiled Potato (grated)
To taste	- Salt
½ tsp	- Turmeric powder
1tsp	- Green chilli (chopped)
1 tbsp	- Green coriander (chopped)
1 tsp	- Ginger (chopped)
½ tsp	- Yellow chilli powder
½ tsp	- Garam masala
½ tsp	- Kutty red chilli
2 tsp	- Cornflour
For binding	- Breadcrumbs
For frying	- Refined oil

METHOD

1. Put boiled jackfruit in a processor, make fine mince and transfer it to a bowl, add grated banana, potato and add all the ingredients in the order listed above, mix thoroughly and keep aside.
2. Divide the mixture into 4-5 equal parts and make balls and then press it between your palm to give it a medallion (tikki) shape.

Cooking

3. Heat oil in a non-stick pan and shallow fry till golden brown on both sides.
4. Serve hot with choice of a salad and chutney.

Tori Ke Shammi

KEBAB OF FINELY MINCED RIDGE GOURD PERFUMED WITH SPECIAL BLEND OF SPICES AND CRISPY FRIED

Cooking time 2-3 minutes Serves 1-2

INGREDIENTS

200 gm	- Tori (ridge gourd)
25 gm	- Channa dal (pre-soaked in water)
½ tsp	- Garam masala

Whole Spice

2 no	- Small cardamom
1 no	- Big cardamom
1 no	- Cinnamon stick
1 no	- Cloves
2 tsp	- Black pepper
To taste	- Salt
30 gm	- Boiled potato (grated)
½ tsp	- Yellow chilli powder
½ tsp	- Garam masala
1 tsp	- Cornflour
For binding	- Breadcrumbs
For frying	- Refined oil

METHOD

1. Clean, wash and peel tori, boil with channa dal, garam masala and whole spices, till tender and water gets evaporates.
2. Remove whole spices, put boiled mixture in a food processor and make a fine mince.
3. Add the remaining ingredients, mix well and keep aside for at least half an hour.
4. Divide the mixture into 4 equal parts and make balls.
5. Press each ball between your palms to give it a medallion (tikki) shape.

Cooking

6. Heat oil in a kadai, deep fry it to golden brown and crisp. Remove on absorbent paper to remove excess oil.
7. Serve hot with choice of a salad and chutney.

Toofa-E-Zameen

THIS MAGNIFICENT KEBAB IS MADE OF YAM AND LOTUS STEM, IS A PERFECT IMITATION OF LUCKNOWI SHAMMI KEBAB

Cooking time 2-3 minutes Serves 1-2

INGREDIENTS

25 gm	- Channa dal (pre-soaked in water)
100 gm	- Jimikand (yam)
50 gm	- Nadru (lotus stem)
50 gm	- Boiled grated potatoes
To taste	- Salt
½ tsp	- Garam masala
1 tsp	- Desi ghee
A pinch	- Elaichi javitri powder
A drop	- Itter/essence
3 tsp	- Roasted channa powder
½ tsp	- Yellow chilli powder
½ tsp	- Dalchini powder
½ tsp	- Kutty red chilli
For binding	- Bread crumbs
½ tsp	- Chaat masala
For frying	- Refined oil

METHOD

1. Boil channa dal, till half cooked, add jimikand, nadru, cook till tender, drain water and let it cool. Transfer to a food processor and make a fine mince.
2. Take mince mixture in a bowl, add all the ingredients in the order listed, mix well and keep aside.
3. Divide mixture into 5 equal parts and make balls.

Cooking

4. Press each ball between your palms to give it a medallion (tikki) shape.
5. Heat oil in a kadai and shallow fry it. Remove to a kitchen paper to drain extra oil. Sprinkle chaat masala.
6. Serve hot with choice of a salad and chutney.

Dahi Ke Shammi (for recipe turn to page no: 244)

Achari Bharwan Khumb Shashlik (for recipe turn to page no: 251)

Tandoori Adraki Gobhi (for recipe turn to page no: 262)

Tandoori Malai Arbi (for recipe turn to page no: 276)

Tandoori bharwan Achari Baigan (for recipe turn to page no: 287)

Rajma Ke Galouti (for recipe turn to page no: 295)

Ankurit Dal Ke Kebab (for recipe turn to page no: 291)

Bhein Ke Kakori

AN ABSOLUTELY SOFT KEBAB MADE OF LOTUS STEM AND INFUSED WITH KAKORI SPICE BLEND

Cooking time 4-6 minutes Serves 1-2

INGREDIENTS

175 gm	- Nadru (lotus stem)
30 gm	- Channa dal
2 tsp	- Desi ghee
To taste	- Salt
30 gm	- Potato (grated)
1/3 tsp	- Ginger garlic paste
½ tsp	- Garam masala
3 tsp	- Brown onion paste
2 tsp	- Roasted channa powder
A pinch	- Elaichi javitri powder
A drop	- Kewra water
½ tsp	- Kakori masala
For binding	- Breadcrumbs

METHOD

1. Peel, wash and slice lotus stems.
2. Heat ghee in a pan, sauté nadru slices, dal for a minute, add water and let it cook till both are tender, remove to cool, transfer to a food processor and make a fine mince.
3. In a bowl take paste, add all the remaining ingredients in the order listed, mix well and keep aside for at least half an hour.
4. Divide the mixture into 4 equal parts and make balls.

Cooking

5. Take a skewer and apply this mixture individually along the skewer with a moist palm in a cylindrical shape (4").
6. Roast in a moderately hot tandoor or over charcoal grill for 4-6 minutes.
7. Serve hot with choice of a salad and chutney.

Kacche Kele Anar Ke Kebab

RAW BANANA AND POMEGRANATE BLENDED WITH POUNDED YELLOW CHILLI

Cooking time 2-3 minutes Serves 1-2

INGREDIENTS

125 gm	- Raw bananas (boiled)
50 gm	- Cottage cheese (grated)
50 gm	- Boiled potato (grated)
½ tsp	- Yellow chilli powder
To taste	- Salt
2 tsp	- Cornflour
For binding	- Breadcrumbs

Stuffing

1 ½ tsp	- Anardana (crushed)
½ tsp	- Ginger (chopped)
1 tsp	- Green coriander (chopped)
½ tsp	- Green chilli (chopped)
For frying	- Refined oil

METHOD

1. In a deep tray grate boiled banana, cottage cheese, potato, add yellow chilli powder, salt, corn flour, breadcrumbs mix well to form a smooth dough and keep aside for at least half an hour.
2. Divide the mixture into 4-5 equal parts and make balls.
3. In a bowl mix anardana, ginger, green chilli, coriander and divide in 5 parts.
4. Press each ball between your palms, place stuffing mixture, seal it and again press to give medallion (tikki) shape.

Cooking

5. Heat oil in a pan or kadhai and deep fry to a golden brown colour.
6. Serve hot with choice of a salad and chutney.

Kathal Ke Shammi

KEBAB OF FINELY MINCED JACKFRUIT PERFUMED WITH ROYAL SPICES
Cooking time 2-3 minutes Serves 1-2

INGREDIENTS

200 gm	- Jackfruit (with out skin)
30 gm	- Channa dal
To taste	- Salt
½ tsp	- Turmeric powder
1 no	- Cloves
1 no	- Black pepper corn
2 no	- Small cardamom
1 no	- Big cardamom
30 gm	- Boiled potato (grated)
¼ tsp	- Ginger garlic paste
½ tsp	- Garam masala
1 tsp	- Green chilli (chopped)
1 tbsp	- Fresh coriander (chopped)
½ tsp	- Ginger (chopped)
½ tsp	- Red chilli powder
2 tsp	- Cornflour
For binding	- Breadcrumbs
For frying	- Refined oil

METHOD

1. In boiling water cook jackfruit with channa dal, salt, turmeric powder, cloves, black peppercorn, small and big cardamom till half done. Drain water, remove excess water and leave to cool and remove whole spices.
2. Put the boiled jackfruit and channa dal in a food processor, make fine mince and transfer it to a bowl, add all the remaining ingredients in the order listed, mix well and keep aside for at least half an hour.
3. Divide the mixture into 5 equal parts and shape each one into a ball and then press it between your palms to give it a medallion (tikki) shape.

Cooking

4. Heat oil in a non-stick pan and shallow fry till golden brown and crisp. Remove to a absorbent paper to drain excess oil.
5. Serve hot with choice of a salad and chutney.

Akhrot Ki Galouti

SOFT AND DELICIOUS KEBAB PERFUMED WITH WALNUT, POTATO AND FLAVOURED WITH FLORAL AROMA AND SUBTLE SPICES
Cooking time 4-6 minutes Serves 1-2

INGREDIENTS

100 gm	- Walnuts (grounded)
50 gm	- Boiled grated potato
To taste	- Salt
½ tsp	- Yellow chilli powder
1 tsp	- Green chilli (chopped)
1 tsp	- Cornflour
½ tsp	- Galouti masala
½ tsp	- Roasted jeera powder
Few drop	- Kewra/Itter
2-3 no	- Clove
1 tsp	- Desi ghee
For cooking	- Desi ghee

METHOD

1. In a bowl take grounded walnuts, add all the remaining ingredients except cloves and desi ghee, mix well to smooth consistency.

Smoking

2. Take a small bowl (katori), place in the middle of the mixture bowl, put 2 pieces of burning charcoal, cloves and pour desi ghee, immediately cover with lid and keep aside for 2-3 minutes.
3. Divide the mixture into 4 equal balls and shape it to a round medallion (tikki) shape.

Cooking

4. Heat desi ghee in a non-stick pan or griddle, place the kebab and shallow fry it on slow fire till golden brown on both sides.
5. Serve hot with choice of a salad and chutney.

Lajawab Achari Arbi

THIS EXTRAORDINARY KEBAB OF COLOCASIA VEGETABLE CHAR-GRILLED WITH MUSTARD SEEDS AND PICKLING SPICES

Cooking time 4-6 minutes Serves 1-2

INGREDIENTS

225 gm (8 no) - Boiled arbi

Marination
4 tbsp	- Hung curd
To taste	- Salt
½ tsp	- Ginger garlic paste
½ tsp	- Yellow chilli powder
A pinch	- Turmeric powder
1 tsp	- Lemon juice
½ tsp	- Roasted besan
2 tsp	- Achaar paste
1 tsp	- Cornflour
2 tsp	- Mustard oil
2 tsp	- Whole achari masala (saunf, kalonji, mustard seeds, methi dana)

METHOD

1. In a bowl whisk hung curd, add all the ingredients in the order listed and mix well.
2. Heat mustard oil in a pan, add whole achari masala. When it starts to crackle immediately add the above mixture.
3. Apply this to arbi, coat well and keep aside for at least 1 hour.

Cooking

4. Take a skewer and skew marinated arbi one by one an inch apart.
5. Roast in a moderately hot tandoor or over charcoal grill for 4-6 minutes.
6. Serve hot with choice of a salad and chutney.

Arbi Khumb Ke Kebab

COMBINATION OF COLOCASIA AND FRESH MUSHROOM INFUSED WITH CARUM SEEDS AND COOKED IN CLAY OVEN

Cooking time 4-6 minutes Serves 1-2

INGREDIENTS

125 gm	- Boiled arbi (colocasia)
50 gm	- Boiled mushroom
50 gm	- Cottage cheese
To taste	- Salt
½ tsp	- Yellow chilli powder
½ tsp	- Green chilli (chopped)
1 tsp	- Fresh coriander (chopped)
½ tsp	- Ginger (chopped)
A pinch	- Ajwain
A drop	- Attar/kewra
For bindin	- Dry breadcrumbs

METHOD

1. Grate arbi, chop mushroom, grate cottage cheese and transfer to a bowl.
2. Put all the remaining ingredients in the order listed above and mix well. Keep aside for at least half an hour.
3. Divide the mixture into 4 equal parts and make balls.

Cooking

4. Take a skewer and apply mixture along it with a moist palm to give cylindrical shape (4").
5. Roast in a moderately hot tandoor or over a charcoal grill for 4-6 minutes.
6. Serve hot with choice of a salad and chutney.

Arbi Akhrot Ke Kebab

A SIMPLE YET DELICIOUS KEBAB MADE OF COLOCASIA AND WALNUT

Cooking time 2-3 minutes Serves 1-2

INGREDIENTS

150 gm	- Boiled arbi (colocasia)
50 gm	- Cottage cheese
To taste	- Salt
½ tsp	- Green chilli (chopped)
1 tsp	- Green coriander (chopped)
½ tsp	- Ginger (chopped)
A pinch	- Ajwain
A pinch	- Turmeric powder
For binding	- Breadcrumbs
1 tsp	- Cornflour
2 tsp	- Grated walnut
½ tsp	- Yellow chilli powder
2 tsp	- Walnut (chopped)
For frying	- Refined oil

METHOD

1. Grate arbi, cottage cheese and transfer to a bowl.
2. Add all the remaining ingredients listed above except chopped walnuts and mix well.
3. Divide mixture into 4-5 parts and make balls.
4. Press each ball between palms, place chopped walnut in centre, close, again press to give it medallion (tikki) shape.

Cooking

5. Heat oil on a griddle and shallow fry till golden brown and crisp.
6. Serve hot with choice of a salad and chutney.

Tandoori Malai Arbi

A CREAMY COLOCASIA VEGETABLE KEBAB FLAVOURED WITH CARDAMOM AND ROYAL CUMIN

Cooking time 4-6 minutes Serves 1-2

INGREDIENTS

225 gm (8no) - Arbi (colocasia)

First Marination

½ tsp	- Ginger garlic paste
To taste	- Salt
1/3 tsp	- White pepper powder

Second Marination

30 gm	- Processed cheese (grated)
2 tbsp	- Cream
½ tsp	- Green corriander (chopped)
½ tsp	- Green chilli (chopped)
1 tsp	- Cornflour
To taste	- Salt
½ tsp	- White pepper powder
½ tsp	- Ginger garlic paste
A pinch	- Elaichi powder
A pinch	- Shahi jeera
For basting	- Clarified butter

METHOD

1. Wash and boil arbi till half done. Drain water and let it cool. Peel arbi and prick it with a toothpick.

First Marination

2. In a bowl mix ginger garlic paste, salt, white pepper powder, apply this to arbi and keep aside for at least 1 hour.

Second Marination

3. In a deep tray mash processed cheese, put all the other ingredients listed and mix well to smooth consistency.
4. Remove excess moisture from arbi and put it into this marinade, coat well and keep aside for at least half an hour.

Cooking

5. Take a skewer and skew marinated arbi leaving an inch apart, apply remaining marinade on them.
6. Roast it at moderate temperature in tandoor or over charcoal grill for 4-6 minutes. Baste with clarified butter and roast for another 2-3 minutes.
7. Remove and serve hot with choice of a salad and chutney.

Nadru Chop

A KASHMIRI DELICACY OF LOTUS STEM INFUSED WITH A VARIETY OF SPICES FROM THE VALLEY

Cooking time 2-3 minutes Serves 1-2

INGREDIENTS

350 gm	- Lotus stem (kamal kakri)

Whole Spice

1 no	- Cinnamon stick
2 no	- Black pepper
1 no	- Big cardamom
2 no	- Small cardamom
1 no	- Bay leaf
1 tsp	- Green coriander (chopped)
½ tsp	- Green chillies (chopped)
A pinch	- Black cumin seeds
½ tsp	- Dry mint powder
A pinch	- Cinnamon powder
½ tsp	- Kashmiri red chilli powder
½ tsp	- Black pepper powder
To taste	- Salt
½ tsp	- Garam masala
For binding	- Breadcrumbs
For frying	- Refined oil

METHOD

1. Peel, wash and cut the stems into slices. Boil it with whole garam masala.
2. In a food processor put boiled lotus stem, make a coarse paste and transfer to a bowl.
3. Add all the remaining ingredients in the order listed, mix well and keep aside for at least half an hour.
4. Divide the mixture into 5-6 equal parts and make balls. Press each ball between your palms to make a medallion (tikki) shape.

Cooking

5. Heat oil in a pan, shallow fry the patties till light brown. Remove with a slotted spoon and drain the excess oil on absorbent kitchen paper.
6. Serve hot with choice of a salad and chutney.

Lauki Ki Galouti

ABSOLUTELY SOFT GALOUTI KEBAB MADE WITH PUMPKIN AND FLORAL AROMA
Cooking time 4-6 minutes Serves 1-2

INGREDIENTS

150 gm	- White pumpkin
25 gm	- Channa dal (pre-soaked in water)
2 no	- Cardamom (small)
1 no	- Cardamom (big)
1 no	- Cinnamon stick
1 no	- Bay leaf
To taste	- Salt
75 gm	- Boiled potato (grated)
½ tsp	- Garam masala
To taste	- Salt
½ tsp	- Yellow chilli powder
For binding	- Breadcrumbs
1 tsp	- Cornflour
1 tsp	- Roasted channa powder
½ tsp	- Cinnamon powder
½ tsp	- Galouti masala
1 tsp	- Desi ghee
2-3 no	- Cloves
For cooking	- Desi ghee

METHOD

1. Wash, peel white pumkin and boil with channa dal, small and big cardamom, cinnamon stick, bay leaf and salt, till cooked and water evaporates.
2. Remove whole masala, put in a processor, make fine paste and transfer to a bowl.
3. Add all the remaining ingredients listed in order except desi ghee and cloves, mix well to smooth consistency.
4. Smoke: Take a small bowl (katori), place in the middle of the mixture bowl, put 2 pieces of burning charcoal, cloves and pour desi ghee, immediately cover with lid and keep aside for 2-3 minutes.
5. Divide the mixture into 4-5 equal parts and make balls.
6. Press each ball between your palms to give the shape of medallion (tikki).

Cooking

7. Heat desi ghee in a non-stick pan or griddle, fry kebab on slow fire till crisp from both side (4-6 minutes).
8. Remove, serve hot with choice of a salad and chutney.

Phaldari Seekh Kebab

AN EXTRAVAGANT COMBINATION OF GARDEN FRESH VEGETABLES, FRUITS AND ENHANCED WITH SUBTLE SPICES AND COOKED IN CLAY OVEN
Cooking time 4-6 minutes Serves 1-2

INGREDIENTS

½ no	- Apple
40 gm	- Boiled carrots and beans
20 gm	- Boiled green peas
1 no	- Boiled raw banana
4 tsp	- Boiled potatoes (grated)
2 tbsp	- Cottage cheese (grated)
5 no	- Fresh cherry (seedless)
2 tsp	- Raisins
2 tsp	- Cashewnut (chopped)
2 tsp	- White pepper powder
To taste	- Salt
A pinch	- Shahi jeera
A pinch	- Elaichi powder
For binding	- Channa powder (roasted)
½ tsp	- Yellow chilli powder
½ tsp	- Green chilli (chopped)
For binding	- Breadcrumbs

METHOD

1. Peal, grate apple and squeeze moisture
2. In a processor, put boiled vegetables, raw banana, and make a coarse mince, transfer this mixture to a bowl.
3. Add the remaining ingredients in the order listed above mix well and keep aside for at least half an hour.
4. Divide this mixture into 4-5 parts.

Cooking

5. Spread each portion of mixture along on a skewer in a cylindrical shape of 4 inch long.
6. Cook in a moderately hot tandoor or over charcoal grill for 4-6 minutes.
7. Remove, serve hot with choice of a salad and chutney.

Syalkoti Subz Kebab

COMBINATION OF VEGETABLES AND SPECIAL SPICES PREPARED WITH RECIPE FROM SYALKOT

Cooking time 2-3 minutes Serves 1-2

INGREDIENTS

1 tsp	- Refined oil
1/3 tsp	- White jeera
8 no	- Curry leaves
1/3 tsp	- Kalonji
3 tsp	- Onion slice
1/3 tsp	- Garlic (chopped)
50 gm	- Boiled potato (grated)
To taste	- Salt
A pinch	- Turmeric powder
½ tsp	- Red chilli powder
1 tsp	- Lemon juice
150 gm	- Carrots and beans (boiled)
1 tsp	- Cornflour
For binding	- Breadcrumbs
For frying	- Refined Oil

METHOD

1. Heat oil in a pan, put kalounji, cumin, curry leaves, add garlic, onion, cook it for a while and add all the remaining ingredients listed above, except carrots and beans, stir fry for a while till all ingredients are mixed and moisture evaporates. Remove to cool.
2. In a food processor put stir fried mixture, boiled vegetables and make a mince.
3. Mix well, add breadcrumbs and cornflour.
4. Divide the mixture into 4 equal parts and make balls.

Cooking

5. Press each ball between your palms to give this shape of a medallion (tikki).
6. Heat oil in a pan and deep fry till golden brown on both sides and crisp. Remove to drain excess oil on absorbent paper.
7. Serve hot along with choice of a salad and chutney.

Tandoori Bharwan Karela

BITTER GOURD STUFFED WITH SPICY POTATO, COTTAGE CHEESE, STEEPED IN PICKLE FLAVOURED MARINADE AND COOKED IN CLAY OVEN

Cooking time 7-8 minutes Serves 1-2

INGREDIENTS

170 gm (4no)	- Karela (bitter gourd) (large)
½ tsp	- Turmeric powder
½ tsp	- Salt
Refined oil	- For frying

Filling

2 tsp	- Oil
2 tsp	- Kalonji and saunf, mustard seeds
½ tsp	- Green chilli (chopped)
½ tsp	- Ginger garlic paste
½ tsp	- Yellow chilli powder
To taste	- Salt
25 gm	- Boiled potato (grated)
25 gm	- Paneer (grated)

Marination

4 tbsp	- Hung curd
½ tsp	- Ginger/garlic paste
To taste	- Salt
½ tsp	- Garam masala
A pinch	- Kasoori methi powder
1½ tsp	- Refined oil
½ tsp	- Yellow chilli powder
1 tsp	- Achari paste
½ tsp	- Roasted besan

METHOD

1. Scrap, wash and cut karela from the middle and de-seed / empty.
2. Apply, turmeric and salt to karela, rub well and keep aside for 1 hour.
3. Wash, pat dry and fry till half cooked. Drain excess oil and keep aside.

Filling

4. Heat oil in pan, add saunf, kalonji, mustard seeds. When it starts crackling add all the remaining ingredients listed above and sauté till mixture is dry and keep to cool.
5. Divide in 4 equal parts and fill each karela to full, tie karela with thread to retain stuffing from falling.

Marination

6. In a bowl whisk hung curd, add the remaining ingredients listed and mix well.
7. Put the stuffed karela into this marinade and keep aside for at least 45 minutes.

Cooking

8. Take a skewer and skew the karela leaving a gap of 1 inch in between
9. Roast in a tandoor at a moderate temperature for 7-8 minutes.
10. Serve hot with a choice of a salad and chutney.

Khumb Palak Seekh

FRESH MUSHROOM AND SPINACH SKEWER COATED WITH CRUNCHY VERMICELLI

Cooking time 4-6 minutes Serves 1-2

INGREDIENTS

75 gm	- Boiled spinach (chopped)
75 gm	- Boiled mushroom (chopped)
30 gm	- Boiled potatoes (grated)
30 gm	- Cottage cheese (grated)
½ tsp	- Green chilli (chopped)
1 tsp	- Fresh coriander (chopped)
1 tbsp	- Roasted channa powder
½ tsp	- Yellow chilli powder
½ tsp	- Kasoori methi powder
To taste	- Salt
For binding	- Breadcrumbs
For coating	- Vermicelli (crushed)

METHOD

1. Squeeze extra moisture from spinach and mushroom.
2. In a deep tray take boiled spinach, mushroom, add all the remaining ingredients in the order listed, mix well and keep aside for at least ½ hour.
3. Divide the mixture into 5 equal parts and make balls.

Cooking

4. Take a skewer and apply each ball on it with a moist palm along the length of the skewer in a cylindrical shape an inch apart, make each kebab 4 inches long and coat with vermicelli.
5. Roast in a moderately hot tandoor or over charcoal grill for 4-6 minutes.
6. Serve hot with choice of a salad and chutney.

Basmati Aur Bhutta Seekh

AN UNUSUAL COMBINATION OF BASMATI RICE AND CORN WITH SAFFRON AND CUMIN

Cooking time 5-6 minutes Serves 1-2

INGREDIENTS

100 gm	- Basmati rice (boiled)
50 gm	- Corn niblets (roughly chopped)
25 gm	- Cottage cheese (grated)
25 gm	- Boiled potatoes (grated)
1 tsp	- Green chilli (fine chopped)
1 tsp	- Ginger (fine chopped)
1 tsp	- Fresh coriander (fine chopped)
½ tsp	- Yellow chilli powder
½ tsp	- Garam masala
A pinch	- Royal cumin seeds
A pinch	- Saffron
To taste	- Salt
1 tsp	- Cornflour

METHOD

1. Take sweet corn, squeeze water by using a dry cloth.
2. In a bowl mash boiled basmati rice, add corn niblets, grated potato, grated cottage cheese, chopped green chilli, ginger, green coriander, yellow chilly powder, garam masala, royal cumin seeds, saffron, cornflour, salt and mix well with help of your palm till smooth and keep aside.
3. Divide this mixture into 4 equal parts and make balls.

Cooking

4. Take a skewer and apply mixture on it with a moist palm in cylindrical shape (4"- 5").
5. Roast in a moderately hot tandoor or charcoal grill for 5-6 minutes or till done.
6. Serve hot with choice of a salad and chutney.

Chawal Bhutte Ke Shammi Kebab

EXCITING MIX OF RICE AND TENDER CORN FLAVOURED WITH CARDAMOM
Cooking time 3-4 minutes Serves 1-2

INGREDIENTS

100 gm	- Basmati rice (boiled)
50 gm	- Boiled corn niblets (roughly chop)
50 gm	- Boiled potato (grated)
1 tsp	- Green chilli (chopped)
1 tsp	- Ginger (chopped)
1 tsp	- Onion (chopped)
1 tsp	- Green coriander (chopped)
½ tsp	- Yellow chilli powder
A pinch	- Cardamom powder
1/3 tsp	- Turmeric powder
To taste	- Salt
1 tsp	- Cornflour
For frying	- Refined oil

METHOD

1. Take corn niblets, squeeze water by using a dry cloth.
2. In a bowl mash boiled basmati rice, sweet corn, potato, chopped ginger, coriander, green chilli and all remaining ingredients in the order listed and mix well, check seasoning and keep aside.
3. Divide this mixture into 4 equal parts and make ball by pressing it between palms and give a shape of medallion (tikki).

Cooking

4. Heat oil in non-stick pan and shallow fry till golden brown and crisp on both sides (3-4 minutes). Remove to an absorbent paper to drain excess oil.
5. Serve hot along with choice of a salad and chutney.

Dahi Ke Kebab

ABSOLUTELY SOFT AND CHEESY KEBAB MADE WITH YOGHURT AND SPECIAL BLEND OF SPICES
Cooking time 3-4 minutes Serves 1-2

INGREDIENTS

1 tbsp	- Warm milk
A pinch	- Saffron threads
1 cup	- Hung curd (double)
1½ tbsp	- Roasted channa powder
A pinch	- Clove powder
½ tsp	- Black pepper powder
A pinch	- Cinnamon powder
½ tsp	- Yellow chilli powder
To taste	- Salt

Stuffing

½ tsp	- Ginger (chopped)
½ tsp	- Mint (chopped)
For frying	- Refined oil

METHOD

1. Soak saffron in warm milk and keep aside.
2. In a bowl take hung curd, add pre-soaked saffron, and all other ingredients listed in order, mix well.
3. Divide the mixture into 4-5 equal parts and make balls.

Stuffing

4. In a bowl mix chopped ginger, mint and divide in 4-5 equal parts.
5. Flatten each ball between wet palms, place a stuffing in centre, fold again flatten in shape of medallion (tikki) and keep aside.

Cooking

6. Heat oil in a pan and shallow fry till golden brown on both sides and crisp. Remove to an absorbent paper to drain excess oil.
7. Serve hot with choice of a salad and chutney.

Palak Dal Ke Shammi

SPINACH AND LENTIL KEBAB IN TRUE LUCKNOWI STYLE
Cooking time 2-3 minutes Serves 1-2

INGREDIENTS

250 gm	- Spinach leaves
25 gm	- Channa dal (pre-soaked in water)
2 no	- Greeen cardamom
2 no	- Cloves
1 no	- Cinnamon sticks
1 no	- Big cardamom
½ tsp	- Yellow chilli powder
A pinch	- Elaichi javitri powder
½ tsp	- Cinnamon powder
Few drops	- Kewra
2 tsp	- Cornflour
To taste	- Salt

Stuffing

30 gm	- Cottage cheese (grated)
2 tsp	- Cashewnut (chopped)
2 tsp	- Chironji (chopped)
½ tsp	- Green chilli (chopped)
1 tsp	- Ginger (chopped)
1 tsp	- Fresh coriander (chopped)
To taste	- Salt

For frying - Refined oil

METHOD

1. Clean, remove hard stem of spinach and wash in running water.
2. Boil spinach with channa dal, green cardamom, cloves, cinnamon sticks, big cardamom and boil it on slow fire till dal is cooked and allow the water to dry up, cool it.
3. In a food processor put spinach and make a paste, transfer to bowl and add all ingredients listed in the order above and mix well.
4. In a bowl mix ingredients of the filling listed above and divide into 4-5 equal parts.
5. Divide the spinach mixture into 4-5 parts, make balls, press each ball between palms, place filling, fold it, again press and give shape of medallion (tikki) and keep aside.

Cooking

6. Heat oil in a non-stick pan and shallow fry kebab till crisp. Drain excess oil on a absorbent paper.
7. Serve hot with choice of a salad and chutney.

Shahi Dahi Palak Ke Shammi

DELICIOUS YOGURT AND SPINACH KEBAB
Cooking time 2-3 minutes Serves 1-2

INGREDIENTS

300 gm	- Boiled spinach
2 no	- Green chilli (chopped)
4 no	- Garlic whole
20 gm	- Ginger
To taste	- Salt
For binding	- Breadcrumbs
1 tsp	- Cornflour

Stuffing

½ cup	- Hung curd (thick)
½ tsp	- Elachi powder
½ tsp	- Cashewnut (chopped)

For frying - Refined oil

METHOD

1. Squeeze excess water from spinach and put in food processor, add green chilli, whole garlic, ginger and make a paste to thick consistency and transfer to a bowl.
2. In a another bowl take hung curd, elaichi powder, chopped cashewnut, mix it for stuffing and keep aside
3. Add salt to spinach, mix well, divide into 4-5 parts and make balls.
4. Flatten each spinach ball between your palms, place hung curd filling and total cover with spinach by making balls and again flatten to give round medallion (tikki) shape.
5. Keep in refrigerator for some time.

Cooking

6. Heat oil in a kadhai and deep fry kebab till crisp. Drain excess oil on a absorbent paper.
7. Serve hot with choice of a salad and chutney.

Tarkari Shammi Kebab

MEDLEY OF GREEN VEGETABLE BLENDED WITH LUCKNOWI SPICES

Cooking time 2-3 minutes **Serves** 1-2

INGREDIENTS

50 gm	- Carrots and beans
30 gm	- Green peas
50 gm	- Boiled potato (grated)
30 gm	- Tomato seedless (chopped)
30 gm	- Bottle gourd (grated)
1 tbsp	- Cashewnut (crushed)
2 tsp	- Refined oil
30 gm	- Onion (chopped)
½ tsp	- Ginger (chopped)
½ tsp	- Green chilli (chopped)
½ tsp	- Red chilli powder
½ tsp	- Garam masala
½ tsp	- Black pepper powder
A pinch	- Turmeric powder
½ tsp	- Amchur powder
1 tbsp	- Refined Oil
To taste	- Salt
For binding	- Breadcrumbs

METHOD

1. Wash all the vegetables, peel and cut them into small dices.
2. Boil carrots, beans, green peas and grated bottle gourd, drain water completely and let it cool.
3. In a food processor put vegetables and make a coarse mince.
4. In a pan, heat oil add chopped ginger, onions, sauté it, add chopped green chilli, and others spices listed above, add this to vegetables mince.
5. Transfer this mixture in a bowl, add the remaining ingredients listed above and mix well.
6. Divide the mixture into 5-6 parts and make balls, press between your palms and make medallion (tikki) shape.

Cooking

7. Heat oil in a non-stick pan and shallow fry kebab till crisp.
8. Serve hot with choice of a salad and chutney.

Bhutta Seekh Kebab

KEBAB MADE UP OF CORN NIBLETS AND SELECTED SPICES

Cooking time 5-6 minutes **Serves** 1-2

INGREDIENTS

100 gm	- Baby corn (fine chopped)
50 gm	- Corn niblets
50 gm	- Boiled potato (grated)
50 gm	- Cottage cheese (grated)
To taste	- Salt
½ tsp	- Yellow chilli powder
½ tsp	- Garam masala
½ tsp	- Green chilli (chopped)
1 tsp	- Green coriander (chopped)
1 tsp	- Mint (chopped)
½ tsp	- Crushed anardana
A pinch	- Turmeric powder
2 tsp	- Cornflour
For binding	- Breadcrumbs

METHOD

1. In a deep tray take baby corn, corn niblets, add all the ingredients in the order listed, mix well to form a smooth dough and keep aside for at least half an hour.
2. Divide the mixture into 4 equal parts and make balls.

Cooking

3. Take a skewer and apply each ball on it with a moist palm along the length of the skewer in a cylindrical shape 2 inches apart, make each kebab 4 inches long.
4. Roast in a moderate temperature over charcoal grill or in tandoor for 5-6 minutes.
5. Serve hot with choice of a salad and chutney.

Khumb Mutter Ke Shammi

FRESH MUSHROOM AND GREEN PEAS PATTIES
Cooking time 2-3 minutes Serves 1-2

INGREDIENTS

120 gm	- Fresh mushroom
75 gm	- Green peas
1 tsp	- Roasted channa powder
½ tsp	- Garam masala
½ tsp	- Yellow chilli powder
¼ tsp	- Black pepper powder
¼ tsp	- Cinnamon powder
1/3 tsp	- Elaichi powder
To taste	- Salt
For frying	- Refined oil

METHOD

1. Cut stem of mushroom, wash thoroughly.
2. Par boil mushroom and green peas, drain water and squeeze excess water from mushroom and green peas with help of kitchen cloth.
3. In a food processor put boiled mushroom, green peas and make coarse paste and transfer to a bowl.
4. Add all the remaining ingredients listed in the order above and mix well.
5. Divide this mixture into 4-5 equal parts, make balls, press each ball between your palms to give a medallion shape (tikki).

Cooking
6. Heat oil in a pan and shallow fry till cooked golden brown and crisp on both sides. Drain excess oil.
7. Serve hot along with choice of a salad and chutney.

Tandoori Aloo Sarson Wale

POTATO WITH GRAIN MUSTARD AND PICKLE SPICES
Cooking time 4-6 minutes Serves 1-2

INGREDIENTS

200- 225 gm - Baby potatoes (8 no)

4 tbsp	- Hung curd
1 tsp	- Roasted besan
½ tsp	- Yellow chilli powder
½ tsp	- Mustard powder
1/3 tsp	- Garam masala
½ tsp	- Grain mustard (crushed)
½ tsp	- Mustard paste
A pinch	- Turmeric powder
To taste	- Salt
2 tsp	- Mustard oil

METHOD

1. Peel, wash and boil potatoes in a pan till ¾ cooked, drain water and cool.

Marination
2. In a bowl whisk hung curd, add all the remaining ingredients in the order listed and mix well
3. Put boiled potatoes into this marinade and mix well. Keep aside for at least 1 hour.

Cooking
4. Take a skewer and skew marinated potatoes one by one an inch apart and roast in tandoor at moderate temperature for 4-6 minutes.
5. Serve hot with choice of a salad and chutney.

Kale Moti Ke Shammi

BLACK GRAM PATTIES STUFFED WITH PROCESSED CHEESE
Cooking time 2-3 minutes Serves 1-2

INGREDIENTS

100 gm	- Black grams
10 gm	- Ginger
4 no	- Garlic cloves
50 gm	- Boiled potato (grated)
½ tsp	- Yellow chilli powder
1 tsp	- Fresh coriander (chopped)
½ tsp	- Garam masala
To taste	- Salt
1 tsp	- Cornflour
For binding	- Breadcrumbs

Stuffing

2 tbsp	- Processed cheese (grated)
½ tsp	- Green chilli (chopped)
1 tsp	- Green coriander (chopped)
1 tsp	- Onion (fine chopped)
To taste	- Salt

METHOD

1. Clean, wash and soak black gram for a couple of hours, boil with ginger, garlic and salt till soft, drain water and let it cool.
2. Put boiled black gram in a food processor and make fine paste, add all the remaining ingredients listed above and mix well
3. Divide the mixture into 5 equal parts or according to desired size and make balls.

Filling

4. In a tray take processed cheese rub well, add chopped onion, green chilli, mix well and divide in 5 parts.
5. Press each ball between wet palms, place filling mixture, seal, press again, give it medallion (tikki) shape and keep in refrigerator for some time.

Cooking

6. Heat oil in a pan and deep fry till golden brown and crisp.
7. Serve hot along with choice of a salad and chutney.

Makkai Akhrot Ki Seekh

DELICIOUS SKEWER OF TENDER CORN AND WALNUTS
Cooking time 4-6 minutes Serves 1-2

INGREDIENTS

50 gm	- Sweet corn (chopped)
50 gm	- Walnuts (chopped)
50 gm	- Lotus rout (nadru)
50 gm	- Boiled potato (grated)
½ tsp	- Green chilli (chopped)
½ tsp	- Green coriander (chopped)
½ tsp	- Yellow chilli powder
½ tsp	- Garam masala
To taste	- Salt
For binding	- Breadcrumbs

METHOD

1. Peel, slice and boil nadru till tender. Drain water and cool it.
2. In a processor put boiled nadhru, make a fine mince and transfer to a bowl.
3. Add chopped sweet corn, chopped walnuts, mince nadru, grated potato add remaining ingredients in the order listed and mix well.
4. Divide this mixture into 4 equal portion and shape each portion into a ball.

Cooking

5. Take a skewer and apply each portion on it along the skewer in cylindrical shape with moist palm and grill over charcoal for 4-6 minutes.
6. Serve hot along with choice of a salad and chutney.

Kathal Ke Galouti Kebab

THE ROMANCE OF THE LATE SPRING AND EARLY SUMMER FOR A GOURMET IN AWADH IS NEVER COMPLETE WITHOUT THE RAW MANGO, AND RAW JACKFRUIT PREPARATIONS WHICH ARE VERY POPULAR IN THE REGION. THE FLESH OF THE JACKFRUIT OR 'KATHAL' IS FIBROUS AND SO THE COOKS DESIGNED THE 'KATHAL KABAB' AS A VEGETARIAN PARALLEL TO THE GALOUTI KABAB PREPARED FROM THE FIBROUS PORTION OF THE MUTTON. THE DEFT BLENDING OF SPICES WITH THE VEGETABLE LENDS THIS KEBAB A FANTASTIC FLAVOUR.

Cooking time 4-6 minutes Serves 1-2

INGREDIENTS

150 gm	- Boiled kathal (jackfruit)
50 gm	- Boiled potato (grated)
To taste	- Salt
½ tsp	- Yellow chilli powder
½ tsp	- Garam masala
A drop	- Itter
1 tsp	- Green coriander (chopped)
½ tsp	- Green chilli (chopped)
1 tsp	- Ginger (chopped)
1 tsp	- Corn flour
3-4no.	- Cloves
1tsp	- Desi ghee
For cooking	- Desi ghee

METHOD

1. In a food processor, put boiled kathal and make a fine mince, transfer to a deep tray, add all the remaining ingredients in order listed except cloves and desi ghee, mix well. Keep aside for atleast ½ hour.
2. Take a small bowl (katori), place in the middle of the mixture bowl, put 2 pieces of burning charcoal, cloves and pour desi ghee, immediately cover with lid and keep aside for 2-3 minutes.
3. Divide the mixture into 5-6 equal parts and make balls. Press each ball between your palm to make a medallion (tikki) shape.

Cooking

1. Heat desi ghee in a non-stick pan or griddle and shallow fry each kebab until golden brown in colour from both sides.
2. Serve hot with choice of a salad and chutney.

Tandoori subz Bahar

SYMPHONY OF SELECT VEGETABLES ON A SKEWER

Cooking time 6-7 minutes Serves 1-2

INGREDIENTS

40 gm	- Cauliflower
40 gm	- Broccoli
40 gm	- Zucchini (cube)
2 no	- Mushroom
2 no	- Potato (cubes)
2 no	- Permal
A pinch	- Turmeric powder

Marination

2 tbsp	- Hung curd
1 tsp	- Roasted basen
½ tsp	- Yellow chilli powder
½ tsp	- Garam masala
½ tsp	- Ajwain
A pinch	- Turmeric powder
To taste	- Salt
1 tbsp	- Refined oil

METHOD

1. Remove stems without disjoining the cauliflower and broccoli. Remove the stems of the mushroom. Peal the potato and cut the upper and lower side of parmal cut the zucchini and wash.
2. Parboil all the vegetables with salt and turmeric. Drain water and let it cool.

Marination

3. In a bowl whisk hung curd and add all the reaming ingredients in the order listed and mix well.
4. Remove excess moisture from boiled vegetables and put them into this marinade and leave for 1 hour.

Cooking

5. Take skewer and skew all the vegetables without leaving a gap.
6. Roast in a tandoor at a moderate temperature for 6-7 minutes.
7. Serve hot with choice of salad and chutney.

Tandoori Bharwan Achari Baigan

STUFFED BABY BRINJALS STEEPED IN A PICKLE FLAVOURED MARINADE AND CHARGRILLED

Cooking time 7-8 minutes Serves 2-3

INGREDIENTS

200-225 gm (6pcs.) Small Egg Plant

Stuffing
50 gm	- Scooped pulp of eggplant
30 gm	- Boiled potato (grated)
50 gm	- Cottage cheese (grated)
2 tsp	- Cashewnet (chopped)
2 tsp	- Small capsicum (diced)
½ tsp	- Yellow chilli Powder
½ tsp	- Garam Masala
1 tsp	- Wole achar masala (Shaunf, kalonji, methidana, mustard seeds)
½ tsp	- Cumin seeds
To taste	- Salt
1 tbsp	- Refined oil

Marination
4 tbsp	- Hung curd
1 tsp	- Ginger garlic past
1 tsp	- Lemon juice
1 tsp	- Roasted besan
½ tsp	- Yellow chilli powder
½ tsp	- Garam masala
2 tsp	- Achar paste
A pinch	- Turmeric powder
2 tsp	- Mustard oil
To taste	- Salt
For basting	- Clarified butter

METHOD

1. Wash, peel alternately upper layer of eggplant, cut the tip from one side, make deep hole.

Stuffing
2. Heat oil in a pan add cumin seeds, achar masala when it starts crackle add scooped pulp of egg plant and cook it for while add grated paneer and all the remaining ingredients, mix it well. Remove and keep aside, cool it.
3. Stuff each eggplant with above stuffing and keep aside.

Marination
4. In a bowl whisk hung curd add ginger garlic paste and all other ingredients listed above and mix well.
5. Put the stuffed eggplant into this marinade, coat well and keep aside for atleast ½ hour.

Cooking
6. Take a skewer and skew marinated eggplant on the to pside.
7. Roast in a tandoor or charcoal grill at a moderate temperature for 7-8 minutes, baste with clarified butter while cooking.
8. Serve hot along with choice of a salad and chutney.

Dal
(Lentils & Beans)

Channa Dal Ke Shammi

FAMOUS LUCKNOWI KEBAB PREPARED WITH LENTIL AND SPICES

Cooking time 2-3 minutes Serves 1-2

INGREDIENTS

100 gm	- Channa dal
5 gm	- Ginger (whole)
5 gm	- Garlic (whole)
2 no	- Red chilli (whole)
To taste	- Salt
40 gm	- Boiled potato (grated)
40 gm	- Cottage cheese (grated)
½ tsp	- Ginger (chopped)
½ tsp	- Green chilli (chopped)
½ tsp	- Green coriander (chopped)
To taste	- Salt
A pinch	- Turmeric powder
2 tsp	- Hung curd
½ tsp	- Yellow chilli powder
A pinch	- Elaichi javitri powder
½ tsp	- Garam masala
For binding	- Dry breadcrumbs
1 ½ tsp	- Cornflour

Filling

2 tsp	- Processed cheese (grated)
1 tsp	- Mint (chopped)
½ tsp	- Green coriander (chopped)
½ tsp	- White till (sesame)
A pinch	- Black cumin seeds

For frying - Refined Oil

METHOD

1. Clean, wash and soak channa dal for at least 1 hour and boil with ginger, garlic, red chilli whole and salt till soft, drain water and let it cool.
2. Put boiled dal in a processor and make fine paste, add all the remaining ingredients listed above and mix well
3. Divide the mixture into 5 or 6 equal parts or according to desired size and make balls.

Filling

4. In a deep tray take processed cheese, rub well, add mint, green coriander, white til, shahi jeera. Mix well and divide into 5-6 equal parts.
5. Press each ball between wet palms, place filling mixture, seal, press again, give it medallion (tikki) shape and keep under refrigerator for some time.

Cooking

6. Heat oil in a pan and deep fry till golden brown and crisp.
7. Serve hot along with choice of a salad and chutney.

Kurkure Malka Kebab

ABSOLUTE, CRUNCHY KEBAB MADE OF LENTIL AND ROLLED IN CORNFLAKES

Cooking time 2-3 minutes **Serves** 1-2

INGREDIENTS

75 gm	- Malka dal (red gram)
10 gm	- Ginger (whole)
5 gm	- Garlic (whole)
3 no	- Red chilli (whole)
To taste	- Salt
40 gm	- Cottage cheese (grated)
40 gm	- Boiled potato (grated)
½ tsp	- Ginger (chopped)
1 tsp	- Green chilli (chopped)
½ tsp	- Green coriander (chopped)
To taste	- Salt
½ tsp	- Yellow chilli powder
A pinch	- Javitri/elaichi powder
1/4 tsp	- Garam masala
For binding	- Dry breadcrumbs
3 tbsp	- Cornflour
For coating	- Cornflakes
For frying	- Refined oil

METHOD

1. Clean, wash and soak red gram for at least 1 hour and boil with ginger, garlic, red chilli whole and salt till done and water gets evaporated, remove to cool.
2. Put boiled dal in a processor, make fine paste, add all the remaining ingredients listed above and only 1 tsp of cornflour (remaining to be used for coating).
3. Divide the mixture into 4-5 equal parts or according to desired size and make balls.
4. Press each ball between your palms to give a medallion (tikki) shape.
5. Dip it in cornflour batter (with water) and then coat with cornflakes.

Cooking

6. Heat oil in a pan and deep fry till golden brown and crisp.
7. Serve hot along with choice of a salad and chutney.

Ankurit Dal Ke Kebab

NUTRITIOUS AND LOW CALORIE KEBAB MADE WITH SPROUTED LENTIL

Cooking time 2-3 minutes **Serves** 1-2

INGREDIENTS

100 gm	- Ankurat dal (moong sprouted)
50 gm	- Paneer (grated)
50 gm	- Boiled potato (grated)
To taste	- Salt
½ tsp	- Yellow chilli powder
A pinch	- Turmeric powder
1 tsp	- Green coriander (chopped)
½ tsp	- Green chilli (chopped)
1/2 tsp	- Garam masala
1 tsp	- Whole achar masala
1/3 tsp	- Shahi jeera (black cumin)
2 tsp	- Cornflour
2 tsp	- Breadcrumb
To sprinkle	- Chaat masala
For frying	- Refined oil

METHOD

1. Coarsely chop ankurat dal and squeeze excess moisture.
2. Take ankurat dal in a deep tray, add paneer and remaining ingredients in the order listed and mix well and keep aside for at least half an hour.
3. Divide the mixture into 4-5 equal parts and make balls. Press each ball between your palms to give it a medallion shape (tikki).

Cooking

4. Heat oil in a non-stick pan and shallow fry till golden brown and crisp (2-3 minutes).
5. Sprinkle chaat masala and serve hot along with choice of a salad and chutney.

Kabuli Shammi Kebab

RICH IN PROTEINS, DELICIOUS CHICK PEAS KEBAB

Cooking time 2-3 minutes Serves 1-2

INGREDIENTS

75 gm	- Kabuli channa (white gram)
40 gm	- Cottage cheese (grated)
40 gm	- Boiled potato (grated)
½ tsp	- Green chilli (chopped)
1 tsp	- Green coriander (chopped)
½ tsp	- Ginger (chopped)
A pinch	- Ajwain
To taste	- Salt
½ tsp	- Yellow chilli powder
½ tsp	- Garam masala
A pinch	- Turmeric powder
A pinch	- Kasoori methi powder
½ tsp	- Channa masala
1/3 tsp	- Amchur powder
1 tsp	- Brown onion paste
For binding	- Dry breadcrumbs
For frying	- Refined oil

METHOD

1. Clean, wash and soak kabuli channa for 2-3 hours and boil till soft, drain water, let it cool.
2. In a food processor put boiled channa and make a fine paste and transfer it to a bowl.
3. Add all the ingredients as listed above and mix well to form smooth dough.
4. Divide the mixture into 4-5 equal parts or as desired and make balls, press each ball between your palms to give a medallion shape (tikki).

Cooking

5. Heat oil in a non-stick pan and shallow fry till golden brown on both sides (2-3 minutes).
6. Serve hot along with choice of a salad and chutney.

Kale Moti Kebab

DARK BLACK BUT DELICIOUS KEBAB MADE OF BLACK GRAMS

Cooking time 5-6 minutes Serves 1-2

INGREDIENTS

100 gm	- Bengal gram (black)
10 gm	- Ginger
5 no	- Garlic cloves
2 no	- Red chilli (whole)
50 gm	- Boiled potato (grated)
50 gm	- Cottage cheese (grated)
To taste	- Salt
½ tsp	- Yellow chilli powder
½ tsp	- Garam masala
1 tsp	- Green coriander (chopped)
½ tsp	- Green chilli (chopped)
A pinch	- Ajwain
2 tsp	- Cornflour
For binding	- Breadcrumbs

METHOD

1. Clean, wash and soak Bengal gram for 2-3 hours and boil with ginger, garlic, cloves, whole red chilli till soft, drain water and let it cool.
2. In a food processor put boiled gram and make paste and transfer to a bowl.
3. Add potatoes, cottage cheese and other remaining ingredients in the order listed, mix well to a smooth dough and keep aside for at least half an hours.
4. Divide the mixture into 4-5 equal parts and make balls.

Cooking

5. Take a skewer and apply each ball on the skewer in cylindrical shape (4"-5") leaving a gap of one inch between them.
6. Roast in a tandoor or charcoal grill for 5-6 minutes till golden brown.
7. Serve hot along with choice of a salad and chutney.

Kale Channe Ke Shammi

DIFFERENT KEBAB MADE WITH BLACK GRAMS IN LUCKNOWI STYLE

Cooking time 2-3 minutes Serves 1-2

INGREDIENTS

75 gm	- Kala channa (black gram)
10 gm	- Ginger (whole)
10 gm	- Garlic (whole)
2 no	- Red chilli (whole)
To taste	- Salt
1 tsp	- Brown onion paste
40 gm	- Boiled potato (grated)
40 gm	- Cottage cheese (grated)
½ tsp	- Ginger (chopped)
½ tsp	- Green chilli (chopped)
1 tsp	- Green coriander (chopped)
To taste	- Salt
½ tsp	- Yellow chilli powder
A pinch	- Elaichi javitri powder
A pinch	- Garam masala
1 ½ tsp	- Cornflour
A pinch	- White cumin seeds
For coating	- Vermicelli (crushed)
For frying	- Refined oil

METHOD

1. Clean, wash and soak kala channa for 2-3 hours and boil with ginger, garlic, red chilli whole, salt and brown onion till soft, drain water and let it cool.
2. In a processor put kala channa, make a fine paste and transfer it to a bowl.
3. Add all the ingredients as listed, mix well and keep aside for half an hour.
4. Divide the mixture into 4-5 equal parts or as desired and make balls, press each ball between wet palms into a medallion (tikki) shape and coat with vermicelli.

Cooking

5. Heat oil in a non-stick pan and shallow fry till golden brown on both sides (2-3 minutes). Remove on an absorbent paper to remove excess oil.
6. Serve hot along with choice of a salad and chutney.

Kurkure Dal Shammi

CRUNCHY, LENTIL KEBAB PREPARED WITH LUCKNOWI TOUCH

Cooking time 2-3 minutes Serves 1-2

INGREDIENTS

75 gm	- Boiled green lentil (moong chilka)
50 gm	- Boiled chickpeas (chopped)
40 gm	- Boiled potatoes (grated)
40 gm	- Paneer (grated)
To taste	- Salt
½ tsp	- Green chilli (chopped)
1 tsp	- Green coriander (chopped)
½ tsp	- Yellow chilli powder
½ tsp	- Garam masala
½ tsp	- Red chilli paste
2 tsp	- Cornflour
For binding	- Breadcrumbs
For coating	- Vermicelli (crushed)
For frying	- Refined oil

METHOD

1. In a processor, coarsly chop boiled green lentils, chickpeas and transfer to a tray.
2. Add remaining ingredients in the order listed and mix well to a smooth dough and keep aside for half an hour.
3. Divide the mixture into 6-7 equal parts and make balls. Press each ball between your palms to give it a medallion (tikki) shape and coat it with vermicelli.

Cooking

4. Heat oil in kadhai and deep fry till golden brown (2-3 minutes). Remove on an absorbent paper to drain excess oil.
5. Serve hot along with choice of a salad and chutney.

Malka Dal Shammi

LUCKNOWI VERSION OF KEBAB MADE WITH POPULAR LENTIL RICH IN PROTEINS

Cooking time 5-6 minutes Serves 1-2

INGREDIENTS

75 gm	- Malka dal (red gram)
10 gm	- Ginger (whole)
5 gm	- Garlic (whole)
3 no	- Red chilli (whole)
To taste	- Salt
60 gm	- Boiled potato (grated)
½ tsp	- Ginger (chopped)
½ tsp	- Green chilli (chopped)
1 tsp	- Green coriander (chopped)
To taste	- Salt
½ tsp	- Yellow chilli powder
½ tsp	- Garam masala
½ tsp	- Dalchini powder
A pinch	- Turmeric powder
½ tsp	- Roasted jeera powder
2 tsp	- Cornflour
For binding	- Dry breadcrumbs

METHOD

1. Clean, wash and soak red gram for a couple of hours, boil with ginger, garlic, red chilli whole and salt till done completely, drain water and keep cool.
2. In a processor put boiled malka dal, make a fine paste and transfer it to a bowl.
3. Add all the remaining ingredients listed above, mix well, keep aside for at least half an hour.
4. Divide the mixture into 4-5 equal parts and make balls.

Cooking

5. Spread mixture on a skewer in a cylindrical shape leaving a gap of one inch between them.
6. Roast in tandoor or charcoal grill for 5-6 minutes till golden brown.
7. Serve hot along with choice of a salad and chutney.

Lajawab Rajma Kebab

AMAZING CONCOCTION OF KIDNEY BEANS INFUSED WITH SPICES AND STUFFED WITH DRY FRUITS FILLING

Cooking time 2-3 minutes Serves 1-2

INGREDIENTS

75 gm	- Rajma (kidney beans)
10 gm	- Ginger (whole)
10 gm	- Garlic (whole)
2 no	- Red chilli (whole)
½ tsp	- Salt
40 gm	- Boiled potato (grated)
To taste	- Salt
½ tsp	- Yellow chilli powder
½ tsp	- Ginger (chopped)
½ tsp	- Green chilli (chopped)
1 tsp	- Green coriander (chopped)
½ tsp	- Coconut powder
A pinch	- Garam masala
1 tsp	- Cornflour
For binding	- Dry breadcrumbs

Filling

5 gm	- Cashewnut (chopped)
5 gm	- Almond (chopped)
For frying	- Refined oil

METHOD

1. Clean, wash and soak rajma for a couple of hours and boil with ginger, garlic, red chilli whole and salt till soft, completely drain water and keep aside.
2. In a food processor put rajma, make a fine paste and transfer it to a bowl.
3. Add all the ingredients as listed and mix well, keep aside for at least half an hour.
4. In a bowl mix chopped cashewnut almonds and divide into 5 parts.

Stuffing

5. Divide the mixture into 4-5 equal portions or as desired make balls. Press each ball between palms, place filling, seal and make medallion (tikki) shape.

Cooking

6. Heat oil in kadhai and deep fry till golden brown (2-3 minutes). Remove on an absorbent paper to drain excess oil.
7. Serve hot along with choice of a salad and chutney.

Rajma Ke Galouti

A CLASSIC LUCKNOWI KEBAB MADE WITH RED KIDNEY BEANS

Cooking time 4-6 minutes Serves 1-2

INGREDIENTS

75 gm	- Rajma (red kidney beans)
10 gm	- Ginger (whole)
5-6 gm	- Garlic (whole)
2-3 no	- Red chilli (whole)
To taste	- Salt
50 gm	- Boiled potato (grated)
1 tsp	- Cornflour
1/3 tsp	- Garam masala
1 tsp	- Coconut powder
A pinch	- Elaichi javitri powder
To taste	- Salt
½ tsp	- Yellow chilli powder
½ tsp	- Ginger (chopped)
½ tsp	- Green chilli (chopped)
1 tsp	- Green coriander (chopped)
1 tsp	- Brown onion paste
½ tsp	- Ginger garlic paste
A drop	- Kewra (Itter)
2-3 no	- Cloves
1 tsp	- Desi ghee
For cooking	- Desi ghee

METHOD

1. Clean, wash and soak rajma for 2-3 hours and boil rajma with ginger, garlic, red chilli whole, salt, till soft, completely drain water and keep to cool.
2. In a processor put rajma, make a fine paste and transfer it to a bowl.
3. Add all the remaining ingredients as listed except desi ghee and cloves, mix well.

Smoking

4. Take a small bowl (katori), place in the middle of the mixture, put 2 pieces of burning charcoal, cloves, pour desi ghee, immediately cover with lid and keep aside for 2-3 minutes.
5. Remove mixture from the bowl and divide into 5-6 parts and make balls.
6. Press each ball between your palms and give a medallion (tikki) shape and keep in refrigerator for some time.

Cooking

7. Heat ghee in a pan or griddle, place kebabs and fry on slow fire till brown on both sides.
8. Serve hot along with choice of a salad and chutney.

Harra Chholia Kebab

THIS NUTRITIOUS WINTER KEBAB MADE OF FRESH GREEN GRAMS BEAUTIFULLY DRESSED WITH SPICES

Cooking time 2-3 minutes Serves 1-2

INGREDIENTS

150 gm	- Boiled green chholia
50 gm	- Boiled potato (grated)
½ tsp	- Green chilli (chopped)
1 tsp	- Fresh Coriander (chopped)
1 tsp	- Ginger (chopped)
1 tbsp	- Roasted channa powder
½ tsp	- Yellow chilli powder
½ tsp	- Garam masala
A pinch	- Elaichi javitri powder
To taste	- Salt
For frying	- Refined oil

METHOD

1. In a food processor make a coarse paste of boiled cholia and transfer to a bowl.
2. Add the remaining ingredients in the order listed and mix well to form fine dough.
3. Divide the dough into 5-6 pieces or desired shape and press each ball between your palms to give a medallion (tikki) shape.

Cooking

4. Heat oil in a kadhai and fry till golden brown and crisp. Remove to absorbent paper to drain excess oil.
5. Serve hot with choice of a salad and chutney.

Lobia Galouti Kebab

LEGENDARY SOFT KEBAB MADE FROM WHITE KIDNEY BEANS AND
FLORAL AROMA OF LUCKNOWI SPICES

Cooking time 4-6 minutes Serves 1-2

INGREDIENTS

75 gm	- Lobia (white kidney beans)
½ tsp	- Ginger garlic paste
½ tsp	- Garam masala
1 tsp	- Galouti masala
½ tsp	- Kasoori methi powder
2 tsp	- Chironji paste
1tsp	- Khus khus paste
Salt	- To taste
Few drops	- Kewra/ittr
4 no	- Cloves
1 tsp	- Desi ghee
For cooking	- Desi ghee

METHOD

1. Clean, wash and soak lobia beans for a couple of hours and boil till soft, drain water, let it cool.
2. Put boiled lobia in a food processor and make a fine paste, transfer to a deep tray, add remaining ingredients listed above expect cloves and ghee, mix well and transfer to a bowl.

Smoking
3. Take a small bowl (katori), place in the middle of the mixture, put 2 pieces of burning charcoal, cloves, pour desi ghee, immediately cover with lid and keep aside for 2-3 minutes.
4. Remove mixture from the bowl and divide into 5-6 parts and make balls.
5. Press each ball between your palm and give a medallion (tikki) shape and keep in refrigerator for some time.

Cooking
6. Heat desi ghee in a lagan or thick-bottomed pan, place kebabs on it and shallow fry on slow fire till brown on both sides.
7. Serve hot along with choice of a salad and chutney.

Spices

If variety is the spice of life, it is spices which lend variety to food. Spices are an integral part of Indian cuisine. It is the numerous combinations of spices which create variety in different dishes.

Spices and Herbs: Their use in food is primarily aromatic rather than nutritional. Spices and herbs are used to flavour food which forms the major part of the meal or dish. Spices play an important role in Indian cookery. Whole spices have a different taste from ground spices and when the spices are dried by roasting they taste entirely different again. Simple dishes may have just one or two spices whereas more eloborate dishes might have ten or twelve. By adding different spices the entire taste of the dish can be changed. All spices have their own characteristics and they are used in varying proportions to make the correct combination for a particular dish. It is an art of blending, mixing and combination of spices / herbs which ultimately matters and one can create a variety of dishes, each different and distinctive.

The magic of kebabs is in the blending of spices and herbs. It is important to know about each spice, its characteristics use in a particular dish. In this book I have used two types of masalas – dry and wet. Dry can be a simple to exotic blend, wet masala is in the form of a paste.

The following are the commonly used spices and ingredients in preparation of kebabs:

Ginger (Adrak): It is the root of a plant with a hot rich flavour, vital to Indian cooking. It is used ground or chopped for curries, pickles, lentils or beans. It helps to counteract flatulence, aids digestion and is also beneficial in disorders connected with the formation of phlegm. It increases body heat if taken with jaggery in vegetables.

Carum Seeds (Ajwain): Also known as Bishop's weed. Used as a part of batters, masalas and in savoury dishes.

Coriander Seeds (Dhania): Used whole and in the powdered form in curries and vegetables and as a part of garam masala.

Cardamom (Elaichi): There are two varieties of cardamom – brown and green. The former is generally used for savoury food. The latter with its cool scented flavour, is equally welcomed in a curry blend and in puddings. It reduces the air and water elements, increases the appetite, and soothes the mucous membrane. The seeds are very hard and should be pounded before use.

Turmeric (Haldi): It is a bright yellow powder of the ground rhizone used as a colouring and flavouring spice essential for curries and pickles. It has a warm, musty flavour. It helps in drawing out and balancing other flavours. It has strong preservative and medicinal properties. Oriental women also used it as a cosmetic.

Cumin seeds (Jeera): Used whole or ground, it imparts a spicy, aromatic flavour to curries, pulaos and raitas. Light roasting in a dry pan enhances the aroma.

Mace (Javitri): It is the dried outer shell of a nut, golden yellow in colour. It has a strong nutmeg flavour. Used whole or ground, it imparts a delicious flavour to sweet and savoury dishes.

Nutmeg (Jaifal): It is a timble-sized and almost egg-shaped kernel of the fruit. The best way to use this spice is by grating it freshly as and when needed. It goes well with egg, meat and spinach. It has digestive properties.

Onion Seeds (Kalonji): Dry onion seeds are used in pickles and as a topping for Naans.

Allspice (Kabab chini): The name Allspice recognizes the fact that the berries smell like a blend of cinnamon, cloves and nutmeg. It is an important ingredient for kebabs. It has a long history as a food preservative especially in meat. It is used either whole or ground, preferably freshly ground.

Black Peppercorn (Kali Mirch): Next to chillies, this is the most commonly used spice throughout India. It has a strong pungent, spicy flavour. A digestive spice, rich in vitamin C, it is used in all meat dishes and some fish and vegetable dishes. It is used whole or ground (preferably freshly ground) and gives an extraordinary lift to the simplest of foods.

Saffron (Kesar/Zaffaran): It is the world's most expensive spice. Deep red-orange in colour, the saffron strands are both a colouring and flavouring spice. They have a pervasive and warm bitter-honey flavour. A small pinch is enough to flavour a dish. Specially cultivated in Kashmir, it is an important ingredient in almost all Awadh recipes – sweet or savoury.

Chillies (Mirch): there are three varieties of chillies used in Indian cuisine – green chillies, red chillies and yellow chillies. The green chillies are the fresh peppers, rich in vitamin C and add a spicy flavour to the food. They can be used chopped, sliced, crushed or slit lengthways. Red chillies are the hottest of all peppery spices and should be used with caution. They are a necessary ingredients of all Indian kebabs and are most commonly used in the powdered form. The Ayurveda recommends it as an aid for digestion and cure for paralysis. Since it aids the saliva and gastric juices, it helps to overcome a weak appetite.

Fenugreek (Methi): It is an aromatic bitter – sweet spice, reddish yellow in colour. Because of its strong flavour it should be used sparingly. Rich in vitamins, iron and protein. In Ayurveda it has been prescribed for reducing fevers and intestinal inflammations.

Salt (Namak): Salt is the first of all seasonings and essential to all dishes. It is a vital preservative for food of all kinds.

Mustard (Sarson/Rai): These are yellow or black and have a sharp and hot flavour. Rich in manganese and vitamin D.

Bayleaf: Although commonly referred to as 'bay leaf' in Indian recipes what is meant is actually the dried leaf of the cassia tree. I like to call it cinnamon leaf. Used in most dishes all over northern India, cinnamon leaves have a mild sweet flavour. They are not edible, so should be removed before serving. should you find it difficult to obtain them, you can use bay leaves instead.

Royal cumin seed: Also called black cumin, these spice seed are very dark brown, long and very thin, and smaller then regular cumin. Their aroma is earthy and strong during cooking. The spice is used extensively in kashmiri cuisine, and in Mughal cuisine as a tempering for meat.

Fennel seed: A very commonly used spice in India, whole or ground fennel seeds add a warm and sweet flavour to all kinds of curries. Fennel seed are also used in pickles and chutney and in desserts. Fennel is thought to have digestive properties, so rosted seed are often served after a rich Indian meal.

Pickling spices: This combination of equal quantities of fennel, carum, onion, fenugreek, mustard and cumin either as whole seed or ground, is used in pickles as well as to flavour sauce and marinades for meat. you can buy ready – made pickling spices in India; elsewhere you will need to mix the spices together yourself.

Dry mint leaves (puddina): Mint leaves are an aromatic herb, which have been used from ancient times.

Cloves (laung): Cloves are the dried flower buds of an evergreen plant. Clove oil contains phenol, which is a good antiseptic and helps in preserving food.

Cinnamon (dalchini): Most Indian food is cooked with cassia bark, which is a good substitute for real cinnamon. However, it has a stronger flavour than that of cinnamon, which is more delicately flavoured.

Garam Masala (King of Spices)

The word literally means "Hot Spice" which enhances the taste of food. This is mostly in powered form. It is a blend of more than one spice. Each spice has a specific and unique aroma. It plays an important role in marinations of kebabs and in gravies.

Garam masalas are often a chef's own combination of spices. To make any blend / mix, it is important to be aware of spices and their characteristics. There are many versions of garam masala. Every chef has his own preferred combination. There are basically two types of garam masalas. One is the chill hot while the other comprises aromatic (Spices and condiments).

Its prime use in kebabs is during marination and in some kebabs it is sprinkled over after cooking to provide aromatic flavouring at the time of serving. One often sees some people sprinkling tandoori masala (spice) over kebabs after cooking. I would not advise this as I personally believe that it over-spices the kebabs, kills the specific aroma of meat and makes all kebabs taste alike.

The art of preparing a garam masala involves grinding or powdering a combination of dried spices and condiments. Spices are lightly roasted on a griller or on a slow flame till a subtle aroma emanates. Remove from fire and grind. Sieve finely. If the masala is still moist, dry it and store in an air-tight jar for further use. For the benefit of the reader who may like to prepare garam masala, I have listed ingredients and the method on next page.

Junglee Masala

INGREDIENTS
Whole red chilli - 500gm
Whole cumin - 500gm
Coriander seeds - 500gm
Shahi jeera - 150gm
Kebab chini - 100gm

METHOD:
1. Put all the ingredients in a mortar and pound with a pestle to make a fine powder.
2. Sieve and store in an air-tight, dry container.

Gross Weight: 1750gm
Yield: 1650gm

Shenshahi Kebab Masala

INGREDIENTS
Cloves - 300gm

Baylead - 250gm
Kebab Chini - 50gm

METHOD:
1. Put all the ingredients in a mortar and pound with a pestle to make a fine powder.
2. Sieve and store in an air-tight, dry container.

Gross Weight: 600gm
Yield: 550gm

Sugandhit Masala

INGREDIENTS
Javitri - 200gm
Cardamom (green) - 200gm

METHOD:
1. Put all the ingredients in a mortar and pound with a pestle to make a fine powder.
2. Sieve and store in an air-tight, dry container.

Gross Weight: 400gm
Yield: 375gm

Gulabi Masala

INGREDIENTS
Dry rose petals - 500gm

METHOD:
1. Clean and slightly dry rose petals to remove excess moisture.
2. Put in a mortar and pound with a pestle to make a fine powder.
3. Sieve and store in an air-tight and dry container.

Gross weight: 500gm
Yield: 440gm

Tandoori Masala (Garam Masala)

INGREDIENTS
Coriander Seeds - 400gm
Cumin - 400gm
Shahi jeera - 100gm
Rose petals - 250gm

Javitri - 150gm
Cinnamon - 150gm
Black pepper - 100gm
Bayleaf - 100gm
Star anise - 60gm
Green cardamom - 30gm
Black Cardamom - 50gm
Cloves - 30gm
Nutmeg - 30gm

METHOD:
1. Clean and slightly dry the aforementioned ingredients to remove excess moisture.
2. Put all the ingredients in a mortar and pound with a pestle to make a fine powder.
3. Sieve and store in an air-tight and dry container.

Gross Weight: 1850 gm
Yield: 1750 gm

Galouti Masala

Stone Flower - 80 gm
Dal Jhare - 30 gm
Bay Leave - 30 gm
Rose Petals - 80 gm
Clove - 40 gm
Cinnamon - 40 gm
Black Pepper - 230 gm
Kebab chini - 50 gm
Mace - 30 gm
Sandal Wood - 40 gm
Black Cardamom - 20 gm
Green Cardamom - 20 gm
Cumin Seeds - 20 gm

METHOD:
1. Clean and slightly dry the aforementioned ingredients to remove excess moisture.
2. Put all the ingredients in a mortar and pound with a pestle to make a fine powder.
3. Sieve and store in an air-tight and dry container.

Gross Weight: 710 gm
Yield: 650 gm

Marinades

The purpose of a marinate is to season the food steeped in it by impregnating it with the flavour of its condiments. It also softens the fibre of meat and enables fish and meat to be kept longer than it is generally possible.

While there is no fixed time allowed for marination, the time factor is important and depends on the following:
- The type of meat, fish or vegetable to be cooked.
- The type of cut/size and texture-whole, tikka, chunks, etc.
- Type of tenderizer being used.

Marinated meat can be kept for 2-3 days in the refrigerator and used when required. The marination should enhance the flavour of what is being cooked, not completely overwhelm the taste of it.

To achieve the best results in tandoori cooking of various kebabs, marination plays an important role, so care must be taken for therein lies the secret of a delicious kebab. Some tips for marination are as follows:
- In hot climate, marinated food should be stored in a refrigerator.
- Do not use aluminum dish to marinate or keep marinated food in.
- The addition of salt during marination needs special attention.
- For whole meat and vegetables, salt is to be added together with the spices in the beginning. As for red meat, salt should not be added with the first marination as the addition of salt releases water and juices from the meat thus making it stringy. Add the salt to red meat twenty minutes before cooking.
- Use freshly ground spices for good results.
- Dry fruits are added to impart a distinctive flavour, richness, softness and texture to kebabs.
- The marinade should be well mixed and should be of coating consistency.
- For better results, food items to be cooked must be steeped in the marinade to ensure proper marinating.

Basic marinades

These are the basic marinades used for preparing any kind of kebabs, i.e. tandoori/tawa/fried:

Red Marination

INGREDIENTS
Hung curd - 500gms
Ginger garlic paste - 1½ tbsp
Red chilli paste - 1½ tbsp
Salt - to taste
Kasoori methi powder - 1 tsp

Garam masala - 1 tsp
Lemon juice - 15 ml
Refined oil - 20 ml

METHOD:
1. In a bowl, whisk hung curd, add ginger garlic paste, red chilli paste, salt, kasoori methi powder, garam masala and lemon juice.
2. Mix them thoroughly until smooth paste and add refined oil

Note: this marination is used for chicken, mutton, paneer shashlik, etc.

Yellow Marination

INGREDIENTS
Hung curd - 500gm
Ginger garlic paste - 1½ tbsp
Salt - to taste
Yellow chilli powder - 2 tbsp
Garam masala - 1 tsp
Mustard oil - 30 ml
Turmeric - 1 tsp

METHOD:
1. In a bowl, whisk hung curd, add ginger garlic paste, salt, yellow chilly powder and garam masala, mix them and keep aside.
2. In a pan, heat mustard oil, add turmeric to it and cook for a while. Pour this oil in the above mixture and mix thoroughly to a smooth paste.

Note: this marination is mainly used for prawns, fish, paneer kebabs, etc.

Green Marination

INGREDIENTS
Mint leaves - 30 gm
Coriander leaves - 150 gm
Spinach boiled - 50 gm
Green chillies - 12 nos.
Hung curd - 200 gm
Ginger garlic paste - 1 tbsp
Salt - to taste
Yellow chilli powder - 2 tbsp
Kasoori methi powder - 1 tsp
Garam masala - ½ tsp
Mustard oil - 30 ml

METHOD:

1. clean, wash mint leaves and coriander paste. In a blender, grind these with boiled spinach and green chilies to a smooth paste.
2. in a bowl, whisk hung curd, add ginger garlic paste, mint leaves, salt, kasoori methi powder, yellow chilli powder and garam masala. Mix thoroughly and add mustard oil.

Note: this marination can be used for chicken, fish and paneer kebabs.

White Marination

INGREDIENTS
Processed cheese - 150 gm
Egg white - 1 no.
Cream - 300 ml
Cashewnut paste - 75 gm
Ginger garlic paste - ½ tbsp
Green chillli - 3 nos.
Coriander roots(Chopped) - 15 gm
Salt - to taste
White pepper powder - 1 tbsp
Elaichi javitri powder - a pinch

METHOD:
1. In a paraat (Flat vessel), grate cheese. Mash it with your plam. Add egg white and mix it with cheese and rub until the cheese dissolves.
2. Add cream gradually in one direction so that it gets blended/ mixed in the cheese.
3. Add cashewnut paste, ginger garlic paste and all the remaining ingredients, them mix them thoroughly.

Note: this is mild yet rich marination used mainly for chicken kebabs.

Tenderizers

Taking off from the famous saying that "history was made when the sausages met the mustard" one could say that "history was remade when meat met the tenderizer".

For cooking meat in the tandoor or charcoal grill only tender meat or the tender part of meat is recommended as the temperature is ranging from 300ºC to 325ºC.

The principle of all tenderizers depends on the range of acid content and enzymes. These readily dissolve sinews and muscle fibres, hence making the meat tender.

The most commonly used tenderizers are:
1. Raw papaya (Kaccha Papita): Generally papaya is an oblong melon-like fruit obtained from a fully grown tree and is used in its raw form. The papaya contains a protein digesting enzyme called papain that gives it its tenderizing property.
2. Kachri (botanical name): Cucumis pubescens – Kachri is a wild variety of cucumis.
3. Raw Pineapple (Ananas): the active enzyme found in pineapple is bromalein which has a very similar tenderizing action to raw papaya.
4. Yoghurt (Dahi): Fresh milk inoculated with the culture of lactobacillus. It is the lactic acid in yoghurt that helps to break down meat fibres and tenders meat soft and succulent when roast/cooked kebabs.
5. Lemon (Nimbu): The citric acid contained in this fruit is what causes the tenderizing. Also used on kebabs, especially when freshly squeezed as the finishing touch to cooked kebab.
6. Vinegar (Sirka): these are of two types, i.e. white synthetic and malt vinegar. Acetic acid in the vinegar gives it its tenderizing action.

Commercially prepared tenderizers: Although a convenient substitute, there's nothing like the natural tenderizer.

Mechanical tenderizing: Often it is the lamb which is beaten with the wooden or rough side of a butcher knife / chopper, to break the tissues, thus facilitating the tenderizing process.

Pastes

Ginger Paste

INGREDIENTS
Ginger - 300 gm
Water - 50 ml
Yield - 325 gm

PREPARATION:
1. scrape, wash and roughly chop ginger.
2. put the chopped ginger in a blender, add water and make a fine paste. Remove and refrigerate.

Garlic Paste

INGREDIENTS
Peeled garlic - 250 gm
Water - 50 ml
Yield - 275 gm

PREPARATION:
1. Wash and roughly chop the peeled garlic.
2. Put the chopped garlic in a blender, add 50 ml of water and make a fine paste. Remove and refrigerate.

Cashewnut Paste

INGREDIENTS
Broken cashewnuts - 250 gm
Water - 125 ml
Yield - 375 gm

PREPARATION:
1. soak the broken cashewnuts in water for 20-30 minutes and drain the water.
2. put soaked cashewnuts in a blender, add 100 ml of water and blend to a paste consistency. Remove and refrigerate.

Hung Curd

INGREDIENTS
Curd - 1 kg
Yield - 600gm

PREPARATION:
1. In kebabs, yoghurt is an important ingredient for marination. It should be hung in a muslin cloth for at least 1½ hours before use to drain out extra water/ whey.

Boiled Onion Paste

INGREDIENTS
Onion - 500 gm
Water - for boiling

PREPARATION:
1. Peel, wash and cut onion in four pieces.
2. In a handi, put the onion pieces and add water.
3. bring to boil and simmer until onions are soft and the liquid has evaporated.
4. cool, put in a blender and make a fine paste.

Almond paste

INGREDIENTS
Almonds - 250 gm
Toned milk - 250 gm
Yield - 475 gm

PREPARATION:
1. Soak almonds in boiling hot water for 10 minutes. Drain water, peel the skin off.
2. Put peeled almonds in a blender, add milk and blend to paste consistency. Remove and refrigerate.

Poppy Seed Paste

INGREDIENTS
Poppy seeds - 250 gm
Water - 150 ml
Yield - 375 gm

PREPARATION:
1. Soak poppy seeds in warm water for 45 minutes and drain.
2. Put seeds in a blender, add water and make a find paste. Remove and refrigerate.

Ingredients

Poppy Seeds (Khuskhus): These tiny ivory coloured seeds are used for their scant flavour and nutty texture. They are generally lightly toasted before grinding for use in gravies. This aromatic spice is rich in protein and stimulates appetite. It imparts a softness in the texture to the meat or vegetables with which it is cooked. It is also a sedative and checks diarrhoea.

Kewra / Keora: Keora essence is extracted from the inner leaves and flower petals of a small kind of palm common to South India. Not only is it used in desserts but also in some meat and rice dishes. It is used to impart a flowery fragrance to a variety of dishes from rice to sweet dishes.

Garlic (Lahsun): Strong in flavour, it is used as a spice for curries. Used chopped or sliced, in whole cloves or ground to a paste, it promotes the success of the other ingredients and is commonly used with ginger. Medically garlic is reputed to aid digestion, reduce high blood pressure, expel catarrh from the chest and acts as an antiseptic. Because of its overpowering flavour and aroma it should be used with discretion.

Mint (Puddina): The aromatic leaves of this herbs are used fresh or dried in chutneys, salads, fruit drinks or as garnish. The strong flavoured leaves have great digestive and cooling properties.

Vinegar (Sirka): A sour pickling agent and preservative prepared usually from sugarcane and rose apple (Jamun). It alleviates bilious tumours. It acts as a prophylactic against cholera and intestinal infections. Also relieves nausea and vomiting. Contains 39% active acid from the oxidation of alcohol.

Almond (Badam): The world's most sought after nuts. Used extensively in sweetmeats. Rich in iron, fats and proteins. In India it is used in savoury dishes and also as garnish.

cashewnut (Kaju): Rich in proteins and vitamin B and used in Sweetmeats and some non-Vegetarian kebabs and curries.

Raisins (Kishmish): Semi-dried white grapes used as garnish for sweets, kheer and vermicelli. Deep fried and used as garnish for some kormas.

Curd (Dahi): Can be used in chutneys, raitas and as the thickening ingredients for a sauce or as a marinade for kebabs. Then, of course, it is also used for sweets or served on its own as a mild accompaniment to hot curries. Extremely versatile and in constant demand for the recipes throughout this book.

Clarified Butter (Ghee): Highest quality cooking fat, made from butter. Old Sanskrit writings suggest that the consumption of ghee could improve a person's appearance, power of speech mental process and digestion. It was a staple dietary recommendation for wrestlers. Best preferred cooking medium in India. When applied on freshly prepared naans and rotis it enhances the taste and aroma. A cheaper ghee substitute is hydrogenated vegetable oil.

Khoya: Khoya is a granular residue obtained by evaporating fresh milk. It is a popular base for sweetmeats and halwas and adds body and richness to any sweet or savoury dish.

Butter (Makkhan): A fat made by churning the cream, rich in vitamins A and D and use for making clarified butter (ghee) which is used as a cooking medium.

Cream cheese (Paneer): Similar to cottage cheese made by curdling the freshly boiled milk by addition of acids, usually lime or vinegar. Rich in vitamins.

Ginger and Garlic: After salt these are probably the most used ingredients in the cooking of delhi and Punjab. they are added to marinades for meat , fish and vegetabel when preparing them for the tandoor as well as being a flavouring in many curries. ginger and garlic are normally made into a paste, which can be done separately or in combination: take about 100g {31|2oz} peeled fresh ginger and 75g {21\2oz} peeled garlic and blend with 175ml {6fl oz} water, using a food processor. the paste can be kept in airtight jar in the refrigerator for up to 5 days .

Coconut: The hard, brown, hairy fruits of the coconut tree contain 'water' which makes a refreshing drink enjoyed straight from the fruit. The crunchy, sweet white flesh is used to make rich coconut milk, which is an important part of many Indian curries . Freshly grated coconut flesh is used in Bengali cuisine, while desiccated coconut features in Muslim cooking .

Kachri: A sour, tomato-like compound fruit native to Rajsthan, this has a hard skin and seed inside. Available fresh and dried. It is used to tenderize meat and in the making of certain chutneys.

Chickpea flour: Also known as besan and gram flour ,this is obtained form husking and then grinding split gram lentils into a powder. It is a very versatile flour, commonly used to make dumpling and batter fritter and in bread dough. Chickpea flour can be kept in airtight jar for up to 6 months .

Chapati flour: This finely ground whole wheat flour is used to make unleavened breads.

Mustard oil: As the name suggests this oil is extracted form mustard seeds . It is pungent in taste and smell and deep in gold colour . Mustard oil is greatly favoured in Bengal and eastern parts of India, and certain Rajsthani dishes get their unique flavour from it. When used, the oil is normally heated almost to smoking point, then cooled down and reheated again, which tones down its aroma.

Rose water and Screwpine essence: Essences have been a part of Indian cookery since antiquity. During the mughal emperors, rare flowers were grown in the royal greenhouses to make attars, or

Seekh Kebab being skewered

Dhuanaar (Smoking)

fragrant oils, and some of these turned up in the kitchen. FLORAL ESSENCES such as rose water and screwpine essence are the most popular today, used to flavour biryanis, pulaos, kebabs, desserts and treats.

Tamarinds:
This sweet and sour fruit is commonly used in south India cooking. As a souring agent and it bring a tangy contrast to mild coconut sauces. It also used for chutney and drinks. Tamarind pulp is sold in dried blocks.

Curry leaves: This is most widely used herb in south India cuisine. As the name suggest, it smell and taste like curry. While the flavour is spicy it is also nutty, a quality brought out when the leaves are lightly fried in oil until crips. curry leaves can also be added to a dish just like any other fresh herbs whole or torn. Buy them whenever you find them fresh, they as can be stored in the fridge wrapped in foil or sealed in a plastic bag.

Pistachios (pista): A relative of the cashew nut, pistachio nuts are often sold roasted and salted in their shells. They are very rich in minerals, vitamins and dietary fibre.

Black pepper: Known as 'black gold' pepper is one of the most widely used spice all over world. Kerala is considered to be its birthplace, because the plant from which the spice come {piper nigrum} is native to Tranvancore. Black peppercorns are the dried almost ripe berries of the plant. Keralan pepper market are attractive place to visit – the spice aroma of the crowded market is carried. It can be used whole or ground for flavouring dishes.

Star anise: Shaped like a star {hence its name}, this spice has a strong liquorice flavour that is warm and sweet . It is wildely used in South East Asian cooking .

Lamb Tikka being skewered

Important Cooking Tips

- Grilling or roasting should be done on constant moderate heat, and not on very high heat. High heat toughens the proteins of the meat or paneer, making the kebabs shrink and turn hard.
- Chill peeled onions before cutting/slicing to prevent tears in eyes.
- It is commonly believed that the only way to cook kebab is in a tandoor or on an open iron grill. It is true but in this book we have created several non-tandoori kebabs, shallow fried or deep fried or broiled on a griddle plate (Tawa).
- Peeled & chopped garlic or onion soaked in oil can be stored for long period.
- Always place the tikkas or the kebabs on the grill or on the wire rack and never directly on a tray. When you place them on a tray, the liquid that drips while grilling keeps collecting around the food and keeps the food wet all the time. This prevents the tandoori food from getting crisp on the outside. Whereas, if the food is placed on the wire rack, the liquid drips down and food remains dry.
- Remember, temperature plays an important part in Tandoori cooking. To maintain an even temperature in the tandoor, it is essential that the charcoal be evenly spread at the bottom.
- Always completely defrost frozen poultry before cooking.
- Place a tray beneath the wire rack on which the tikkas or any tandoori food is placed.
- Peppercorn freshly crush gives better flavour.
- Always grease/brush the wire rack or grill nicely with oil to avoid the kebabs from sticker to the grill.

Chiken Drumsticks being skewered

- Roasted kebabs should never be reheated, as they tend to get dry.
- When cream or Dahi (Yoghurt) is used, add a little refined flour or Gram flour (Besan) to prevent it from curdling.
- The size of the tikkas should not be too small, because after getting cooked they shrink. A very small piece after getting cooked can turn hard after some time.
- While skewering or placing pieces of chicken, mutton, fish or even vegetable, the pieces should be arranged such that there is atleast 1" gap between them so that each piece can get it's own space and heat all around to get cooked properly.
- When skewering delicate meats like fish and prawns or vegetables, it is advisable to use thinner skewers, then there is less chance of the vegetable or fish to break.
- Whole spice should be correctly pounded whenever possible to bring out the true flavour/aroma.
- Pastes like raw papaya paste, ginger-garlic paste, onion paste, coriander paste or chilli paste should be made with as little water as possible.
- Do not chop fresh dhania (coriander)/pudhina (mint) in a mixy/food process as it looses its colour & texture.
- To keep the tandoori food soft and succulent, baste food with some melted butter/oil or sometimes with the left over marinade. To baste, just pour the oil/melted butter on the food that is being barbecued when it is a little more than half done.
- While grinding red chilli put little oil so it does not harm eyes and hand.
- While grilling tikkas, turn them only after they are half done, otherwise they tend to break if

Shammi Kebab being flattened

they are shifted again & again. To check if meats is fully cooked, break a little. If it breaks off easily, it is done, otherwise it needs to be cooked more.
- Do not store acidic food/ingredients in aluminium and copper utensils.
- The marination should be a thick paste to coat the meat or vegetables well.
- Do not leave boiled potatoes in its water as it become sticky mashy.
- Pan should be quite hot before placing meat to cook as it does not stick, it seals and retain juices.
- Whenever Dahi (Yoghurt) is to be used for marination, it should be hung in a muslin cloth for atleast 1 ½ hours before use to drain out extra whey.
- Never put frozen meat for cooking as it toughens.
- To make smooth paste of nuts, soak it in warm water for atleast 1 hour.
- After cutting eggplant/always place them in cold water to prevent discolouration.
- To store fresh ginger, wrap it in clean wrap/papper towel and then refrigerate.
- Lemon juice taste best when it is freshly squeezed.
- Kebabs should not be over-cooked, as they tend to become dry and not remain succulent.
- To attain better colour of saffron soak it in warm water.
- Grease the skewer before skewing meat to avoid sticking.
- Roast sesame seeds to inhance its flavour.
- To peel garlic easily, dip it in water.
- To remove bitterness of karela (bitter gourd) apply salt, turmeric and keep for sometime before cooking.

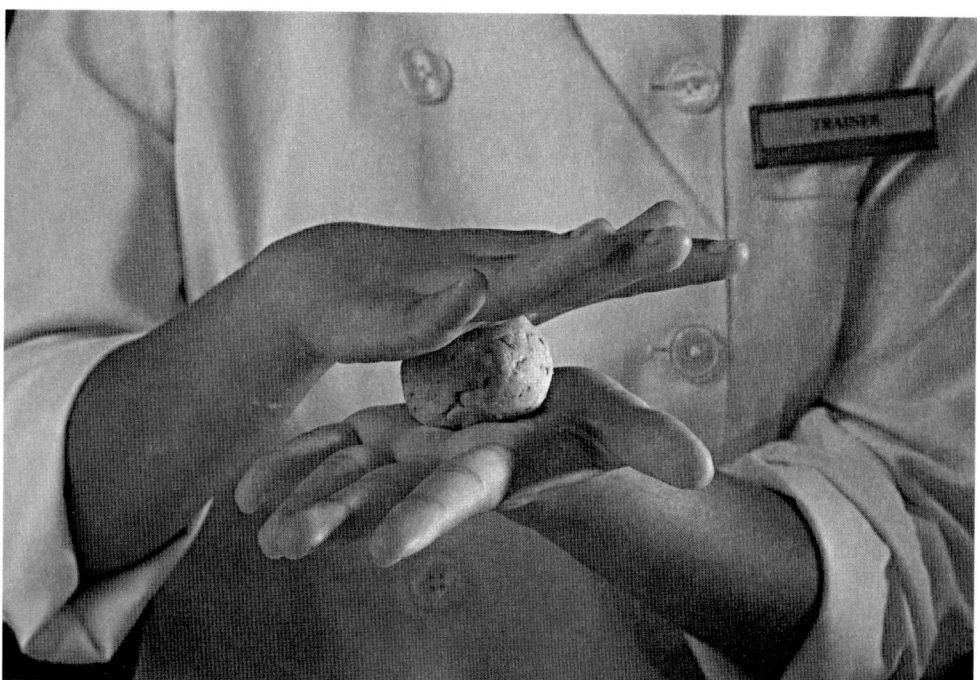

Vegetable Kebab being shaped

- Frozen food once thawed should not be frozen again.
- Always fry any vegetable kebab in hot oil to ensure absorption of less oil.
- To remove fish smells, marinate or wash fish with lemon juice/salt.
- Prick roti in the tandoor to prevent puffing.
- Always points/seal seekh kebab at both ends to prevent slipping.
- Spices should be coarsely pounded to bring out its true flavour.
- Substitute food colour to any kebab marination with the following:
- Red - Red chilli paste
- Green - Spinach paste
- Yellow - Saffron/turmeric
- Before transferring meat, fish or vegetable from first marinade to second marinade, must ensure that excess moisture is squeezed with the help of both palms.
- Cooking in an oven/grill:

- You may also use electric domestic type grill for roasting kebabs.
- For roasting any kebab in oven, use a wire wrack/grill.
- Pre heat oven at 180°c
- Place marinated meat or seafood or vegetable & keep basting during cooking.
- Grilling or roasting should be done on constant moderate heat otherwise it toughens the portion of the meat, making the kebab shrink.
- Cover the skewers with aluminum foil to avoid excess colouring or drying of kebab.
- Keep basting and turning kebab from time to time.

Glossary (English to Hindi)

SPICES

ENGLISH NAME	HINDI NAME
Alkanet Root	Ratan Jot
Alum	Fitkari
Anise Seed	Choti Saunf, Suwa, Shopa
Asafoetida	Hing
Basil Leaf	Tulsi
Bay Leaf Indian	Tej Patta
Black Cumin / Royal Cumin	Shahi Jeera, Kala Jeera
Black Mustard Seeds	Rai
Black onion Mustard seeds Cracked	Kalonji, Rai Kuria
Black Peppercorn	Kali Mirch
Black Rock salt	Sanchal, Kala Namak
Cardamom Black	Bari Elaichi
Cardamom Green	Choti Elaichi
Carum Seed	Ajwain
Cassia buds	Kebab chini
Cayenne Pepper	Lal Mirch
Celery seeds	Ajmud
Cilantro	Hara Dhania Patta
Cinnamon	Dalchini
Cloves	Laung, Lavang
Coriander seeds	Dhania
Cumin seeds	Jeera
Curry Leaves	Curry Patta
Dill	Soa
Dry rose petal	Sukhi gulab ki pattiyan
Fennel	Moti Saunf, Saunf
Fenugreek Leaves dried	Kasoori Methi
Fenugreek seeds	Methi dana
Garcinia indica	Kokum
Garlic Fresh	Lassun
Ginger Fresh	Adrak
Ginger Dried	Saunth
Gum Katira Sap	Gond Katira
Green Chili	Hari Mirch
Elaichi	Choti elaichi
Licorice	Mulaethi, Jethi-madh
Lime Pickling	Paan-Choona
Long Pepper	Pippali
Lotus seed pops	Makhna

Jaggery	Gur, Raw sugar cake Sources: Sugarcane, Palm
Mace	Javitri
Mango powder	Amchoor, Amchur .... Dried Tar Green Mango Powder
Mustard Seeds	Sarson
Mustard Oil	Sarson Tel
Namak	Salt
Nutmeg	Jaifal
Onion	Piyaz
Paprika (Kashmiri Paprika)	Degi Mirch
Pomegranate seeds	Anar-daana
Poppy Seeds	Khuskhus
Red Chili	Lal Mirch
Rose water	Gulab jal
Sage	Kamarkas
Saffron	Kesar, Zaafraan
Salt	Namak
Salt Sea	Saindha Namak
Salt Sanchal Black	Kala Namak
Silver leaves	Chandi ka varq
Star Anis	Chakraphool
Sugar	Chini
Sumac	Sumaq
Tamarind	Imli
Turmeric	Haldi
Thyme	Ajwain ke phool. Ajwain is Carum
Vinegar	Sirka
White pepper corn	Safed mirch
Yeast	Samunder Jhag (Sea Foam) Traditional Cuttle Stone soft rock
Yellow chilli	Peeli mirch

DRIED FRUITS AND NUTS

ENGLISH NAME	HINDI NAME
Apricot dried	Khumani
Almonds	Badaam
Cantaloupe seed/Melon seeds	Kharbooza ke beej/magaz
Cashews	Kajoo
Dates	Khajoor
Dates Dry skin	Chhohara
Coconut	Naarial
Fig	Anjeer
Gooseberry Indian (Emblica)	Amla
Peanuts/groundnuts	Mungphali

Pine Nuts	Chilgoza
Pistachio Nuts	Pista
Pistachio Soft	Chironghi
Prunes	Manukka
Raisins	Kishmish
Sesame Seed	Til
Watermelon seed	Tarbooj ke beej
Walnuts	Akhroat/Akhrot
Rose Essence	Gulab-Jal
Screwpine Essence	Kewra
Sultana	Munnakka
Vetiver Essence	Khas

FRUITS

Apple	Seb
Apricot	Jardaloo
Avocado	Makhanphal
Banana	Kela
Cantaloupe	Kharbooja
Cranberry	Karonda. In realty, Karonda is 'Natal Plum'
Grapes	Angoor
Grapefruit	Chakutra
Guavas	Amrood
Jackfruit	Kathal
Java Plum	Jamoon
Lemon	Nimboo
Mango	Aam
Mulberry	Shehtoot
Natal Plum	Karonda
Olives	Zetoon
Orange	Santra
Orange - Navel	Mosambi
Papaya	Papeeta
Papaya green	Kachcha papeeta
Peach	Aadoo
Pear	Nashpati
Pineapple	Anna-naas
Plum	Aloo-bukhaara
Pomegranate	Anar
Raw mango	Amia
Sweet Lime	Musambi
Watermelon	Tarbooj

GRAINS

Barley	Jaun
Bengal gram	Channa dal
Buckwheat	Kuttu
Chickpeas/white gram	Chana, Desi Chana, Kabuli Chana
Cracked Wheat/Porridge	Dalia
Flour - Bread	Atta. Durum wheat wholemeal coarse flour
Flour - Chickpea	Besan
Flour - Pastry	Maida. Super refined soft wheat flour
Legume - Red gram	Masoor
Legume - Green gram	Moong
Legume - Black (Black Matpe)	Urad
Legume - Yellow gram	Arhar, Toor
Maize	Makki
Millet - Finger	Ragi
Millet - Pearl	Bajara
Oats	Vilaiti Jaun
Rice	Chawal
Semolina	Sooji
Sorghum	Jowar
Split gram lentil	Channe ki dal
Tapioca/Sago	Saboo-daana
Vermicilli	Sevaiyan
Wheat	Gehoon

MEATS

Boti	Boneless cube of lamb
Chicken	Murghi
Chicken wings	Pankhari
Baby chicken	Chooza
Duck	Battakh
Drum stick	Tangri
Egg	Anda
Fish generic	Machli
Goat	Bakra ka Gosht
Goose	Bada-Battakh
Guinea fowl	Bada-Teetar
Leg of kid lamb	Raan
Lobster	Lobster
Meat generic	Gosht
Mussels	Teesari
Prawn	Jhinga
Quail	Battar

ORGANS

Bone	Haddi
Kidney/Sweet bread	Gurda
Liver	Kaleja
Marrow	Guda
Tongue	Jeeb

VEGETABLES

Aloe	Gawar Patha
Banana raw	Kachcha kela
Beet root	Chukandar
Bell Pepper/capsicum	Simla Mirch
Broad beans	Sem ki phali
Celery	Ajmud
Cabbage	Bandh-Gobi
Carrot	Gaajar
Cauliflower	Phool-Gobi
Cilantro	Hara Dhania
Cluster beans	Guar-phali
Colocasia	Arbi
Corn Kernel	Makki
Corn on the cob	Bhutta
Cowpea	Lobhia
Cucumber	Kheera, Kakri
Eggplant/Brinjal	Baingen
Fresh fenugreek	Methi
Gourd, Ash	Petha
Gourd, Bitter	Karela
Gourd, Bottle	Ghiya. Lauki
Lettuce	Salad patta
Lotus stem	Bhein/Kamal kakri
Mushrooms	Khumbi
Mustard Greens	Sarson Patta
Okra/Gumbo	Bhindi
Onion	Piyaaz
Pointed gaurd	Parmal
Peas	Mattar
Peppermint Leaves Fresh	Hara Podina
Potato	Aloo
Pumpkin	Kaddu
Radish	Mooli
Scallion/Green onion	Hari Piyaz
Spinach	Palak
Sweet Potato	Shakar-kandi

Tomato	Tamatar
Turnip	Shalgam
Water Chestnuts	Singhaara
Yam	Zimikand

TASTE EXPRESSIONS

Aroma	Khush-boo, Sugandh
Bad	Kharaab
Burnt	Jalaa
Bland	Feeka
Cold	Thunda
Fresh	Taaza
Good	Bhariya … "Achha is just okay"
Hot	Garam
Raw	Kuchaa
Heeks	Bad-boo
Ripe	Pukka
Rotten	Galaa
Salty	Namkeen
Savory	Chat-pata
Sharp	Teekha
Sour	Khatta
Sweet	Meetha
Tasty	Swaad

COMMON DAIRY PRODUCTS

HINDI	ENGLISH
Chachh	Churned homemade Yogurt with butter removed
Chenna	Cheese similar to small curd cheese
Dahi	Homemade Yogurt
Doodh	Milk
Ghee	Rendered butter
Khoya	Reduced whole milk
Kheer	Rice Pudding
Lassi	Churned homemade Yogurt
Makhan	Butter
Malai	Cream
Paneer	Cottage cheese

the last ISLAND

A Naturalist's Sojourn on Triangle Island

Written and illustrated by
Alison Watt

Harbour Publishing

Text and illustrations copyright © 2002 Alison Watt

All rights reserved. No part of this publication may be reproduced, stored in a retrieval system or transmitted, in any form or by any means, without prior permission of the publisher or, in case of photocopying or other reprographic copying, a licence from CANCOPY (Canadian Reprography Collective), 214 King Street West, Toronto, Ontario M5H 3S6.

Published by
HARBOUR PUBLISHING CO. LTD.
P.O. Box 219
Madeira Park, BC Canada
V0N 2H0
www.harbourpublishing.com

Cover and page design by Roger Handling
Edited by Shane McCune

Printed in Canada

Harbour Publishing acknowledges the financial support of the Government of Canada through the Book Publishing Industry Development Program (BPIDP) and the Canada Council for the Arts, and the Province of British Columbia through the British Columbia Arts Council, for its publishing activities.

National Library of Canada Cataloguing in Publication Data

Watt, Alison, 1957-
  The last island

Includes bibliographical references.
ISBN 1-55017-296-4

1. Watt, Alison, 1957- –Journeys–British Columbia–Triangle Island.
2. Natural history–British Columbia–Triangle Island. 3. Triangle Island (B.C.)–Description and travel. I. Title.
QH106.2.B7W37 2002   508.711'2   C2002-910765-2